First World War
and Army of Occupation
War Diary
France, Belgium and Germany

63 (ROYAL NAVAL) DIVISION
190 Infantry Brigade
Headquarters
1 May 1916 - 30 April 1917

WO95/3116

The Naval & Military Press Ltd
www.nmarchive.com
Published in association with The National Archives

Published by

The Naval & Military Press Ltd

Unit 10 Ridgewood Industrial Park,

Uckfield, East Sussex,

TN22 5QE England

Tel: +44 (0) 1825 749494

www.naval-military-press.com

www.nmarchive.com

This diary has been reprinted in facsimile from the original. Any imperfections are inevitably reproduced and the quality may fall short of modern type and cartographic standards.

© Crown Copyright
Images reproduced by permission of The National Archives, London, England, 2015.

Contents

Document type	Place/Title	Date From	Date To
Heading	63rd (RN) Division 190th Infy Bde Brigade Headquarters May 1916-Apr 1917		
Heading	WO95/3116		
Heading	War Diary Of 3rd Brigade Royal Nasal Division From 1st May 1916 To 31st May 1916		
War Diary	Lemnos	01/05/1916	14/05/1916
War Diary	Marseilles	19/05/1916	19/05/1916
War Diary	Abbeville	20/05/1916	21/05/1916
War Diary	Vieulaine	22/05/1916	31/05/1916
Heading	War Diary Of 3rd Infantry Brigade Royal Naval Division. From June 1st 1916 to June 30th 1916.		
War Diary	Neulaine	01/06/1916	01/06/1916
War Diary	Barlin	02/06/1916	12/06/1916
War Diary	Bajus	13/06/1916	30/06/1916
Operation(al) Order(s)	Operation Order No.8 by Lieut-Colonel E.J. Stroud, R.M.L.I., Commanding 3rd Bde, R.N.D.S Appendix A	04/06/1916	04/06/1916
Operation(al) Order(s)	Operation Order No. 9 by Lieut-Colonel E.J. Stroud, R.M.L.I., Commanding 3rd Bde, R.N.D.S Appendix B	04/06/1916	04/06/1916
Operation(al) Order(s)	Operation Order No.11 by Lt. Col. E.J. Stroud, R.M.L.I., Commanding 3rd Bde., R.N.D. Appendix C	07/06/1916	07/06/1916
Operation(al) Order(s)	Operation Order No.10 by Lt. Col. E.J. Stroud, R.M.L.I., Commanding 3rd Bde., R.N.D. Appendix C1	07/06/1916	07/06/1916
Operation(al) Order(s)	Training Order No.1. by Lieut Colonel E.J. Stroud, R.M.L.I., Commanding 3rd Bde. R.N.O. Appendix D	09/06/1916	09/06/1916
Operation(al) Order(s)	3rd. Bde.Order No. 12 by Lieut. Col.E.J. Stroud, R.M.LI.,Commanding 3rd Bde., R.N.D. Appendix E	10/06/1916	10/06/1916
Operation(al) Order(s)	3rd. Infy Bde. R.N.D. Order No. 13 by Lt. Col. E.J. Stroud R.M.L.I. Commanding 3rd Infy. Bde., R.N.D. Appendix F	11/06/1916	11/06/1916
Operation(al) Order(s)	Training Order No 2 by Brigadier General C.N. Trotman, C.B. Commanding 3rd Bde. R.N. Divn. Appendix G.	17/06/1916	17/06/1916
Diagram etc	Sketch of Suggested Bayonet fighting Ground		
Operation(al) Order(s)	3rd. Bde Order No 14 by Brigadier General C.N. Trotman, C.B., Commanding 3rd. Bde., R.N.D. Appendix H	24/06/1916	24/06/1916
Heading	War Diary of 190th Infantry Brigade From July 6th 1916 to July 31st. 1916 Volume 2		
War Diary	Fresnicourt	06/07/1916	06/07/1916
War Diary	London	07/07/1916	18/07/1916
War Diary	Boulogne	22/07/1916	22/07/1916
War Diary	Barlin	23/07/1916	27/07/1916
War Diary	Hersin	27/07/1916	31/07/1916
Heading	War Diary of 190th Infantry Brigade From August 1st 1916 to August 31st 1916. Volume III		
War Diary		01/08/1916	01/08/1916
War Diary	Hersin	02/08/1916	29/08/1916
War Diary	Bully Grenay	30/08/1916	31/08/1916

Operation(al) Order(s)	190th. Infantry Bde. Order No. 1. by Brigadier General C.N. Trotman, C.B. Commanding 190th. Bde 63rd (R.N) Div. Appendix 1	25/07/1916	25/07/1916
Operation(al) Order(s)	190th. Infantry Bde. Order No. 2. by Brigadier General C.N. Trotman. C.B. Commanding 190th. Infy. Brigade. Appendix 2	03/08/1916	03/08/1916
Miscellaneous	March Table (Supplement to Brigade Order No.2)		
Operation(al) Order(s)	190th. Infantry Brigade Order No. 3. by Brigadier General C.N. Trotman, C.B., Commanding 190th. Infantry Brigade. Appendix 3	10/08/1916	10/08/1916
Miscellaneous	March Table (To accompany Brigade Order No.3)	10/08/1916	10/08/1916
Operation(al) Order(s)	190th. Infantry Brigade Order No. 4. by Brigadier General C.N. Trotman, C.B., Commanding 190th. Infantry Brigade. Appendix 4	15/08/1916	15/08/1916
Miscellaneous	March Table (To accompany Brigade Order No.4)	15/08/1916	15/08/1916
Operation(al) Order(s)	190th. Infantry Brigade Order No.5. by Brigadier General C.N. Trotman C.B., Commanding 190th. Infantry Brigade. Appendix 5	22/08/1916	22/08/1916
Map	Map E		
Map			
Miscellaneous	March Table (To accompany 190th Infantry Bde. Order No.5)	22/08/1916	22/08/1916
Operation(al) Order(s)	Brigade Order No.9 by Brigadier General C.N. Trotman C.B. Commanding 190th Infantry Brigade. Appendix 6	28/08/1916	28/08/1916
Miscellaneous	March Table (To accompany Brigade Order No.9.	28/08/1916	28/08/1916
Operation(al) Order(s)	Brigade Order No 8. by Brigadier General C.N. Trotman. C.B. Commanding 190th. Infantry Brigade. Appendix 7	27/08/1916	27/08/1916
Miscellaneous	March Table (To Accompany 190th. Infantry Brigade Order No.8)	27/08/1916	27/08/1916
Miscellaneous	Casualties for the month of August. Appendix 9		
Miscellaneous	Appendix A. Working Parties Found for the 255th Tunnelling Coy. R.E. by the Battalion in Brigade Support Calonne.		
Map	Appendix 8		
Heading	War Diary of 190th. Infantry Brigade. from 1st Sept 1916 to 30th Sep 1916 Vol 4		
War Diary	Bully-Grenay	01/09/1916	16/09/1916
War Diary	Hersin	17/09/1916	17/09/1916
War Diary	Bajus	18/09/1916	18/09/1916
War Diary	Roellecourt	20/09/1916	30/09/1916
Operation(al) Order(s)	Brigade Order No.10. by Brigadier General C.N. Trotman C.B. Commanding 190th Infantry Brigade. Appendix 9	01/09/1916	01/09/1916
Miscellaneous	March Table (to accompany 190th Infantry Brigade Order No. 10.)	01/09/1916	01/09/1916
Operation(al) Order(s)	Brigade Order No.11 by Brigadier General C.N. Trotman. C.B. Commanding 190th Infantry Brigade Appendix 10.	05/09/1916	05/09/1916
Miscellaneous	March Table (to accompany 190th Infantry Brigade Order No.11.	05/09/1916	05/09/1916
Operation(al) Order(s)	Brigade Order No. 12. by Brigadier General C.N. Trotman. C.B. Commanding 190th Infantry Brigade. Appendix 11.	09/09/1916	09/09/1916
Miscellaneous	March Table. (to accompany 190th Infantry Brigade Order No.12.)	09/09/1916	09/09/1916

Operation(al) Order(s)	Brigade Order No.14. by Brigadier General C.N. Trotman C.B. Commanding 190th Infantry Brigade. Appendix 12	13/09/1916	13/09/1916
Miscellaneous	March Table (to accompany Brigade Order No.14.)		
Operation(al) Order(s)	Brigade Order No.13. by Brigadier General C.N. Trotman C.B. Commanding 190th Infantry Brigade.	13/09/1916	13/09/1916
Operation(al) Order(s)	190th Infantry Brigade Order No. 15. by Lieutenant Colonel R.E. Hutchison C.M.G. R.M.L.I. Appendix 13.	16/09/1916	16/09/1916
Miscellaneous	March Table (to accompany Bde Order No. 15.)		
Operation(al) Order(s)	Brigade Order No.16. by Lieut. Colonel A.R.H. Hutchison, C.M.G., Commanding 190th. Inf. Brigade. Appendix 14.	17/09/1916	17/09/1916
Miscellaneous	March Table (to accompany Brigade Order No.16).	17/09/1916	17/09/1916
Operation(al) Order(s)	Addenda to 190th. Infantry Brigade Order No.16.	17/09/1916	17/09/1916
Operation(al) Order(s)	Brigade Order No.17. by Lieutenant Colonel A.R.H. Hutchison. C.M.G., Commanding 190th Infantry Brigade. Appendix 15.	18/09/1916	18/09/1916
Miscellaneous	March Table (to accompany 190th Inf. Bde Order No.17.)		
Miscellaneous	Casualties for the month of September 1916. Appendix 16		
Heading	190 1 B Vol 5 October 1916		
Heading	War Diary of 190th. Infantry Brigade from 1st October 1916 to 31st October 1916.Vol V		
Miscellaneous	190th Infantry Brigade Vol V		
War Diary	Roelecourt	01/10/1916	02/10/1916
War Diary	Varennes	03/10/1916	07/10/1916
War Diary	Mailly-Mallet	08/10/1916	17/10/1916
War Diary	Lealvillers	18/10/1916	18/10/1916
War Diary	Puchevillers	19/10/1916	20/10/1916
War Diary	Varennes	21/10/1916	29/10/1916
War Diary	Englebelmer	30/10/1916	31/10/1916
Operation(al) Order(s)	190th. Infantry Brigade Order No.18. by Brigadier General C.N. Trotman. C.B., Commanding 190th. Infantry Brigade.	02/10/1916	02/10/1916
Miscellaneous	Appendix "A"		
Operation(al) Order(s)	190th. Infantry Bde. Order No.19. by Brigadier General C.N. Trotman, C.B. Commanding 190th. Infantry Brigade.	02/10/1916	02/10/1916
Miscellaneous	Headquarters, 190th Infantry Brigade. Appendix 17	02/10/1916	02/10/1916
Operation(al) Order(s)	Brigade Order No. 22. by Brigadier General C.N. Trotman C.B. Commanding 190th Infantry Brigade.	05/10/1916	05/10/1916
Operation(al) Order(s)	190th Inf. Brigade Order No.23. by Lieutenant Colonel A.R.H. Hutchison.C.M.G., R.M.L.I. Commanding 190th Infantry Brigade. Appendix 18	07/10/1916	07/10/1916
Miscellaneous	March Table.		
Miscellaneous	Appendix "A"		
Miscellaneous	Appendix "B" Working parties etc		
Operation(al) Order(s)	Addenda to 190th Infantry Brigade Order No 23.		
Map	Redan Sector.		
Operation(al) Order(s)	190th Infantry Brigade Order No.24 by Lieutenant Colonel A.R.H. Hutchison. C.M.G. Commanding 190th Inf. Bde. Appendix 19	10/10/1916	10/10/1916
Miscellaneous	March Table	10/10/1916	10/10/1916

Type	Description	Date	Date
Operation(al) Order(s)	190th. Infantry Brigade Order No.25. by Lieut. Colonel A.R.H. Hutchison. C.M.G., R.M.L.I., Commanding 190th Inf. Bde. Appendix 20	11/10/1916	11/10/1916
Operation(al) Order(s)	Corrigenda to 190th. Inf. Bde. Order No.25.		
Miscellaneous	Appendix. 21.		
Operation(al) Order(s)	190th. Infantry Order No.25. by Lieut. Colonel A.R.H. Hutchison, C.M.G., R.M.L.I., Commanding 190th. Inf. Bde. Appendix 22	16/10/1916	16/10/1916
Miscellaneous	March Table for 17th. October 1916.		
Miscellaneous	March Table for 16th Oct.		
Miscellaneous	Headquarters, 190th Infantry Brigade.	17/10/1916	17/10/1916
Operation(al) Order(s)	Brigade Order No.26 by Brigadier General C.N. Trotman C.B. Commanding 190th Infantry Brigade Appendix 23	18/10/1916	18/10/1916
Miscellaneous	March Table.		
Operation(al) Order(s)	Brigade Order No.27. by Brigadier General C.N. Trotman. C.B. Commanding 190th Infantry Brigade Appendix. 24	19/10/1916	19/10/1916
Miscellaneous	March Table.		
Operation(al) Order(s)	Brigade Order No.28. by Brigadier General C.N. Trotman C.B. Commanding 190th Inf. Bde. Appendix 25	21/10/1916	21/10/1916
Operation(al) Order(s)	Brigade Order No. 29. by Brigadier General C.N. Trotman C.B. Commanding 190th Inf. Bde. Appendix 26	21/10/1916	21/10/1916
Miscellaneous	Headquarters 190th Infantry Brigade Appendix 27	30/10/1916	30/10/1916
Miscellaneous			
Miscellaneous	Barrage Table for Attack of 63rd Division. Appendix 1.		
Miscellaneous	Appendix 2.		
Operation(al) Order(s)	190th. Infantry Brigade Order No.29. by Brigadier General C.N. Trotman, C.B. Commanding 190th. Infantry Brigade. Appendix 27	23/10/1916	23/10/1916
Miscellaneous	Appendix 1. Barrage Table.		
Operation(al) Order(s)	Addenda to 190th Inf. Bde. Order No. 29.	23/10/1916	23/10/1916
Map	Map "B"		
Map			
Miscellaneous	Time Table of 63rd Division Attack.		
Operation(al) Order(s)	Addenda and Corrigenda 2. to 190th Infantry Brigade Order No. 29.	28/10/1916	28/10/1916
Miscellaneous	Appendix 11.		
Miscellaneous	Supply of Hot Food.	25/10/1916	25/10/1916
Miscellaneous	Appendix III.		
Operation(al) Order(s)	190th Infantry Brigade Order No.30. by Brigadier General the Hon. C.J. Sackvill West C.M.G. Commanding the 190th Infantry Brigade. Appendix 28	28/10/1916	28/10/1916
Miscellaneous	March Table.		
Operation(al) Order(s)	Addenda to 190th. Inf. Bde. Order No.30.		
Miscellaneous	Information for Battalion relieving Hamel Sector. Left Battalion.	29/10/1916	29/10/1916
Operation(al) Order(s)	190th Inf Bde Order No 20. by Lieut Colonel C.N. Trotman C.B.	03/10/1916	03/10/1916
Operation(al) Order(s)	190th Inf Bde Order No 21 by Brig General C.N. Trotman C.B H.Q. 190th Inf. Bde.	03/10/1916	03/10/1916
Miscellaneous	Schedule		
Miscellaneous	Headquarters, 190th Infantry Bde.	24/10/1916	24/10/1916
Miscellaneous	Headquarters, 190th Inf. Bde.	26/10/1916	26/10/1916

Miscellaneous	Headquarters, 190th Infantry Brigade	28/10/1916	28/10/1916
Heading	D.A.G. G.H.Q 3rd Echelon		
Heading	HQ 190 Infy Bde Vol 6 November 1916		
Heading	War Diary of 190th Infantry Brigade. from 1st November to 30th November 1916 Inclusive		
War Diary	Englebelmer	01/11/1916	07/11/1916
War Diary	Puchevillers	08/11/1916	10/11/1916
War Diary	Varennes	11/11/1916	11/11/1916
War Diary	Mesnil	12/11/1916	14/11/1916
War Diary	Englebelmer	15/11/1916	20/11/1916
War Diary	Occoches	21/11/1916	23/11/1916
War Diary	Nouvion.	24/11/1916	30/11/1916
Miscellaneous	63rd Div. No.G.130/22/	12/11/1916	12/11/1916
Miscellaneous	63rd Div. G.945/22/3.	08/11/1916	08/11/1916
Miscellaneous	63rd Div. No.G.945/22/3.	08/11/1916	08/11/1916
Miscellaneous			
Miscellaneous	Report on Patrol of 190th Infantry Brigade night of 7/8th Nov	08/11/1916	08/11/1916
Operation(al) Order(s)	190th Infantry Brigade Order No.32. by Brigadier General W.G. Heneker D.S.O., A.D.C. Commanding 190th Infantry Brigade. Appendix 30	02/11/1916	02/11/1916
Miscellaneous	March Table.		
Miscellaneous	Defence Scheme for Hamel Sector Whilst held by the 190th Inf. Bde. Appendix 31	02/11/1916	02/11/1916
Operation(al) Order(s)	190th Infantry Brigade Order No.32. by Brigadier General W.C.G. Heneker D.S.O., A.D.C. Commanding 190th Infantry Brigade. Appendix 32	05/11/1916	05/11/1916
Operation(al) Order(s)	190th Infantry Brigade Order No.33. by Brigadier General W.C.G. Heneker D.S.O., A.D.C. Commanding 190th Inf Bde. Appendix 33	06/11/1916	06/11/1916
Miscellaneous	March Table. for 6th Inst.		
Miscellaneous	Hd. Qrs. 190th Inf. Bde.	06/11/1916	06/11/1916
Miscellaneous	Appendix A. 190th Infantry Brigade Defence Scheme Hamel Sector. Machine Gun Emplacements	04/11/1916	04/11/1916
Operation(al) Order(s)	190th Infantry Brigade Order No 35 by Brigadier General W.C.G. Heneker D.S.O., A.D.C., Comdg. 190th Inf Brigade.	06/11/1916	06/11/1916
Miscellaneous	March Table		
Operation(al) Order(s)	190th Infantry Brigade Order No.36.	10/11/1916	10/11/1916
Miscellaneous	March Table.		
Miscellaneous	Report on Hamel Beaucourt Road from	12/11/1916	12/11/1916
Operation(al) Order(s)	190th Infantry Brigade Order No.37.	11/11/1916	11/11/1916
Operation(al) Order(s)	Amendments to Brigade Order No.37	12/11/1916	12/11/1916
Miscellaneous	Amended Time Table of 63rd (RN) Division Attack		
Miscellaneous	Report on the action of 190th Infantry Brigade. During the 13th and 14th November.1916. Appendix 36	20/11/1916	20/11/1916
Miscellaneous	Position of 190th Inf. Bde at Zero hour 13th Inst Rough Diagram Not Scale. Appendix A		
Miscellaneous	190th Bde Communications at Zero. Appendix B.		
Miscellaneous	190th Bde Communication With Hd Qrs at Hamel Appendix C		
Miscellaneous	Appendix D. Liaison Officers.		
Map	Hamel Section Scale 1/10,000.		
Map	Tanks		
Map			

Miscellaneous	Report on the action of 190th Infantry Brigade. during the 13th and 14th November 1916. Appendix 36	20/11/1916	20/11/1916
Miscellaneous	Position of 190th Inf Bde at Zero hour 13th Inst. Appendix A		
Miscellaneous	190th Bde Communications at Zero. Appendix B.		
Miscellaneous	190th Bde Communications With Hd Qrs. at Hamel Appendix C		
Miscellaneous	Appendix D. Liaison Officers.		
Map	Hamel Beaucourt Road		
Operation(al) Order(s)	190th Infantry Brigade Order No.38. Appendix 37	14/11/1916	14/11/1916
Miscellaneous	Barrage Table.		
Operation(al) Order(s)	190th Infantry Brigade Order No.39. Appendix 38	14/11/1916	14/11/1916
Operation(al) Order(s)	190th Infantry Brigade Order No.41. Appendix 39	18/11/1916	18/11/1916
Miscellaneous	March Table.		
Operation(al) Order(s)	190th Infantry Brigade Order No.42. Appendix 40	20/11/1916	20/11/1916
Miscellaneous	Table.		
Operation(al) Order(s)	190th Infantry Brigade Order No.43. Appendix 41	21/11/1916	21/11/1916
Miscellaneous	March Table.		
Operation(al) Order(s)	190th Infantry Brigade Order No.41. Appendix 42	22/11/1916	22/11/1916
Miscellaneous	Table.		
Operation(al) Order(s)	190th Infantry Brigade Order No.45. Appendix 43	22/11/1916	22/11/1916
Miscellaneous	Table		
Miscellaneous	Headquarters, 190th Infantry Bde.	23/11/1916	23/11/1916
Operation(al) Order(s)	190th Infantry Brigade Order No.46. Appendix 44	24/11/1916	24/11/1916
Miscellaneous	Casualties for November. Appendix 45.	30/11/1916	30/11/1916
Heading	190th Inf Bde Officer i/c All Office Base		
Heading	December 1916		
Heading	War Diary of 190th. Infantry Brigade from Dec 1st 1917 to Dec 31st 1917. Vol VII		
War Diary	Nouvion	01/12/1916	12/12/1916
War Diary	Noyelles-Sur-Mer	13/12/1916	31/12/1916
Heading	Headquarters, 190th Inf. Bde (63rd Div.) January 1917. Vol 8.		
Heading	War Diary of 190th. Infantry Brigade from 1-1-17 to 31-1-17 Vol 8		
War Diary		01/01/1917	31/01/1917
Miscellaneous			
Operation(al) Order(s)	190th Infantry Brigade Warning Order No.47. Appendix A.	01/01/1917	01/01/1917
Operation(al) Order(s)	190th Infantry Brigade Order No.48 Appendix B	08/01/1917	08/01/1917
Miscellaneous	March Table		
Operation(al) Order(s)	190th Infantry Brigade Order No.49. Appendix C	12/01/1917	12/01/1917
Miscellaneous	March Table.		
Miscellaneous	March Table		
Operation(al) Order(s)	190th Infantry Brigade Operation Order No.50. Appendix D	23/01/1917	23/01/1917
Miscellaneous	March Table.		
Operation(al) Order(s)	190th Infantry Brigade Order No.51. Appendix E	25/01/1917	25/01/1917
Miscellaneous	March Table to accompany 190th Infantry Brigade Order No.5.	26/01/1917	26/01/1917
Miscellaneous	March Table to accompany 190th Infantry Brigade Order No.51.	27/01/1917	27/01/1917
Miscellaneous	190th Infantry Brigade Administrative Instructions Issued With reference to 190th Infantry Brigade Order No.51.	26/01/1917	26/01/1917
Operation(al) Order(s)	190th Infantry Brigade Order No. 52. Appendix F	29/01/1917	29/01/1917

Operation(al) Order(s)	190th Infantry Brigade Order No. 52.	29/01/1917	29/01/1917
Heading	Historical Section C.I.D. Infantry Branch 2 Cavendish Square W.C.		
Heading	Headquarters 190th Inf. Bde (63rd Div.) February 1917 Vol.9		
Heading	War Diary of 190th. Infantry Brigade from 1-2-17 to 28-2-17 Volume IX		
War Diary		01/02/1917	28/02/1917
Miscellaneous	Summary of Casualties-February 1917.	28/02/1917	28/02/1917
Operation(al) Order(s)	190th Infantry Brigade Order No. 53. Appendix I	31/01/1917	31/01/1917
Miscellaneous	March Table to accompany 190th Infantry Bde Order No. 53.		
Miscellaneous	Working Party Reliefs.	31/01/1917	31/01/1917
Operation(al) Order(s)	190th Infantry Brigade Order No.54. Appendix II	07/02/1917	07/02/1917
Miscellaneous	Headquarters, 190th Infantry Brigade	07/02/1917	07/02/1917
Operation(al) Order(s)	190th Infantry Brigade Order No.55. Appendix III	11/02/1917	11/02/1917
Operation(al) Order(s)	190th Infantry Brigade Order No.57. Appendix IV	13/02/1917	13/02/1917
Miscellaneous	March Table (to Accompany Bde Order No.57.)		
Miscellaneous	Headquarters, 190th Infantry Brigade.	13/02/1917	13/02/1917
Operation(al) Order(s)	190th Infantry Brigade Order No.58. Appendix V	17/02/1917	17/02/1917
Operation(al) Order(s)	190th. Infantry Brigade Order No.59. Appendix VI	18/02/1917	18/02/1917
Operation(al) Order(s)	190th Infantry Brigade Order No.60. Appendix VII	20/02/1917	20/02/1917
Miscellaneous	March Table to accompany 190th Infantry Brigade Order No.60		
Miscellaneous	Appendix "A" Arrangements for Relief of Working Parties.		
Miscellaneous	Headquarters, 190th Infantry Brigade.	21/02/1917	21/02/1917
Operation(al) Order(s)	190th Infantry Brigade Order No.62. Appendix VIII.	24/02/1917	24/02/1917
Operation(al) Order(s)	Addendum No.1. to 190th Brigade Order No.62.	24/02/1917	24/02/1917
Miscellaneous	Headquarters, 190th Infantry Bde.	24/02/1917	24/02/1917
Operation(al) Order(s)	Addendum No.2 to 190th Brigade Order No.62.	24/02/1917	24/02/1917
Operation(al) Order(s)	190th Infantry Brigade Order No. 63. Appendix IX	25/02/1917	25/02/1917
Operation(al) Order(s)	190th Infantry Brigade Order No. 64. Appendix X	25/02/1917	25/02/1917
Operation(al) Order(s)	190th Infantry Brigade Order No 65. Appendix XI	26/02/1917	26/02/1917
Operation(al) Order(s)	Addendum No 1 to 190th. Inf. Bde. Order No.64.	25/02/1917	25/02/1917
Miscellaneous	March Table to Accompany 190th. Infantry Brigade Order No.64.		
Heading	Historical Section Committee of Internal Defence 2 Cavendish Sq W. 1.		
Heading	Headquarters, 190th Inf. Bde. (63rd Div.) March 1917 Vol 10.		
Heading	War Diary of 190th Infantry Brigade. from 1-3-17. to 31-3-17. Vol 10		
War Diary		01/03/1917	31/03/1917
Operation(al) Order(s)	190th Infantry Brigade Order No.66. Appendix I	01/03/1917	01/03/1917
Miscellaneous	March Table to Accompany 190th. Infantry Brigade Order No.66.		
Operation(al) Order(s)	190th. Infantry Brigade Order No.67. Appendix II	16/03/1917	16/03/1917
Miscellaneous			
Miscellaneous	March Table to Accompany 190th Inf. Bde. Order No.67.		
Miscellaneous	Headquarters, 190th Infantry Brigade.	16/03/1917	16/03/1917
Operation(al) Order(s)	Addendum No.1. to 190th Inf. Bde. Order No.67. Appendix III		
Miscellaneous	March Table.		

Type	Description	Date From	Date To
Operation(al) Order(s)	Amendment No.1. to 190th Infantry Brigade Order No.67.		
Operation(al) Order(s)	190th Infantry Brigade Order No.69. Appendix IV	20/03/1917	20/03/1917
Miscellaneous	March Table to Accompany 190th Infantry Brigade Order No.69		
Operation(al) Order(s)	190th Infantry Brigade Order No.70. Appendix V	20/03/1917	20/03/1917
Miscellaneous	March Table to accompany 190th Infantry Brigade Order No. 70		
Operation(al) Order(s)	190th. Infantry Brigade Order No. 71. Appendix VI	23/03/1917	23/03/1917
Miscellaneous	March Table to Accompany 190th Inf. Bde. Order No.71.		
Miscellaneous	Billeting List for 25th. Inst.		
Miscellaneous	Billeting List for 26th. Inst.		
Operation(al) Order(s)	190th Inf. Brigade Order No. 72. Appendix VIII	23/03/1917	23/03/1917
Miscellaneous			
Miscellaneous	March Table.		
Miscellaneous	General Idea. Appendix IX		
Miscellaneous	Special Idea North.		
Miscellaneous	Special Idea South.		
Heading	On His Majesty's Service.		
Heading	HQ 190 Infy Bde (63rd Div.) Vol XI April 1917.		
Heading	War Diary of 190th Infantry Brigade. from 1-4-17 to 30-4-17. Volume XI		
War Diary		01/04/1917	30/04/1917
Miscellaneous	Headquarters, 190th Inf. Bde., Appendix I	31/03/1917	31/03/1917
Miscellaneous	190th. Infantry Brigade. Presentation of Ribbons Bt G.O.C. Division. on 1st April 1917.		
Miscellaneous	General Idea. Appendix II		
Miscellaneous	Special Idea South.		
Miscellaneous	Special Idea North.		
Miscellaneous	Communication between Aeroplane And Infantry. Appendix III	03/04/1917	03/04/1917
Miscellaneous	Hd. Qrs. 190th. Inf. Bde. Appendix III	02/04/1917	02/04/1917
Miscellaneous	Brigade Communication Scheme Appendix IV		
Operation(al) Order(s)	190th. Infantry Brigade Order No.72. Appendix V	06/04/1917	06/04/1917
Operation(al) Order(s)	Amendment No.1 to 190th. Inf. Bde. Order No.72.	07/04/1917	07/04/1917
Miscellaneous	March Table to Accompany Amendments No. 1 to Bde Order No.72.		
Miscellaneous	All Units of Brigade Group.	09/04/1917	09/04/1917
Operation(al) Order(s)	190th Infantry Brigade Order No.73. Appendix VI	11/04/1917	11/04/1917
Miscellaneous	March Table.		
Miscellaneous	Headquarters, 190th Infantry Brigade.	12/04/1917	12/04/1917
Operation(al) Order(s)	190th. Infantry Brigade Order No.74. Appendix VII	13/04/1917	13/04/1917
Miscellaneous	Bus Table to Accompany 190th. Infantry Brigade Order No. 74.		
Miscellaneous	March Table for Transport and Mounted Hen. to Accompany 190th Infantry Brigade Order No.74.		
Miscellaneous	Relief Table to Accompany 190th. Infantry Brigade Order No.74.		
Operation(al) Order(s)	190th Inf Bde Order No 76. Appendix VIII	15/04/1917	15/04/1917
Operation(al) Order(s)	190 Inf. Bde. Order No 72 Appendix IV	16/04/1917	16/04/1917
Miscellaneous			
Operation(al) Order(s)	190th Infantry Brigade Order No. 78. Appendix X	19/04/1917	19/04/1917
Operation(al) Order(s)	190th Infantry Brigade Order No.81. Appendix XI	21/04/1917	21/04/1917
Operation(al) Order(s)	190th. Infantry Brigade Order No.82. Appendix XII	22/04/1917	22/04/1917
Miscellaneous	Headquarters, 190th. Infantry Brigade. Appendix XIIa	28/04/1917	28/04/1917

Operation(al) Order(s)	190th. Infantry Brigade Order No. 83 Appendix XIII	23/04/1917	23/04/1917
Operation(al) Order(s)	190th. Infantry Brigade Order No. 84. Appendix XIV	23/04/1917	23/04/1917
Operation(al) Order(s)	190th. Infantry Brigade Order No.85. Appendix XV	24/04/1917	24/04/1917
Operation(al) Order(s)	Addendum to 190th Infantry Brigade Order No 86.	24/04/1917	24/04/1917
Operation(al) Order(s)	190th. Infantry Brigade Order No.86. Appendix XVI	27/04/1917	27/04/1917
Operation(al) Order(s)	190th. Infantry Brigade Order No.88. Appendix XVII	28/04/1917	28/04/1917
Operation(al) Order(s)	190th Infantry Brigade Order No.89. Appendix XVIII	29/04/1917	29/04/1917
Miscellaneous	March Table to accompany 190th. Inf. Bde. Order No. 89.		
Operation(al) Order(s)	190th. Infantry Brigade Order No.90. Appendix XIX	30/04/1917	30/04/1917
Miscellaneous	March Table.		
Heading	D.A.G. 3rd Echelon		

63RD (RN) DIVISION
190TH INFY BDE

BRIGADE HEADQUARTERS
MAY 1916 - APR 1917

63RD (RN) DIVISION
190TH INFY BDE

WO 95/2116

CONFIDENTIAL

May.
3rd Bde
R.N.Bn 3
Vol 1

Head Quarters 3rd
Royal Naval
3rd July 1916

WAR DIARY
of
3rd Brigade Royal Naval Division

from

1st May 1916
to
31st May 1916

To/ H.Q. Office
    [illegible]

                                O.[illegible]
                                Brigade Major
                                for G.O.C.
                                3rd Bde R.N.Div.

Note:- This Bat. was originally the 2W.R—R RNDiv
and was altered to 3rd Bat. on the 28th May 1916.
(S.) The duplicate for [illegible]

Army Form C. 2118.

WAR DIARY of 2nd Bn Royal Naval Bn

INTELLIGENCE SUMMARY.

(Erase heading not required.)

Instructions regarding War Diaries and Intelligence Summaries are contained in F.S. Regs., Part II. and the Staff Manual respectively. Title pages will be prepared in manuscript.

Hour, Date, Place	Summary of Events and Information	Remarks and references to Appendices
Aug 1st LEMNOS	Bns at Training	
" 2nd "	Drake Bn arriving from IMBROS and attached temporally to 2nd S.N.Bde	
" 3rd "	Special Orders issued to BNS and NCO Details on 5 days Journey.	
	Lt Bayfield Bde Sig and Offers	
" 4th, 5th "	Bns at Drill — Arrangem Bn commenced hurriedly.	
" 6th "	Received orders that in relief of Division in TRENCHES and	
	that Bn was to be ready again up to strength up to FRANCE.	
" 7th "	Owing to firde elections all troops were employed within Division lines	
	A number of progress from 1/Royal marines and those 2n RNVR being	
1400	placed along the beaches and Station boats ↑ the area.	
	at 1400 men were viewed to embark for (2) ORM bn on boy	
	and two Veluches arrivals in HM Transport "Partia"	
	9/ Royal marines and those 2n RNVR were ordered to embark for Partia	
	left these three.	
	By 1900 all troops and stores were embarked and within ½ left	
	for MARSEILLES — being whilst 7/6 in bay.	
	Congratulatory signals in the offset of the Embarkation were received	
	by the Division from the Vice Admiral and Sr E Med Sqd. The	
	Port admiral and DND.	
1900	Bns Training	
" 8th & 12th "	1st Bn NDOs having arrived from IMBROS + Nelson, Hood	
" 13th "	and Drake Bns RNVR were attached from 2nd Bde.	

WAR DIARY
or
INTELLIGENCE SUMMARY.
(Erase heading not required.)

Army Form C. 2118.

N 3rd (1st & 2nd) Bn RWR

Instructions regarding War Diaries and Intelligence Summaries are contained in F.S. Regs., Part II. and the Staff Manual respectively. Title pages will be prepared in manuscript.

Hour, Date, Place	Summary of Events and Information	Remarks and references to Appendices
14th May LEMNOS	Bde HQrs, 1/Royal hames, Anson Bn (less 2 Coys) and 1 Coy More Bn RNVR Embarked in S.S. Aragon.	
0700 19th May MARSEILLES	arrived at MARSEILLES at 0700.	
1130	No orders were received on arrival + M.L.O.(?) Gen(?) would probably go into camp to start this trip. However about 1130 orders were received to entrain and move immediately.	
1500	By 1500 all troops were entrained. HQ Staff, Anson Bn H & 1 Coy Bn and Bde hqrs (commanded by Lt Col Stanley RMLI) and 7 Bde PARIS & ABBEVILLE arriving at 11) 10 had train via PARIS & ABBEVILLE	
20 May ABBEVILLE	20 May 1915 C.Y. O.C. RN Dn	
21 May	reported to MEUDLAINE where Bde HD Qrs were established in Billets	
22 " MEUDLAINE	1/Royal haves arrived on the 21st & went into Billets at LONGPRÉ when 2/Royal haves were already Billeted. Anson Bn (less 2 Coys) arrived on 21st and went into Billets at AIRAINES. More Bn detached from Brigade which now becomes 3rd Bty Bde RN Bn consisting of 1/Royal haves – 2/Royal haves – 1/ Anson RN Br – 9/ Anson RNVR namer — 1/ Anson RN Br – 9/ Anson RNVR (not yet arrived from England) is a new formation.	

WAR DIARY
— or —
INTELLIGENCE SUMMARY.
(Erase heading not required.)

Army Form C. 2118.

Hour, Date, Place	Summary of Events and Information	Remarks and references to Appendices
23rd May VIEULAINE	Remainder of 1/Royal and Batt. Hdrs arrived	
24th May "	Bde reorganising and mostly day in Billets	
25th " "	Brig. Gen. C.W. Trotman CB arrived at VIEULAINE and resumed command of 3rd R.M. Bde. Capt (Temp. Major) C.F. Jerram R.M.L.I. relieves Maj F.G. Saunders D.S.O. R.M.L.I as Bde Major - Maj. Saunders being appointed to command 1/4 RMB.	
26th May "	Received orders to H.Q. 2/Royal reserve in readiness to proceed to forming area. Bde leaving today new billets. Staff Capt. and Billeting party of 2/Royal remain handy in BARLIN. Bus at Rifle quarters, lorry, and leaving 2/Royal horses returned for BARLIN presently to 7PM	
27th "		
28th "	R.E.M.T. by march route. Staff Capt. returned.	
29th " "	Training continued. Brig. Gen. Trotman Hon CB on leave by 31st May.	
30th " "	ENGLAND – Lt. Col. E.J. Stood RMH assumed Cmd of the Bde	
31st " "	Adjointed Bridging parties from Bde H.Q. to 1/RM & 2/ home, Hours provided to BARLIN.	

A.J. Jerram Bde Major
3rd Inf. Bde R.M. Bde

CONFIDENTIAL

Head Quarters 3rd Brigade
Royal Naval Division
3rd July 1916.

WAR DIARY
of
3rd Infantry Brigade - Royal Naval Division.
from
June 1st 1916
to
June 30th 1916.

To/ The A.G.'s Office
3rd Echelon.

A R H Hutchison.
Lt Col. R.M.L.I.
Commanding
3rd Bde R.N. Div.

Army Form C. 2118.

WAR DIARY P 32 Inf Bn
R.N. Div
INTELLIGENCE SUMMARY.

(Erase heading not required.)

Instructions regarding War Diaries and Intelligence Summaries are contained in F. S. Regs., Part II. and the Staff Manual respectively. Title pages will be prepared in manuscript.

Hour, Date, Place	Summary of Events and Information	Remarks and references to Appendices
1st June NEULAINE	Bn HQ Gro and 1/Anson RNVR at 1030; Signal Section and 1/Royal Marines at 1330 entrained at PONT REMY arriving at BARLIN at 1900 and 2400 1/2 June and marched to BARLIN.	
2nd June BARLIN	Bn HQrs established at FOSSE VII BARLIN 1/Royal Marines " HERSIN 2/Royal Marines " HERSIN 1/Anson RNVR " BARLIN with 2 Coys at FOSSE VII Officers (40) and men detailed for various courses of instruction at Corps and 2.3 Bn Schools. 2/Royal Marines working parties 350 every am 230 pm. The Bn is placed under the 28 2 Bn for training & works.	
3rd June "	Ratios. Received orders that 4 Coys are to proceed to trenches tonight. In 28 Bn for training.	
4th June "	Acting Brigadier and Bde Major proceeded with GSO, Bn HQ Gro B 24 the 4 + 68 to fy Bde and 6 Q3 Bn to HQ Gro B 24 Bn to proceed to 24th Bde Area arriving 4pm. 2 Lieut 1/Royal Marines 2 Lieut 1/Anson to 68th Bde Area tomorrow. The former dispersed in forenoon, the latter in afternoon. During the afternoon the two Coys 2/RM were put through the Gas Chamber, and arrangements made to put the	GSO spec for this part attached. Appendices A + B

Forms/C. 2118/10

WAR DIARY

Army Form C. 2118.

3rd ?/?th Battn

INTELLIGENCE SUMMARY.

(Erase heading not required.)

Hour, Date, Place	Summary of Events and Information	Remarks and references to Appendices
April (contd)	The Coys. 1/Rhon though & their way to the trenches. They have are provided to the trenches before they are properly equipped. After having been in 3 days / a few without and not off the men have never found them. They have no steel helmets. Their gas helmets have been so wet too, than a week and their field with them P.H. undergarment. Instruct St. Reynold P. Ken officer of his damagers. French knorn and bomb formed an army attached & to their ten them timepro and sent to huir his training B.H.	
5th June BARLIN	2 Coys 1/Rhon to 24th L.F. B.H. 9 Coys 1/Roye Wanies to B 8 to Reh in 2 Draw?.Some no m. further training tore byo or offers into sections had hardly returned to army Bns.	
6 June in BD1 major provide to 24th Lf Reh all Cos for further experience and to the touches		

Army Form C. 2118.

WAR DIARY
or
INTELLIGENCE SUMMARY.
(Erase heading not required.)

Instructions regarding War Diaries and Intelligence Summaries are contained in F.S. Regs., Part II. and the Staff Manual respectively. Title pages will be prepared in manuscript.

Hour, Date, Place	Summary of Events and Information	Remarks and references to Appendices
6th June (cont)	Some further heavy firing which went [from] LEMNOS relieving Reinforcements:- 3 Officers and 52 OR to 1/Royal Marines 1 " " 45 " " 2/ " 2 " " 22 " " 1/Anson RNVR.	
7th June, BERLIN	Stores are coming in very slowly. Maps arrived and distributed.	
8th June "	Advance of 500 a day with 4 Portuguese, 2 Coys 1/RM and 2 Coys 1/Anson relieved two Btns by 9p in the trenches	Appendices C and G (Both Orders 10 & 11)
	Bde HQrs and 2/Royal Marines went through for chambers Bde HQrs repaired from 2d to St Bde. Considered him how became carried to relief in the trenches	
9th June "	Some of Trans went engaged in their (not their caps not into this attached to others that there was no answer with advanced trenches in front 5th Wilts. Every support was made to establish with wire across the p'e. p'e 2-3.4.	
	Div. - 2/C RN Bn. - 2d and 8-6 th Lt Bdes here at [illegible] from to the try day up to the trenches Majl. Capt Garrand RMLI to Lt Col Capt Rde HQ for tomorrow.	

10th June "

Forms/C. 2118/10

Army Form C. 2118.

WAR DIARY
or
INTELLIGENCE SUMMARY.
(Erase heading not required.)

Instructions regarding War Diaries and Intelligence Summaries are contained in F. S. Regs., Part II. and the Staff Manual respectively. Title pages will be prepared in manuscript.

Hour, Date, Place	Summary of Events and Information	Remarks and references to Appendices
11th June.	Arrangements made for 1/Royal Marines and 1/Anson R.N.V.R. to proceed to trenches as before. Also orders (attached) for change of Billets with 2 Bde R.N.Bn. Above orders cancelled and new ones issued to effect that Brigade HQrs and 1/Anson proceed to DIEVAL. These were again altered at midnight 11/12.X. to cancel orders as regards Bde HQrs and 1/Anson.	Appendix D.D1 {Appendix E 2 Bde Order No 12 {~~Appendix~~ ~~2/Bn~~ ~~Royal Marines Order~~ {Appendix F {Bde Order No V.13.
12th June.	1/Anson R.N.V.R. from trenches to Billets at BARLIN. 1/Royal Marines 2 Coys to BOIS DE LA HAIE when they came under the orders of G.E. 4th Corps. Brigadier, Bde Major and some 50 men attended lecture at 23rd Ind. Gas School and went through gas chamber. Bde HQrs proceed to BAJUS.	
13th June. BAJUS	1/Anson R.N.V.R. to LA COMTÉ. Remainder 1/Royal Marines from trenches to BOIS DE LA HAIE. 2 Coys 2/Royal Marines to trenches.	

Army Form C. 2118.

WAR DIARY
INTELLIGENCE SUMMARY.
(Erase heading not required.)

Instructions regarding War Diaries and Intelligence Summaries are contained in F.S. Regs., Part II. and the Staff Manual respectively. Title pages will be prepared in manuscript.

Hour, Date, Place	Summary of Events and Information	Remarks and references to Appendices
14th June BAVIS	2/Royal Munsters temporally attached to 2/RWFus RWDn. Pongarani and Bole, hop on side Bomb Training area and close site for Bols Bomb School and other training grounds. Bole Trench mortar Battery (3rd T.M. Batt RWD) formed under command of Lieut. Campbell, R.W.R. 11/1 Anon. 2/Lt Young lent from 2nd Bn. to start the Bole Bomb School. 2/Lt Pound of RMLI appointed Bole Bomb Officer. Great delay in training owing to constant Brigade orders for moves. All arrangements having been made for training grounds, but School etc Ords was received this evening that the Brigade was to move into a different area probably in two days time.	
15th June "		

Army Form C. 2118.

WAR DIARY

INTELLIGENCE SUMMARY

(Erase heading not required.)

Hour, Date, Place	Summary of Events and Information	Remarks and references to Appendices
16-17 June 18th June	Bde Bomb School formed and first Class of 50 started. Training. Bde H.Q. moved to FREVILLERS. 3rd Trench Mortar Battery to HERMIN. Bomb School to CUVIGNY Farm - Training (programme arranged). Evening:- orders received for 1/Anson RNVR. (forward) to ESTRÉE - CAUCHIE. This again seriously interferes with training. This Bn requires more training than any and arrangements has been made for them to go to HOUVLIN where there are good training grounds, and which place is close to Bde. H.D. Qrs. 1/Anson moved at 2.3 pm from LA COMTÉ to ESTRÉE: Brigadier inspected them on the march Lt H.F. Boulogo RNVR. from 1/ANSON RNVR attached Bde H.Q. for duty.	Appendix "G".
19th June		

Army Form C. 2118.

WAR DIARY
or
INTELLIGENCE SUMMARY.
(Erase heading not required.)

Instructions regarding War Diaries and Intelligence Summaries are contained in F.S. Regs., Part II. and the Staff Manual respectively. Title pages will be prepared in manuscript.

Hour, Date, Place	Summary of Events and Information	Remarks and references to Appendices
20 June	6 Officers + 370 men of 1/R.M. withdrawn from working parties at Bois de la Haie (BOIS DE LA HAIE) for training under Captain Foley.	
	R.M.L.I. at FREVILLERS consisting of Bomb parties — Lewis guns — Scouts — Snipers — Signallers and wiring parties. I have been, as yet, unable to obtain any wire for instructional purposes.	
pm	Major Campbell from 3rd Army Schools lecture to Officers + N.C.O.'s of 1st Cavan RNVR on modern Bayonet fighting. A most instructive lecture. The Divisional Commander and Brigadier were present.	
21 June	Bde H.Q. moved from FREVILLERS to FRESNICOURT	
22 June	Training of 1/ANSON + specialists of 1/Royal Marines	
23	Continuing. Heavy Rain	

WAR DIARY
or
INTELLIGENCE SUMMARY.
(Erase heading not required.)

Army Form C. 2118.

Hour, Date, Place	Summary of Events and Information	Remarks and references to Appendices
24 June	Very heavy rain. During the night 23/24 2/Royal Marines were relieved in the trenches and marched to Billets and Huts at FRESNICOURT arriving at 9.10 a.m. In many places they had to wade over their waists in water and were wet through.	
25 June	1 Royal Marines were relieved in the Bois DE LA HAIE by the 14 Worcester Pioneer Bn, and marched into to FREVILLERS where they went into billets.	Appendix "H"
26 June	The IVth Corps Commander inspected the Brigade at their training visiting the Brigade Bomb School, Trench Mortar battery and parties of 1/ + 2/ Royal Marines at work. A Company of the 2/Royal Marines and one of the 1/Anson RNVR were inspected on the march. Corps Commander was to have inspected the 1/Anson RNVR at their training but this was postponed on account of rain.	
27 June		
28 June	Very wet.	

Army Form C. 2118.

WAR DIARY
or
INTELLIGENCE SUMMARY.
(Erase heading not required.)

Instructions regarding War Diaries and Intelligence Summaries are contained in F. S. Regs., Part II. and the Staff Manual respectively. Title pages will be prepared in manuscript.

Hour, Date, Place	Summary of Events and Information	Remarks and references to Appendices
29 June	Corps Commander inspected 1/Anson Battn R.N.V.R at their work.	
30 June	Brigadier & Bde Major attended conference by Divl Commander - Subject reorganisation of the Division. The 1st Brigade is to be broken up again and one Bn going to the 2nd and one to 3rd Bde. The other Bde is to be an army one.	
1 July	The offensive by the British and French on the Somme commenced	
2 July	Nothing to report	

A.R.H. Hutchison
Lt Col. R.M.L.I.
Comm'g 3rd Bde
R.N. Div

3/7/16.

APPENDIX A

SECRET　　　　OPERATION ORDER No.8
　　　　　　　　　　　　by
LIEUT. COLONEL E. J. STROUD, R.M.L.I., COMMANDING 3RD. BDE. R.M.B.

H.Q., 3rd.Bde.
4.6.16.

Edition 6

Ref.Map.France, Sheet 36B, 1:40,000.

1. TRAINING.
　　A & C Coys of 1/R.M. will proceed into the trenches occupied by the 24th.Infy.Bde. tomorrow, for further training.

2. REGTS. TO WHICH ATTACHED.
　　A Coy. will be attached to the Sherwood Foresters, C.Coy. to the E.Lancs Regt.

3. RENDEZVOUS.
　　Guides will meet Coys. at the Cross Roads at R 3 C 25.

4. TIME.
　　The head of A Coy. will be at Rendezvous at 0900.
　　　"　"　"　C　"　　"　"　　"　　　"　　0915.

5. ROUTE.
　　March Route via SAINS – EN – COHELLE. Coys. to move at ½hr interval to SAINS – EN – COHELLE; on entering which place they will divide into Sections in file, one rank on each side of road, 100 yards between Sections and will so proceed to Rendezvous.

6. GAS HELMETS.
　　Gas Helmets must all be carefully overhauled, and those any way unserviceable are to be discarded.

7. DRESS.
　　Marching Order with Pack and W.P.Sheet, but no blanket.

8. RATIONS.
　　1 Iron ration, unexpired portion of day's ration and Tuesday's ration to be taken, after which, coys. will be rationed by 24th.Bde.

9. TRANSPORT.
　　Wagons with the one Day's supplies will proceed with each Coy

10. HELMETS.
　　Steel Helmets will be issued prior to the move, if possible.

11. COOKING.
　　All Cooking will be done in Canteens; Dixies will NOT be taken.

12. QUARTERMASTER'S STAFF.
　　Either the Q.M. or Q.M.S. will proceed with one of the Coys. and will be attached to the Regtl.Q.M. for training.
　　The other will proceed when B & D Coys. go up to the trenches.

　　　　　　　　　　　　　　　　　　　　　C.F.Jerram　Major.
　　　　　　　　　　　　　　　　　　　　　　　Bde.Major.

1. Retained.
2. 23rd.Dn.
3. 24th.Infy.Bde.(Through 23rd.Dn).
4. 1/R.M.
5. R.N.D.

1915   Appendix B

OPERATION ORDER NO.9.

LIEUT. COLONEL H.O. STROUD, K.M.L.I., COMMANDING 3RD. BDE., R.N.D.

                                                    H.Q., 3rd.Bde,
                Edition 6.   4.6.16.
Ref.Map, France, Sheet 36B, 1:40,000.

1. TRAINING.
    B & C Coys. 1/Anson will proceed into the trenches occupied by the 68th.Bde, tomorrow, for further training.

2. RENDEZVOUS.
    Guides will meet Coys. at the Six Cross Roads R.? M.18.

3. TIME.
    Head of B Coy. will be at Rendezvous at 1750 } Note:- these boys will have been
    "   " C "   "   "   "   "   " 1745 } through gas school prior to this
                                                 } time.

4. ROUTE.
    March Route via BARLIN & HERSIN. Coys. to move at ½ hour interval.

5. HALTS.
    The Coys. will halt for one hour about one mile beyond Rendezvous; during this halt the men will have tea.

6. GAS HELMETS.
    Gas Helmets must all be carefully overhauled, and those in any way unserviceable are to be discarded.

7. DRESS.
    Marching order with Pack and W.P. Sheet, but no blankets.

8. RATIONS.
    1 Iron Ration, unexpired portion of day's ration and Tuesday's ration to be taken, after which, Coys. will be rationed by 68th.Bde.

9. TRANSPORT.   Wagons for
    ~~~~~~~~~~~~~~~~~~~~~~~~~~~~~~ supplies will proceed with each Coy. cookers may proceed as far as halting place and will then return.

10. HELMETS.
    Steel Helmets will be issued prior to the move, if possible.

11. COOKING.
    All Cooking will be done in Cookers: Dixies will NOT be taken.

12. QUARTERMASTERS STAFF.
    The R.Q.M.S. will proceed with one of the Coys. and will be attached to the Bde. Q.M. for training.
    The other will proceed when A & D Coys. go up to the trenches.

13. The transport officer and a member of the Q.M.'s Staff will proceed to 68th Bde H.Q. in the forenoon to find out details as to how far Ration carts may go etc.

                                                    C.R.Jerram. Major,
                                                    Bde.Major.

1. Retained.
2. 23rd.Bn.
3. 68th.Inf.Bde. (through 23rd Div.)
4. 1/Anson.
5. R.N.D.

Appendix C

OPERATION ORDER NO. 11
BY
LT. COL. E. J. STROUD, R.M.L.I., COMMANDING 3RD. BDE., R.N.D.

Hd. Qrs. 3rd. Bde.,
June 7th 1916.

Ref. Map. France, Sheet 36B, Edition 6, 1:40,000.

1. **TRAINING.**
   A. & D. Coys of 1/Anson Bn. will proceed into the trenches occupied by the 68th. Bde., tomorrow for futher training.

2. **RENDEZVOUS.**
   Guides will meet Coys. at BOYEFFLES. R 18.b.44.

3. **TIME**
   Head of A Coy. will be at rendezvous at 1730
   "   " D "   " "   "   "   1745.

4. **ROUTE.**
   March Route via BARLIN and HERSIN. Coys to move at ½hr. interval.

5. **HALTS.**
   The Coy. will halt for 1 hour at Rendezvous, during this halt the men will have tea. Cookers may proceed as far as the halting place, where the men have tea, and cookers return.

6. **GAS HELMETS.**
   Gas Helmets must be carefully overhauled and those defective in any way discarded.

7. **DRESS.**
   Marching order with packs, W.P. Sheet but no blankets.

8. **RATIONS.**
   1 Iron Ration, unexpired portion of day's ration to be taken, after which Coy's will be rationed by 68th. Bde.

9. **COOKING.**
   All cooking will be done in Canteens, dixies will not be taken.

10. **Q.M. Staff.**
    The Q.M. or Q.M.S. will be attached to the Regimental Q.M. for training.

11. **MEDICAL.**
    The Medical Officer and half of his Staff will accompany the Coy's to the trenches for training.

12. **RELIEF.**
    The 68th. Infy. Bde. will be relieved by the 69th. Infy. Bde. on Friday, 9th. inst.

1. Retained.
2. 23rd. Division.
3. 68th. Infy. Bde. (23rd. Division.)   E. J. B. Tagg, Capt. R.M.L.I
4. 69th. Infy. Bde.   "   "   for Bde. Major.
5. 1/Anson Bn.
6. R.N.D.

SECRET   Appendix C.

OPERATION ORDER No.10
BY
LIEUT. COLONEL S.J.STROUD, R.M.L.I., COMMANDING 3RD. BDE. R.N.D.

H.Q., 3rd. Bde.
7th. June 1916.

Map France Sheet 36B, Edition 6, 1:40,000.

1. **TRAINING.**
   B. & D Coys. of 1/R.M. will proceed into the trenches occupied by the 24th. Infy. Bde. tomorrow for further training.

2. **REGIMENTS TO WHICH ATTACHED.**
   B. Coy. will be attached to Sherwood Foresters.
   D. "   "   "   "   " East Lancashire Regt.

3. **RENDEZVOUS.**
   Guides will meet Coys. at the Cross Roads, R.8.c.2.5.

4. **TIME.**
   The head of B Coy. will be at Rendezvous at 0900.
     "   "   " D "   "   "   "   "   " 0915.

5. **ROUTE.**
   March Route via SAINS-EN-GOHELLE. Coys. to move at ¼ hour interval to SAINS-EN-GOHELLE, on entering which place they will divide into Sections in file, one rank on each side of the road, 100 yards between sections and will   so proceed to Rendezvous.

6. **GAS HELMETS.**
   All Gas Helmets must be carefully overhauled, and those defective in any way to be discarded.

7. **DRESS.**
   Marching Order with Pack, T.B. Sheet but no blanket.

8. **RATIONS.**
   One Iron Ration, unexpired portion of day's ration will be taken, after which, Coys. will be rationed by 24th. Bde.

9. **COOKING.**
   All Cooking will be done in Canteens, Dixies will not be taken.

10. **Q.M.STAFF.**
    The Q.M. or Q.M.S. will be attached to the Regimental Q.M. for Training.

11. **MEDICAL.**
    The Medical Officer and half of his Staff will accompany B & D Coys. to the trenches for training.

1. Retained.   E.J.D.Ware, Captain, R.M.L.I.
2. 23rd. Dn.
3. 24th. Infy. Bde. (23rd. Dn).   For Bde. Major.
4. 1/R.M.
5. R.N.D.

Appendix D

SECRET.

TRAINING ORDER NO.1.
by
LIEUT. COLONEL E.J.STROUD, R.M.L.I., COMMANDING 3RD. BN. R.M.B.

H.Q., 3rd. Bde,
9.6.16.

Ref. Maps France. Sheets 36B, 36C. 1:40,000.

1. **RELIEF.**
    1/Royal Marines will take over ANGRES 1 Subsection of the 24th. Infantry Brigade, on June 11th.

2. **DETAIL.**
    B.Coy. now in the line goes into Reserve Coy. trenches.
    D.Coy. moves across from ANGRES 11 and relieves the RIGHT Coy. in ANGRES 1, both under arrangements made by the 24th.Infantry Bde.
    C.Coy. moves from HERSIN and relieves CENTRE Coy.
    A.Coy. relieves LEFT Coy.
    Bn.H.Q. relieve Bn.H.Q. at MECHANICS.

3. **COMMAND.**
    O.C. 1/Royal Marines takes Command of ANGRES 1 Subsection under G.O.C., 24th.Infantry Bde.

4. **ROUTE.**
    C & A Coys. move up COLONS D'AIX communication trench, arriving at the commencement of this trench at BULLY-GRENAY at:-
        C. Coy. at 1400.
        A. "   " 1430.

5. **FORMATION ON MARCH.**
    As far as SAINS-EN-GOHELLE, Coys. will march in Column of Route, ¼ hour interval between Companies, thence in Sections in file on both sides of road, 100 yards between sections.

6. **GUIDES.**
    Guides will meet Coys. at the BULLY-GRENAY entrance to COLONS D'AIX trench.

7. **TRANSPORT.**
    Remains parked at HERSIN.

8. **RATIONS.**
    Are taken up by half limbers after dark, by sunken road to the line of MECHANICS trench, thence they are carried up by a working party from the reserve or "C" Coy.

9. **RETURN.**
    The 1/R.M. will return to their Billets on the 15th.inst, being relieved by a Battalion from the 24th.Infantry Bde.

                                        E.P.Jerram Major.
                                            Bde.Major.

1. Retained.
2. 63rd. Division.
3. R.N.D.
4. 24th.Infantry Bde.
5. 1/R.M.

Appendix E

SECRET

3RD. BDE. ORDER NO. 12.
BY
LIEUT. COL. E. J. STROUD, R.M.L.I., COMMANDING 3RD. BDE., R.N.D.

Headquarters,
3rd. Bde.
10.6.16.

Ref. Maps. France, Sheets 36B. 1:40,000.
1. **MOVES.**
   The following moves will take place:-
   12th. June. 1/Royal Marines from trenches to HERSIN.
     "   "   1/Anson, R.N.V.R.   "   "   BARLIN.
   13th. "   Bde. H.Q. from FOSSE VII to BAJUS.
     "   "   1/Royal Marines from HERSIN to BOIS-DE-LA-HAIE.
     "   "   1/Anson, R.N.V.R. from BARLIN to LA-COMTE.

2. **RELIEF.**
   The 1/Royal Marines will be relieved in the Sector of Defence by a Bn. of the 24th. Infy. Bde., during daylight.
   The 1/Anson Bn. by a Bn. of the 69th. Infy. Bde., after dark.

3. **BILLETS.**
   1/R.M. will take over the Camp now occupied by Howe Bn. of the 2nd. Infy. Bde., R.N.Divn., and will be clear of their billets by 1000 on the 13th. inst.
   They will come directly under the command of the Chief Engineer of the First Army.
   An advanced party is to be sent to take over the Camp by 0800, 13th. inst.
   The O.C. 1/R.M. will communicate with Howe Bn. as to duties, etc., prior to taking over.
   1/Anson Bn. will take over the billets now occupied by Hawke Bn. of the 2nd. Infy. Bde., R.N.Divn., and will be clear of their present billets by Noon, 13th. inst.
   Advanced billeting parties will be at LA COMTE by 0800.

4. **BDE. & SIGNAL OFFICES.**
   Bde. and Signal Offices will close at FOSSE VII at 0900 and open at BAJUS at 1200, 13th. inst.

5. **BILLETING PARTIES.**
   Billeting parties of Howe and Hawke Bns. will arrive at HERSIN and BARLIN at 0830 and 1000 respectively.

1,2,&3. Retained.   C. F. Jerram, Major.
4. R.N.D.   Bde. Major.
5. 23rd. Divn.
6. 24th. Infy. Bde.
7. 69th. "   "
8. 2nd.   "   " , R.N.Divn.
9. 1/R.M. Bn.
10. 1/Anson Bn.
11. 2/R.M. Bn.
12. O.C. Bde. Signal Section.

SECRET.   Appendix F
                                                                         Copy No. 1
Issued at 10.30 a.m.
                          3rd.Infy.Bde., R.N.D. Order No.13.

               Lt.Col.E.J.Stroud, R.M.L.I., Commanding 3rd.Infy.Bde., R.N.D.

                                                          H.Q., 3rd.Bde.
   Ref.Map France Sheet 36B. 1:40,000.   11th.June 1916.
1. 3rd.Bde.Order No.10 of 10.6.16 is cancelled.

2. MOVES.
     The following moves of the Bde. will take place:-
   12th.June. 1/Anson Bn.R.N.V.R. from trenches to BARLIN & FOSSE V11.
        "   H.Q.& 2 Coys.1/R.M. from trenches to HERSIN.
   Note:- The two Coys. to come out will be detailed by the 24th.Infy.Bde.
   13th.June. Bde.H.Q. from FOSSE V11 to DIEVAL.
        "   1/Anson from BARLIN & FOSSE V11 to DIEVAL.
        "   1/R.M. from HERSIN & trenches to BOIS DE LA HAIE.
        "   2 Coys. 2/R.M. from HERSIN to trenches.
3. DETAIL.
     The 1/Anson Bn.R.N.V.R. will be relieved after dark on 12th. by a Bn.
   of the 69th.Infantry Bde. and will return to Billets.
     They will march to DIEVAL on 13th. being clear of their Billets by
   noon.
     1/R.M. H.Q. & 2 Coys. will return from 24th.Infy.Bde.Area to Billets
   in daylight, 12th.inst. as may be arranged by 24th.Infy.Bde.
     Remaining two Coys. will be relieved by two Coys. 2/R.M., a.m. 13th.
   inst. and proceed direct to Camp at BOIS DE LA HAIE.
     H.Q. & 2 Coys. will proceed from Billets to BOIS DE LA HAIE 13th.
   inst. and take over Camp from Howe Bn.
     They will be clear of Billets by 10 a.m. On arrival at BOIS DE LA HAIE
   this Bn. will come under the orders of Lt.Col.Hawkes, 4th.Royal Welsh
   Fusiliers for work on rearward lines.
     2/R.M. Two Coys. will relieve two of 1st.R.M. in the sector occupied by 24th.Infy.Bde.
   on the morning of the 13th.inst. Guides will meet Coys. at Cross Roads
   R 3c. 2.6. at 9 a.m. & 9.15 a.m.
     Coys. will move at ½ hour interval to SAINS EN GOHELLE thence in
   Sections in file both sides of road.   100 yards between Sections.
     Rations for the 14th.inst. will be taken, after which they will be
   rationed by Bns. to whom attached. The Bn. will come under the orders of
   the G.O.C., 2nd.Infy.Bde., R.N.Division, on and from the 13th.inst.
4. BILLETING PARTIES.
     Advanced parties of Howe & Hawke Bns. will arrive at HERSIN & BARLIN
   at 0830 and 1000 respectively.
5. BDE. & SIGNAL OFFICES.
     Will close at FOSSE V11 at 9 a.m. and open at DIEVAL at 2 p.m. 13th.
   inst.

                                                    C.F.Jerram, Major.
                                                        Bde.Major.

1,2,3 Retained.
4. R.N.D.
5. 23rd.Bn.
6. 24th.Infy.Bde.
7. 69th.Infy.Bde.
8. 2nd.Infy.Bde.R.N.D.
9. 1/R.M.
10. 2/R.M.
11. 1/Anson Bn.
12. O.C. Sig.Sec.

                                                  Please acknowledge.

Issued at 6.0 pm   Appendix G.   Bde Major.

TRAINING ORDER NO 2
BY
BRIGADIER GENERAL C.N. TROTMAN, C.B. COMMANDING 3RD BDE. R.N. DIVN.

Headquarters, 3rd Bde.
17th June 1916.

1. **WIRE.**

   (a) 1 Sergt. and 1 Corpl. or L/Corpl. and corresponding R.N.V.R. ranks in each Coy. and 6 men in each Platoon are to be trained as expert wire parties.
   After their preliminary training they will, normally, work as ordinary infantry except when there is work on wire to be done and their infantry training should not be allowed to deteriorate. They should, however, be kept up to the mark by frequent wire exercises.

   (b) Their duties will be:-
   1. Constructing wire entanglements.
   2. Repairing   "   "
   3. Cutting our own and enemy's wire as may be necessary.

   (c) The following is suggested as a progressive form of training:-
   1. Uses of wire; types of entanglements (our own & enemy); types of Stakes (Screw etc.); French wire and mixtures of French and English.
   2. Putting out wire by Drill Method in daylight.
      (Note:- Drill for this has been issued to Bns.)
   3. Ditto by night.
   4. Cutting through wire by day.
   5. Ditto by night.
   6. Constructing very complicated entanglements by day, mixed French and English wire.
   7. Cutting through this by night.
   8. Repairing by night a badly cut about and complicated bit of wire.
      Note:- Absolute quietness and silence must be impressed on the men whilst carrying out these exercises both by day and night. If men do not accustom themselves to working in silence by daylight they will not be quiet by night.
      During these exercises men might be placed in trenches on the enemy's side of the wire, which being cut or erected, who would report subsequently what they had seen or heard.

   (d) An Officer is to be detailed in each Bn. to give the necessary instruction.

   (e) Indents for material required should be made on R.E. through Bde. Hd. Qrs.

2. **DRILL.**

   Steady Drill is to be practised for disciplinary purposes Every possible man in the Bn. should be given at least half an hours steady drill daily, either in Bn., Coy., or Platoon; Arm Drill, marching past etc. particular care being taken as to the smartness and correctness of the way in which it is carried out. A good time for this Drill is on the return from other instruction and open formation, before the men dismiss.

3. **BAYONET FIGHTING.**

   Certain Officers and N.C.O's in each Bn. have been through a course of Bayonet Fighting at the Corps School. These are now to be detailed as instructors in the Bns.
   The attached diagram is a suggestion, which Bns. can make in their own areas.

4. BOMBING.

5. BDE. SCHOOLS.

C.F. Jerram, Major,
Brigade Major.

1, 2 & 3. Hawkins(?)
4. R.N.D.
5. 1/R.M.Bn.
6. 2/R.M.Bn.
7. 1/Anson Bn.
8. 3/T.M.Battery.
9. 2/Anson Bn.
10. Bde. M.G. Coy.

Sketch of Suggested Bayonet Fighting Ground

Direction of attack ↓

Bags of straw representing men

Fire Trench

Strong Timber →

Sacks of Straw

Support Trench

All alike, but at least 3 lines should be made

17/6/16

Belchnay
3rd Batt'n Res. Div.

Copy No. 1.

Appendix H

SECRET.

3RD. BDE. ORDER NO.14
BY
BRIGADIER GENERAL C.N.TROTMAN, C.B., COMMANDING 3RD. BDE., R.N.D.

H.Q. 3rd. Bde.,
24th. June.16.

Ref. Map France 36B. 1:40,000

1. The 14th. Pioneer Bn. Worcestershire Regt. is moving today to BOIS DE LA HAIE in relief of 1/Royal Marines. They will bivouac there on the night of the 24/25th. in a site selected by O.C. 1/Royal Marines.
   On the 25th. they will move into the Camp now occupied by 1/R.M.

2. Guides from 1/Royal Marines will report to Staff Capt. at Bde. Hd. Qrs. at FRESNICOURT at 11.30a.m. to-day to guide Pioneer Bn. to BOIS DE LA HAIE; they will bring an haversack ration with them.

3. The 1/Royal Marines will move on the 25th. inst. to billets at FREVILLERS.

4. The 1/Royal Marines will hand over to the Pioneer Bn. all plans and programmes of work they may have, and will help them in every way possible.

5. When the 1/Royal Marines march out on the 25th., they will leave behind 1 N.C.O. and 4 Pte's per Coy., to act as guides.
   This party will be incharge of an Officer, and will rejoin its Bn. on the 26th. inst.

Copy to:-
1, 2, & 3 Retained.
4. R.N. Divn.
5. 1/R.M.
6. Pioneer Bn. (For information)
7. 2/R.M. Bn.
8. 1/Anson Bn.
9. 3rd. T.M. Battery.
10. Bde. Signal Officer.

C.F. Jerram. Major.
Bde. Major.

63/ July
190 Inf Bde Vol 2

SECRET

Headquarters 190th Inf Bde.
1st August 1916.

WAR DIARY
of
190th Infantry Brigade
from
July 6th 1916.
to
July 31st 1916.

Volume 2.

To
Headquarters
63rd (RN) Division.

C.F. Jerram
Brigade Major
190th Inf Bde.

Army Form C. 2118.

WAR DIARY of 3rd Inf Bde Royal Naval Div and 190th Inf Bde.

INTELLIGENCE SUMMARY.

Place	Date	Hour	Summary of Events and Information	Remarks and references to Appendices
FRESNICOURT	6th July	—	Received orders that Brigadier and Staff of 1st R.N. Bde were to take over this 3rd Inf Bde R.N. Division, which was to become the 1st Bde; and that present Staff was to proceed to England to take over a new ARMY Bde to be known as 3rd Bde R.N. Division.	
LONDON	9th do.	—	Brigadier and Bde Major proceeded to BOULOGNE and arrived LONDON @ 9.P.M.	
	8th do.	—	Brigadier and Bde Major proceeded to WAR OFFICE and called on A.G.I. R.N. Div: to be known as 63rd (R.N.) Division BRIGADES. 188th 189th 190th 190th Bde. 7th ROYAL FUSILIERS now @ FALMOUTH. 4th BEDFORDSHIRE REGIMENT - FELIXSTOW 10th DUBLIN FUSILIERS - DUBLIN 11st H.A.C. - FRANCE in FRANCE. The 4th BEDFORDS are only 300 Strong. They received a draft of 250 on the 12th from the DUKE OF BEDFORDS training centre, and a further 300 on arrival in FRANCE. The other BATTALIONS are stated to be up to strength. Orders have been given for them to mobilize @ once and go to FRANCE early next week.	

Army Form C. 2118.

WAR DIARY of 190th Inf Bde.

INTELLIGENCE SUMMARY.

(Erase heading not required.)

Place	Date	Hour	Summary of Events and Information	Remarks and references to Appendices
	8th July 1915		At present they are certainly only partially trained and have no transport. The DUBLIN FUSILIERS have not done any musketry.	
	9th July		Remainder of Staff arrived in LONDON. H.Qrs of B/Qr. Office established @ 91. YORK St. WESTMINSTER. Men sent on leave. Arrangements made for Brigadier and his Staff Officer to inspect 4th BEDFORDS on 11th. DUBLIN FUSILIERS 13th - 7th R.F. on 16th.	
	11th July		Brigadier and Bde Major proceeded to FELIXSTOWE. Found that draft had not arrived yet, and most of remainder were on leave. About 90 men on parade.	
	13th do		Brigadier and Staff Captain proceeded to DUBLIN to inspect 10th DUBLIN FUSILIERS	
	18th do		Brigadier accompanied by Bde Major inspected 7th Royal Fusiliers @ FALMOUTH. All the above named BATTALIONS require a great deal of training before taking their place in the line.	
BOULOGNE	22nd do		Bde Headquarters proceeded overseas via FOLKESTONE to BOULOGNE	
BARLIN	23rd do		Bde Headquarters established at FOSSE VII BARLIN. 1st H.A.C. @ COUPIGNY with 2 Coys in BOIS DE VERDREL.	
	26th do		7th ROYAL FUSILIERS arrived and billeted @ VERDREL. 30 Officers 980 other ranks.	

Army Form C. 2118.

WAR DIARY

INTELLIGENCE SUMMARY

(Erase heading not required.)

1/190 Inf Bde

Place	Date	Hour	Summary of Events and Information	Remarks and references to Appendices
HERSIN	27th July	-	Bde Headquarters relieved 141st Bde Headquarters @ HERSIN and Bde took over duties of Divisional Reserve. 1st H.A.C. moved from COUPIGNY to BOUVIGNY HUTS in the Bois de BOUVIGNY. - 4th BEDFORD REGIMENT arrived @ BARLIN and went into Billets and Huts @ COUPIGNY	Appendix I.
	28th July	-	Units Training. Detailed training areas.	
	30th do	-	300 reinforcements arrived for 4th BEDFORDSHIRE REGIMENT.	
	31st July	-	Brigadier inspected 4/Bedfordshire Regt.	

A. Sueran
Bde. Major
190th Inf Bde.

1/8/16.

190 Bde Vol 3

SECRET.

Headquarters 190th Inf Bde.
1/9/16.

WAR DIARY
of
190th Infantry Brigade
From
August 1st 1916
to
August 31st 1916.

VOLUME III

To
Hd. Qrs 63rd Div.

Charles Futman
Brig. General.
Commanding
190th Inf Bde.

Army Form C. 2118.

WAR DIARY
or
INTELLIGENCE SUMMARY.
(Erase heading not required.)

Instructions regarding War Diaries and Intelligence Summaries are contained in F.S. Regs., Part II. and the Staff Manual respectively. Title pages will be prepared in manuscript.

Place	Date	Hour	Summary of Events and Information	Remarks and references to Appendices
HERSIN	Aug 1st 2nd	—	Training	
do.	3rd	—	Orders for attachment of H.A.C. by Companies to Units in the line. Sent out.	Ibid APPENDIX 2.
	4th	—	Two Coys. I.H.A.C. went for instruction to BOUCHEZ sector 189th Infantry Brigade. They were distributed by platoons, and attached to Coys in the line.	Ibid
	5.6.7.8th		Training	Ibid
	9th		190th T.M. Battery proceeded to PERNES for live round firing. 300 rounds allowed. Night of 8/9th 2 Coys H.A.C. (relieved other two Coys. Six guns 1st Motor M.G. Battery came out of the line on 8th inst. and were attached to 190th Infty. Bde. Four of these Guns immediately detached again to 189th Bde in defence of LORETTE RIDGE. Four Hotchkiss Guns Brig Edwards horse attached 190th Bde. on same day and billeted in COUPIGNY.	
	10th 11th		Deep dug-out Platoons of 7th Royal Fusiliers and 4th Bedfordshire Regiment attached to Engineers for training.	Ibid
	12th		Training. Two Companies 1st Honourable Artillery Company attached to 189th Infantry	Ibid

1577 Wt.W10791/1773 500,000 1/15 D.D.&L. A.D.S.S./Forms/C. 2118.

Army Form C. 2118.

WAR DIARY
or
INTELLIGENCE SUMMARY.
(Erase heading not required.)

Place	Date	Hour	Summary of Events and Information	Remarks and references to Appendices
	August			
	12th Cont.		Brigade for further Trench training till 16th; then the other two until the 20th inst.	
				APPENDIX 3.
	13th & 14th		Training. Weather changing to S.W. winds and showery. Wet.	
	15th Aug.		Brigadier visited the SOMME Battlefields, returning the same day. After	
	16th do.		Two Companies 7th ROYAL FUSILIERS to ANGRES Section of the Divisional Area held by the 188th Infantry Brigade.	APPENDIX A.
			IVth Corps Commander visited the Brigadier in the afternoon and saw the ordinary training going on.	
	17 Aug.		Training	
	18 Aug.			
	19 Aug.		10/ Royal Dublin Fusiliers arrived in France. Schifftrain & wire cutting by "Bangalore" Torpedoes	
	20 Aug.		attended by Brigadier & staff. Also several Micros & Bros. Very interesting experiment and bars well cut.	
	21 Aug.		Lecture by C.R.E. to Officers from each Bn on Revetments at 11 a.m. Lecture by Capt Capper	

Army Form C. 2118.

WAR DIARY
or
INTELLIGENCE SUMMARY.
(Erase heading not required.)

Place	Date	Hour	Summary of Events and Information	Remarks and references to Appendices
	22 Aug		P.T. Staff to 1/RF 4/Bedfordshire Regt. and 1/HAC M. Bayonet fighting.	
	23 Aug		Train up found taken.	
	24 Aug		During night of the 20/21 ult Gas was discharged from AN.6. RE 8 & 11 ? And section against the Enemy. This was first in heavy yapre gas since Indian.	
	25 Aug		Until last night, the wind has been unfavourable.	
	26 Aug		Training. 1st Army Com.dr inspected the Brigade 1/HAC enfiltrated their trenches by comp. in the trenches. 4/Bedfordshire Regt commenced to take over CH ONIVE section on the Orders received the prevent 63rd Div trench, or its NORTH side.	MGSection 3
	27 Aug		28th int.f later altered to 35th west. Officers visited the new line. 2 Bns and a M.G. Coy to be attached to 73rd Bn for a few days pending the further	

WAR DIARY
or
INTELLIGENCE SUMMARY.

Army Form C. 2118.

Place	Date	Hour	Summary of Events and Information	Remarks and references to Appendices
	28 Aug		Training of 4/Beds Regt and 10/R. Sus. Fus. 7/Royal Fusiliers have to go to the trenches to take over a subsection without ever having gone in by Coys. Orders for relief at nt. Considerable confusion Carried owing to (portion of) Headquarters - subdivisions being constantly changed. The new subsection being taken over from another Corps. Finally decided that the 10/R. Sus. would NOT be taken over and new ones went (?) in BULLY-GRENAY accordingly much change of by rail. wires, transport arranged &c &c. 11th M.G. Coy. moved to HERSIN and attached 1902 to Bde	Appendices 6 + 7
	29th Aug		1/Honourable Artillery Company moved to HERSIN. 13/Kings Royal Rifle Corps to PETIT-SAINS.	

WAR DIARY
INTELLIGENCE SUMMARY
(Erase heading not required.)

Army Form C. 2118.

Place	Date	Hour	Summary of Events and Information	Remarks and references to Appendices
BULLY GRENAY	30 May		13/ Royal Fusiliers to HERSIN - The two latter on attachment to 195th Inf Bde. 111th Bde. M.G. Coy. and 190 L.T.M. Battery to trenches. In the afternoon an exceptionally heavy thunderstorm and rain. A flood of water passing through HERSIN waist high. The 13/KRR who were passing through at the time were unable to proceed and a large regim was carried off its wheels.	Appendix 6.
	31 May		Relieved 120 Inf Bde in the CARDWNE SECTOR according to APPENDIX 6. Relief completed 2.51 p.m. Very wet and clingy half a gale. Quiet night but right Coys slightly down. Refs N Section attached. Fine day and light W & N.W.	Appendix 6. Appendix 9.
			CASUALTIES	

J.F.... Bde hd
130th Inf Bde.
1/9/16.

Appendix I

SECRET.   190th. Infantry Bde. Order No. 1.
by
Brigadier General C.N.Trotman, C.B. Commanding 190th.Bde. 63rd(R.N)Div.

H.Q., 190th. Bde.
25/7/16.

Reference Map FRANCE Sheet 36B
1/40,000

1. The 190th.Infantry Bde. will relieve the 141st.Infantry Bde. in 63rd. Divisional Reserve on the 27th.inst.

2. Bde.Headquarters will arrive at HERSIN at 7.30 a.m. where they will relieve 190th.Infantry Bde. Hd.Qrs.
   1/H.A.C. will arrive at BOUVIGNY HUTS at 7.30 a.m. and relieve 17th.London Regt.
   Transport will NOT accompany Bn.but will move to BOYEFFLES where it will take over the lines of the 17th.London Regt.

3. Movement of 1/H.A.C. is to be by Companies at ½ hour interval to a line drawn N and S through G of BOUVIGNY - BOYEFFLES; thence by Platoons at 100 yards interval.
   Road or Roads may be used as found convenient.

4. Prior to this move, Officers of the 1/H.A.C. are to reconnoitre roads to BOUVIGNY HUTS.

5. Whilst in BOUVIGNY HUTS, in Divisional Reserve, 1/H.A.C. is allotted to the Defence of the LORETTE RIDGE and will be prepared on receipt of instructions from Bde.H.Q., to occupy the MARBURE line on the LORETTE Ridge from St.NAZAIRE River to R.35.c. 6.4.
   All Officers are to make themselves acquainted with the various routes to this line.
   A great part of this spur is under direct observation of the enemy.

6. 190th.Infantry Bde.Office will close at Fosse V11 at 5.30 a.m. and open at HERSIN at 7.30 a.m.

                                             C.F.Jerram.   Major.

Copy.No.1. 63rd.(R.N)Div.   Bde.Major.
        2. 141st.Infantry.Bde.
        3. 1/H.A.C.
        4. 190th.T.M.Battery (for information)
        5. File.
        6,7,8, War Diary.

Appendix 2

SECRET.   190th. Infantry Bde. Order No.2.
                              by
        Brigadier General C.N.Trotman, C.B. Commanding 190th.Infy.Brigade.

                                                    H.Q.190th.Bde,
Reference Map FRANCE Sheet 36b   3/8/16.
              1/40,000.

1. Companies of the 1/H.A.C. will be attached for further training to the 189th.Infantry Brigade in the SOUCHEZ Sector as follows:- Two Companies from the night of the 4/5th to the night of the 8/9th; Two Companies from the night of the 8/9th to the night of the 12/13th.

2. One of these Coys. will be attached to each Bn. in the line and will be split up into Sections each of which will be attached to a different Platoon.
    Officers, N.C.O's and Specialists will be attached to individuals of equal rank etc., in the Bns.

3. The "Dugout Platoons" attached to R.E. will be withdrawn to their Bn. this evening and will go into the trenches with their Coys.

4. Companies will move in accordance with attached March Table.

5. Further orders will be issued as to attachment of whole Companies to Bns. in the line.

6. Coy. Officers will reconnoitre the safest routes to AIX NOULETTE.

7. Individuals of Bn. Headquarters, Medical Officer, Transport Officer and Q.M.Staff will arrange to visit the line whilst the Coys. are under training.

8. Rations for the 5th will be taken; after which Coys will be rationed by Coys to which attached.

                                        C.F.Jerram.   Major.
                                              Brigade Major.

    Copies to:-
      1. Retained.
      2. 63rd.Div.
      3. 189th.Infy.Bde.
      4. C.R.E. (for information, Para.3)
      5. 1/H.A.C.
      6. 7/Royal Fusiliers.) for
      7. 4/Bedfordshire Regt.) information.
      8.) War Diary.
      9.)

MARCH TABLE.(Supplement to Brigade Order No.2)   3/8/16.

Unit.	Coy.	Subsection.	Unit to which attached.	Place for guides to meet.	Time.	Date.	Date of relief.
H.A.C.	1.	SOUCHEZ.1.	Hood Bn.R.N.V.R.	March in AIX-NOULETTE.	9-30 p.m.	4/8/16.	Night of 8/9th.
"	2.	SOUCHEZ.2.	Hawke Bn. R.N.V.R.	-ditto-	10.p.m.	4/8/16.	-ditto-
"	3.	SOUCHEZ.1.	Drake Bn. R.N.V.R.	-ditto-	9-30 p.m.	8/8/16.	Night of 12/13th.
"	4. *	SOUCHEZ.2.	Nelson Bn.R.N.V.R.	-ditto-	10.p.m.	8/8/16.	-ditto-

NOTES * These numbers refer to order of going in and NOT to definite Companies of Bn. Coys.will march by Platoons at 100 yards interval.

C.F.Jerram. Major.
Brigade Major.

SECRET.

Appendix 3

190th. INFANTRY BRIGADE ORDER NO.3.

BY

BRIGADIER GENERAL C.N.TROTMAN, C.B., COMMANDING 190th. INFANTRY BRIGADE.

H.Q.190th.Inf.Bde,
10/8/16.

Reference Map FRANCE 36B.
1/40,000.

1.   Two Coys. of the 1/H.A.C. will be attached to 189th.Inf. Bde. for further training in the trenches from the night of the 12/13th to the night of the 18/19th.inst.
One Coy. will be attached to each Bn. in the line and will complete the relief with that Bn.

2.   Lewis Guns and detachments (2 Guns per Coy) will relieve on the night of the 11/12th.

3.   The Q.M.,1/H.A.C. will arrange as to rations with the Q.M's of the Hood and Hawke Bns.

4.   Coys. will move in accordance with attached March Table.

C.F.Jerram, Major.
Brigade Major.

Copies to:-
1. 63rd.Div.
2. 189th.Inf.Bde.
3. 1/H.A.C.
4. 7/Royal Fusiliers.) for information.
5. 4/Bedfordshire Regt)
6. Retained.
7.)
8.) War Diary.
9.)

MARCH TABLE (To accompany Brigade Order No.3)

10/8/16.

Unit.	Coy.	Subsection.	Unit to which attached.	Place for guides to meet.	time.	Date.	Date of relief.
H.A.C.	*1.	SOUCHEZ.1.	Hood Bn.	H.Q.Hood ABLAINS-S-NAZAIRE	8.p.m.	12th.Aug.	18/19th.Aug.
"	2.	SOUCHEZ 11.	Hawke Bn.	H.Q.Hawke (R27.b.2.3)	8 p.m.	12th.Aug.	18/19th.Aug.
"	Lewis Guns of 1.	SOUCHEZ 1	Hood Bn.	Road Junction (R22.a.9.8.)	9.p.m.	11th.Aug.	
"	Lewis Guns of 2.	SOUCHEZ 11.	Hawke Bn.	—ditto—	9 p.m.	11th.Aug.	

* Refers to order of going in and not to definite Coys.

C.F.Jerram, Major.

Brigade Major.

APPENDIX. 4.

SECRET.

190th. INFANTRY BRIGADE ORDER NO.4.

BY

BRIGADIER GENERAL C.N.TROTMAN, C.B., COMMANDING 190TH. INFANTRY BRIGADE.

H.Q.190th.Inf.Bde.
15/8/16.

Reference Map FRANCE 36B.
1/40,000.

1. "A" and "B" Coys.7/Royal Fusiliers will be attached to the 188th.Inf.Bde. for trench training from the 16th. to the 20th.inst.
"C" and "D" Coys. from the 20th. to 24th.inst.

2. Coys.will move in accordance with attached March Table.

3. Lewis Gun Crews, two crews per Coy, will go up with their Coys, but guns will NOT be taken.
They will move with the leading platoons of their respective Coys.

4. Scouts and Snipers will NOT go to the trenches, but will continue their training.

5. Rations for the 17th.will be carried.
Coys.will be rationed by their own Units.
Rations will be made up in bags for each section and for each pair of Lewis Guns Crews. These bags, clearly marked, will be handed by the Q.M. to the Q.M's of the Bns, in the line, who will distribute to the Advanced Dumps.
One man from each section and pair of Lewis Guns of the 7/Royal Fusiliers, will accompany the nightly ration parties of the Coys.to whom they are attached.

6. Dress will be Marching Order.

7. On relief, Coys.will march back to their billets.

C.F.Jerram, Major.

Brigade Major.

Copies to:-
1. 63rd.(R.N)Division.
2. 188th.Inf.Bde.
3. 7/Royal Fusiliers.
4. 4/Bedfordshire Regt.)
5. 1/H.A.C.   )For information.
6. 190th.T.M.Battery.   )
7. File.
8,9,10 War Diary.

SECRET.

Reference Map FRANCE Sheet 36B.   MARCH TABLE (To accompany Brigade Order No.4)
1/40,000.

15/8/16.

Unit.	Coy.	Sub-sectⁿ to which attached	Place for guides to meet.	Date	Time.	Route.	Remarks.
7/Royal Fusiliers.	A	ANGRES 1	BULLY GRENAY Church. R11.a.4.8.	16/8/16.	4. p.m.	COUPIGNY – HERSIN – R7.b.1.8.– SAINS-EN-COHELLE – R3.d.1.7. – R4.d.9.9	(1) Coys.at quarter hour interval to SAINS-EN-COHELLE, thence by platoons at 100^x interval.
"	B	ANGRES 2	ditto	"	4.15p.m.	ditto	(2) There will be one guide for each section and 1 for each pair of Lewis Guns Crews.
"	C	ANGRES 1	"	20/8/16	4.0 p.m.	"	
"	D	ANGRES 2	"	"	4.15 p.m.	"	

C.F.Jerram, Major.
Brigade Major.

Appendix 5

Copy No. 9

SECRET.

190th. INFANTRY BRIGADE ORDER NO.5.

BY

BRIGADIER GENERAL C.N.TROTMAN C.B., COMMANDING 190TH. INFANTRY BRIGADE.

H.Q.190th.Inf.Bde,
22nd.August 1916.

Reference Map FRANCE 36B.
1/40,000.

1. "A" and "B" Coys. 4/Bedfordshire Regt. will be attached to Bns. in SOUCHEZ Section for further training and will move in accordance with the attached March Table.

2. Specialists will be attached to similar Units in the line. Lewis Gun Crews will be similarly attached, but guns will NOT be taken.

3. Coys. will be split up in Platoons.

4. The Regimental Q.M. will arrange with the Q.M's of the Bns. to which Coys. are attached, as to the method of rationing.

5. Coys. will NOT pass a line drawn N. and S. through BOYEFFLES until after 8 p.m.

6. The Roads to be taken as far as the rendezvous are to be thoroughly reconnoitred.

Major.

Brigade Major.

Issued to Signals at 11 am

Copy No. 1. 4/Bedfordshire Regt.
"   " 2. 189th.Inf.Bde.
"   " 3. 7/Royal Fusiliers.
"   " 4. 10/Royal Dublin Fusiliers.
"   " 5. 1/Honourable Artillery Company.
"   " 6. 190th.T.M.Battery.
"   " 7. 63rd(R.N)Division.
"   " 8. File.
9,10,11   War Diary.

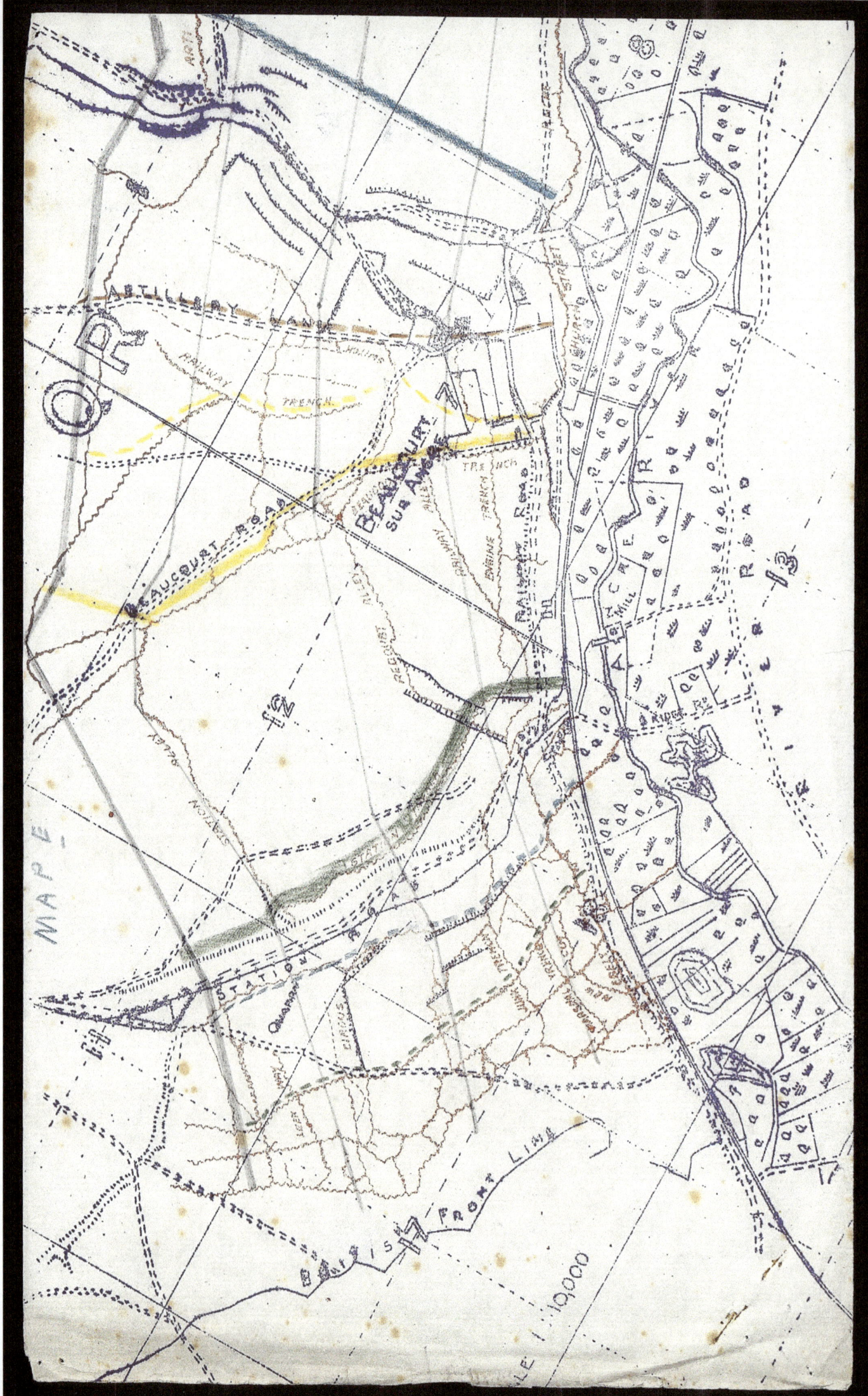

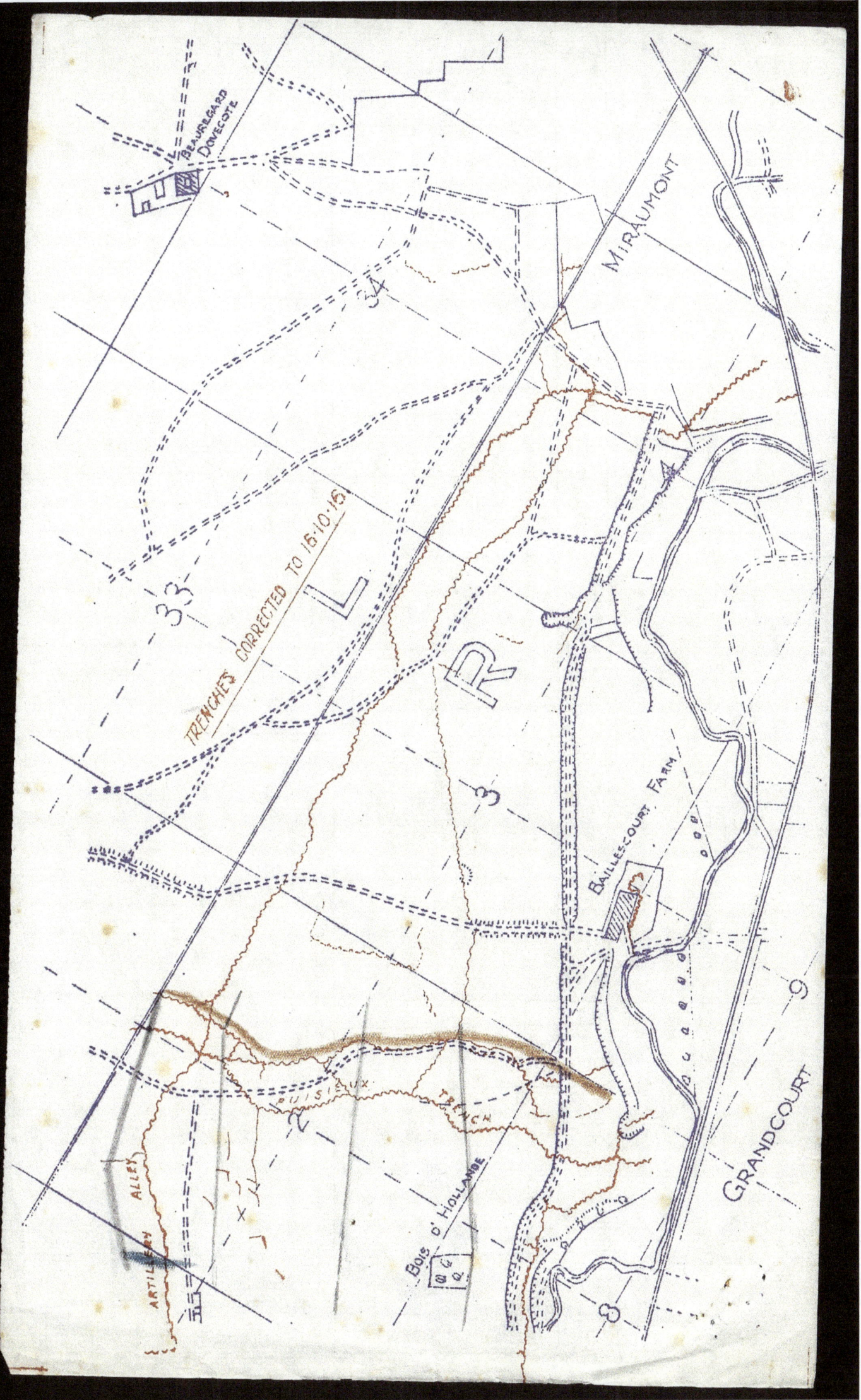

SECRET.

22/8/16.

MARCH TABLE. (To accompany 190th.Infantry Bde.Order No.5)

Reference map FRANCE Sheet 36B.
1/40,000.

Date.	Unit.	Coy.	Unit to which attached.	Sub-Section.	Place for guides to meet.	Time.	Remarks.
Night 24/25th.	4/Bedfordshire Regt.	A.	Hawke Bn.	SOUCHEZ 11.	Road Junction R22.A.9.8.	9 p.m.	Guide takes Coy. to FRENCH DUMP where 1 guide per Platoon will be provided.
Night 25/26th.	ditto.	B.	Hood Bn.	SOUCHEZ 1.	ditto.	9 p.m.	Meets Bn. here and proceeds with them.

[signature]
Major.

Brigade Major.

Appendix 6

SECRET.   Copy No......
                    BRIGADE ORDER NO.9.
                            by
BRIGADIER GENERAL C.N.TROTMAN C.B. COMMANDING 190TH. INFANTRY BRIGADE.
                                    Brigade Headquarters,
                                    28th. August 1916.

Ref. Map FRANCE 36B.
     1/40,000.

1.   The 4/Bedfordshire Regt. and 10/Royal Dublin Fusiliers will be attached by Coys. to Units in the line for training as in 63rd.Div.No.G.443/2 of 25th.August forwarded to Bns.by 190th.Inf. Bde. No.723/16.

2.   Attached March Table shows moves up to and including the 30th.inst, after which arrangements will be made direct between Brigades and Bns. concerned.

3.   In all cases the supply of rations will be arranged between Q.M's concerned.

4.   Specialists will be attached to similar Units in the line. Lewis Guns will NOT be taken whilst Coys.are split up in sections but will be taken up when whole Coys are in the line.
     In all cases the personnel will proceed to the trenches for attachment to similar personnel.

5.   Arrangements for attachment of individuals of Bn.Headquarters will be arranged by Bns. with the Brigades to which they are attached.
     Opportunity being taken for Q.M. and Transport Officer to go up with the rations at least once in each Section.

6.   The Coys. joining the 188th.Inf.Bde. on the 29th. will take on the person the rations of the 30th.
     Rations for the 31st.and following days will be delivered at Trench Railhead by the Q.M. 10/Royal Dublin Fusiliers, at 8 pm daily and will go up with Bn. rations.

7.   From the 30th.inst. the 4/Bedfordshire Regt. and 10/Royal Dublin Fusiliers become Divisional Troops until they take their place in the line with the 190th.Inf.Bde.
     In order to preserve continuity the usual states will be rendered through Brigade Headquarters, and Brigade Headquarters will continue to send Routine Orders.

                                        Major.
                                    Brigade Major.

Issued to Signals....9 Am

Copies to:-
1. 63rd.Div.
2. 188th.Inf.Bde.
3. 189th.Inf.Bde.
4. 7/Royal Fusiliers.
5. 4/Bedfordshire Regt.
6. 10/Royal Dublin Fusiliers.
7. 1/H.A.C.
8. 13/Royal Fusiliers.
9. 13/Kings Royal Rifle Corps.

28/9/16.

MARCH TABLE (to accompany Brigade Order No.9.

Unit.	Coy.	Unit to which attached.	Date of joining.	Sub-Section.	Remarks.
10/Royal Dublin Fusiliers.	A	13/K.R.R.	29th.	CALONNE 11.	Billets at FOSSE 10 PETIT SAINS with 13/K.R.R. on night of 29/30th and proceeds with them on 30th.
do	C	Anson Bn.	29th.	ANGRES 1.	Report to Anson Bn., and billet, at FOSSE 10. night of 29/30th.
do	D.	2/Royal Marines.	29th.	ANGRES 11.	Nos.1&2 platoons billet FOSSE 10 night of 29/30th, reporting their arrival to 2/Royal Marines at BULLY GRENAY by wire. They will arrive by 3 pm. Nos.3 & 4 Platoons move direct to BULLY GRENAY and report to 2/Royal Marines by 3.30 pm. They will move, after passing SAINS-EN-GOHELLE by Sections at 10 minutes interval. Billeting parties "C" & "D" Coys. loss 2 platoons to report to Town Major FOSSE 10 by 10 am.

NOTES:- Coys. will be split up into sections and distributed amongst Coys. in the front line System.

SECRET.   Appendix 7.

BRIGADE ORDER NO 8.
by
BRIGADIER GENERAL C.N.TROTMAN, C.B. COMMANDING 190th. INFANTRY BRIGADE.

Brigade Headquarters,
27/8/16.

Ref.Map FRANCE Sheets 36B - 36C.
1/40,000.

1. The 190th.Inf.Bde. will relieve the 120th.Inf.Bde. in the CALONNE Section on the 29th.and 30th.August. in accordance with the attached March Table.

2. The following units will be attached to the 190th.Inf.Bde. from the 29th.August inclusive,
   - 13th.Royal Fusiliers.
   - 13th.Kings Royal Rifle Corps.
   - 111th.Brigade Machine Gun Coy.

3. Advanced parties of Bns, 1 Officer per Bn. and 1 N.C.O. per Coy. will be at GRENAY Bridge (M.1.d.8.2.) 36C at 6 p.m. on August 29th, except the 13thRoyal Fusiliers who will detail a billeting party to be at the GRANDE PLACE, BULLY GRENAY at 6 am on August 30th. Guides of the 120th.Infantry Brigade will meet the various parties.

4. Carrying parties, from the Support Bn. (7/R.F), for the 255th.Tunnelling Coy. R.E., will relieve the present party of Argyle and Sutherland Highlanders.
   The 1st.relief will parade at the Hd.Qrs. of the Support Bn. at 4 pm, 30th.August, whence guides conduct them to the place of rendezvous.
   For composition of parties see Appendix A.

5. Lewis Guns of 13/R.F. will move with their Bn.

6. The Bde.Intelligence Officer and Brigade Scouts (8); The Bn. Scout Officer 8 Observers and 4 snipers each of the 1/H.A.C. 7/R.F. and 13/K.R.R. will parade at GRENAY Bridge at 10 am on the 29th. and will take over the observation and snipers posts, each in their own Bn. area.

7. Signals will be taken over on the 30th.August - all arrangements being made between Brigade Signal Officers concerned.

8. Bde.stores will be taken over on August 30th.under arrangements to be made between Staff Captains concerned.

9. The disposition of transport and Q.M.Stores and all questions of victualling will be communicated to Units in due course by the Staff Captain.

10. There are certain control posts, Tunnel Sentries etc throughout the area; they will be relieved by Bns. concerned.

11. Units will take over all trench stores, log-books, trench maps etc and the defence scheme which will continue to be used pending further instructions.

12. No.1 M.M.G.Battery and the K.E.Horse Hotchkiss M.G.Battery will remain at the present stations and will come under the orders of the 189th.Inf.Bde.

13. 1 Coy.Royal Dublin Fusiliers will be attached to 13/K.R.R. for training. They will be split up into sections and attached to Coys.in the front line. Arrangements for their rations will be made between Q.M's concerned.

63rd.Div.	7. 4/Bedford Regt.	14. Staff Capt.
120th.Inf.Bde.	8. 10/R.Dublin Fus.	15. Bde.Intell.Off.
188th. "	9. 13/K.R.R.C,	16. Bde.Sig.Off.
189th. "	10. 111th.Bde.M.G.Coy.	17. " Bomb "
7/R.F.	11. 190th.T.M.Batt.	17. 1st HAC
13/R.F.	12. 1st.M.M.G. "	
	13. Hotchkiss Gun Det.	

Brigade Major
Major.

MARCH TABLE (TO ACCOMPANY 190th.INFANTRY BRIGADE ORDER NO.8)

27/8/16.

Relieving Unit.	Unit to be relieved.	Date.	Guides Number.	Guides Place.	Time.	Remarks.
111th.M.G.Coy.	120th.M.G.Coy.	August 29th.	1 per gun.	GRENAY CH.	3 pm.	
Lewis Guns. 1/H.A.C. 13/K.R.R. 7/R.F.	Lewis Guns. 13/E.Surry Regt. 11/R.Lancs Regt. 14/A&S Highlndrs	Aug.29th.	1 per gun.	do.	4 pm.	NOTE:- A distance of 200X is to be maintained between platoons – Sections of Machine or Lewis Guns and sections of Light T.M. Battery after passing SAINS-EN-GOHELLE. 2. Units will move via the road which runs through L.33 Central.
120th.T.M.B.	120th.T.M.B.	do.	1 per Mortar	do	5 pm.	
1/H.A.C. less Lewis guns.	13/E.Surrey Regt. less Lewis Guns. R.Sub-section.	Aug.30th.	1 Bn.H.Q. 1 per platoon	do	6 am	
13/K.R.R. & 1 Coy, R.Dublin Fus. less Lewis guns.	11/Royal Lancs Regt. less Lewis Guns left-Sub-section	do	do	do	8 am	
7/R.F. less Lewis guns.	14/A&S Highlanders less Lewis guns. Support Sectn	do	do	do	12 noon.	
13/R.F.	14/H.L.I. Reserve Sectn. billot.	do	do	GRANDE PLACE BULLY GRENAY	9 am.	

APPENDIX 9

Casualties for the month of August.

	Killed	Wounded	Missing	Total
Officers	-	1	-	1
OR.	5	31	-	36
Total.	5	32	-	37

APPENDIX A.

WORKING PARTIES FOUND FOR THE 255TH TUNNELLING COY. R.E. BY THE BATTALION IN BRIGADE SUPPORT CALONNE.

Party No.	Strength N.C.O's	Men.	Place of Rendezvous.	Time of Rendezvous	Report to
1.	1	20	MARBLE ARCH M.14.d.1.1½	4 pm	No.4 Soctn.
2.	1	20	do	12 midnight	do
3.	1	20	do	8 am	do
4.	1	20	do	9.30 pm	No.2 Soctn.

Appendix 8

36°S.E.2. 36°S.W.1
Cité des Alouettes
Fosse 11 de Béthune
Cité du Nº 11
Corons d' Aix
Cité Calonne
Fosse 10 de Lens
Cité de la Plaine
Cité des Champs Grenette
Fosse 3 de Lens
Cité des Cornailles
Cabaret des Jardins
Dynamite House
Mersey Tunnel
Pit Prop Corner
Essex Trench
Hoxton Road
Railroad Alley
Calonne North
Calonne South
Chapel Alley
Village Line
Reserve Line
Morocco North
Potters Bar
Tamworth Trench
Bully Alley
Ham Lane
Magnetic
13°28' 1918.

Vol IV

Vol 4

S.E C R E T.

Headquarters, 190th. Inf. Brigade,
1st October 1916 Date.

W A R   D I A R Y
of
190th. Infantry Brigade.

From 1st Sept 1916
To 30th Sep 1916

[signature] Major.

Brigade Major,
190th. Infantry Brigade.

To:- A.G. 3rd Echelon.
       Troops 63rd Division.

S.E C R E T.

Army Form C. 2118.

WAR DIARY 19th L/F Bat
of
INTELLIGENCE SUMMARY.
(Erase heading not required.)

Instructions regarding War Diaries and Intelligence Summaries are contained in F. S. Regs., Part II. and the Staff Manual respectively. Title pages will be prepared in manuscript.

Place	Date	Hour	Summary of Events and Information	Remarks and references to Appendices
BULLY-GRENAY	Sept. 1st		During the night of the 31st Aug./1st Sept. the Reserve Bde practiced manning the "VILLAGE LINE" – their battle station. The section has been left in an appallingly bad state. No work appears to have been done during the summer months in the way of upkeep of trenches and the winter is now fast approaching. Our patrols were active at night examining the state of "No man's land". The Bde were relieved appear to have the ground well in hand, but has left few records. In three places we have salients viz: M.15.d. central – HAUNTED HOUSE and M.10 central. our trenches have been nearly blotted out by continual Minenwerfer fire – Schemes are being got out to dig a strengthening trench to cut off these salients, whilst continuing to hold the latter at night. And draining and repairing being done.	APPENDIX 6. (See August Vol.)
	2nd		Patrols and work as usual. – The trenches mentioned above have, in two places, been commenced.	

Army Form C. 2118.

WAR DIARY of 1/4th Northumberland Bde
or
INTELLIGENCE SUMMARY.
(Erase heading not required.)

Place	Date	Hour	Summary of Events and Information	Remarks and references to Appendices
	Sept. 2nd (cont.)		The sap leading from BURNING BING close to PIT PROP corner caught fire last night and all efforts to quell the fire were unavailing and the sap was abandoned. BURNING BING is a trench cut along the top of a slag heap which is always smouldering. The trench is revetted with very dry wood and is liable to burst into flames at any moment, — so as it is on our front and only line here it is of no importance. The flames in this case were 10 to 30 feet high. A scheme is being prepared to rivet the whole with a double row of sandbags filled with earth backed by steel frames, but it will be a difficult, dangerous and lengthy piece of work. Internal relief carried out.	APP. 6. (see Aug. Vol)
	3rd		The fire at BURNING BING has died down, but appears to be starting again in the actual trench — steps are being taken to check it by packing the place with earth.	APP. 9

Army Form C. 2118.

WAR DIARY
or
INTELLIGENCE SUMMARY.
(Erase heading not required.)

Place	Date	Hour	Summary of Events and Information	Remarks and references to Appendices
	Sept.			
	3rd (cont.)		Enemy sprang a mine yesterday at 3 p.m. at about M.20.c.6.5½. damaging our advanced shaft and burying one man. No crater found.	
	4th		The enemy Heavy Trench Mortars are very active in this section on our present allowance of T.M. ammunition does not permit of silencing them. Very much work going on. little has been done in this section during the Summer. Our three Salients RAILWAY — HAUNTED HOUSE and PICKAXE are being strengthened by new fire trenches behind them. BURNING BING has been taken in hand. The work consists of digging out the burning slag to a depth of 6 feet and replacing with bags of earth with steel frames behind.	
	5th		Work continuing — our wire in being constantly strengthened it was in very bad condition. Our patrols report that "No mans land" does not appear to be used by the Enemy	

Army Form C. 2118.

WAR DIARY
or
INTELLIGENCE SUMMARY.
(Erase heading not required.)

P/GW Ryles

Instructions regarding War Diaries and Intelligence Summaries are contained in F. S. Regs., Part II. and the Staff Manual respectively. Title pages will be prepared in manuscript.

Place	Date	Hour	Summary of Events and Information	Remarks and references to Appendices
	Sept 6.	(A.M.)	One of our patrols came upon an enemy wiring party. Lewis guns opened fire and the enemy dispersed.	
	"	4 p.m.	At 4 p.m we blew a CAMOUFLET near Dozen 209 just breaking surface. At the same time our Trench Mortars opened a heavy fire on the supposed positions of enemy mine shafts.	APP. 6. (See Aug Vol)
	"	6.30 p.m	At 6.30 p.m. we carried out an organised bombardment of the enemy lines round PUITS 16 bis with Howitzers, Stokes, Trench Mortars and Rifle Grenades - with much success. One enemy light T.M. was knocked out and it is believed one Minenwerfer. The enemy reply was feeble.	APP. 10.
	7.		Work continued. Relief carried out.	
	8.	11. a.m. to 2. p.m.	From 11.a.m. to 2. p.m. the enemy shelled CALONNE with 5.9" and 4.2" doing little damage. A large percentage of "Duds" were noticed. Our artillery retaliated on his front line and billets.	

WAR DIARY
INTELLIGENCE SUMMARY.

(Erase heading not required.)

Army Form C. 2118.

Place	Date	Hour	Summary of Events and Information	Remarks and references to Appendices
	Sept.			
	9.		Our Trench Mortars by their activity are wearing down the enemy T.M's. but in place of it he is far more active with his 5.9" and 4.2" artillery, which however has up to date done little damage. Our patrols are active in "No mans land", and report no enemy patrols appear to be out. Our improvements to BURNING BING continue; but stirring it up is dangerous work and four fires broke out during the night which were got under.	
	10.		Our patrols report the enemy wire abnormally thick, 4 feet high and at least 15 yards thick. Never have we seen such wire. A fatal accident occurred with our heavy Trench Mortar, a bad charge caused the bomb (150 lbs) to fall in our support line on a Coy. Hd. Qrs. of the 1/H.A.C. seriously wounding the Coy Commdr. and killing a Subaltern.	

WAR DIARY
or
INTELLIGENCE SUMMARY.

(Erase heading not required.)

Army Form C. 2118.

Place	Date	Hour	Summary of Events and Information	Remarks and references to Appendices
	Sept			
	11th		Carried out internal relief, completed by 11.30 p.m. last night in a successful bombing raid on a Sap head the 188th Inf. Bde. on our RIGHT captured a German for identification purposes.	App. 11.
	12th		During the night of 11th/12th enemy shelled BULLY with H.E. in the neighbourhood of Bde. Hd. Qrs. 27 shells were fired of which 11 were blind. Our Stokes Mortars retaliated for any enemy activity by a rapid concentration on that part of the enemy front line from which direction fire came. In all we fired 109 rounds. Our patrols continue to report no enemy activity in front of their trenches, wire and sap-air continue very satisfactory.	
	13th		Our artillery fired a seven minutes burst on THOMPSONS CRATER immediately on our RIGHT at 5.58 p.m. Our T.M's continue active replying to enemy fire at the rate of about 20 to 1, altogether our Stokes today fired 650 rounds.	

WAR DIARY or INTELLIGENCE SUMMARY.

Army Form C. 2118.

(Erase heading not required.)

Place	Date	Hour	Summary of Events and Information	Remarks and references to Appendices
	Sept. 13th- cont.		We sprung a camouflet near HAUNTED HOUSE; the enemy were working within 10 feet of us at the time. Brigadier went to Hospital.	
	14th		Lt.Col. Ilchester Empey JPR arrived Cambrai.	
	15th 16th		The weather turned suddenly colder.	
	17th		Colder but fine. Carried out internal relief. H.Col.Ilchester C.M.G. R.M.L affiliated temporarily to the Brigade vice Brig Gen Pollard C.B. D.S.O. 1.30 a.m. 17th orders were received that the Brigade was to be relieved by the 111th Inf. Bde. and march back to billets in	App. 12.
HERSIN	18th		HERSIN. Relief completed by 7 p.m.	App. 13.
BAJUS			Brigade moved from HERSIN to village round BAJUS. The Division is concentrating in this area for training. We do not yet know where we are eventually going. Very wet throughout the day.	App. 14.
			Orders received that we again move on the 20th to billets a few miles further South, with Bde H.d Qrs at BAILLEUL- aux - CORNAILLES.	
RŒLLECOURT	20th 21st		Moved to new billets. Heavy showers. Training in the MONCHY-BRETON training area commenced.	App. 15.

Army Form C. 2118.

WAR DIARY of 1/6th R/f/Rle.
— or —
INTELLIGENCE SUMMARY.

(Erase heading not required.)

Instructions regarding War Diaries and Intelligence Summaries are contained in F. S. Regs., Part II. and the Staff Manual respectively. Title pages will be prepared in manuscript.

Place	Date	Hour	Summary of Events and Information	Remarks and references to Appendices
	Sept			
	21st cont.		Bn. at open warfare training	
	22nd		} Coy and Battalion Training	
	23rd			
	24th			
	25th			
	26th			
	27th		Brigade Training – An attack as in open warfare.	
	28th		Brigade Training – An attack on enemy trenches and communication with aeroplane.	
	29th		Divisional Training – Attack on enemy trenches.	
	30th		Divisional Route March.	
			Casualties for the Month.	App: Six 16.

Charles Fitzman
Lieut Col
Commanding 1/6th R/f/Rle.

1577 Wt.W10791/1773 500,000 1/15 D. D. & L. A.D.S.S./Forms/C. 2118.

Appendix 9

SECRET.   Copy No...23...

BRIGADE ORDER No. 10.
by
BRIGADIER GENERAL C.N.TROTMAN.C.B.COMMANDING 190th INFANTRY BRIGADE.

Brigade Headquarters.
1st Sept. 1916.

Ref. Maps 36B. 36C.
    1/40,000.
and Section trench map of CALONNE SECTION.

1. Reliefs will be carried out on the 3rd instant according to the attached March Table.

2. Trench Stores, log books etc will be handed over in situ.

3. Lewis Guns of incoming Bns. will take over the same positions occupied by the outgoing Bn.

4. Guides will be provided at the rate of 1 per Bn.Hd.Qrs. and 1 per Coy.

5. The O.C. CALONNE Defences will be Lt. Col. E.TREFFRY. 1st H.A.C.

6. Code word for completion of relief will be TREGENNA.

Issued to Signals 5-0pm

Major.
Brigade Major.

Copies to:-
1. 63rd Division.
2. 188th Inf. Bde.
3. 121st Inf. Bde.
4. 7th Royal Fusiliers.
5. 13th Royal Fusiliers.
6. 13th K.R.R.
7. 1st H.A.C.
8. 4th Bedfordshire Regt.
9. 10th Royal Dublin Fusiliers.
10. Left Group Artillery.
11. 1st Field Coy. Divl. Engrs.
12. 1st Field Ambulance.
13. 255th Tunnelling Coy. R.E.
14. Pioneer Bn.Worcester Regt.
15. 111th Bde M.G.Coy.
16. 190th T.M.Battery.
17. Signal Section.
18. Bde. Transport Officer.
19. Bde Bombing Officer.
20. Bde Intelligence Officer.
21. Staff Captain.
22. File.
23. War Diary. (B)

1/9/16.

MARCH TABLE (to accompany 190th Infantry Brigade Order No. 10.)

Unit relieving	Unit relieved	Date.	Guides. Place	Time.	Subsection.	Remarks.
7th Royal Fusiliers	1st H.A.C.	3rd Sept.	By Bn. Arrangement		CALONNE 1.	Relief to be completed by 9.0.am.
1st H.A.C.	7th Royal Fusiliers.	3rd Sept.	-ditto-		CALONNE Defences.	
13th Royal Fusiliers	13th K.R.R.	3rd Sept.	Hd.Qrs. Reserve Bn. R.5.d.0.1.	8.30.am	CALONNE 11.	
13th K.R.R.	13th Royal Fusiliers.	3rd Sept.	By Bn. Arrangement		Reserve.	

APPENDIX. 10.

SECRET.........   Copy No. 26

BRIGADE ORDER No. 4
by
BRIGADIER GENERAL C.N.TROTMAN.C.B.COMMANDING 190th INFANTRY BRIGADE.

Headquarters,
190th Infantry Brigade.
5/9/16

Ref. Maps. 36B. 36C. 1/40,000 and Sectional
Map of CALONNE SECTION.

1. Reliefs will be carried out on the 7th instant according to the attached March Table.

2. Trench Stores, Log-books etc will be handed over in situ.

3. Lewis Guns of incoming Bns. will take over the same positions occupied by the outgoing Bn.

4. The O.C. CALONNE DEFENCES will be MAJOR.A.E.GREENWELL, 4th Bedfordshire Regt.

5. The rationing of attached units will be arranged between Q.MS. concerned.
   The 18th R.E. detachment in FOSSE 10. will continue to be rationed by the 10th R.E.

6. Code word for relief PERRAN.
   "   "   " completion of relief WELL.

Major.
Brigade Major.

Copies to:-
1. 7th Royal Fusiliers.
2. 13th Royal Fusiliers.
3. 4th Bedfordshire Regt.
4. 10th Royal Dublin Fusiliers.
5. 10th Royal Fusiliers.
6. 1st H.A.C.
7. 63rd (R.N.) Division.
8. 120th Infantry Bde.
9. 188th "   "
10. 111th Bde M.G.Coy.
11. 190th Light Trench Mortar Battery.
12. 1st Field Coy. Div. Engrs.
13. Div.T.M.Officers.
14. 1st Field Ambulance.
15. Left Group Artillery.
16. G.R.E.
17. 255th Tunnelling Coy. R.E.
18. Signal Section.
19. Brigade Transport Officer.
20. 190th Bde. Bombing Officer.
21. 190th Bde. Bomb School.
22. 190th Bde. Intelligence Officer.
23. Staff Capt.
24. File
25. War Diary.

MARCH TABLE (to accompany 190th Infantry Brigade Order No.11. 5/9/16.

Unit relieving	Unit relieved.	Date	Subsection.	GUIDES. Time	GUIDES. Place.	Remarks.
4th Bedfordshire Regt.	1st H.A.C.	Sept. 7th	CALONNE DEFENCES.	6.0.am	GRENAY BRIDGE.	This relief will be carried out as the 1st H.A.C. are relieved in CALONNE DEFENCES.
1st H.A.C.	7th Royal Fusiliers.	"	CALONNE 1.	By Battalion arrangement.		
10th Royal Fusiliers.	13th Royal Fusiliers.	"	CALONNE 11.	10.0am	GRENAY BRIDGE.	On relief 13th Royal Dublin Fusiliers march to COUPIGNY where they will take over billets vacated by 4th Bedfordshire Regt. Billeting party to report Hd.Qrs. 111th Inf. Bde. by 5.0.pm 6th inst. "E" Coy. 10th Royal Dublin Fusiliers now attached 13th Royal Fusiliers will be formed as a Coy. on the afternoon of the 6th inst and will take over a Coy. frontage; remaining in the line on the 7th attached to 10th Royal Fusiliers. "A" Coy. 10th Royal Dublin Fusiliers will join 10th Royal Fusiliers by 5.0.pm 6th inst and will proceed into the line with them as a complete Coy. To adjust numbers 2 Coys. 10th Royal Fusiliers will on the evening of the 6th instant march to FOSSE.10. (The mining village in R.2.3.8.and 9. and billet there. Map ref. of detachment Hd.Qrs. to be sent to Bde.Hd.Qrs. on arrival. Advanced billeting party, report to Town Major FOSSE.10.
7th Royal Fusiliers.	10th Royal Fusiliers.	"	Reserve.	—	—	Billeting party of 7th Royal Fusiliers to take over billets at 7.0.am

Note.- All movements in roads to be by Platoons at 200x interval.

Major.
Brigade Major.

APPENDIX. II.

SECRET.   Copy No.....

BRIGADE ORDER. No. 12.
by
BRIGADIER GENERAL.C.H.TROTMAN.C.B.COMMANDING 190th INFANTRY BRIGADE.

                                                                Headquarters,
                                                                    190th Infantry Brigade.
                                                                    9/9/16.

Ref. Maps 36B. 36C. 1/40,000.
    Sectional Trench Map CALONNE Section.

1. Reliefs will be carried out on Monday 11th inst according to attached March Table.

2. Trench Stores, Log-books etc will be handed over in situ.
   In order to obtain continuity of work all work in progress or proposed will be carefully handed over by outgoing Bns.

3. Lewis Guns of ingoing Bns. will take over the positions of outgoing Bns.

4. The O.C.CALONNE DEFENCES will be Lt.Col.D.E.PRIDEAUX-BRUNE. Commdg 13/Rifle Brigade.

5. Code word for relief PEDN.
   "   "   " completion of relief PORTH.

Issued to Signal at... 7.30 pm

                                                                            Major.
                                                                    Brigade Major.

Copies to:-
1. 7th Royal Fusiliers.
2. 10th Royal Fusiliers.
3. Detachment of 10th Royal Fusiliers at FOSSE.10.
4. 4th Bedfordshire Regt.
5. 10th Royal Dublin Fusiliers.
6. 13th Rifle Brigade.
7. 1st H.A.C.
8. 111th Bde.M.G.Coy.
9. 190th M.G.Coy.
10. 190th Light T.M.Battery.
11. 1st Field Coy. Divl.Engrs.
12. 3rd Field Ambulance.
13. Left Group Artillery.
14. 255th Tunnelling Coy. R.E.
15. Signal Section.
16. Brigade Transport Officer.
17. 190th Bde. Bombing Officer.
18. 190th   "   "   School.
19. 190th   " Intelligence Officer.
20. Staff Capt.
21. 63rd Division.
22. 111th Infantry Bde.
23. 120th   "   "
24. 188th   "   "
25. Divl. T.M.Officer.
26. File.
27. War Diary.
28. Rev. Dr. Davies.
29. Rev. S.A. Thornton.

MARCH TABLE.(to accompany 190th Infantry Brigade Order No.12.)

Unit relieving	Unit relieved.	Date.	Subsection.	GUIDES Time	GUIDES Place	Remarks
7th Royal Fusiliers.	1st H.A.C.	Sept 11th	CALONNE 1	6.0.am	GRENAY BRIDGE	13th Rifle brigade Billet on night of 10/11th at FOSSE.10. (PETIT SAIN R.2.3 8 & 9.
1st H.A.C.	7th Royal Fusiliers.	"	Reserve.	-	-	
13th Rifle Brigade	4th Bedfordshire Regiment.	"	CALONNE DEFENCES	8.0.am	GRENAY BRIDGE.	This relief will be carried out under Bn. Arrangements as the 4th Bedfordshire Regt. are relieved by the 13th Rifle Brigade. On relief 10th Royal Fusiliers will march to billets in VERDREL, picking up their 2 Coys at FOSSE.10 en route. Advanced billeting party report VERDREL pr 10th inst. The 2 Coys 10th Royal Dublin Fusiliers attached to 10th Royal Fusiliers will rejoin their Bn. on relief.
4th Bedfordshire Regiment.	10th Royal Fusiliers.	"	CALONNE II.	By Bn. Arrangement.	x	

All movements E. and S. of SAINS-EN-COHELLE to be by platoons at 200x interval.

[signature]
Major.
Brigade Major.

APPENDIX. 12.

SECRET.   Copy No. 27

BRIGADE ORDER No.14.
by
BRIGADIER GENERAL.C.N.TROTMAN.C.B.COMMANDING 190th INFANTRY BRIGADE.

Headquarters,
190th Infantry Brigade.
13.9.16

Ref. Maps 36B.36C. 1/40,000
and Sectional Trench Map CALONNE Section.

1.   Reliefs will be carried out on Friday 15th Sept according to the attached March Table.

2.   Lewis Guns of ingoing Bns. will take over the positions of outgoing Bns.

3.   The Reserve and CALONNE Bns. will man their battle stations within 12 hours of the time they take over.

4.   The O.C.CALONNE DEFENCES will be Lt.Colonel R.J.I.HESKETH Comdg 7th Bn. Royal Fusiliers.

5.   Code word for relief NAN.
Code word for completion of relief CARROW.

Issued to Signals......5/-

Major.
Brigade Major.

1. 7th Royal Fusiliers.
2. 4th Bedfordshire. Regt.
3. 10th Royal Dublin Fusiliers.
4. 13th Rifle Brigade.
5. 1st H.A.CM
6. 111th Bde.M.G.Coy.
7. 190th BDE.M.G.Coy.
8. 290th T.M.Battory
9. 1st Field Coy Divl.Engrs.
10. 3rd Field Ambulance.
11. Left Group Artillery.
12. 255th TUnnelling Coy.R.E.
13. Signal Section.
14. 190th BDe Transport Officer.
15. 190th Bde Bombing Officer.
16. 190th BdeBomb School.
17. 190th Bde Intelligence Officer.
18. Staff Capt.
19. 63rd Division.
20. 120th Infantry Brigade
21. 188th Infantry Brigade.
22. Divl T.M.Officer.
23. Rev.Dr.Davies.
24. Rev.Father Thornton.
25. File.
26. War Diary (3)

MARCH TABLE (to accompany Brigade Order No.14.) 13/9/16.

Unit relieving.	Unit relieved.	Date.	Subsection	GUIDES.		Remarks.
				Time	Place	
1st H.A.C.	7th Royal Fusiliers	15th Sept.	CALONNE 1	6.0.am	GRENAY BRIDGE	These Bns. will move into their new areas by small units as they are relieved in the areas they now hold. The guards and control posts found by the Reserve Bn. will be taken over by the 4th Bedfordshire Regt. by 6.0.am 15th instant.
7th Royal Fusiliers.	13th Rifle Brigade.	"	CALONNE DEFENCES	By Battalion Arrangement.		
13th Rifle Brigade.	4th Bedfordshire Regt.	"	CALONNE 11.			
4th Bedfordshire Regiment.	1st H.A.C.	"	Reserve.			

Major.
Brigade Major.

SECRET.   Copy...............

BRIGADE ORDER No. 13.
by
BRIGADIER GENERAL C.N.TROTMAN.C.B. COMMANDING 190th INFANTRY BRIGADE.

                                                                  Headquarters,
                                                                  190th Infantry Brigade.
                                                                      13.9.16.

1. The Officers and O.R. of the 190th Bde. M.G.Coy now attached to 111th Bde.M.G.Coy will be relieved by the remaining details 190th Bde.M.G.Coy. on Thursday 14th inst.

2. On Sunday 17th instant the 190th Bde.M.G.Coy will relieve the 111th Bde. M.G.Coy in the CALONNE SECTION

3. Details will be arranged direct between O.C.Coys. concerned.

4. Completion of relief will be notified to these Hd.Qrs. by the code word AUTUMN.

    Issued to Signals .... 5.0 pm

                                                          C.F.Jerram, Major.

                                                          Brigade Major.

1. 111th M.G.Coy.
2. 190th M.G.Coy.
3. 7th Royal Fusiliers.
4. 4th Bedfordshire Regt.
5. 10th Royal Dub,in Fusiliers.
6. 1st H.A.C.
7. 13th Rifle Brigade.
8. 190th T.M.Battery.
9. 1st Field Coy. Divl. Engrs.
10. 3rd Field Ambulance.
11. Left Group Artillery.
12. Signal Section.
13. 190th Brigade Transport Officer.
14. 190th Bde.Bombing Officer.
15. 190th Bde Intelligence Officer.
16. Staff Capt.
17. 111th Infantry Brigade.
18. 120th Infantry Brigade.
19. 188th Infantry Brigade.
20. 63rd Division.
21. File.
22. War Diary (3)

APPENDIX. 13.

SECRET.   Copy. No. 30

190th INFANTRY BRIGADE ORDER No. 15.
by
Lieutenant Colonel A.E.Hutchison C.M.G. R.M.L.I.

Headquarters,
190th Infantry Bde.
16.9.16.

Ref. Maps 36B & 36C. 1/40,000 and
Sectional Trench Map of CALONNE SECTION.

1.   The 190th Infantry Brigade will be relieved by the 111th Infantry Brigade in CALONNE SECTION on the 17th instant according to the attached March Table.

2.   The 13th Rifle Brigade and 111th Bde.M.G.Coy will remain in their present position.

3.   Carrying parties from 13th Royal Fusiliers for the 255th Tunnelling Coy R.E. will relieve the present party of the 7th Royal Fusiliers. The first relief will report at Headquarters of the Bn. in the CALONNE DEFENCES at 11.0.am whence guides of the 7th R.F. will conduct them to their work.

4.   Signal Section will relieve under mutual arrangements between O.C. Signal Sections. The 190th Bde. Signal Section is to be completely out of the line by 6.30.pm.

5.   Lewis Guns will move with their Bns.

6.   The Bde. Intelligence Officer of the 111th Inf.Bde. and 8 Brigade Scouts; the Bn. Scout Officer of the 13th Royal Fusiliers and 13th K.R.R. and 8 observers and 4 snipers of each of those Bns. will meet the 190th Inf.Bde. Intelligence Officer at 190th Inf. Bde. Hd. Qrs at 10.0.am. and will take over the observation and snipers' posts.

7.   Brigade Stores will be handed over under arrangements to be made between Staff Captains concerned.

8.   Units will turn over all trench stores, log-books, trench maps etc and the Defence Scheme to relieving units; duplicate lists signed by both relieving and relieved units are to be sent to 190th Inf. Bde. Hd. Qrs. as soon as possible after relief.

9.   All Officers and men, including Staff, of the Bomb School will rejoin their units by 6.0.pm 17th inst. An Bn. Stores to be taken back to Bns. Further orders will be issued as to disposal of bombs etc.

10.   The men attached to the Engineers and deep dug-out platoons will rejoin their Bns after breakfast 17th instant.
        Bde. details such as canteen men etc will rejoin their units as soon as relieved.

11.   190th Inf. Bde. will rest one night at HERSIN and will march during forenoon of 18th instant for new billets.

O.Ferrann
Bde.Maj.

(over)

Copy No. 1 7th Royal Fusiliers.
2. 4th Bedfordshire Regt.
3. 10th Royal Dublin Fusiliers.
4. 1st H.A.C.
5. 13th Rifle Brigade.
6. 190th M.G.Coy.
7. 190th T.M.Battery.
8. 111th M.G.Coy.
9. 1st Field Coy Divl. Engrs.
10. 3rd Field Ambulance.
11z 255th Tunnelling Coy R.E.
12. Left Group Artillery.
13. 190th Bde. Signal Section.
14. 190th Transport Officer.
15. 190th Bde Bombing Officer.
16. 190th Bde. Bomb School.
17. 190th Bde Intelliegence Officer
18. Staff Captain.
19. 63rd Division.
20. 111th Infantry Brigade.
21. 120th Infantry Bde.
22. 188th   "   "
23. Divl T.M.Officer.
24. 14th Bn. Worcester Regt., Pioneers.(CALONNE)
25. C.R.E.
26. Rev Dr Davies.
27. Rev Father Thornton.
28. File.
29. War Diary. (3)

Issued to Signals at
am 17/9/16.

MARCH TABLE (to accompany Bde Order No. 15.)

Unit to be relieved.	Relieving Unit.	Date.	Subsection.	GUIDES. Number.	Place.	Time.	Remarks.
7th Royal Fusiliers	13th Royal Fusiliers	17th Sept.	CALONNE DEFENCES.	1 for H.Q. 1 per platoon 1 per section of Lewis Guns.	GRENAY BRIDGE	10.0.am	7th R.F. march to billets in HERSIN.
1st H.A.C	13th K.R.R.	"	CALONNE 1.	"	"	2.30.pm	1st H.A.C "
190th T.M.Battery	111th T.M.Battery	"	------	1 per gun.	"	1.30.pm	190th T.M.Battery "
4th Bedfordshire Regt.	10th Royal Fusiliers	"	Reserve.	Nil	------	3.30.pm	Billeting party 10th R.F. report to Hd.Qrs 4th Bedfordshire Regt at 11.30.am. 4th Bedfordshire Regt march to billets in COUPIGNY HUTS.
190th Bde M.G.Coy.	----------	"	------	------	------	------	Will march to billets in HERSIN leaving BULLY GRENAY at 1.30.pm
190th Bde Hd Qrs.	111th Bde. Hd.Qrs.	"	------	------	------	3.0.pm	190th Bde.Hd.Qrs march to billets in HERSIN.
1st Field Coy Divl. Engrs.	?	"	------	------	------	------	Will clear BULLY GRENAY at 5.0.pm and march to billets in HERSIN.
1.Coy 14th Worcester Regt.	?	"	------	------	------	------	Will clear BULLY GRENAY at 5.15.pm and march to HERMIN where they will rejoin their Bn.

(over)

Notes:- (a) All movements E and S of SAINS-EN-COHELLE to be by platoons at 200X interval.
  (b) "UP" Trench CALONNE NORTH.
      "DOWN Trenches CALONNE SOUTH.
  (c) Advanced billeting parties of units of 190th Inf.Bde. and 1st Field Coy will report to Bde. Hd.1rs. at 9.0.am 17th instant.

APPENDIX 14.

SECRET.   Copy No. 11

BRIGADE ORDER NO.16.
BY
LIEUT.COLONEL A.R.H.HUTCHISON, C.M.G., COMMANDING 190th.INF.BRIGADE.

Headquarters, 190th.Inf.Bde,
17/9/16.

Ref.Map 36B. 1/40,000.

1.   The 190th.Inf.Bde.will move into billets on the 18th.inst. according to the attached March Table.

2.   Baggage wagons will accompany units.

3.   No.4 Coy.Divisional Train is attached to the Brigade. Its position will be notified later. All indents for baggage wagons and supplies will be made on this Coy.

E. B. Tagg
for Major. Staff Capt
Brigade Major.

Issued to Signals 2-30pm

Copies to:-
1. 7/Royal Fusiliers.
2. 4/Bedfordshire Regt.
3. 10/Royal Dublin Fusiliers.
4. 1/H.A.C.
5. 190th.M.G.Coy.
6. 190th.T.M.Battery.
7. 1st.Field Coy. Div Engineers.
8. No.4 Coy.Div.Train.
9. 63rdDiv.

SECRET.   17/9/16.

MARCH TABLE (to accompany Brigade Order No.16).

Unit.	Date.	From.	To.	Route.	Head of Column will pass.	At.	Remarks.
10/Royal Dublin Fusiliers.	18th.Sep.	MAISNIL	DIEVAL	HOUDAIN - DIVION - OURTON	Cross Roads J.36.c.1.2.	8 am	) O.C.10/R.D.F.will) detail Billeting) Areas for these) Units.
4/Bedfordshire Regt.	"	COUPIGNY	"	BARLIN - MAISNIL - thence as per 10/R.D.F.	Cross Roads Q.5.b.1.2.	"	
190th.Bde.M.G.Coy.	"	HERSIN	"	- ditto -	- ditto -	8.30am	
190th.T.M.Batty.	"	"	La COMTE	BARLIN - MAISNIL - RANCHICOURT	- ditto -	9.am	Billeting area will be allotted by 1/H.A.C.
190th.Inf.Bde.H.Q.	"	"	CHATEAU O.10.b.5.8	BARLIN-MAISNIL-RANCHICOURT-LA COMTE.	- ditto -	9.30am	
1/H.A.C.	"	"	LA COMTE	BARLIN - MAISNIL - RANCHICOURT	- ditto -	9.45am	Will allot billet area to T.M.Batty.
7/Royal Fusiliers.	"	"	BEUGIN	BARLIN - MAISNIL -	- ditto -	10.15am	
1st.Field Coy. Div.Engineers.	"	"	BAJUS	HOUDAIN. BARLIN - MAISNIL - RANCHICOURT - LA COMTE.	- ditto -	10.45am	

NOTES:- (a) Troops are to keep an uniform speed of 2¾ miles per hour including halts, except as in (b).
(b) Troops not already arrived at destination will halt for dinner from 12.30 pm to 1.15pm. The road must be left clear for traffic.
(c) Billeting parties will march two hours ahead of their units.
(d) Blocking parties to show the correct roads, under an officer will be provided as follows:-
1. 10/Royal Dublin Fusiliers provide their own, which will close after Bn. has passed and follow on in rear.
2. 4/Bedfordshire Regt. will provide for Bn. and M.G.Coy.-Follow in rear of M.G.Coy.
3. 1/H.A.C.will provide for T.M.Batty.and Bde.H.Q.(as far as LA COMTE) and 1/H.A.C. This party will move 5 minutes ahead of T.M.Batty. and will close and follow 1/H.A.C. as they pass.
4. 7/Royal Fusiliers and 1st.Field Coy. each provide their own.

ADDENDA TO 190th. INFANTRY BRIGADE ORDER NO.16.

Headquarters, 190th.Inf.Bde,
17/9/16.

Add new para.4. Refilling Point for 190th.Infantry Bde.on 19th inst. will be OURTON DIEVAL Road I.34.c. at 8 am.

    5. Transport. 1 guide from each Unit except 10/Royal Dublin Fusiliers and No.4 Coy.Div.Train is to be at Bde.Headquarters, Q.5.b.4.1. at 6.30am 18th.September to guide Motor Lorries to Units.

March Table.Column 4 lines 5 & 6 for CHATEAU O.10.6.5.8. read BAJUS.

Notes:- Add new note (e). No Unit of the 190th.Inf.Bde. is to be on the road between the points J.36.d.4.5. (fork roads) and J.36.C.1.1. (Cross Roads) between the hours of 11.0 and 11.30 am. Units EAST of the first named point will halt from 11.0am to 11.30 am, well into the RIGHT of the road leaving passage for troops of another Division to pass.
    This halt is not to be included in the uniform speed of $2\frac{3}{4}$ miles per hour.

Major.

Brigade Major.

1. 7/Royal Fusiliers.
2. 4/Bedfordshire Regt.
3. 10/Royal Dublin Fusiliers.
4. 1/H.A.C.
5. 190th.M.G.Coy.
6. 190th.T.M.Battery.
7. 1st Field Coy.
8. No. 4 Coy. Div Train.
9. 63rdDiv.
10. Signal Section.
11. Staff Captain.

APPENDIX. 15.

SECRET.   BRIGADE ORDER No.17.   Copy No.... 11
                    by
LIEUTENANT-COLONEL.A.R.H.HUTCHISON.C.M.G.COMMANDING 190th INFANTRY
                                                        BRIGADE.

                                        Headquarters,
                                        190th Infantry Bde.
                                        18.9.16.

Ref. Map 36B 1/40,000.

1.   The 190th Infantry Brigade will move on the 20th inst into
     billets according to attached March Table.

2.   Baggage wagons will accompany units.

3.   Refilling point will be announced later.

Issued to Signals................

                                        Major.
                                        Brigade Major.

1. 7th Royal Fusiliers.
2. 4th Bedfordshire Regt.
3. 10th Royal Dublin Fusiliers.
4. 1st H.A.C.
5. 190th M.G.Coy.
6. 190th T.M.Battery.
7. No.4.Coy.Div. Train.
8. Signal Section.
9. Staff Capt.
10. Staff File.
11. War Diary (3)
12. 63rd Division.

MARCH TABLE. (To accompany 190th Inf.Bde. Order No.17.)

Unit.	Date.	From	To	Route.	Time leaving	Remarks.
7th Royal Fusiliers.	20th Sept.	BEUGIN	BAILLEUL-AUX-CORN-AILLES	LA COMTE-MAGNICOURT	9.15.am	Billeting Areas will be allotted by Staff Capt.
190th Bde. M.G.Coy.	"	DIEVAL	-ditto-	N25 (Central)-LA THIEULOYE-MONCHY BRETON-U.8.	9.15.am	
190th Inf. Bde.Bd.Ors.	"	BAJUS	-ditto-	HOUVLIN-MAGNI-COURT	9.30.am	
1st H.A.C.	"	LA COMTE	MARQUAY.	HOUVLIN-MONCHY BRETON	8.45.am	1st H.A.C. will allot billeting area to T.M.Battery.
190th T.M. Battery.	"	-ditto-	-ditto-	-ditto-	9.0.am	
10th Royal Dublin Fusiliers.	"	DIEVAL	OSTREVILLE	BRYAS	9.0.am	
4th Bedfordshire Regt.	"	"	SAVENCOURT	N.25.-LA THIEU-LOYE-MONCHY BRETON.	9.30.am	

Notes.- (a) Troops will keep an uniform speed of 2¾ miles per hour.
(b) Troops dining en route may be passed by units which are following them.
(c) Billeting parties will march two hours ahead of their units.
(d) Road blocking parties will be provided by units concerned; except that parties for 1st H.A.C. and T.M.Battery will be found by 1st H.A.C.

APPENDIX 16.

Casualties for the month of September 1916

	Killed	Wounded	Total
Officers	1	3	4
Other Ranks	9	34	43
Total	10	37	47

190/3 Vol 5
October 1916

SECRET.

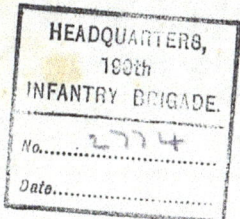
HEADQUARTERS,
190th
INFANTRY BRIGADE.
No. 274
Date.

Headquarters, 190th. Inf. Brigade,
1st November 1916. Date.

. VOL. V .

WAR DIARY
of
190th. Infantry Brigade.

From 1st October 1916
To 31st October 1916.

[signature]
Major.
Brigade Major,
190th. Infantry Brigade.

To:-
Officer i/c
A G's Office
Base.

Note:- Appendix 27.
will be appended to Vol. VI.

WAR DIARY of 190th Infantry Brigade
or INTELLIGENCE SUMMARY. Vol V

Army Form C. 2118

APPENDIX 29.

Summary of Casualties for October 1916.

Unit	Killed Officers	Killed OR	Wounded Officers	Wounded OR	Missing Officers	Missing OR
190th Infantry Brig. HQ.	–	–	1	–	–	–
7th Royal Fusiliers	–	2	–	7	–	1
4th Bedfordshire Regt.	–	1	–	6*	–	–
1st H.A.C.	–	5	2	9=	–	–
10th Royal Dublin Fusiliers	–	6	2	45%	1	3
190th Machine Gun Co.	–	–	–	–	–	–
190th Trench Mortar Battery	–	–	–	–	–	–
	–	14	5	67	1	4

* ⎫ includes 1 accident
= ⎬ wounded
% ⎭

Army Form C. 2118.

WAR DIARY of 190th Infantry Brigade. Vol V
or
INTELLIGENCE SUMMARY.
(Erase heading not required.)

Place	Date	Hour	Summary of Events and Information	Remarks and references to Appendices
ROELECOURT	1916 Oct 1.		Training	
	2.		Received orders that the Division was to move on the 3rd and 4th inst. to the Reserve Army area and form part of the VII th Corps. Brig. Gen. C. Trotman, C.B. returned from Hospital and resumed command of the Brigade.	Appendix 17.
VARENNES	3 4 5		Moved to Achieux district in accordance with appendix 17. Great delay both by train and road, mainly owing to the bad weather. Brig. Gen. C. Trotman. C.B. sick on 5th inst. Lt. Col. Hakett, Commanding 7/R.F. Commanded Brigade on the 5th inst. Lt. Col. Hutchison. C.M.G., R.M.L.I. appointed to temporarily command the Brigade.	
	6		Orders received that we were to take over the SERRE and REDAN Sectors with all four Battalions in the line on the 8th inst. Brigade Major and Officers from each unit visited the line. Units disposed as follows:— Brigade Headquarters VARENNES 7/Royal Fusiliers " 1/H.A.C. "	

Army Form C. 2118.

WAR DIARY of 190th Infantry Brigade
or
INTELLIGENCE SUMMARY. Vol V

Place	Date	Hour	Summary of Events and Information	Remarks and references to Appendices
VARENNES	1916 Oct 6 cont'd		Disposal of units - continued:- 190th Brigade M.G. Company VARENNES 190th T.M. Battery " 4/Bedfordshire Regt. " 10/Royal Dublin Fusiliers LEALVILLERS	
"	Oct 7		4/Bedfordshire Regt. and 10/R.Dublin Fusiliers moved to HEDAUVILLE. Instructions received that we are only to take over the REDAN section instead of REDAN and SERRE.	
MAILLY-MAILLET	" 8		Relieved 5th Infantry Brigade in REDAN Section. Relief completed by 7.15 p.m. Appendix 18 Much congestion on roads owing to various moves. Headquarters MAILLY-MAILLET Very wet weather with S.W. wind.	
"	" 9		In the LEFT Subsection the fire line and immediate support have been blown in some time ago and are not occupied. Attempts have previously been made to clean them but they are full of dead. We hold our third line here, the old communication trenches being used as raps. The enemy wire opposite this front in the thickest we have yet seen.	

WAR DIARY of 190th Infantry Brigade Vol. V

INTELLIGENCE SUMMARY

Place	Date	Hour	Summary of Events and Information	Remarks and references to Appendices
MAILLY-MAILLET	Oct.9 cont.		Our Artillery is very active here, the enemy repl[y] being more or less feeble; he occasionally puts in a short sharp burst.	
"	Oct.10		Fine day. Our artillery active, including heavies. Evening very quiet.	
"	" 11		Carried out internal relief; position of Troops now as follows:- 10/R.Dublin Fus. - RIGHT Subsection. 1/ H.A.C. - LEFT " 7/ R.F } MAILLY WOOD 4/ Bed. Rgt } Some shelling of our lines during relief.	Appendix 19
"	Oct.12		A demonstration was carried out by the V Corps and Corps to our LEFT with the purpose of assisting the operations of the IVth Army and harassing the enemy prior to ascertain intensity etc. The orders given by this Brigade & result of observations are attached - Appendices 20 + 21. On their way to view the operations, the Divisional Commander Sir A PARIS, K.C.B. was severely wounded and Major SKETCHLEY, D.S.O., R.M.L.I. G.S.O₂ killed by shell fire. The casualties in the Brigade were very slight:- 1 man severely wounded, 3 men	Appendix 20 Appendix 21

WAR DIARY or INTELLIGENCE SUMMARY.

of 190th Infantry Brigade Vol V

Army Form C. 2118.

Place	Date	Hour	Summary of Events and Information	Remarks and references to Appendices
MAILLY-MAILLET	1916 Oct 13	contd 12	shell shock. Enemy heavily shelled the SUGAR FACTORY and portions of our front trenches. Weather mild dull + misty.	
"	14		During the night of the 13/14th the enemy made an organized raid on our outpost position at the REDAN. This is the remains of an old unoccupied British Salient full of shell holes and ending in a series of craters, in which we have recently placed by night a Lewis gun and two bombing posts. For a reason which cannot be accounted for the Lewis gun officer on this occasion took his gun out half an hour before his bombing escort were due at the Rendezvous. Whilst getting the gun into position the crew were surprised by an enemy bombing party and dispersed. One sergeant got back. The officer, 3 men and gun are missing. One of the bombing posts, which by this time were on its way out, was also attacked and the Officer and 3 men wounded. In spite of his wounds Lt HENCHY 10/Royal Dublin Fusiliers, sprung up a bank and bombed the enemy placing one bomb between two of them; the remaining 5 then ran towards their	Appendix 22 (map)

Army Form C. 2118.

WAR DIARY of 190th Inf. Brig.
or
INTELLIGENCE SUMMARY. Vol V.
(Erase heading not required.)

Place	Date	Hour	Summary of Events and Information	Remarks and references to Appendices
MAILLY/MAILLET	1916 Oct 14 (contd)		own line. Owing to the severe nature of his wound this officer was unable to do more, and the post was withdrawn bringing its wounded with it. The O.C. 10/R.D.F. organised a working reinforcement which reached the ground till dawn without being able to find any of the missing men, gun or wounded enemy.	
		2.46 pm	At 2.46 pm our troops made an attack some distance to the North of us and the Brigade on our RIGHT made a smoke screen and demonstration. They were heavily shelled by H.E. but in that area, at any rate, there was nothing which could be called a barrage. Some heavy minenwerfer were added to the usual allotment of shell put over by the enemy against our front today.	
	Oct 15		During the night of the 14/15th further search was made for the missing Lewis gun and crew. The ammunition, a revolver and a belt, the officer's helmet and an unexploded German grenade were found, but none of the men. The enemy have very badly damaged our fire, support and forward communication trenches. We dig these out by night but are quite unable to at present to keep pace with it.	

WAR DIARY of the 190th Infantry Brigade.

or INTELLIGENCE SUMMARY. Vol. V.

Army Form C. 2118.

(Erase heading not required.)

Place	Date	Hour	Summary of Events and Information	Remarks and references to Appendices
MAILLY-MAILLET	Oct 16	(contd)	The whole line is being prepared for a forward advance and is crammed with our 2" Trench mortars. It is this fact probably which draws the enemy fire, and so far our guns are doing little firing on the enemy front lines. About 8 p.m. the enemy opened a very heavy fire on our front and support lines mainly on the RIGHT Subsection with heavy artillery and Minenwerfer. It is estimated that between 300 + 400 Minenwerfer bombs were thrown on this area alone; at the same time cheering was heard in the enemy line. Our artillery was called for and opened heavily, the enemy fire dying down about 8.35 p.m. British S.O.S Signals were, at the same time, sent up some distance to our RIGHT; and to NORTH of us also a very heavy enemy fire was answered by our artillery with a sharpnel barrage. Received orders that the Brigade was to be relieved by the 99th Infantry Brigade on the 16th+17th October and march to RAINCHEVAL and ARQUEVES.	
	Oct. 17		Support and Reserve Battalions moved to ARQUEVES and RAINCHEVAL respectively. Carried out relief in accordance with appendix 22, orders being received during the	Appendix 22

WAR DIARY of 190th Infantry Brigade
Vol V
INTELLIGENCE SUMMARY

Army Form C. 2118.

Place	Date	Hour	Summary of Events and Information	Remarks and references to Appendices
MAILLY-MAILLET LEALVILLERS	Oct 17/(cont) Oct 18		night of the 16th/17th that the whole Brigade was to concentrate at LEALVILLERS. Orders received at 1·5am that the Brigade was to move to PUCHEVILLERS clearing LEALVILLERS by noon. Brigade cleared starting point by 11·20 am and arrived at PUCHEVILLERS by 1·30 pm. A good deal of congestion on the road.	Appendix 23.
PUCHEVILLERS	Oct 19		Officers from Brigade HQ, Battalions and M.G.C? visited trenches occupied by the 188th and 189th Brigades. It is from these trenches, immediately NORTH of the ANCRE River, that the Division will attack from in forthcoming operation.	
		10·35pm	Orders received to move tomorrow; Brigade HQ and one Battalion to VARENNES and one Battalion to HEDAUVILLE.	
	Oct 20		Brigade H.Q., 7 Royal Fusiliers and 4/Bedfordshire Regt moved in accordance with Appendix 24	
VARENNES	Oct 21.		1/HAC and 10/Royal Dublin Fusiliers moved to HEDAUVILLE. Fine frosty weather.	Appendix 24 Appendix 25
	Oct 22		190th M.G. Coy and 190th L.T.M. Battery moved to VARENNES. Preliminary orders received from the Division for the attack. It is probable that this attack will	Appendix 26

WAR DIARY of 190th Infantry Brigade Vol V
INTELLIGENCE SUMMARY

Army Form C. 2118.

Place	Date	Hour	Summary of Events and Information	Remarks and references to Appendices
VARENNES	Oct 22 (cont)		The delivered on the 25th inst. Brigadier attended Corps and Divisional Conferences and then assembled a conference of O.Cs. at 9 p.m. Brigade orders for attack issued at 9 a.m. Foggy weather, wind S.E.	Appendix 27
	" 23		Evening, further orders received from the Division which definitely gives the day of attack as 26th inst.	
	" 24		Brigadier General C. N. TROTMAN C.B. left The Brigade and was relieved by Brigadier General The Honourable SACKVILLE-WEST, C.M.G. Attack postponed 48 hours, weather wet and foggy.	
	" 25		Assembly area of 190th Brigade for forthcoming operations taped out and marked. Operations postponed till 28th October, weather very wet, the country and roads being in a very wet bad state in consequence. Brigadier inspected Brigade by units. Weather still wet.	
	" 26		Evening, received orders that in the event of operations being again postponed, the 190th Infantry Brigade would relieve the 188th and 189th Infantry Brigades in the line.	
	" 27			
	" 28		Weather continues very wet.	

WAR DIARY of 1/190th Infantry Brigade Vol V.
or
INTELLIGENCE SUMMARY.

Army Form C. 2118.

Place	Date	Hour	Summary of Events and Information	Remarks and references to Appendices
	1916			
VARENNES	29 Oct		Orders received to take over the HAMEL SECTOR now occupied by the 138th and 189th Infantry Brigades. The Brigadier and Brigade Major together with the Brigadiers of the 189th Infantry Brigade went up to the trenches to inspect the Sector with a view to taking over. Whilst standing in a trench an enemy H.E. shell exploded amongst, and partially buried, the party. Brig. General Sackville West was wounded in the jaw, but was able to walk to the dressing station, whence he was evacuated. At 4 p.m. Brig-General HENEKER, D.S.O., A.D.C. arrived and took command of the Brigade.	Appendix 28
ENGLEBELMER	Oct 30		Relieved the HAMEL Sector by 3.10 p.m. Very wet and a high wind.	
"	" 31		Better day, high wind with heavy showers. The trenches are in a revolting bad state. Nothing has been done to them for months and they are taking in everywhere and knee-deep in mud and water. The two front trenches are in many places disconnected whilst the 3rd line is so blown in that it is merely a line of shell holes. There are enormous amount of ammunition etc. lying about, which will have to be salvaged.	

Heneker Bob Brig
Brigadier General
Commanding 190th Inf (Brigade)

SECRET

Copy No. 13

190th. Infantry Brigade Order No.18.
by
Brigadier General C.N. Trotman, C.B., Commanding 190th. Infantry Brigade.

H.Q. 190th. Inf. Bde,
2/10/16.

Ref. Map LENS SHEET 1/100,000.

1. The 190th. Inf. Bde. as part of the 63rd. Division will be transferred to the Vth. Corps, Reserve Army.

2. The Details of the Brigade, not shewn in Appendix A, will move in accordance with a March Table to be issued later.
   Those Units are to be prepared for an early start on the 3rd. inst. and will be billeted on the night of the 3/4th in the FREVENT – REBREUVIETTE Area.

3. Supply wagons of Units marching by road will deliver supplies in billets on the evening of the 3rd. Inst. for consumption on the 4th. inst. Supply wagons of Units proceeding by Train and Baggage wagons of all Units other than Brigade Headquarters will, as soon as supplies for the 4th. inst. have been delivered and baggage wagons have been packed, be parked as ordered by O.C. No.4 Coy. Div. Train, and will march under that Officer's orders at a time to be notified by him.
   The above wagons must be packed by 8 am.

4. Supply Railhead will be
   4th. October   at TINQUES.
   5th.   "   in Reserve Army Area.

5. Personnel, animals and vehicles shewn in Appendix "A" will move by Tactical Trains on the 4th. October under arrangements to be notified later.

6. Troops will move with one Iron Ration and the unexpired portion of the days ration. Troops entraining P.M. are to have the following day's ration with them in addition to the ration carried by the supply wagons.

7. Units will report <u>at once</u> to Brigade Hd. Qrs. amount and nature of ammunition being taken.

8. Transport detailed to entrain and a working party of 100 Officers and men from each Bn. and 20 from M.G. Coy. will be at the Entraining Station of their Unit 3 hours before the Train is due to leave. The remainder of the Bn. or Unit will be at the Station 1½ hours before the Train leaves.
   <u>Note</u>:- A covered truck takes 8 horses or 40 men. 3 men go in each horse truck in charge of horses.

9. The R.T.O. is responsible for loading the train and his orders are to be implicitly obeyed.

10. Entraining States for each Unit or part of each Unit (shewing numbers of personnel, horses, vehicles (by nature) are to be handed to R.T.O. 3 hours before departure of train. Duplicate copy being handed to Officer of Bde. Hd. Qrs.

11. Breast and Head ropes for tying up horses are provided by Units, lashings for vehicles by Railway authorities.

12. The 7/Royal Fusiliers, 4/Bedfordshire Regt, and 1/H.A.C. will each detail 1 Officer and two orderlies, all provided with bicycles to report to an officer of Bde. Hd. Qrs. at the Entraining Station 3 hours before the departure of the 1st. Train.
    One officer and 2 orderlies will always be on duty. They will proceed in the last train.

These orderlies should know the billets of each unit of the Bde.

13. Blankets will be carried on the man.

14. Further orders as to time, stations etc, will be issued.

                                              Major.
                                        Brigade Major.

Issued to Signals........

Copies to:-

1. 7/Royal Fusiliers.
2. 4/Bedfordshire Regt.
3. 10/Royal Dublin Fusiliers.
4. 1/H.A.C.
5. 190th.M.G.Coy.
6. 190th.T.M.Battery.
7. No.4 Co. Div. Train.
8. Staff Captain.
9. Signal Section.
10. 63rd.Division.
11. File.
12. War Diary (3).

APPENDIX "A"

Personnel, Animals, and vehicles to proceed in each series of three tactical trains.

Unit.	Officers	Other Ranks.	Animals.	Limbered G.S. or R.E.	2 wheel carts	Cookers.	Trench Mortars.	In which train to travel.	Remarks.
190th.Bde.H.Q.	(less 4 officers and transport)							1 & 2.	
Bde.H.Q.Transport (part of)	4	9	8	1	-	-	-	3	
Bde.Sig.Sec.	1	26	8	3	-	-	-	3	
190th.M.G.Coy (part of)	9	130	41	8	-	-	-	3	
190th.T.M. Battery.	4	46	-	-	-	-	8	3	
1/H.A.C. } 7/R.F. }	complete (less transport)							1.	With Lewis Guns and hand-carts.
4/Bed. } 10/R.D.F.)	ditto							2.	ditto
Transport of 4 Bns.(part of)		24	44	4*	4⁄	16	-	3	
Pack animals (2 per Coy.)		32	32	-	-	-	-	3	
1 Field Coy.	(dismounted personnel)							1,2&3	)Distribution to)trains will be)given later.
1 Field Ambco	(dismounted personnel)							1,2&3	
H.Q.& No.1 Sec.Sig.Coy.		40						1	1st.Series only
Pioneer Bn.	complete (less transport)							1,2&3.	)Distributed amongs)trains in accordan)with orders to be)issued later.)Lewis Guns & hand)carts by train.
Pioneer Bn.		23	280	1	1	4	-	3	

For information only.

* 1 per Bn. for S.A.A. ⁄ 1mess cart per Bn.
ø includes 17 pack animals.

N.B. All Personnel, bicycles, animals and vehicles not included in above table will proceed by March Route on 3rd.October.

SECRET.   190th. Infantry Bde. Order No.19.   Copy No. 16
                                   by
Brigadier General C.N.Trotman, C.B. Commanding 190th. Infantry Brigade.

                                                     H.Q.190th. Inf. Bde.
        Ref. Map LENS. 1/100,000.   2/10/16.

1.   In continuation of 190th.Inf.Bde.Order No.18.
        The details proceeding by road will march as follows under the
        Command of the Bde.Transport Officer:-
        The portion of Transport proceeding by road of all Units will
        parade at LA BELLE EPINE, head at first E² in EPINE at 8 am. 3rd.inst
        and will come under the Command of the Bde.Transport Officer at that
        time.
        Transport of each Unit will be accompanied by its Transport
        Officer.

2.   Transport will march to LA COUTURE via TERNAS-BUNEVILLE-
        SIBIVILLE-MONVAL-REBREUVE clearing TERNAS by 9.30 am.

3.   Transport will move at an average rate of 2½ miles per hour
        including halts. Halts will be made between 10 minutes before the
        clock hour and the clock hour.

4.   It is presumed that orders as to future movement will be
        received by the Bde.Transport Officer at LA COUTURE. D.H.Q.Transport
        will be at SIBIVILLE and if no orders arrive, the Bde.Transport
        Officer will communicate with them.

5.   The attached personnel of the M.G.Coy. and T.M.Battery will
        entrain with the Units to which they are attached and NOT with the
        Bns.
        This will alter the numbers given in Appendix "A" but not the
        actual number in the Troop Train. The whole of these Units, there-
        fore, except Transport of M.G.Coy. will move by Troop Train.
        Hand-carts of T.M.Battery will entrain with Unit.

6.   In Appendix "A" for Sig.Section "3 wagons" read "1 wagon".

7.   Following are supply arrangements for Troops moving by road.
        Supply vehicles move full and issue rations to Units at their
        new billets on the evening of the 3rd.inst.

8.   Supply arrangements for those moving by Troop Train.
    (a) Troops entraining before noon on 4th.will take their rations
        for 4th. with them and will be issued with rations for 5th.inst.
        on arrival at destination.
    (b) Troops entraining afternoon 4th.inst.will take rations for
        5th. in addition to rations for 4th.inst. Rations for 5th.will
        be dumped at the Railway Station. Quartermasters and necessary
        O.R. are to arrive at Entraining Station in ample time to take
        over these rations and make arrangements for them to be loaded
        on Troop Train.
        Rations for 6th.will be received in new Area.

9.   Railway Station and time of trains will be notified.

        Note for Bde.Transport Officer.
                Transport of Bde.H.Q. consists of,
                        2 Tool carts.
                        1 Baggage wagon.
                        5 led horses.
                under 2nd.Lieut.Marriott, 7/R.F.

Issued to Signals. 11.45/-
Copies to:-
1. 7/Royal Fusiliers(2)
2. 4/Bedfordshire Regt.(2)
3. 10/Royal Dublin Fusiliers(2)   C.F.Jerram.   Major.
4. 1/H.A.C.(2)   Brigade Major.
5. 190th.M.G.Coy.(2)   10. Staff Captain.
6. 190th.T.M.Battery.   11. 2nd.Lt.Marriott.
7. Signal Section.   12. 63rd.Division.
8. Bde.Transport Officer. 13. File.
9. No.4 Coy.Div.Train.   14. War Diary(3)

        NOTE:- D.H.Q.have been asked about Transport for Kits and
Mob.Stores of T.M.Battery, and kits of surplus officers.
        Instructions will be issued as soon as received.

APPENDIX 17

SECRET.

Headquarters,
190th Infantry Brigade.
2/10/16.

1. The Brigade as part of the 63rd Division will move to the vicinity of ETREE - WAMIN by Tactical Trains on the 4th instant.

2. The Division will then form part of the Vth Corps, Reserve Army.

3. Further orders will be issued.

4. Acknowledge.

                                        Major.
                                Brigade Major.

7th Royal Fusiliers.
4th Bedfordshire Regt.
10th Royal Dublin Fusiliers.
1st H.A.C.
190th M.G.Coy.
190th T.M.Battery.
Staff Capt.
Intelligence Officer.
Bombing Officer.
Signals.
War Diary.

SECRET.

War Diary

BRIGADE ORDER NO. 22.   Copy No. 13
by
BRIGADIER GENERAL C.N.TROTMAN C.B. COMMANDING 190th INFANTRY BRIGADE.

Headquarters,
190th Infantry Brigade.
5/10/16.

Ref Map 1/40,000
Sheet 57D

1. The 190th Infantry Brigade will take over the line at present held by the 2nd Division on or about the 8th instant for about one (1) week.

2. All four Bns will be in the front line.

3. Officers and N.C.Os as follows will proceed to the Brigade Hd. Qrs. at the CAFE JORDON, MAILLY MALLET. to be there by 9.0am tomorrow whence guides will shew them their area.
   Brigadier, Brigade Major, O.C.,M.G.Coy, O.C.,190th T.M.Battery will proceed round the whole area.
   Bn. Commanders, Company Commanders and 1 N.C.O. from each Coy. will proceed round their Bn. fronts.

4. Transport for the conveyance of the Officers and N.C.Os. from VARENNES will be at 190th Bde. Hd. Qrs VARENNES at 8.30.am; transport to take those from LEALVILLERS will be outside 63rd Divisional Hd. Qrs LEALVILLERS at 8.0.am.

5. Bns will be in the line as follows:-

   From the RIGHT.   4th Bedfordshire Regt.
                     7th Royal Fusiliers.
                     10th Royal Dublin Fusiliers
                     1st H.A.C.

Time issued to Signals. 7.30 pm

Major.
Brigade Major.

1. 7th Royal Fusiliers.
2. 4th Bedfordshire Regt.
3. 10th Royal Dublin Fusiliers.
4. 1st H.A.C.
5. 190th M.G.Coy.
6. 190th T.M.Battery.
7. Staff Captain
8. Intelligence Officer.
9. 190th Bde Bombing Officer.
10. 190th Bde Transport Officer.
11. 63rd Division.
12. File.
13. War Diary (3)

SECRET.   Copy No............
                                                              20.
190th INF. BRIGADE ORDER No.23.
                    by
LIEUTENANT COLONEL A.R.H.HUTCHISON.C.M.G.,R.M.L.I.COMMANDING 190th
                                              INFANTRY BRIGADE.

Appendix 18

                                        Headquarters,
                                        190th Infantry Bde.
                                        7/10/16.

1.   The 190th Infantry Brigade will relieve the 5th Inf.
Bde. in the REDAN Section ob the 8th instant and will move
in accordance with the attached March Table.

2.   A group of the 2nd Div. Artillery will support this
section.

3.   At the conclusion of relief distribution of the Bde.
will be as follows:-

        4th Bedfordshire Regt.   RIGHT Sub Section.
        7th Royal Fusiliers   LEFT Sub section
        10th Royal Dublin Fusiliers. MAILLY WOOD EAST.
        1st H.A.C.   -ditto-.
        M.G.Coy. & T.M.Batt. in the line.

4.   Details as to Transport, supplies etc are attached
Appendix "A".

5.   Details as to working parties required Appendix "B"

6.   The 4th Bedfordshire Regt will detach 1 Company to
garrison the strong points ELLIS SQUARE (Coy. less 1 Platoon)
and FORT HORSTED (1 Platoon). 25% of the garrison is always
to be within the limits of the post. The O.C. Coy will command
both posts and will be appointed by name; name being rendered
to Bde Hd. Qrs. by 10.0 an 8th inst.

7.   All movements EAST of MAILLY WOOD are to be by Platoons
at 200 yards interval; if there is enemy shelling these
Platoons should automatically shake out into sections.

8.   The 5th Inf. Bde. will leave one man with each Machine
gun and one with each group of Stoke's Guns until the morning
of the 9th instant when these men will be sent to rejoin their
Bns.

9.   The road from HEDAUVILLE to MAILLY-MALLET must be
clear of all details of 190th Inf. Bde. by 12.30 pm.

10.   Blankets of troops not moving to trenches will be carried
on the person. Those of troops moving to trenches will be left
at unit Hd. Qrs. under a loading party and will be collected
under Bde. arrangements later in the day and taken to Bn. Q.M.
Stores (in the case of M.G. and T.M.B. to billets in MAILLY
MALLET.

11.   Bde. Hd. Qrs. will close at VARENNES at 12 noon and open
at CAFE JORDAN, MAILLY-MALLET at 4.0. pm 8th instant.

Issued to Signals......... 12.30.A.M.
                                                        Major.
                                                   Brigade Major.
Copies to:-   15. No.4 Coy. Div. Train
1. 7th Royal Fusiliers.   16. 2   th Field Coy. R.E.
2. 4th Bedfordshire Regt.   17. File.
3. 10th Royal Dublin Fusiliers. 18. War Diary. (3)
4. 1st H.A.C.
5. 190th M.G.Coy.
6. 190th T.M.B.
7. Bde. Transport Officer.
8. "   Intelligence Officer.
9. "   Bombing Officer
10. Signal Section
11. Staff Capt.
12. 63rd Division.
13. 5th Inf. Bde.
14. 188th Inf. Bde.

MARCH TABLE.

Unit relieving.	Unit relieved.	Destination.	Route.	Time	GUIDES. Place	Number.	Remarks.
190th M.G.Coy.	5th M.G.Coy.	REDAN Section	FORCEVILLE.	9.30am	Bde.H.Q.	1 per gun	Guns not in the line will take over the billets now occupied by 5th Bde. M.G.Coy.
190th T.M.B. 10th R.Dublin Fusiliers.	5th T.M.B. Nil	ditto MAILLY WOOD EAST	ditto P.23.d.	9.30am Nil	CAFE JOR DAN,MAILLY MALLET. ditto Nil	1 per gun Nil	Will clear HEDAUVILLE at 9.0.am & take over bivouacs from Bn. 188th Bde. Billeting parties to proceed two hours ahead of Bn.
4th Beds. Regt.	2/H.L.I.	RIGHT SUB-SECTION	P.23.d.	1.30pm	Bde.H.Q. CAFE JOR DAN	1 per platoon & 1 per L.G.	Will clear HEDAUVILLE at 10.0.am and halt for dinner off the road in P.12.c or d. Advanced party will select suitable place.
1.Coy.4th Beds/Rgt.	Nil.	ELLIS SQUARE & FORT HORSTED	ditto	2.0pm	ditto	ditto	Moves with Bn. to halting place as above. Will not take over from anyone as this position is not at present held.
7/Royal Fus.	24/Royal Fus.	LEFT SUB-SECTION MAILLY WOOD EAST	FORCEVILLE ditto	2.30pm	ditto Nil	ditto Nil	Will clear VARENNES at 9.0am & take over bivouacs from Bn. of 188th Inf. Bde. Billeting parties proceed two hours ahead of Bn.
1st H.A.C.	Nil			Nil			
190th Inf BDE Hd.Qrs.	5th Inf Bde Hd.Qrs	CAFE JORDAN MAILLY MALLET	FORCEVILLE	Nil	Nil	Nil	Arrives by 3.0pm

Note.- On moving off from CAFE JORDAN Bns going into line will move with all Lewis Guns leading Bns.

APPENDIX "A".

Transport.
All 1st Line Transport of 190th Inf. Bde. with the exception of Bde Hd. Qrs will be situated in HEDAUVILLE P.34.d. and V.4.a.
Lines will be allocated by Bde. Transport Officer.
Personnel will be housed in tents.

Quartermaster's Stores.
Quartermaster's Stores will be situated in MAILLY-MALLET Q.7.c.
Q.M.Stores will be taken over as follows:-
7th Royal Fusiliers take over from 24th Royal Fusiliers.
4th Bedfordshire Regt take over from H.L.I.
10th R.D.Fusiliers) take over from remaining two Bns of
1st H.A.C.   )   5th Inf. Bde.

190th M.G.Coy.   take over from 5th M.G.Coy.
190th T.M.Battery   "   "   " 5th T.M.Battery.

Method of Supply when in Tranches.
Rations are taken up by road in limbers after dark and dumped as below:-

        RIGHT Bn. Dump............ WHITE CITY.
        LEFT Bn. Dump............ CHEEROH AVENUE.

From these Dumps supplies are carried up and distributed under Bn. arrangements.
All transport will be regulated and under the control of the Bde. Transport Officer who will issue times of starting and regulations as to the necessary distances to be kept between vehicles.
All usual precautions are to be taken, no smoking, no lights etc.
190th M.G.Coy and 190th T.M.Battery will take over the arrangements for ration supply from the units they relieve.

R.E.Stores.
Indents for R.E.material must be sent to Bde. Hd. Qrs. by 8.30am daily for approval and transmission to No. 5 Field Coy R.E. situated at BEAUSSART P.11.a. Such material as is available will be notified to Bde Hd. Qrs. who will then inform Transport Officer of Unit concerned. Unit Transport Officer should then get into touch with R.E. Dump No. 5. Field Coy. at BEAUSSART and send such transport as is necessary to take material up to Ration Dump with rations where it will be turned over to unit concerned.

Brigade Bomb Dump.
Bde Bomb and Ammunition Store is situated in QUARRY off SOUTH AVENUE close to and South of SOUTH AVENUE and SUCRERIE.
Any Trench Mortar Ammunition carrying parties required should be asked for from Bde Hd. Qrs.

Motor Transport.
One Motor Lorry will be available for 190th Inf. Bde. to take blankets etc to Q.M.Stores in MAILLY-MALLET. It will report as follows:-
        190th M.G.Coy......) 8.15.am.
        190th T.M.Battery..)
        4th Bedfordshire Regt 10.30.am
        7th Royal Fusiliers   1.0.pm
        190th Inf. Bde. Hd. Qrs.2.30.pm
Guides are to accompany lorry in all cases and should it be finished with earlier than the times laid down, it should be sent to report to the next unit mentioned in Table.

(over)

APPENDIX "B"

Working parties etc

1.　　　　The orders as to deep dugout parties and additional men are cancelled.

2.　　　　The 4th Bedfordshire Regt and 8th R.F. will each detail one officer and 144 O.R. formed from their deep dug-out platoons with additional men for deep dugout work under Engineers.
　　　　These will be a permanent party but will live with and form part of the garrison. They will work under the 226th Field Coy R.E. in shifts; the first shift will take on direct from similar parties of the 5th Inf. Bde. on relief.

3.　　　　The 10th R.D.F. will find two parties each of two officers and 100 O.R. to report to 226th Coy. R.E. at 9.30am and 10.30am as shewn in detail issued to them with this order.
　　　　Those parties will march off, without their packs, in time to give them a good rest before commencing work.
　　　　Their packs will be brought over as may be found convenient later.
4.　　　　The 1st H.A.C. will provide similar parties at 6.0.pm and 7.0.pm as shewn in the detail issued to them.

4.　　　　The 1st H.A.C. will take over the following posts afternoon on the 8th instant.
　　　　XXXXXXXXXX
　　　　COLIN CAMPS Control Post 1 N.C.O. 3 men.
　　　　COURCELLES water guard 1 N.C.O. 3 men.
　　　　MAILLY Baths.

Secret

ADDENDA to 190th Infantry Brigade Order No.23.

<u>Para 6.</u>   This Garrison will be found by 7th Royal Fusiliers
and NOT by 4th Bedfordshire Regt.
   The O.C. will be Captain CLARKE 7/R.F..

<u>March Table.</u>
   Col. 1. line 5. for 1. Coy. 4/Bedfordshire Regt read
1.Coy 7/R.F..
   Delete first two lines of Remark and add "This Coy will
move from CAFE JORDAN in rear of 4th Bedfordshire Regt.

Note:- The 6oy. of 4/Bedfordshire Regt which was to have gone to
   ELLIS SQUARE is to be accommodated in and around WHITE CITY.
   Bns. will report if they are too crowded in the front lines.

                                            Major.
                                      Brigade Major.

7th Royal Fusiliers.
4th Bedfordshire Regt.
10th Royal Dublin Fusiliers.
1st H.A.C.
190th M.G.Coy.
190th T.M.Battery.
Bde Transport Officer.
 " Intelligence Officer.
 " Bombing Officer.
Signal Section
Staff Capt
63rd Division
5th Inf. Bde.
188th Inf Bde.
No.4.Coy Div Train.
226th Field Coy. R.E.
File.
War Diary (3)

REDAN SECTOR.

Appendix 19

SECRET.   Copy No. 19

190th Infantry Brigade Order No.24
by
LIEUTENANT COLONEL.A.R.H.HUTCHISON.C.M.G.COMMANDING 190th INF. BDE.

Headquarters,
190th Infantry Brigade.
10/10/16.

Ref. Map HEBUTERNE.
1/10,000 (SECRET)

1. Internal reliefs will be carried out in the REDAN SECTION tomorrow as shown in attached Table.

2. Arrangements are to be made by Bn. Commanders whereby all permanent parties, such as "dugout parties" etc relieve each other without any stoppage of work.

3. Billeting parties of 7/R.F. and 4th Bedfordshire Regt will take over the billets of the 1/H.A.C. and 10/Royal Dublin Fusiliers. respectively at 9.0.am.

4. The 7/R.F. on relief become the SUPPORT Bn.
The 4th Bedfordshire Regt. on relief become the RESERVE Bn.

5. The Reserve Coys should have had breakfast before moving out as they will probably be required to find working parties.

6. The continuity of work is of the first importance.

Issued to Signals......5 p..

Major.
Brigade Major.

1. 7th Royal Fusiliers.
2. 4th Bedfordshire Regt.
3. 10th Royal Dublin Fusiliers.
4. 1st H.A.C.
5. 190th M.G.Coy.
6. 190th T.M.Battery.
7. Staff Capt.
8. Bde Bombing Officer.
9. Bde.Transport Officer.
10. Bde Intelligence Officer.
11. 63rd Division.
12. 63rd   "   Train.
13. 9th Inf. Bde.
14. 116th Inf. Bde.
15. 226th Field Coy. R.E.
16. 2nd Div. Artillery.
17 File
18 } War Diary
19 }
20 }

MARCH TABLE.

10/10/16.

Unit relieving	Unit relieved	Subsection	GUIDES Time	GUIDES Place	Route	Remarks.
10th Royal Dublin Fus.	4th Bedfordshire Regt.	RIGHT	7.30.am	Bde.H.Q.	VIth AVENUE to VALLADE CORNER	1 Coy to VIEW TRENCH 2 platoons of which will garrison FORT HORSTED. All Lewis Guns will lead the Bn.
4th Bedfordshire Regt.	10th Royal Dublin Fus.	Billets in MAILLY WOOD EAST.		-Nil-	BORDEN AVENUE / VIth AVENUE.	Reserve Coy will march out clearing VIth AVENUE by 7.30am less 1 platoon which will garrison FORT HORSTED until relieved by 10/R.D.F.
1st H.A.C. Lewis Guns	7th R.F. Lewis Guns	LEFT	8.0.am	Bde.H.Q.	VIth AVENUE — BORDEN AVENUE.	Follow last Coy of 10/R.D.F.
1st H.A.C.	7th Royal Fusiliers	LEFT	1.0.pm	Bde.H.Q.	VIth AVENUE — BORDEN AVENUE.	1 Coy to ELLIS SQUARE 2 platoons of which will form the garrison
7th Royal Fus.	1st H.A.C.	Billets in MAILLY WOOD EAST.		-Nil-	CHEERO AVENUE	Reserve Coy will march out clearing CHEERO by 7.30.am leaving 1 platoon to garrison ELLIS SQUARE until relieved by 1st H.A.C.

Note:- (a). All movements out of trenches to be by Platoons at 200x interval. In case of enemy shelling those should automatically shake out into sections.
(b) VIth AVENUE is NOT to be used as a DOWN trench from 1.0.pm until completion of relief. Any of RIGHT Subsection going down after 1.0.pm will use ROMAN Rd or CHEERO.

SECRET.   190TH. INFANTRY BRIGADE ORDER NO.25.   Copy No... 16
BY
LIEUT.COLONEL A.R.H.HUTCHISON,C.M.G.,R.M.L.I.,COMMANDING 190th.INF.BDE.

Ref.Map.HEBUTERNE & BEAUMONT.   Appendix 20   H.Q.190th.Inf.Bde.
1/10,000.   SECRET.   11/10/16.

1.   The IVth.Army will be engaged on active operations tomorrow the 12th.Oct.

2.   The 190th.Inf.Bde.in co-operation with the Bde.on our LEFT and the Royal Artillery will make a demonstration with a view to drawing and locating the enemy's barrage, cutting wire and damaging his strong points.

3.   Infantry action will be as follows:-

Zero - 15 minutes.   All troops will be withdrawn under cover except those demonstrating and sentries as follows:-
Numbers at discretion of Bn.Comdrs but not more than 1 per 200 yds.of Fire line and 1 per 50 of Support and Local Reserve Trench, 2 in ELLIS SQ.and 1 at FORT HORSTED.
Men will be withdrawn from Saps, and all working parties cease work.
Sentries should be posted near Dugouts and in the safest portions of the trenches.

Zero +3 mins. Infantry demonstrating parties will fix bayonets and shew them over the parapets (as under) as if they were about to advance.
Parties will be distributed along the fire and support lines in the vicinity of dugouts; as many parties as possible being employed, allowing for dugout accommodation.
Machine Guns will search probable assembly points behind enemy line and any known good targets.
Smoke screen commences as follows:-
About 40 bombers of 1/H.A.C. under Bn.Bombing Officer will throw "P" bombs from MONK Trench between FLAG AVENUE and DELAUNEY Trench.
About 40 bombers of 10/R.D.F. under Bn.Bombing Officer will throw "P" Bombs from Fire line between WATLING ST. and ROMAN RD.
The Bde.Bombing Officer will personally give fuller and detailed instructions to the Bn.Bombing Officers.

Zero + 6 minutes.   Infantry demonstrating parties will take cover in dugouts.
"P"Bombers will get into dugouts.
A proportion of machine guns will sweep the enemy front and support lines, where they will bear, to catch any enemy who may man his parapet.

Zero + 8 minutes.   M.G.Fire ceases.
Zero + 9 minutes.   M.G's sweep enemy front, support and reserve lines.
Zero + 9½ minutes.   Cease Fire.

4.   The Artillery programme is as follows:-
Zero   Barrage German Front Trench.
Zero + 3 minutes.   Lift to Support Line.
Zero + 6 minutes.   "   " 3rd.Line.
Zero + 8 minutes.   Back to Support Line.

5.   The Infantry will resume their normal occupations when any enemy fire has died down.

6.   There must be accommodation in dugouts 12 & 40 in the RIGHT and 5, 14 and 15 in the LEFT Sub-sections for the Bombing parties.

7.   Bn. Comdrs.will cause all working parties, R.E. etc., in their areas to be warned to take cover by Zero - 15 minutes.

8.   All dugouts whether finished or not may be used.

9.   All dugouts are to have in them at least 2 picks and 4 shovels by noon 12th.inst.

2.

10. All ranks taking part in the demonstration and sentries are to be most carefully instructed in their duties or some confusion is bound to arise; each man for instance should know exactly where he is to stand and where he is to go when ordered to cover.

11. Mens lives are NOT to be unnecessarily wasted and should the enemy put a barrage on our trenches the Infantry Demonstrating parties will take cover at once, keeping their bayonets up whilst moving in the trench. Bombers will continue to throw unless the barrage becomes severe when they also will take cover. Sentries MUST remain but should be provided with periscopes and be sheltered as much as possible.
Sentries should be warned that our M.G's will be firing over their heads.

12. Smoke Screen will NOT be made unless the wind is between S.W. and N.N.W.

13. Watches will be synchronised by Divisional time at 9 am. & noon.
Bde.Signals will be responsible for passing time to all Units.

14. Light Trench Mortars will remain under cover and will NOT take part in the Demonstration.

15. The Bde.M.G.Officer may move any of his Reserve Guns to positions in the line.

16. Bns. will report as soon as possible after operations on the points mentioned in para.2.

17. ZERO Hour is 2.5 pm.

Major.
Brigade Major.

Issued to Signals. 12.10 am

1. 1/H.A.C.
2. 10/Royal Dublin Fusiliers.
3. 190th.M.G.Coy.
4. 190th.T.M.Battery.
5. 7/Royal Fusiliers.
6. 4/Bedfordshire Regt.
7. 116th.Inf.Bde.
8. 9th.Inf.Bde.
9. 63rd.Division.
10. No.2 Field Coy, R.N.D.E.
11. Staff Captain.
12. Intelligence Officer.
13. Bde. Bombing Officer.
14. Bde. Signals.
15. File.
16,17,18. War Diary.

Copy No. 13

SECRET.   Corrigenda to 190th.Inf.Bde.Order No.25.

    Para.3.   The Infantry Demonstrating parties will fix bayonets and shew them over the parapet as if they were about to advance at Zero - 5 minutes instead of Zero + 3 mins.

    NOTE:- There MUST be cover for all parties employed; dugouts allotted to M.G's, Officers, Signals, etc., should be used temporarily to accommodate troops in addition.

    Add new Para.18.   The Bde. Intelligence Officer will distribute his scouts to report on
        a. Time of enemy barrage.
        b. Position.
        c. Time and position of any lifts.
        d. Intensity.
        e. Calibre of guns firing and type of shell.
        f. Time ceases.

P Bombers will continue to throw until Zero+12 provided enemy fire is not causing casualties.

                                                              , Major.

Issued to Signals... 10.30 am   Brigade Major.

1. 1/H.A.C.
2. 10/R.D.F.
3. 190th M.G.Coy.
4. 190th T.M.Battery.
5. 116th Inf. Bde.
6. 9th Inf. Bde.
7. 63rd Division.
8. Intelligence Officer.
9. Bombing Officer.
10. Signals
11. File.
12. War Diary. (3)

Army Form C. 2118.

WAR DIARY
or
INTELLIGENCE SUMMARY.
(Erase heading not required.)

Appendix. 21.

Instructions regarding War Diaries and Intelligence Summaries are contained in F.S. Regs., Part II. and the Staff Manual respectively. Title pages will be prepared in manuscript.

Place	Date	Hour	Summary of Events and Information	Remarks and references to Appendices
			Report on activity of the enemy and damage done to his trenches and wire during demonstration 12th October.	
			REDAN Right Sub Section	
			Enemy Artillery.	
			The enemy appeared to be a long time before he started his barrage on our front and support lines. He opened with Minenwerfer at 2.10.pm which was immediately followed by shrapnel and 5.9's on our front line. This barrage was heavier on the left front. Green Rockets went up at short intervals. The enemy fire switched off at intervals to our support and local reserve lines, but at no time did their fire form a really complete barrage. No enemy shells fell in rear of our local reserve lines during the period. Enemy fire ceased at 3.15.pm. Many enemy shrapnel burst very high.	
			Damage to Enemy trenches and wire.	
			Owing to the smoke the effect of our artillery fire on enemy trenches was almost impossible to observe several hits however were reported. Enemy wire reported damaged along whole sub-section front but no apparent gaps have been made but points at K.35.a.35.25. and K.35.c.45.55. appeared to suffer most.	

T2134. Wt. W708-776. 500000. 4/15. Sir J. C. & S.

Army Form C. 2118.

WAR DIARY
or
INTELLIGENCE SUMMARY.
(Erase heading not required.)

Instructions regarding War Diaries and Intelligence Summaries are contained in F. S. Regs., Part II. and the Staff Manual respectively. Title pages will be prepared in manuscript.

Place	Date	Hour	Summary of Events and Information	Remarks and references to Appendices
REDAN.			Right Sub-Section (continued)	
			Damage caused by Enemy Fire.	
			Casualties - Three men suffering from shell-shock.	
			Damage to trenches. The whole front line is badly damaged, more particularly the ~~enemy~~ left Coy's front line. Left Coy. Hd.Qrs. badly damaged by minenwerfer falling on entrances. CHATHAM ST. is blocked in two places, BUSTER ST. and FREDDY TR. have also been damaged considerably. SIXTH AVENUE is blocked in two places between MOUNTJOY and front line. Our wire has been cut in many places also a rubber water pipe at junction VALLADE and SIXTH AVENUE.	
			Enemy seen.	
			At 2.30.pm a few enemy were seen looking over their parapet opposite RIGHT COY.	

Army Form C. 2118.

WAR DIARY
or
INTELLIGENCE SUMMARY.
(Erase heading not required.)

Instructions regarding War Diaries and Intelligence Summaries are contained in F. S. Regs., Part II. and the Staff Manual respectively. Title pages will be prepared in manuscript.

Place	Date	Hour	Summary of Events and Information	Remarks and references to Appendices
REDAN.				
			LEFT Sub Section.	
			Enemy Artillery.	
			The enemy methods in this Sub Section were the same in all respects as in the Sub Section. Only our front, support and reserve lines were shelled and no proper barrage was put up.	
			Damage caused by Enemy Fire.	
			Casualties - One man seriously wounded; four men partially buried.	
			Damage to Trenches. - Two shells burst in ROMAN ROAD doing slight damage. Some damage was done in EGG ST and VALLADE TRENCHES. DELAUNEY TRENCH and LEGEND TRENCH damaged in several places.	
			Damage to Enemy Trenches and Wire	
			Our shells were seen bursting well in the enemy trenches on our RIGHT Coy. Front. Enemy wire between K.35.a.5.4. and K.35.a.8.9. has been badly damaged but no actual gaps can be seen. This is confirmed by two other Officers.	
			Sgd. Alex.F.Knight. Lieut, Intelligence Officer. 190th Inf. Bde.	

SECRET.   Copy No. 22

190th. Infantry Order No.25.

by

Lieut.Colonel A.R.H.Hutchison,C.M.G.,R.M.L.I.,Commanding 190th.Inf.Bde.

                                                     Headquarters,
                                         190th.Infantry Brigade,

Ref.Maps HEBUTERNE (Secret) 1/10,000   16/10/16.
and Sheet 57D 1/40,000.

1.   The 190th.Inf.Bde. will be relieved in the REDAN Section by the 99th.Inf.Bde. on the 16th.& 17th.inst.according to attached Tables.

2.   Garrisons of FORT HORSTED and ELLIS SQUARE (2 Platoons each) will be found by the RIGHT Bn.of 99th.Inf.Bde.

3.   All movement E.of VIth.AVENUE to be by parties of not more than 10.
       WEST of this point and E.of MAILLY-MAILLET by Platoons at 200 yards interval.

4.   2 Baggage and 3 blanket wagons are available for each Bn.
       1 wagon each for M.G.Coy. and T.M.Battery.

5.   Rations will be delivered to Units at RAINCHEVAL and ARQUEVES on the day of move.

6.   Bde.Hd.Qrs. will close at MAILLY-MAILLET at 2 pm. and re-open at ARQUEVES at 5 pm.

                                                         Major.
                                                Brigade Major.

Issued to Signals.... 4 pm

Copies to:-
1. 7/Royal Fusiliers.   } Advanced Copy at 1.30 pm.
2. 4/Bedfordshire Regt.
3. 10/Royal Dublin Fusiliers.
4. 1/H.A.C.
5. 190th.M.G.Coy.
6. 190th.T.M.Battery.
7. Bde.Transport Officer.
8. Bde.Intelligence Officer.
9. Bde.Bombing Officer.
10. Staff Captain.
11. Signal Section.
12. 36th.Bde.R.F.A.
13. No.2.Field Coy.R.N.D.E.
14. No.1. " " "
15. 63rd.Division.
16. 189th.Inf.Bde.
17. 5th.Inf.Bde.
18. No.4 Coy.Div.Train.
19. Bde.Bombing Officer VIth.Bde.
20. File.
21,22 & 23. War Diary.
24. 99th Inf Bde

MARCH TABLE FOR 17th OCTOBER 1916.   190th.Inf.Bde.

Unit relieved.	Unit relieving	Sub-section.	Guides: Time.	Guides: Place.	Guides: Number.	Forming up place.	Route.	Destination	Route.	Remarks.
190th.M.G. Coy.	99th.M.G. Coy.	—	7.30am	190th M.G.Coy H.Q. MAILLY-MAILLET	1 per Gun.	J.30.d. Clear of road.	ROMAN RD. or NEWGATE ST. - COLINCAMPS.	RAINCHEVAL.	COURCELLES -BERTRANCOURT -LOUVENCOURT -ARQUEVES.	)))
190th.T.M. battery.	99th.T.M. battery.	—	99th.T.M.Battery will have no guns in the line.			MAILLY-MAILLET (Clearing at 10.am.)	—	-do-	FORCEVILLE -ACHEUX -LEALVILLERS -ARQUEVES.	) Billeting) parties) 2 hours) in) advance) of Unit.
10/Royal Dublin Fusiliers.	23/R.F.	RIGHT.	9.am.	Bde.H.Q.* CAFE JOURDAIN	1-for H.Q. 1 per platoon 1 per Lewis Gun.	P.18.a. Clear of road.	ROMAN RD. -K32 Central -Q.1.b. - WINDMILL (MAILLY MAILLET)	ARQUEVES.	FORCEVILLE -ACHEUX -LEALVILLERS.	)))))
1/H.A.C.	22/R.F.	LEFT.	10.30am	-do-*	-do-	J.30.d. Clear of road.	NEWGATE St. COLINCAMPS	RAINCHEVAL.	COURCELLES -BERTRANCOURT -LOUVENCOURT -ARQUEVES.	))))
190th.Bde. H.Q.	99th.Bde. H.Q.	—	—	—	—	CAFE JOURDAIN	—	ARQUEVES.	FORCEVILLE -ACHEUX -LEALVILLERS.	190th.Inf Bde.H.Q. leaves at 2.pm.

NOTE:-
* Up Trenches VIth.AVENUE and CAMERON for RIGHT & LEFT respectively.
" Down. " " " " " NEWGATE
" " " ROMAN RD.

MARCH TABLE for 16th Oct.   190th Infantry Bde.

Unit marching out.	Unit marching in.	GUIDES Place	GUIDES Time	GUIDES Number.	Remarks	Destination	Route	Starting point.	Time
7th Royal Fus.	23/Royal Fus.	P.12.c.9.1.	5pm	1 off.	7/RF leave RAINCHEVAL 1 NCO & 6 men to turn over camp to 23/RF.	RAINCHEVAL	FORCEVILLE -ACHEUX- LEALVILLERS -ARQUEVES	P.12.8.9.1.	2.30.pm
4/Bed Regt.	22/ Royal Fus.	do	5.15pm	do	4/Bed Rgt. leave 1 NCO.6 men to turn over camp to 22/RF.	ARQUEVES	ditto	ditto	3.0.pm

Note:- Transport moves during the afternoon to same villages as Battalions.

(OVER)

HEADQUARTERS,
190th
INFANTRY BRIGADE.

No. 2301

Date..................

Headquarters,
190th Infantry Brigade.
17/10/16.

Reference Brigade Order No.25 of the 16th instant, it has now been ordered that the Brigade concentrates at LEALVILLERS on the 17th instant.

The following alterations are therefore to be made in the above Order.

Table for 17th October Column 9 read "LEALVILLERS" throughout.

Column. 10. Shorten accordingly.

M.G.Coy and 1/H.A.C. move to LEALVILLERS direct from BERTANCOURT.

7th Royal Fusiliers and 4th Bedfordshire Regt will move to LEALVILLERS today.

No Unit is to arrive at destination until 2.0.pm. 17th inst

Major.

Brigade Major.

1. 7th Royal Fusiliers.
2. 4th Bedfordshire Regt.
3. 10th Royal Dublin Fusiliers.
4. 1st H.A.C.
5. M.G.Coy.
6. T.M.Battery.
7. Staff Capt.
8. Bde Bombing Officer
9. Intelligence Officer.
10. Bde Transport Officer
11 No4 Coy Train.
12 Signal Master
13. 63rd Division.
14. File.
15. War Diary.

No. 2>01

Headquarters,
190th Infantry Brigade.
17/10/16.

Reference Brigade Order No.25 of the 16th instant, it has now been ordered that the Brigade concentrates at LEALVILLERS on the 17th instant.

The following alterations are therefore to be made in the above Order.

Table for 17th October Column 9 read "LEALVILLERS" throughout.

Column. 10. Shorten accordingly.
M.G.Coy and 1/H.A.C. move to LEALVILLERS direct from BERTANCOURT.

7th Royal Fusiliers and 4th Bedfordshire Regt will move to LEALVILLERS today.

No Unit is to arrive at destination until 2.0.pm. 17th inst

Major.

Brigade Major.

1. 7th Royal Fusiliers.
2. 4th Bedfordshire Regt.
3. 10th Royal Dublin Fusiliers.
4. 1st H.A.C.
5. M.G.Coy.
6. T.M.Battery.
7. Staff Capt.
8. Bde Bombing Officer
9. Intelligence Officer.
10. Bde Transport Officer
11 No4 Coy Train.
12 Signal Master
13. 63rd Division.
14. File.
15. War Diary.

Appendix 23

SECRET.   BRIGADE ORDER No.26.   Copy No..........
                              by
BRIGADIER GENERAL.C.N.TROTMAN.C.B.COMMANDING 190th INFANTRY BRIGADE

                                          Headquarters,
                                          190th Infantry Brigade.
                                          18/10/16.

Ref. Map:
  57 D.1/40,000

1.   190th Infantry Brigade will move from LEALVILLERS to PUCHEVILLE
        in accordance with attached March Table.

2.   1st Line Transport will move with Units.

3.   Details as to allotment of baggage and blanket wagons will be
        issued by Staff Capt as soon as possible.

4.   Billeting parties to proceed an hour ahead of Units.

5.   Should units not receive their baggage wagons in sufficient time
        to move with Bns they will move independently following the last
        of the Brigade.

Time issued to Signals. 9.45 a.m.

                                          G.F.Jerram. Major.
                                          Brigade Major.

1. 7th Royal Fusiliers.
2. 4th Bedfordshire Regt.
3. 10th Royal Dublin Fusiliers.
4. 1st H.A.C.
5. 190th M.G.Coy.
6. 190th T.M.Battery.
7. No4.Coy Divl Train.
8. 63rd Division
9. Staff Capt.
10. Bde Intelligence Officer.
11. Bde Transport Officer
12. Bde Bombing Officer.
13. File
14. War Diary.

MARCH TABLE.

Unit.	Unit forming up place.	Starting point.	Time for head to pass starting point.	Destination.	Route.
7th Royal Fus.	Rd.O.17.c. (rear of bn. at -)	O.16.a.1.7. (Belle Eglise Rm.Rd.Junction)	10.30.am	PUCHEVILLERS.	ARQUEVES-RAINCHEVAL.
4th Bedfordshire. regt.	Rd.O.17.c.d. (head of Bn. at +)	ditto.	10.39.am	ditto.	ditto.
10th R.Dublin Fus.	Rd. running N.E & S.W. through LEALVILLERS (head of Bn.on Church.)	ditto.	10.48.am	ditto.	ditto.
1st H.A.C.	Rd.O.17.d.(head of Bn.on X roads O.23.b.6.8.	ditto.	10.57.am	ditto.	ditto.
190th M.G.Coy.	In rear of 10/R.D.F.	ditto.	11.6.am	ditto	ditto.
190th T.M.Battery	In rear of 1st H.A.C.	ditto	11.11am	ditto	ditto.
190th Bde.H.Q.	Bde H.Q.	ditto	11.15.am	ditto	ditto.

Note.- Brigade will move at a uniform speed of 2½ miles per hour including halts. Halts to be made from 10 minutes to clock hour to clock hour.

SECRET.   Copy No. 14
                        BRIGADE ORDER No.27.
                                by
BRIGADIER GENERAL C.N.TROTMAN.C.B.COMMANDING 190th INFANTRY BRIGADE

                                                    Headquarters,
                                                    190th Inf. Bde.
                                                    19/10/16.
Ref. Map. 57.D.
      1/40,000.

  1.   190th Infantry Bde. Hd.Qrs., 7th Royal Fusiliers and 4th
          Bedfordshire Regt will move tomorrow (20th inst) in accordance
          with attached Table.

  2.   Speed 2½ miles per hour.
          Halts from 10 minutes to clock hour, to clock hour after passing starting
          point.

  3.   Baggage and blanket waggons (5 in all per Bn.) will be at
          Bde. Hd.Qrs. at 8.0.am whither guides are to be sent to
          conduct to units.

  4.   1st Line and Train Transport of each unit will march with
          the unit to which it is attached

  5.   Rations will be delivered at new destination.

  6.   Billeting parties will proceed by 8.0.am.

Time issued to Signals. 9.40 pm

                                                              Major.
                                                         Brigade Major.

    1.7th Royal Fusiliers.
    2.4th Bedfordshire Regt.
    3.10th Royal Dublin Fusiliers.
    4.1st H.A.C.
    5.190th M.G.Coy.
    6.190th T.M.Battery.
(a) 6.Staff Capt.
    7.Bde Intelligence Officer.
    8.Bde. Transport Officer.
    9.Bde. Bombing Officer.
   10.No.4.Coy Divl Train.
   11.Signal Section.
   12.63rd Division.
   13.File.
   14.War Diary. (3)

MARCH TABLE.

Unit.	Starting Point.	Time for head to pass starting point.	Destination.	Route.
7th Royal Fus.	QUESNOYE (N.29.d.)	9.30.am	HEDAUVILLE.	TOUTENCOURT - HARPONVILLE - VARENNES.
4th Bedfordshire Regt.	--do--	9.45.am	VARENNES.	TOUTENCOURT - HARPONVILLE.
Bde. Hd. Qrs.	--do--	11.0.am	VARENNES	--ditto--

SECRET   Copy No....

Brigade Order No.28.
by
Brigadier General C.N.Trotman C.B.Commanding 190th Inf. Bde.

Headquarters,
190th Inf. Bde.
21/10/16.

1/H.A.C and 10/Royal Dublin Fusiliers will move to HEDAUVILLE, today; 1/H.A.C. leaving PUCHEVILLERS at 10-30am 10th Royal Dublin Fusiliers. at 1.0.pm

Route.- TOUTENCOURT - HARPONVILLE and VARENNES.

Baggage and Blanket Waggons will be sent to Bns. Should they not have arrived by starting times, loading parties will be left behind and Waggons will follow as soon as possible.

Billeting parties will proceed by 8.30.am.

C.F.Jarram. Major.
Brigade Major.

1. 1/H.A.C.
2. 10th Royal Dublin Fusiliers. ⎫ Advanced copy forwarded
3. Signal Section.   ⎬   2.40.am
4. 63rd Division.   ⎭
5. Retained
6. 7th Royal Fusiliers.
7. 4th Bedfordshire Regt.
8. 190th M.G.Coy.
9. 190th T.M.Battery.
10. No.4.Coy Div. Train.
11. War Diary (3)

Appendix 26

SECRET.   Copy No.......
              Brigade Order No. 29.
                       by
     Brigadier General C.N.Trotman C.B.Commanding 190th Inf. Bde.

                                        Headquarters,
                                          190th Infantry Bde.
                                            21/10/16.

Ref. Map 57D
     1/40,000.

1.   190th Bde M.G.Company and 190th T.M.Battery will
           move from PUCHEVILLERS to VARENNES tomorrow 22nd inst,
           clearing PUCHEVILLERS by noon.

2.   O.C.190th M.G.Coy will arrange order of march.

3.   Route:- TOUTENCOURT - HARPONVILLES.

4.   1 Wagon per unit will be at PUCHEVILLERS Church at
           8.0.am 22nd, units will send guides there at that time.

                                                 Major.
Time issued to Signals.......
                                              Brigade Major.

1. 190th M.G.Coy.
2. 190th T.M.Battery.
3. 7th Royal Fusiliers.
4. 4th Bedfordshire Regt.
5. 10th Royal Dublin Fusiliers.
6. 1st R.M.C.
7. No.4.Coy.Div.Train.
8. 63rd Division.
9. File.
10. War Diary. (2)

APPENDIX 27

HEADQUARTERS, 190th INFANTRY BRIGADE.
No. 2694
Date............

SECRET&
                                          Headquarters
                                      190th Infantry Brigade
                                              30/10/16.

Ref. 190th Inf. Bde. Order No.29. 23/10/16.

"Z" day is postponed until the 4th November.

                                                Major.
                                        Brigade Major.

7/Royal Fusiliers.
4/4/Bedfordshire Regt.
10/R.Dublin Fusiliers.
1/H.A.C.
190th M.G.Coy.
190th T.M.Battery.
1st Field Coy. Div Eng.
14/Worcester Regt.(Pioneer Coy. attached.
Staff Capt.
Bde Transport Officer.
Bde Intelligence Officer.
Bde. Bombing Officer.
No.3.Field Coy.R.N.D.E.
Signal Section.
No.4.Coy. Divl. Train.
63rd Division.
188th Inf. Bde.
Q189th Inf. Bde.
File.
War Diary.
Artillery Laison Officer.
Laison Officer. 1.
    "   "   11.

2.

8. Assembly:— The Brigade (less 1 Coy of 1/H.A.C.) will assemble in the assembly lines shown in Map "B" on "Y" night and will march from their billets so as to be at the following points at the times mentioned:—
1/H.A.C. (less 1 Coy.) pass MESNIL CHURCH at 6.30.pm and move via HAMEL ROAD.
7/Royal Fusiliers ditto at 8.0.pm.
190th M.G.Coy,Hd.Qrs. and 3 sections-ditto - 9.30pm
4/Bedfordshire Regt. enter GABION AV. at point Q.16.c.9.2. at 6.30.pm
10/R.Dublin Fusiliers ditto at 8.0.pm
M.G.Coy.,1Section ditto at 9.30.pm

Note:—In the case of heavy shelling, the troops moving by the MESNIL - HAMEL Road will be diverted into JACOB'S LADDER.
As soon as troops are formed up in their assembly areas they will inform Bde.H.Q. by runner or by the code word TRESCO by telephone.
1/Coy. of 1/H.A.C. will be attached to the 189th Inf. Bde. and will join this Brigade without further orders on "Y" day.
This Coy. will, moving by the MESNIL - HAMEL Road form up in four waves on the RIGHT of the "Hood" Bn. by 2.0pm on Y/Z night.
The "Hood" Bn. will be formed up in the new trenches which have been dug in Q.18.c.
The Coy. 1/H.A.C. will advance at the same time as the "Hood" Bn., moving up the road and RAILWAY, clearing the dugouts in the RAILWAY EMBANKMENT and protecting the RIGHT flank of the 189th Inf. Bde.
On reaching the NORTHERN END of the Trench, which runs back from Q.18.c.5.2. to Q.24.a.8.9. a strong bombing party with a support and 1 Lewis Gun will clear this trench, which will be "Barraged" by the artillery and Stokes Mortars before the bombing party enters it.
On completion of this duty the party will follow and rejoin their Company on the DOTTED GREEN LINE.
On arrival at the DOTTED GREEN LINE the company will wait for and rejoin their Bn., becoming a reserve Coy. in the hands of the Bn. Commander.
5 Lewis Guns of the 14/Worcester Regt (Pioneers) will be attached to this Company by the 189th Inf. Bde. until their arrival at the DOTTED GREEN LINE, when they will rejoin the attacking infantry of the 189th Inf. Bde.
The orders given by the 189th Inf. Bde. to the Stokes Mortar Battery are as follows:—
"The Light T.M.Battery will bombard the trench running back from Q.18.c.5.2. to Q.24.a.8.9. from ZERO to ZERO + 5' when it will be entered by a bombing party of the H.A.C.
It will assist this party in their attack on the trench as far as visibility permits.
At ZERO + 10, 4 guns will advance and assist the H.A.C. in capturing the dugouts on the RAILWAY EMBANKMENT and the infantry in bombing along MARSHAL TRENCH, if not already captured.............."

9. Attached Units:— 2 Sections of No.3. Field Coy. R.N.D.E. and a half Coy. of the 14/Worcestershire Regt. (Pioneers) are attached to the Brigade and are allocated as follows:—
½ Section Engineers will be attached to each Bn. and will join these Bns., without further orders, by 11.0.am on "Y" day, forming up with them.
They will bring with them one day's ordinary and two iron rations.
The ½ Coy. of the 14/Worcestershire Regt will, on Y/Z night, form up in HAMEL VILLAGE, without further orders with Hd.Qrs. at the Road junction Q.23.d.5.9.
They will move into position passing MESNIL CHURCH at 10.0.pm.

They will be divided into two parties known as "A" and "B", each under an officer.
They will follow the infantry when they advance, at a distance of 50 yards, to the BLUE LINE.
After the capture of the BROWN LINE they will open up the two communication trenches leading from the BLUE to the BROWN LINE; one party working on each trench, "A" on the RIGHT; "B" on the LEFT.
These trenches run forward from:-
   (1) R.2.a.10.25. to R.2.b.10.65.
   (2) R.8.a.20.00. to R.8.b.40.60. and thence by the road to PUISIEUX Trench.
These trenches must be opened up as rapidly as possible.

10. "Tanks":- Three groups of "TANKS" will be working with the 63rd Divn., namely :-
   Groups. 1V. V. and Vl.
Their routes are shewns on Map "D"

11. Advance of the Brigade.-
(a) The Brigade in four waves will advance from its assembly lines on "Z" day at 0 hour 35', so as to ensure the leading wave crossing the British front line trench at 0 hour 50'
The 1st and 2nd waves will be 10 to 15 yards, the remainder 50 yards apart.
The Brigade will replace the 188th and 189th Inf. Bdes. in the support and reserve trenches of the enemy's first system.
The first two waves will occupy the enemy "Reserve" trench.
The 3rd and 4th waves, the enemy "Support" trench.
The two sections of M.G.Coy. with the advanced infantry will move in rear of the 4th wave.
The Headquarters and two sections of the M.G.Coy., which are in reserve, will move forward at the discretion of the O.C. M.G.Coy., taking advantage of all cover, with a view to getting into action as soon as possible after the capture of the BROWN LINE.
The O.C.M.G.Coy. will establish communication, by runner, with the TELEPHONE POST keeping two men there until such time as he moves forward.

Note:- The waves above mentioned are the most convenient formation for any possible offensive action, but Bn. Commanders should at any time that they think it to be advisable adopt artillery formations and subsequently again deploy into "waves".

(b) The Company of the 1/H.A.C. attached to the 189th Inf. Bde. will, here, rejoin its Bn.

(c) At 1 hour 50' the Brigade commences to advance on GREEN LINE, the occupation of which should be completed by 2 hours 20'
The first "wave" will be in the enemy trench:
The second "wave" about 10 yards behind.
The Third and Fourth "waves" at distances of about 50 yards, taking advantage of any cover which may exist.

(d) Between 2 hours 20' and 3 hours 25' two intermediate lines and the BLUE LINE will be occupied by the 189th and 188th Inf. Bdes.
Between these hours the 190th Inf.Bde. will advance from the GREEN to the BLUE LINE.
The Brigade will halt immediately in rear of the troops, which are consolidating the BLUE LINE, the formation being in four waves as in the initial advance.

(e) At 3 hours 40' the 190th Inf. Bde. will pass through the 189th and 188th inf Bdes. and advance on BROWN LINE, which will be captured by them.
The first and second "waves" will advance straight through to the further line and consolidate it.
The third and fourth waves will halt at and "Clean up" PUISIEUX TRENCH.

(f) The "Barrage" Time Table for the whole operation is attached APPENDIX 1.
It must, however, be clearly understood that the times are published merely as a guide to the infantry and are NOT orders for the exact time of the assault.
It is of paramount and vital importance that the infantry keeps close up to the artillery barrage and advance whenever it lifts.

4.

Note :- It will be noticed that, during the halts on the
GREEN and YELLOW LINES there will be two (2) pauses
each of 5 minutes.

The re-opening of intense fire after the
SECOND of these pauses will be the signal for the
infantry to advance, in each case.

Great care must be taken on both the GREEN and YELLOW
LINES that the infantry advance is NOT resumed at the
end of the FIRST pause, or our men would be caught by
the fire of their own barrage.

This does not apply to the 190th Inf. Bde. unless they
are drawn into the fight on or before arrival at the
GREEN LINE.

(g) Strong points will be made as follows:-
By 1/H.A.C. and attached Engineers at (or about) R.8.b.5.8.
" 7/Royal Fusiliers. " " " " " R.2.d.45.50.
" 4/Bedfordshire Regt. " " " " " R.2.d.3.8.
"10/Royal Dublin Fusiliers B " " " R.2.b.1.5.
The guns of the 190th M.G.Coy will be alloted primarily, for
the defence of these points.

(h) All trenches approaching flanks of positions, and which
are NOT occupied by our troops are to be blocked.

(i) Battle patrols will, as soon as possible be pushed out
to the front to keep touch with the enemy.

(j) Every available machine and Lewis gun will be brought
into position for immediate action.

12. Consolidation:- The rapid consolidation of all ground won is of the utmost
importance, in order to meet successfully any counter
attacks, which may be made.

13. Action if   It must be impressed on all subordinate Commanders that
    troops on   they must NOT halt because units on their flanks are held
    Flanks are   up; they must rather assist those units by advancing and
    held up :-   taking the enemy in flank or rear.

14. Communications:- (a) A buried cable will run from Brigade Headquarters to
near our front line trench; the advanced end will be known
as "TELEPHONE POST" and be clearly marked as such; its
position will be Q.17.d. (Central) mine shaft immediately
S.E. of junction of ROBERTS and LOUVERCY TRENCHES.
This post must be known to all runners.

(b) From this point lines will be run to flank Bns. as they
advance.

(c) The two Bns. on the RIGHT will combine to form a system
of runners on the relay system, and a similar precedure
will be adopted by the two LEFT Bns.
The relay posts should be on the cable line and the runner
will carry out with them one shovel per pair of runners
to dig themselves in.

(d) One cable detachment from the Hd. Qrs. section (Div. Sig.
Coy. will be attached to Brigade Hd.Qrs. and will come
under the orders of the O.C. Bde.Si .Section.
Following the advance of the infantry this section will
run out a line to the proposed advanced Bde. Hd.Qrs. in the
YELLOW LINE.
An officer from Brigade Hd.Qrs. will accompany this line
and chose the sight for Hd.Qrs.

(e) When the 190th Inf. Bde.Hd.Qrs. move forward to the YELLOW
LINE, the despatch riders at MESNIL will move forward as
far as HAMEL Q.23.d.4.9. to which point Brigade runners will
carry their messages.

(f) The O.C.Bde. Signal Section will arrange for 10 Bde.
Runners for use as required in carrying despatches to
Division and Brigades.
3 Motor Cyclists D.R. will be attached to the Brigade.

(g) All runners and mounted despatch riders will carry despatches in the LEFT hand breast pocket.
Anyone seeing a dead or wounded D.R. will search him for despatches and hand them in as soon as possible to the nearest runner post or Signal Officer.

(h) Pigeons:- Two HEDAUVILLE birds will be issued to each Bn. by the Bde. Signal Officer on "Y" day.
These birds must be used with the greatest discretion. They will only be employed for very important messages and then only when all other means of communication has failed. Only one bird should be released at a time.

(i) Aeroplanes:- Contact aeroplanes will be employed to fix positions gained by the infantry.
Flares will be lighted:-
(1) On gaining each objective.
(2) Whenever hung up.
(3) When an Aeroplane sounds its "Klaxon" horn.
(4) Just before dark and in the early morning if an aeroplane is about.

It must be remembered that it is ONLY the most advanced troops which light these flares.
Red flares only will be used.

(j) "S.O.S." Rockets are "White", "Green", "White".

15. Communication Trenches.-

"UP"
JACOB'S LADDER.
McMAHON AV.
PECHE ST.
GABION AV.
LONG SAP.

"DOWN"
LOUVERCY ST.
ROYAL AV.
POTTAGE TR.
CHARLES AV.
LONG ACRE.
CONSTITUTION HILL
KNIGHTSBRIDGE.
RAILWAY.

16. Equipment.
Troops will attack in Battle Order and will carry the following:-
4 Sandbags per man (passed through the belt, two on each side)
2 Iron rations.
Unexpired portion of days ration.
Gas Helmet.
1 Flare.
1 Very Light.
Mills Grenades at the rate of two per man: twelve to be carried by each bomber, remainder to be distributed amongst infantry.
In addition to above, each man of the rear wave of the attacking troops will carry 2 tools (1 pick to 10 shovels)
Men carrying wire-cutters will wear yellow armlets.
S.O.S. Rockets and "P" Bombs will be carried under Bn. arrangements.
Runners will be lightly equipped and will NOT carry rifles; they will wear a blue armlet with a white stripe.
Pack will NOT be carried.
Great Coats will be carried to the assembly trenches and then put on.
Coats will be removed at 5.0am; each section will make a bundle; tie with rope to which will be attached a strong label showing the No. of the Section etc.
The bundles will be packed on the RIGHT of each platoon and 2 men per Bn. left in charge.

6.

Medical Arrangements:-	1 bearer sub-division of No.1. Field Ambulance will work with the Brigade; they will assemble in POTTAGE Trench in HAMEL.

Route JACOBS LADDER which will be entered at 10.30.pm on Y/Z night.
Bearer sub-divisions will clear wounded as follows:-
  (a) From present front line to A.D.S. at MESNIL and COOKERS:-
      2 bearer Sub Divisions of 3rd F.A.
  (b) From "GREEN" LINE to present front line:-
      2 bearer Sub Divisions of 2nd F.A.
  (c) From YELLOW LINE to GREEN LINE :-
      1 Bearer Sub Division of 2nd F.A.
      1   "   "   "   3rd F.A.
  (d) From BLUE to YELLOW LINE:-
      2 bearers Sub Divisions of 1st F.A.
  (e) From BROWN to BLUE LINE :-
      1 bearer SubDivision of 1st F.A.
      (Surgeon WALKER R.N.)

Bearer and collecting posts will be established as far forward as possible in the above areas and will be marked by sign beards.

Medical — Regimental Officers will, as soon as the objective has been reached, select positions for Regimental Aid posts in the vicinity of Bn. Hd.Qrs.
These posts should be clearly marked with the Red Cross and letters R.A.P.
Reserve stretchers and dressings will be brought up to Regimental Aid Posts bt the bearer Sub Divisions.
Bearer Sub Divisions have orders to keep in close touch with Regtl Medical Officers.
The Regtl stretcher bearers are NOT required to assist in the evacuation of the wounded during movement. When established,
When halted, however, and the regtl Aid Posts, the regtl stretcher bearers will be responsible for clearing the wounded in front of the Regtl Aid posts and for taking them to that post.
The bearer Sub Divisions will collect the wounded from the Regtl Aid Posts and from the rear.
Should it be necessary for Regtl stretcher bearers to assist in the evacuation of wounded from the Regtl Aid posts, they will carry only so far as the nearest bearer posts and return to their unit.

Administrative Orders:-	Are as issued by Staff Captain.
19	A mine will be sprung by us in "No Man's Land" at ZERO hour.
20 Watches.	Watches will be synchronised by telephone from D.H.Q, at 1.15.pm, 5.15pm and 8.45.pm on "Y" day and at 5.0.pm on "Z" day.
21 Bde.Hd.Qrs.	Will be established at MESNIL Q.28.c.9.9. at 5.0.pm on "Y" day and will move forward after capture of the BROWN LINE to about point R.7.a.0.3.
22 Appendices.	Appendix 1. Barrage Table.

                        "   11. List of Compass bearings.
                        Maps   A.)
                        "   B.) To be detached from order No.29 and attached
                        "   C.) here.
                        "   D.)

23. Notes
    a. The ground over which the attack is to take place must be carefully studied and bearings taken of any points which may assist commanders in keeping direction.
    b. Special mopping up parties, detailed from the 3rd wave must be told off to deal with all trenches between the BLUE and BROWN objectives.
    c. It must be impressed on all ranks that it is of the utmost importance to the success of the operations that no movement takes place in the assembly area during dawn on "Z" day prior to ZERO hour.
During the night of Y/Z there should be as little noise as possible and no loud talking.
Matches must be carefully screened and every precaution taken to conceal the fact of our assembly for attack.
    d. A proportion of the reserve personnel for Machine and Lewis guns should be left behind and not taken into action.
    e. Officers and N.C.Os. must move IN the ranks of their platoons
    f. Bns. must have a special carrying party detailed for S.O.S. Rockets and Very Lights in addition to the one of the latter carried on the man.
    g. No papers etc shewing position of Hd.Qrs. Dumps or other important information are to be taken into action.
Maps of enemy trenches **not** giving above information may and should be taken.

24. This order cancels all previous orders on this subject. Previous orders except maps should be destroyed.

Time issued to Signals... 11 pm

                                                  Major.
                                        Brigade Major.

Copies to:-
1. 7/Royal Fusiliers.
2. 4/Bedfordshire Regt.
3. 10/Royal Dublin Fusiliers.
4. 1/H.A.C.
5. 190th M.G.Co,
6. 190th T.M.Batty.
6. Staff Captain.
7. Bde Intelligence Officer.
8. " Bombing Officer,
9. " Transport Officer.
10. No. 3 Field Coy.
11. 14/Worcester Regt.
12. Signal Section.
13. No. 4 Coy Div. Train
14. 63rd Division.
15. 188th Inf. Brigade.
16. 189th " "
17. A.D.M.S.
18. Art. Liason Officer.
19. File.
20. War Diary (3)
21. Spare (5)

2.

2 hours 20'	Barrage re-opens 150 yards beyond YELLOW LINE	Advance towards DOTTED YELLOW LINE.
2 hours 22'	Barrage moves back at rate of 100 yards in 4 minutes to DOTTED YELLOW LINE ; stays there 4 minutes, and then lifts 150 yards beyond it, where it dwells till 2 hours 30'	
2 hours 34'		Complete capture of DOTTED YELLOW LINE.
2 hours 39'	Barrage moves back to DOTTED BROWN LINE at 100 yards in 4 minutes stays there 4 minutes and then lifts to 150 yards beyond it, where it dwells till 3 hours 00'	
2 hours 55'		Complete capture of DOTTED BROWN LINE and advance close up to barrage.
3 hours 00'	Barrage moves back to BLUE LINE at the rate of 100 yards in 4 minutes; stays there 4 minutes and then lifts to 150 yards beyond it, where it dwells till 3 hours 35'	
3 hours 25'		Complete capture of BLUE LINE.
3 hours 35'	Barrage pauses for 5 minutes.	
3 hours 40'	Barrage re-opens 150 yards beyond BLUE LINE.	Advance towards BROWN LINE.
3 hours 42'	Barrage moves back to BROWN LINE at the rate of 100 yards in 4 minutes; stays there 4 minutes and then lifts to 150 yards beyond it.	
4 hours 20'		Complete capture of BROWN LINE.

APPENDIX 1.

Barrage Table for attack of 63rd Division.

Time.	Artillery (18 pounders)	Infantry
Zero.	Barrage on enemy front line, and 25% on "No Man's Land", 50% on our side of it	Assaulting Infantry Advance.
0 hour 1'	All guns on enemy front line.	
0 hour 4'	Barrage lifts from front line, and moves back to DOTTED GREEN LINE at the rate of 100 yards in 4 minutes; stays there 4 minutes and then lifts 150 yards beyond it, where it dwells till 0 hour 23'.	Assault front line.
0 hour 18'		Complete capture of DOTTED GREEN LINE.
0 hour 23'	Barrage moves back to GREEN LINE at the rate of 100 yards in 4 minutes; stays there 4 minutes and then lifts to 150 yards beyond it, where it dwells till 0 hour 50'.	Advance towards GREEN LINE.
0 hour 40'		Complete capture of GREEN LINE.
0 hour 50'	Barrage pauses for 5 minutes.	
0 hour 55'	Fire resumed 150 yards beyond GREEN LINE.	
1 hour 05'	Barrage pauses for 5 minutes.	
1 hour 10'	Fire resumed 150 yards beyond GREEN LINE.	Advance towards YELLOW LINE.
1 hour 12'	Lifts 100 yards and moves back at the rate of 100 yards in 4 minutes to YELLOW LINE; stays there 4 minutes and then lifts 150 yards beyond it, where it dwells till 2 hours 00'.	
1 hour 50'		Complete capture of YELLOW LINE.
2 hours 00'	Barrage pauses 5 minutes.	
2 hours 05'	Barrage re-opens 150 yards beyond YELLOW LINE.	
2 hours 15'	Barrage pauses 5 minutes.	

APPENDIX. 2.

True bearing of various Map References

A. NORTH DIVISIONAL BOUNDARY.
(For Magnetic Bearings <u>add</u> 1⅓ to the values given)

From end of SHAFTESBURY AVE.(Q.17.a.35.30) to ENEMY'S FRONT LINE (Q.17.a.75.85.)	32°
From end of SHAFTESBURY AVE. to Q.6.c.75.35.	37°
" ENEMY'S FRONT LINE (Q.17.a.75.85.) to Q.6.c.75.35 (Crossing Green Line on route)	38°
" Q.6.c.75.35. to Q.6.d.15.35. (Crossing Yellow Line on route)	90°
" Q.6.d.15.35. to R.1.a.90.20.(Crossing dotted Yellow and dotted Brown Lines on route.)	64½°
" R.1.a.90.20. to R.1.b.65.35.	82½°
" R.1.b.65.35. to R.2.a.15.85.,(Crossing Blue Line on route)	44°
" R.2.a.15.85. to R.2.b.15.99. (Brown Line)	82°

B. Other Bearings.

From end of LOUVERCY ST. (Q.17.d.45.65. to ENEMY'S FRONT LINE (Q.17.b.70.10.)	31°
From end of LOUVERCY ST (Q.17.d.45.65.) to Q.17.b.9.4. (Dotted Green Line)	31°
From Q.17.b.9.4. (Dotted Green Line) to Q.12.c.8.1. (Green Line)	52½°
" Q.12.c.8.1. (Green Line) to R.7.a.10.45. (Yellow Line)	42½°
" R.7.a.10.45. (Yellow Line) to R.8.a.10.80. (Blue Line)	80½°
" R.8.a.10.80. (Blue Line) to R.2.d.40.50. (PUISIEUX TRENCH)	60½°
" R.2.d.40.50. (PUISIEUX TRENCH) to R.2.d.80.45. (Brown Line)	92°

SECRET.　　　　　　　　　APPENDIX 27　Copy No. 20

190th. Infantry Brigade Order No.29.
by
Brigadier General C.N.Trotman, C.B. Commanding 190th. Infantry Brigade.

Hd.Qrs.190th.Inf.Bde.
23rd.Oct. 1916.

Ref. Maps:- HAMEL 1/10,000 (A).
　　　　　　Map B. (Assembly Trenches).
　　　　　　Map C. (Enemy Trenches).
　　　　　　Map D. (Tank Map).

1.　　The Reserve Army is to attack the enemy's positions on both sides of the RIVER ANCRE.

2.　　To the 63rd.Division is allotted the task of capturing the PUISIEUX Trench and its immediate Support line from the RIVER ANCRE on the SOUTH to L32.c.8.0.
　　　The 2nd.Division will be on our LEFT.

3.　　The objectives allotted to the Division are shown on Map C.

4.　　There are four separate objectives, known as :-
　　　　(a) GREEN LINE.
　　　　(b) YELLOW LINE.
　　　　(c) BLUE LINE.
　　　　(d) BROWN LINE.
　　　The capture of "a" "b" and "c" is allotted to the 189th.and 188th.Inf.Bdes. on the SOUTH and NORTH respectively.
　　　The capture of "d" is allotted to the 190th.Inf.Bde.
　　　The final objective is about 1400 yards long and about 4200 yds. from the front assembly trench of the 190th.Inf.Bde.

5.　　The Day of Attack will be known as "Z" day and the hour of attack "ZERO".

6.　　The attack will be preceded by an intense bombardment on X and Y.

7.　　The order of battle for the 190th.Inf.Bde. will be from RIGHT to LEFT.
　　　　1/Honourable Artillery Company (less one Coy.)
　　　　7/Royal Fusiliers.
　　　　4/Bedfordshire Regiment.
　　　　10/Royal Dublin Fusiliers.
　　　190th. Machine Gun Company:- Headquarters and 2 sections in rear of
　　　　　　　　　　　　　　　　　　the centre of the Brigade.
　　　　　　　　　　　　　　　　　1 Section in rear of the RIGHT Bn.
　　　　　　　　　　　　　　　　　1　"　　"　"　"　"　LEFT　".
　　　190th. Light Trench Mortar Battery:- 4 Guns in reserve.
　　　　　　　　　　　　　　　　　　　　　4　"　　" rear of centre of the
　　　　　　　　　　　　　　　　　　　　　　　　　　Brigade.

8.　　The Brigade, less one Company of the 1/H.A.C. will assemble in the assembly lines shown in Map "B" on "Y" night and will march from their billets so as to be at the following points at the times mentioned.
　　　　1/H.A.C.(less 1 Coy.) enter WEST end of JACOBS LADDER at 6.30 pm.
　　　　7/Royal Fusiliers -ditto- at 8 pm.
　　　　4/Bedfordshire Regt. enter GABION AVENUE at point$
　　　　Q16.c.9.2. at 6.30 pm.
　　　　10/Royal Dublin Fusiliers -ditto- at 8 pm.
　　　　M.G.Company, Headquarters and 3 Sections enter JACOBS
　　　　LADDER at 9.30 pm.
　　　　1 Section enter GABION AVENUE at Q 16.c.9.2. at 9.30 pm.
　　　　T.M.Battery; Enter JACOBS LADDER at 10 pm.
　　　　1 Coy. of 1/H.A.C. will be attached to the 189th.Inf.Bde, until after the capture of the first objective. Orders as to this Coy. will be issued as soon as received.

2. Brigade Order No.29.

9. 2 Sections of No.3 Field Company R.N.D.E. and a half Company of the 14/Worcester Regt (Pioneers) are attached to the Brigade and are allocated as follows:-
½ Section Engineers and 2 Sections of Pioneers will be attached to each BN., and will join these Bns. by 11.0.am on "Y" day; they will bring with them 1 days ordinary ration and two Iron rations.
The Officers will be distributed as evenly as possible, preference as regards Engineer Officers being given to the flank Bns.

10. Three groups of "TANKS" will be working with the 63rd Division namely :-
Groups IV. V. and VI.
Their routes are shown on Map "D".

11. (a) The Brigade in four waves will advance from its assembly lines on "Z" day at 0 hour 35'.
So as to ensure the leading wave crossing the British front line trench at 0 hour 50'.
The 1st and 2nd waves will be 10 to 15 yards, the remainder 50 yards apart.
The Brigade will replace the 188th and 189th Inf. Brigades in the support and reserve lines of the enemy First system of trenches.
The first two waves will occupy the enemy "Reserve" trench.
The 3rd and 4th waves, the enemy "Support" trench.
The Machine Guns and Trench Mortars will be in the "Support" Trench, thus leaving the enemy front trench unoccupied.
(b) The Company of the 1/H.A.C., attached to the 189th Inf. Bde. will, here, rejoin its Bn. and become reserve Coy to that Bn.
(c) At 1 hour 50' the Brigade will commence to advance on "GREEN" Line the occupation of which should be completed by 2 hours 20'.
The first wave will be in the enemy trench;
The second wave about 10 yards behind.
The third and fourth waves at distances of about 50 yards, taking advantage of any cover, which may exist.
(d) Between 2 hours 20' and 3 hours 25', two intermediate lines and the "BLUE" Line will be occupied by the 188th and 189th Inf. Bdes.
Between these hours the 190th Inf. Bde. will advance from the "GREEN" to the "BLUE" line.
The Brigade will halt immediately in rear of the troops, which are consolidating the "BLUE" line, the formation being in four waves as in the initial advance.
(e) At 3 hours 40' the 190th Inf.Bde will pass through the 188th and 189th Inf. Bdes. and advance on "BROWN" line, which will be captured by them.
The first and second waves will advance straight through to the further line and consolidate it.
The third and fourth waves will halt at and "Clean up" PUSIEUX TRENCH.
(f) The barrage Time Table for the capture of the "BROWN" line is attached, Appendix 1.
It must, however, be clearly understood that the times are published merely as a guide to the infantry, and are not orders for the exact time of the assault.
It is of paramount and vital importance that the infantry keeps close up to the Artillery Barrage and advance whenever it lifts.
(g) Strong points will be made as follows:-

By 1/H.A.C. at (or about) ......R.8.b.5.8.
By 7/Royal Fus. at (or about) R.2.d.45.50.
By 4/Bed.Regt. " " " R.2.d.3.8.
By10/Royal D.Fus. " " " R.2.t.1.5.
(Dublin)

3. Brigade Order No.29.

    (h) All trenches not occupied by our troops, approaching flanks of positions are to be blocked.
    (i) Battle Patrols will as soon as possible be pushed out to the front to keep touch with the enemy.
    (j) Every available Machine and Lewis Gun will be brought into position for immediate action.

12.   The rapid consolidation of all ground won is of the utmost importance, in order to meet successfully any counter attack which may be made.

13.   It must be impressed on all Subordinate Commanders that they must not halt because units in their flanks are held up. They must rather assist those units by advancing and taking the enemy in flank or rear.

14. Communication.
    A buried cable will run from Brigade Headquarters to near our front line trench.
    From this point lines will be run to flank Bns. as they advance.
    The two Bns. on the RIGHT will combine to form a system of runners on the relay system and a similar procedure will be adopted by the two LEFT Bns.
    The relay posts should be on the cable line, and the runners will each carry out with them one shovel in order to dig in the posts.

15.   Watches are to be synchronised on "Y" day at 6.0.pm and on "Z" day at one hour before ZERO.

16.   Brigade Hd.Qrs. will be at MESNIL about Q.28.c.9.9. and will advance to the "YELLOW" Line as soon as the "BROWN" line is occupied.

17.   Equipment. Troops will attack in battle order and will carry the following.
    4 sandbags per man (passed through the belt 2 on each side)
    2 Iron rations.
    Unexpended portion of days rations.
    Gas Helmet.
    1 Flare.
    1 Verys Light Cartridge.
    2 Hand Grenades.
    If preferred special men may be detailed to carry buckets of grenades.
    In addition to the above 50% of the attacking troops will carry a shovel, a few picks being also carried.
    As many wire cutters as possible will be issued beforehand by Bde. Hd.Qrs. Men carrying wire cutters will wear yellow armlet. S.O.S. Rockets and "P" Bombs will be carried under Battalion arrangements.
    The pack is to be worn and is to contain the following ONLY :-

        1 Greatcoat.
        1 W.P.Sheet.
        2 Iron rations.
        Unexpended portion of days ration.
        Canteen.

    Runners will be lightly equipped and will not carry rifles and will wear a blue armlet with a white stripe.

18.   Administrative orders will be issued separately.

4. Brigade Order No. 29.

19. Communication "UP".   JACOBS LADDER.
    Trenches.   Mc MAHON AVENUE.
                         PECHE STREET.
                         GABION AVENUE.
                         LONG SAP.
            "DOWN"   LOUVEROY ST.
                         ROYAL AVENUE.
                         POTTAGE TRENCH.
                         CHARLES AVENUE.
                         LONG ACRE.
                         CONSTITUTION HILL.
                         KNIGHTS BRIDGE.
                         RAILWAY.

20. Stokes Mortars. Stokes Mortar Ammunition will be carried at the rate of 40 rounds per mortar.

21. Aeroplane Co-operation. Contact Aeroplanes will be employed to fix positions gained by the infantry.
    Flares will be lighted.
    (a) On gaining each objective.
    (b) Whenever hung up.
    (c) When an aeroplane sounds its "Klaxon" horn.
    (d) Just before dark and in the early morning, if an aeroplane is above.
    It must be remembered that it is ONLY the most advanced troops which light these flares.

22. "S.O.S." - The S.O.S. Rockets are white, green, white.

23. Medical Arrangements. - 1 Bearer sub-division of No.1 Field Ambulance will work with the Brigade.
    Regimental Medical Officers, will, as soon as the objective has been reached select positions for Regtl. Aid. Posts, in the vicinity of Bn. Hd. Qrs.
    These posts should be clearly marked with the Red Cross and letters R.A.P.

24.   Notes:- a. The ground over which the attack is to take place must be carefully studied and bearings taken of any points which may assist commanders in keeping direction.
    b. No papers likely to be of value to the enemy are to be taken over the parapet.

Time issued to Signals........

                                               Major.

                                         Brigade Major.

Copies to:-
1. 7th Royal Fusiliers.
2. 4/Bedfordshire Regt.
3. 10/Royal Dublin Fusiliers
4. 1/H.A.C.
5. 190th M.G.Coy.
6. 190th T.M.Battery.
7. Staff Capt.
8. Bde. Transport Officer.
9. Bde Intelligence Officer.
10. Bde. Bombing Officer.
11. No.3.Field Coy. R.N.D.E.
12. 14/Worcester Regt.
13. Signal Section.
14. No.4.Coy. Div.Train.
15. 63rd Division.
16. 188th Inf.Bde.
17. 189th Inf.Bde.
18. File.
19. War Diary.
20.
21.

22 Artillery Liaison Officer
23 Liaison Officer I
24 Liaison Officer II

APPENDIX 1.

BARRAGE TABLE.

TIME.	ARTILLERY.	INFANTRY.
3 hours 25'	Barrage 150 yards beyond BLUE line.	188th & 189th. Inf.Bde. complete capture of BLUE Line.
3 hour 35'	Barrage pauses for 5 mins.	
3 hour 40'	Barrage reopens 150 yds. beyond BLUE Line.	Advance towards BROWN Line.
3 hour 42'	Barrage moves back to BROWN Line. at rate of 100 yds in 4 mins, stays there 4 mins, and then lifts to 150 yds. beyond it.	
4 hours 20'		Complete capture of BROWN Line.

SECRET.

Copy No... 21

ADDENDA to 190th Inf. Bde. Order
No. 29.

Hd Qrs. 190th Inf. Bde.
23rd October 1916.

Para 5.   Add:- "Z" day will be the 26th October 1916 and Zero hour, probably, shortly after 6 a.m.

Para 8.   Add:- As soon as troops are formed up in their assembly area they will inform Bde. Hd. Qrs. by runner or by the Code word
"TRESCO"
via TELEPHONE POST, if open.

Para 11.   Sub para (a). Add:- The Hd. Quarters and 2 Sections of M.G.Coy. in Reserve will NOT move forward until they receive instructions to do so from Bde. Hd. Qrs.
The O.C. M.G.Coy will establish communication by runner to the TELEPHONE POST, keeping two men there until such time as he moves forward.

Para 11.   in order, sub para. (c):-
After last line, add - These "waves" are the most convenient formation for any possible offensive action, but Bn. Commanders should, at any time that they think it to be advisable, adopt Artillery formation, and subsequently again deploy into "waves".

Para 14.   After second line add:-
This point will be known as "TELEPHONE POST". Its exact position will be made known to all Units on "Y" day, and should be understood by Runners.

Para 15.   Delete, and substitute:-
Watches will be synchronised by Telephone from D.H.Q. at 1.15 p.m., 5.15 p.m. and 8.45 p.m. on "Y" day, and at 5.0 p.m. on "Z" day.

Para 21.   Add:- Rod flares only will be used by the attacking infantry of the 63rd Division.

Para 23.   Add:-
Bearer Sub-divisions will be alloted for clearing wounded as follows:-
(a) From present front line to A.D.S. at MESNIL and COOKERS:-
2 Bearer Sub-divisions of 3rd Field Ambulance.
(b) From "GREEN" line to present front line:-
2 Bearer Sub-divisions of 2nd Field Ambulance.
(c) From "YELLOW" line to "GREEN" line:-
1 Bearer Sub-division of 2nd F.A.
1 "   "   "   " 3rd F.A.
(d) From "BLUE" line to "YELLOW" line:-
2 Bearer Sub-divisions of No. 1 F.A.
(e) From "BROWN" line to "BLUE" line:-
1 Bearer Sub-division of No. 1 Field Ambulance.
(SURGEON WALKER. R.N.)
The assembly position alloted to (e) is POTTAGE TRENCH, in HAMEL.
Route JACOBS LADDER which will be entered in rear of Trench Mortar Battery at 10.30 p.m. on Y/Z night.
Bearer and Collecting posts will be established as far forward as possible within the above area and will be marked by Signboards.

2. Addenda to Bde. Order No. 29.

Para 23 (continued).
Reserve stretchers and dressings will be brought up to Regimental Aid Posts by the Bearer Sub-divisions, whenever possible.
Bearer Sub-divisions have orders to keep in close touch with Regimental Medical Officers.
The Regimental stretcher bearers are not required to assist in the evacuation of wounded during movement. When halted, however, and the Regimental Aid Post is established, the Regimental Stretcher Bearers will be responsible for clearing the wounded in front of the Regl. Aid Post and for taking them to that Post.
The Bearer Sub-divisions will collect the wounded from the Regimental Aid Posts and from the rear.
Should it be necessary for Regimental Stretcher bearers to assist in the evacuation of wounded from the Regl. Aid Posts, they will carry only so far as the nearest bearer post and return to their Unit.

Major,
Brigade Major.

Time issued to Signals 9.15am

Copies to:-
1. 7/Royal Fusiliers,
2. 4/Bedfordshire Regt.
3. 10/Royal Dublin Fusiliers,
4. 1/H.A.C.
5. 190th M.G.Coy.
6. 190th T.M.Batty.
7. Staff Captn.
8. Bde Transport Officer.
9. Bde Intelligence Officer.
10. Bde Bombing Officer.
11. No. 3 Field Coy. R.N.D.E.
12. 14/Worcester Regt.
13. Signal Section.
14. No. 4 Coy. Div. Train.
15. 63rd Division. (2 copies)
16. 188th Inf. Bde.
17. 189th Inf. Bde.
18. File.
19. War Diary.
20. -do-
21. -do-
22. Artillery Laison Officer.
23. Laison Officer. I.
24. -do- II.
25. A.D.M.S.

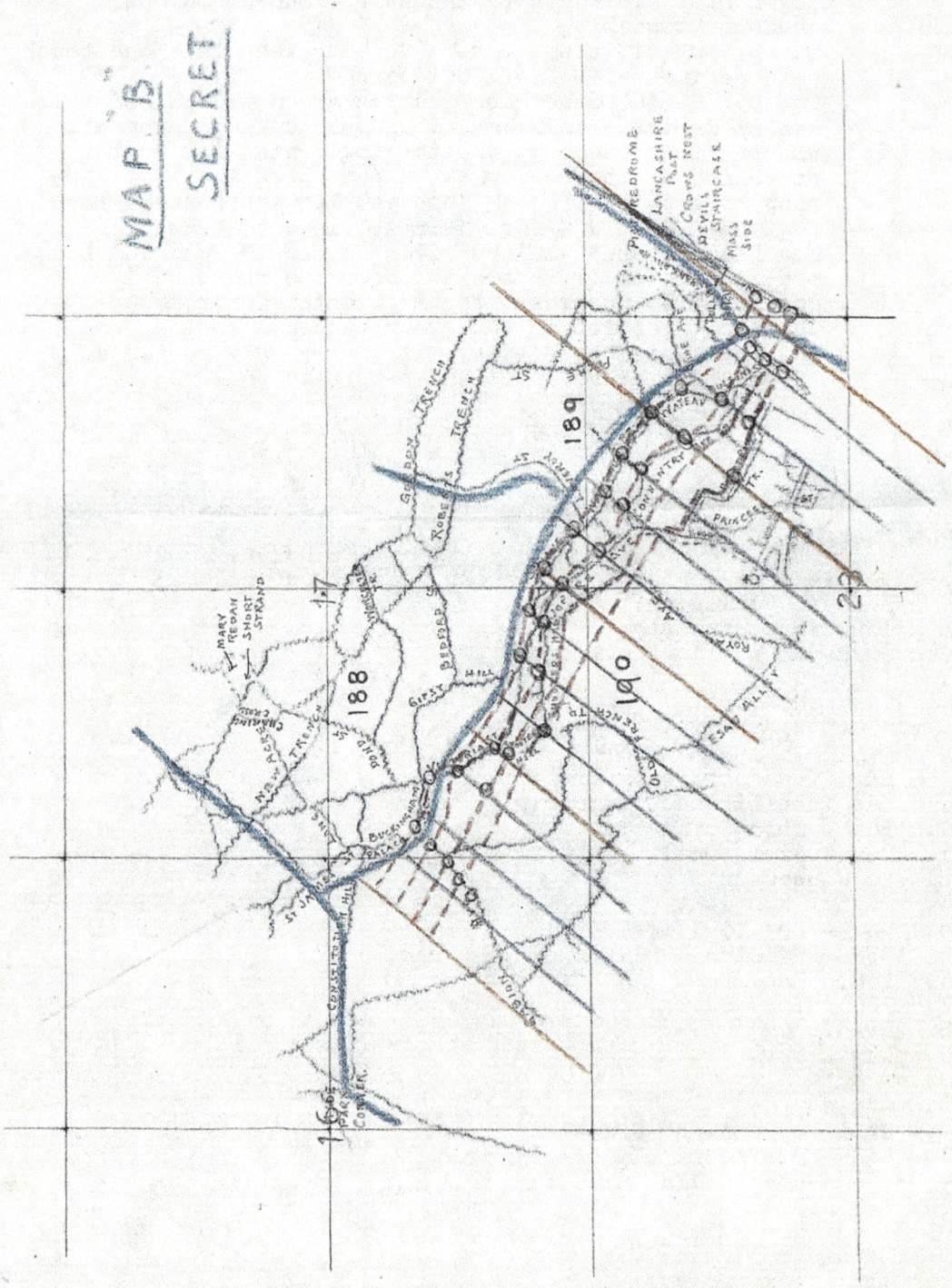

TIME TABLE OF 63rd DIVISION ATTACK.

Time	Artillery (18-Pdrs.)	Infantry.
ZERO	Barrage on enemy front line, and 25% on No Man's Land 50 yards in front of it.	Assaulting Infantry advance
0 hour 1'	25% lifts to front line.	
0 hour 4'	Barrage lifts from front line, and moves back to DOTTED GREEN LINE at rate of 100 yards in 4 minutes; stays there 4 minutes, and then lifts 150 yards beyond it, where it dwells till 0 hour 23' yards	Assault front line.
0 hour 18'		Complete capture of DOTTED GREEN LINE.
0 hour 23'	Barrage moves back to GREEN LINE at rate of 100 yds in 4 minutes; stays there 4 minutes, and then lifts to 150 yds beyond it, where it dwells till 0 hour 50'.	Advance towards GREEN LINE.
0 hour 40'		Complete capture of GREEN LINE.
0 hour 50'	Barrage pauses for 5 minutes.	
0 hour 55'	Fire resumed 150 yds. beyond GREEN LINE.	
1 hour 05'	Barrage pauses for 5 minutes.	
1 hour 10'	Fire resumed 150 yards beyond GREEN LINE	Advance towards YELLOW LINE.
1 hour 12'	Lifts 100 yards and moves back at rate of 100 yards in 4 minutes YELLOW LINE; stays there 4 minutes, and then lifts 150 yards beyond it, where it dwells till 2 hours 00'.	
1 hour 50'		Complete capture of YELLOW LINE.

2.

Time.	Artillery (18-Pdrs)	Infantry.
2 hours 00' 2 hours 05' 2 hours 15' 2 hours 20'	Barrage pauses 5 minutes. Barrage re-opens 150 yards beyond YELLOW LINE Barrage pauses 5 minutes. Barrage re-opens 150 yards beyond YELLOW LINE	Advance towards DOTTED YELLOW LINE.
2 hours 22'	Barrage moves back at rate of 100 yards in 4 minutes to DOTTED YELLOW LINE; stays there 4 minutes, and then lifts 150 yards beyond it, where it dwells till 2 hours 39'.	
2 hours 34'		Complete capture of DOTTED YELLOW LINE.
2 hours 39'	Barrage moves back to DOTTED BROWN LINE at 100 yards in 4 minutes, stays there 4 minutes, and then lifts to 150 yards beyond it, where it dwells till 3 hours 00'.	
2 hours 55'		Complete capture of DOTTED BROWN LINE and advance close up to barrage.
3 hours 00'	Barrage moves back to BLUE LINE at rate of 100 yards in 4 minutes; stays there 4 minutes and then lifts to 150 yards beyond it, where it dwells till 3 hours 35'	
3 hours 25'		Complete capture of BLUE LINE.
3 hours 35' 3 hours 40' 3 hours 42'	Barrage pauses for 5 minutes Barrage re-opens 150 yards beyond BLUE LINE. Barrage moves back to BROWN LINE at 100 yds. in 4 minutes; stays there 4 minutes, and then lifts to 150 yards beyond it.	Advance towards BROWN LINE.
4 hours 20'		Complete capture of BROWN LINE.

SECRET.

Addenda and Corrigenda 2. to 190th Infantry Brigade Order. No.29.

Add new para:-
25. Appendix 11. Table of Barrages for the whole operation and Appendix 111. Compass Bearings.
Map E. Showing dotted lines and lines of demarcation between Battalions, are attached.

Add new para:-
26. A tunnel running forward from our trenches towards the enemy line will be opened up by a mine after ZERO on "Z" day, the exact time will be notified.
The mine will NOT be fired until the 190th Inf. Bde. have passed over NO MAN'S LAND.
The spot where the Crater will be formed will be marked, prior to the explosion, by a Red Flag; and two Green Flags about 50 yards apart will be placed on our present front line parapet.
Troops coming up in rear of the Brigade must NOT pass between these Green Flags and must keep 50 yards clear of the Red Flag until after the mine has been fired.

Para 7. Add; The map references of Headquarters in the assembly area will be:-

        Bde. Hd.qrs.......Q.28.c.9.9.
        7/Royal Fusiliers.Q.23.a.78.28.
        4/Bedfordshire Rgt. Q.23.a.40.85.
        10/R.Dublin.Fus.   Q. ?
        1/H.A.C.,,,,,,,,. Q.23.b.35.25.
        190th Bde.M.G.Coy... Q.23.a.9.2.

Para.8. Ref. last 3 lines. This Company will, moving by the MESNIL-HAMEL Road form up in four waves on the RIGHT of the Hood Bn. by 9.c.pm on Y/Z night.
The Hood Bn. will be formed up in the new trenches which have been dug in Q.18.c.
The Company 1/H.A.C. will advance up the Railway and road, clearing the dugouts in the Railway Embankments, and protecting the RIGHT Flank of the 189th Inf. Bde., searching the ground where the Marsh is passable.
On reaching the NORTHERN END of the trench which runs back from Q.18.c.5.2. to Q.24.a.8.9. a strong bombing party with a support and 1 Lewis Gun will clear this trench which will be barraged by the artillery and Stokes Mortars before the bombing party enter it. On completion of this duty the party will follow and rejoin their Company on the"dotted" GREEN LINE.
On arrival at the "Dotted" GREEN Line the Company will wait for and rejoin their Bn, becoming a Reserve in the hands of the Bn. Commander.
5 Lewis Guns of the 14/Worcester Regt(Pioneers) will be attached to this Company by the 189th Inf. Bde. until their arrival at the "Dotted" GREEN Line, when they will rejoin the Attacking Infantry of the 189th Inf. Bde.
The orders given by the 189th Inf Bde. to the Stokes Mortar Battery are as follows:-
"The Light T.M.battery will bombard the trench running back from Q.18.c.5.2. to Q.24.a.8.9. from ZERO to ZERO + 5 when it will be entered by a bombing party of the H.A.C.
It will assist this party in their attack on the trench as far as visibility permits.
        At ZERO +10, 4 guns will advance and assist the H.A.C. in capturing the dugouts on the Railway Embankment and the Infantry in bombing along MARSHAL Trench, if not already captured........"

5A The Units detailed to proceed via JACOB'S LADDER will move, instead by the MESNIL-HAMEL Road,the Road passing MESNIL CHURCH at the times allotted for entering JACOB'S LADDER.

2.

Should the road be heavily shelled these troops will proceed via JACOB'S LADDER.

Para.9. Line 4. Erase "and 2 sections of Pioneers".
Add:- The ⅔ Coy. 14/Worcestershire Regt. (Pioneers) will, on Y/Z night form up in HAMEL VILLAGE with Headquarters at the road junction Q.23.d.5.9.
They will move into position passing MESNIL Church, immediately, in rear of the 190th T.M.Battery at 10.15.pm.
They will be divided into two parties, each under an Officer. After the Capture of the BROWN Line they will, on receipt of instructions from Bde.Hd.Qrs., move forward and open up the two communication trenches leading from the Blue to the BROWN Line; one party working on each trench.
These trenches run forward from :-
(a) R.2.a.10.25. to R.2.b.10.65. and
(b) R.8.a.20.00. to R.8.40.60. and thence by road to PUISIEUX TRENCH.
These trenches must be opened up as rapidly as possible.

Para.11.Sub para (a) Cancel the first 3 lines of addenda of 23rd October, and substitute:-
The Headquarters and 2 Sections in Reserve will move forward at the discretion of the O.C. 190th Bde. M.G.Coy., taking advantage of all cover, with a view to getting into action as soon as possible after the Capture of the BROWN Line.

Para.14. The TELEPHONE POST will be at Q 17 d (central) Mine shaft immediately SE of junction of ROBERTS & LOUVERCY Trenches.

Para.16. Bde. Hd. Qrs will be established at MESNIL at 5.0.pm on "Y" day. The point to which Bde.Hd.Qrs. will move will be about R.7.a.0.3.

Para.17. Line.12. The proportion picks to shovels will be one in ten.

Para.24. Notes:- Add:-
c. Special mopping up parties, detailed from the 3rd wave, must be told off to deal with all trenches passed over by the Brigade.
d. It must be impressed on all ranks that it is of the utmost importance to the success of the operation that no movement takes place in the assembly area during dawn on "Z" day prior to ZERO hour.
During the night of Y/Z there should be as little noise as possible, no loud talking.
Matches must be carefully screened and every precaution taken to conceal the fact of our assembly for attack.

e. A proportion of the Reserve personnel for Machine and Lewis Guns should be left behind and not taken into action.
f. Officers and N.C.Os. must move IN the ranks of their platoons.
g. Bns. must have a carrying party specially detailed to carry S.O.S. Rockets and Very's Lights in addition to the one (of the latter) carried on each man.
h. No map, papers etc showing the position of Hd.Qrs. Dumps or other important points are to be taken into action.

Major.
Brigade Major.

Time issued to Signals.............

Copies to:-
1. 7th Royal Fusiliers
2. 4/Bedfordshire Regt.
3. 10/R.Dub.in Fus.
4. 1/H.A.C.
5. 190th M.G.Coy.
6. 190th T.M.Battery
7. Staff Capt.
8. Bde Transport Officer.
9. Bde.Intelligence Officer.
10. Bde.Bombing Officer.
11. No.3.Field Coy.R.E.
12. 14/Worcestershire Regt.
13. Signal Section
14. No.4.Coy Div Train
15. 63rd Division.
16. 188th Inf. Bde.
17. 189th Inf.Bde.
18. File
19. War Diary (3)
22. Artillery Laison Officer.
23. Laison Officer 1.
24. Laison Officer 11.
25. A.D.M.S.

APPENDIX. 11.
****

Preliminary Bombardment:-

The attack will be proceeded by an intense bombardment on X and Y days, beginning at 5.0.am and becoming intense at 6.0.am.

On "Z" day the fire of the Heavy Artillery batteries will commence as usual at 5.0.am. At ZERO the whole of the 18 pounder batteries will open fire simultaneously on the enemy front line and 50 yards in front of it and the assaulting infantry of the 188th and 189th Inf. Bdes. will at once advance.

At ZERO + 1 the 18 pdrs firing 50 yards in front of the enemy front line will lift back to the front line.

At ZERO + 4 the whole of the 18 pdrs will lift off the enemy front line and the infantry will assault.

It will be noticed that, during the halts on the GREEN and YELLOW Lines there will be two (2) pauses each of 5 minutes.

The reopening of intense barrage after the SECOND of these pauses will be the signal for the infantry to advance.

Great care must be taken on both the GREEN and YELLOW LINES that the infantry advance is NOT resumed at the end of the FIRST pause, or our men would be caught by the fire of their own barrage

----

Secret

HEADQUARTERS,
190th
INFANTRY BRIGADE
2521
25/10/16

Headquarters,
190th Infantry Brigade.
25/10/16.

SUPPLY OF HOT FOOD.

1. The G.O.C. wishes arrangements made for all men to have hot tea about 11.0.pm and hot soup and rum about 4.0.am on the morning on which operations commence.
    Field Cookers will be brought up to the following places after tea on "Y" day which are as close as possible to the Position of Assembly :-

    7/Royal Fusiliers)
    1/H.A.C.   ) HESNIL XXXXXX. Q.28.d.7.7.

    4/Bedfordshire Regt.)
    10/R.Dublin Fus.   ) Q.22.a.9.9. near KNIGHTSBRIDGE DUMP.

    190th M.G.Coy will be provided as follows:-

    Details M.G.Coy. in PRINCESS STREET by 1/H.A.C.
    "   M.G.Coy. at POTTAGE STREET by 7/Royal Fusiliers.
    "   M.G.Coy. at CARNALEA   by 10/R.Dublin Fus.

    190th T.M.Battery will be provided for by 4/Bedfordshire Regt.

    O.Cs. 190th M.G.Coy and 190th T.M.Battery will confer with O.C.Battalions as to provision of tea and rum for O.Rs. of their units.
    Attached details of Pioneer Bn and R.N.Div.Eng. are to be provided for by units to whom attached.
    Carrying parties will be arranged by O.C.Bns. Transport and Cooks are to be utilized for this. 190th M.G.Coy and 190th T.M. Battery will arrange for their own carrying party from cookers
    An officer should be sent to reconnoitre these places so as to get to them without confusion after dark.
    Field Cookers will return at once to their transport lines as soon as dixies belonging to them have been returned. Water carts may be taken with Cookers.

    1000 Oxo Cubes,
    12 tins Pea Flour.
    20 lbs Meat Extract.
    14 lbs Lentil Soup

has been obtained from various sources and will be divided equally amongst Bns. It must be understood that the proportion due to 190th M.G.Coy. and T.M.Battery.,R.N.D.Eng. and attached Pioneers are included in the above.

E.J.B.Tagg. Captain.
Staff Captain

1. 7th Royal Fusiliers.
2. 4th Bedfordshire Regt.
3. 10/R.Dublin Fus.
4. 1/H.A.C.
5. 190th M.G.Coy.
6. 190th T.M.Battery
7. 14/Worcesters
8. 3rd Field Coy. R.N.D.E.
9. 33rd Division.
10. Bde Transport Officer.
11. File.
12. War Diary.

SECRET.   APPENDIX. III.

              TRUE BEARINGS AND MAP REFERENCES OF NORTH OF
                        DIVISIONAL BOUNDARY.
                   =*=*=*=*=*=*=*=*=*=*=*=

         (For magnetic bearings add 12-1/3° to the values given)

From end of SHAFTESBURY AVE (Q.17.a35.30) to ENEMY'S
                              FRONT LINE (Q.17a75.85)   32°

(From end of SHAFTESBURY AVE to Q.6.c.75.35   37°

  " ENEMY'S FRONT LINE (Q.17a75.85) to Q6c75.35
                          (crossing Green Line on route)   38°

  " Q.6c75.35 to Q.6d15.35 (crossing Yellow Line
                                        on route)   90°

  " Q.6d15.35 to R.1a 90.20 (crossing dotted yellow
                      and dotted brown lines on route)   64½°

  " R.1a 90.20 tp R.1b 65.35   82½°

  " R.1b 65.35 to R.2a 15.85 (crossing blue line
                                        on route)   44°

  " R.2a 15.85 to R.2b 15.99 (Brown Line)   82°

APPENDIX 28

17

SECRET. Copy No.........

190th Infantry Brigade Order No.30.
by
Brigadier General The Hon. C.J.Sackville West.C.M.G.Commanding the 190th
Infantry Brigade.

Headquarters,
190th Infantry Bde.
28/10/16.

Ref.Map 57D 1/40,000.
Trench Map HAMEL 1/10,000.

1. **Relief.** The 190th Infantry Brigade will be held in readiness to relieve the 188th and 189th Infantry Brigades in the HAMEL Section at short notice, according to the attached table.
Date will be notified as soon as known.

2. **Subsections.** RIGHT Subsection:-
The river ANCRE exclusive to LOUVERCY STREET inclusive.
LEFT Subsection:-
LOUVERCY STREET exclusive to SHAFTESBURY AVENUE inclusive.

3. **Disposition.** The 7/Royal Fusiliers and 1/H.A.C. will hold the RIGHT Subsection.
The 4/Bedfordshire Regt. and 10/R.Dublin Fusiliers the LEFT Subsection.

4. **Brigade Headquarters.** Brigade Hd.Qrs. will be at ENGLEBELMER Q.19.c. (Central).

5. **Route.** Units will march via HEDAUVILLE and ENGLEBELMER.
The 7/Royal Fusiliers and 1/H.A.C. will be clear of HEDAUVILLE by 8.0.am and 9.0.am respectively.
That portion of the M.G.Coy. marching to ENGLEBELMER, and the 4/Bedfordshire Regt. will not pass the Cross Roads P.34.c.1.9. until 8.0.am and 9.0.am respectively.
The 190th T.M.Battery will move immediately in rear of the 4/Bedfordshire Regt.,times of starting being arranged between C.Os.

6. The upkeep of the new assembly trenches of the 188th and 189th Inf. Bdes., for forthcoming operations, is to be taken in hand by the Bns. in the line; it is of the greatest importance that these trenches should be kept in good condition.
The various ration, water and store dumps which have been placed in the line for the same purpose will be taken over by Bns. in the line and a sentry posted on each.
On no account are these stores to be depleted.

Time issued to Signals....4.20 p.
Major.
Brigade Major.

1.7/Royal Fusiliers.
2.4/Bedfordshire Regt.
3.10/R.Dublin Fusiliers.
4.1/H.A.C.
5.190th Bde. M.G.Coy.
6.190th T.M.Battery.
7.63rd Division.
8.188th Inf. Bde.
9.189th Inf. Bde.   13.Bde Transport Officer.
10.Staff Capt.   14.No.4.Coy Div Train.
11.Bde.Intelligence Off.15.File.
12.Bde.Bombing Officer. 16.War Diary. (3)

MARCH TABLE.

Unit relieving.	Unit relieved	subsection	Place	GUIDES	Time.	Remarks.
GUNS 4/190th Bde.M.G.Coy.	GUNS 4/189th Bde.M.G.Coy.	RIGHT	Cross Rds Q.28.c.5.9.		9am	
6 Guns " "	6/188th Bde.M.G.Coy.	LEFT.	(Town Major's (Office (ENGLEBELMER.		9am	Remaining guns in reserve.
190th L.T.M.Battery	188th and 189th L.T.M.Batteries.	Whole Soctor	MESNIL CHURCH and Town Major's Office ENGLEBELMER.		10.30am 9.0.am	Guns will be taken ever in the line; half from 188th Inf.Bde. and half from 189th Inf.Bde.
7/Royal Fusiliers.	Drake Bn.	RIGHT.	MESNIL Church.		10.0.am	
1/H.A.C.	Hood Bn.		Billets in MESNIL.		11.0.am	Billeting party to arrive at MESNIL by 9.0am
4/Bedfordshire Regt.	1/Royal Marines	LEFT.	Town Major's Office. ENGLEBELMER.		10.0.am	
10/R.Dublin Fusiliers.	Anson Bn.		Shelters in ENGLEBELMER.		11.0.am	Billeting party to arrive at ENGLEBELMER by 9.0.am

Note:- All movement EAST of ENGLEBELMER to be by platoons at 200 yds. distance.

SECRET.   Copy No. 20

Addenda to 190th Inf.Bde.Order No.30.

1. The Relief will take place on the 30th inst.

2. Lewis guns will move at the head of Bns. so as to relieve first.

3. No.1. Field Coy. R.M.D.E. will be attached to the 190th Inf. Brigade commencing noon 30th inst. Map Ref. of this Coy. is Q.32.c.(Central).

4. Work will be concentrated on the construction, improvement, and maintenance of the trench system, including the new assembly trenches dug by the 188th & 189th Inf.Bdes.
The Bns. in the line will be responsible for GORDON and ROBERTS Trenches, their Extensions and Communication trenches back to VICTORIA ST.- SLOAN ST. and WATEAU ROAD exclusive.
The last 3 named trenches will be improved and made good under Brigade arrangements by parties detailed from the Support Bns.
The O.C.No.1.Field Coy. will survey these trenches and superintend the work, rendering the result of his survey and suggestions for work to Brigade Hd.Qrs. as early as possible.
All work behind the above line is being undertaken under Divisional arrangements.

5. Orders as to Transport, Stores etc., will be issued by the Staff Capt.

6. Guides of all units will meet Billeting parties of incoming units of the 189th Inf. Bde. at 9.0.am at their own unit Hd.Qrs. to point out the billets.
On completion of this duty the guides will rejoin their units.

7. The permanent working party attached to the R.E.Dump at VARENNES will be withdrawn under Bn. arrangement on the 31st inst.
The road working parties reporting to Town Majors will be found by this Brigade until noon tomorrow.
They will rejoin their units during the afternoon under Bn. arrangements.

8. Owing to the 4/Bedfordshire Regt. being considerably stronger than the Bn. it is relieving; one Coy. of this Regt. will be accommodated in the shelters of the 10/Royal Dublin Fusiliers.
Additional shelters can be obtained if required, by applying to Bde.Hd.Qrs.

9. The Lewis Gunners of the 14/Worcestershire Regt. attached to 1/H.A.C. will rejoin their own unit after Breakfast tomorrow.

10. Units will report to Bde. Hd.Qrs. as early as possible the exact disposal of their men, and guns.
    In the case of detached posts or strong points giving the exact numbers of the Garrison.

11. pBrigade Hd.Qrs. will close at VARENNES at noon and open at ENGLEBELMER at 2.pm. 30th inst.

Issued to Signals......... 9.45 pm.

Major.

Brigade Major.

1. 7/Royal Fusiliers.
2. 4/Bedfordshire Regt.
3. 10/R.Dublin Fusiliers.
4. 1/H.A.C.
5. 190th M.G.Coy.
6. 190th T.M.Battery.
7. 63rd Division.
8. 188th Inf. Bde.
9. 189th Inf. Bde.
10. 14/Worcestershire Regt.
11. 1st Field Coy. R.N.D.E.
12. Staff Capt.
13. Bde. Signalling Officer.
14. Bde. Intelligence Officer.
15. Bde. Bombing Officer.
16. Bde. Transport Officer.
17. No.4.Coy. Divl Train.
18. File.
19. War Diary (3)

Information for Battalions relieving HAMEL SECTOR.
LEFT BATTALION.
=*=*=*=*=*=*=

> HEADQUARTERS,
> 190th
> INFANTRY BRIGADE
> No. 2686
> Date 29-10-11

1. RATIONS are taken nightly to KNIGHTSBRIDGE DUMP Q.16.c.9.1. via ENGLEBELMER by well defined track through Q.20.b. & Q.15.c.

2. WATER. Sole supply by watercarts which are left at KNIGHTSBRIDGE DUMP. These can be refilled by day from standpipes at CEMETERY MESNIL & at MARTINSART. Watercarts & vehicles going to KNIGHTSBRIDGE DUMP must approach it by MESNIL along road running through Q.28.a., Q.22.c, Q.22.a.

Soup Kitchen has been established at KNIGHTSBRIDGE TRENCH. Staff is being left by 188th Inf. Bde.. Any help required is to be supplied by left Bn.

KITCHENS for Battalions in the line have been established in KNIGHTSBRIDGE TRENCH Q.16.d. Oil Drums for ovens will be turned over and a site found for them after relief.

Engineer Stores can be got on indent from KNIGHTSBRIDGE DUMP.

Ammunition Bombs etc Bde. Bomb & Ammunition Dump is situated at FORT JACKSON Q.16.d.4.1.

Guards etc. FORT MOULIN Q.21.b.3.3., 1.N.C.O. and 3.O.R. as Guards on Ammunition, Rations etc.

RIGHT BATTALION
=*=*=*=*=*=*=

1. RATIONS are taken by limbered wagon to Battalion Ration Dump HAMEL (Q.23.d.5.5. near Engineer Dump) via ENGLEBELMER and MESNIL.

2. WATER is got from a good well in HAMEL. Medical Officer to see this well is properly chlorinated.
Well Guard should have strict orders to prevent fouling as it is the only supply. If this is not sufficient, water carts can be taken up by night.

3. SOUP KITCHEN. 2 Soyers stoves are established in HAMEL for making soup etc for troops in the line. This Kitchen is maintained by the Right Bn. Staff 1.N.C.O. and 3 cooks.
HAMEL will be reconnoitred with a view of installing 2 Field Cookers for the Bn. in the front line.
A certain number of oil drums are being turned over to make ovens but a suitable place has yet to be found.

Engineer Stores can be got on indent from a large Engineer Dump in HAMEL Q.23.d.5.4.

Ammunitions Bombs etc. can be got on indent from Brigade Bomb Dump at Q.23.d.5½.5½.

General Notes.

Left Support Bn. in shelters at ENGLEBELMER Q.26.a.6.7.

Rations. Normal conditions.
Water. From ENGLEBELMER.
Field Kitchens etc. Normal conditions.

1. Transport, Q.M. Stores will remain in their present positions.

2. Surplus Officers will be left behind in present billets

2.

<u>Right Support Bn. in MESNIL.</u>
    Billets are siuated in cellars and houses of MESNIL and in dugouts along the Railway at Q.28.a.
    3 Coys. in MESNIL and 1 Coy. in dugouts.

<u>Field Kitchens</u> can be brought up into MESNIL.

<u>Water</u> from standpipes by MESNIL CEMETERY   Q.34.a.2.8. and in MARTINSART.

                                      E.J.B.Tagg Captain
                                          Staff Captain.

SECRET   Copy No ___

190th Inf. Bde Order No. 20.

by

Brig: General J. M. Trotman C.B.

Ref. Map LENS.   H.Q. 190th Inf. Bde
    1/100.000   3/10/16.

1. The march of the troops moving by road will
   be continued as follows:—
   The localities in which Units will be billeted is
   not yet known.

2. Transport of 190th Inf. Bde will move from
   LA COUTURE to (not known) via REBREUVIETTE –
   Starting Point – BEAUDRICOURT – LACHEUX –
   MONDICOURT – PAS.

3. Starting point cross roads immediately WEST of
   ETREE – WAMIN STN midway between the first E
   of ETREE – WAMIN and the W of WAMIN

4. Time of passing starting point – 9-38 a.m.

5. Halts and rate of march as before.

Copy No 1. Bde Transport. Off (issued 9 am).
        2. 4/RF.
        3. 4/Bedford Regt.
        4. 10/KRF.
        5. 1/HAC.
        6. 190th M.G. Coy.
        7. Mort T.M. Batty.
        8. Signals.
        9. A/A Marriott.
       10. Staff Capt.
       11. 63rd Div.
       12. File
       13. War Diary (2).

                                    C H Jerram.
                                    Major.
                                    B de Major.

SECRET   Copy No. 18

190th Inf Bde Order No 21
by
Brig. General C. N. Fotnam C.B

H.Q. 190th Inf Bde.
3/10/16

Ref Map LENS
  1/100,000 and 36 B 1/40,000

1. In continuation of previous move orders. The entraining Stn is LIGNY-S-FLOCHEL (T.23.a.6.0 map. 36.B) attached schedule shews train loads time of leaving and probable time of arrival.

2. Troops entraining in Trains 'A' and 'B' must arrive at the station not less than 1½ hours before time of departure. Troops entraining in Train 'C' 3 hours before time of departure.

3. Forming up place will be the road N. of main road, from T.29.b.0.7 to T.29.b.7.9. Troops will fall in facing N. first named Unit on schedule on the RIGHT, last named LEFT.

4. An advanced party from each Unit entraining consisting of one officer and for each 100 men entraining one (1) other rank will report to Train Adjutant at the Station at 9 pm, 10.30 pm 3 Oct and 12.15 am 4th Oct for trains A, B, C respectively. These will act as markers and are in addition to a pilot already ordered.

5. Working parties. Para 8 of Bde Order No 18 of the 2nd inst is cancelled except the tots. The troops will arrive as in Para 2 of this order (Bde Order 21)
   Working parties for:
   Train A for blankets
     20 men M.Gy. Coy.
     20   Y.H. R.
     20   Y.R. 7.
   Train B for blankets
     20 men 4th Bedf Regt.
     20   6th R.D.7.
   Reporting to Train Adjt at 8 pm & 9.30 pm respectively. The 190th M.G. Coy. will provide a working party of 100 officers & men for Train C who will report to Train Adjutant at 12.15 am 4/10/16 for all

(2)

loading and unloading work

The same working parties will unload the train.

6. OC Trains and Train Adjutants will be as follows:-

    Train 'A' C.O. Lt. Col HESKETH 7/R.F.
                 Adj: Adjutant of 4/H.A.C.

    Train 'B' C.O. Lt Col SMITH 10/R.D.F
                 Adj: Adjutant of 4/Bed Regt

    Train 'C' C.O. Capt BASTIN. R.M.L.I.
                 Adj: An Officer of Bde M.G.Coy

7. The Officer representing Bde HQrs at the Station will be 2/Lt STOPFORD. 4/Bed Regt attached Bde H.Qrs. He will report to R.T.O at 7.30 pm. 3rd inst.

8. The numbers given in the Schedule are based on the latest information. Should units have more details than laid down in the Schedule they are to be entrained with them.

9. Troops should take all possible lanterns with them to the Station - especially for Train 'C'

10. Motor cyclists will proceed by road - destination time and route later.

11. The instructions contained in this order are to be carried out and in all cases where they conflict with previous orders - the previous order is to be considered cancelled.

12. Blanket lorries will be provided as follows:-
    1 per Bn.
    1 between Bde HQrs. M.G.Coy & T.M. Bty.
Baggage of surplus Officers - baggage and hos. Stores of T.M. Bty will be conveyed in these lorries to entraining Stn.
These lorries will be at Batt HQrs about 4 pm
Blankets of Bde H.Qrs, Sig Sect, M.G. Coy T.M.Bty 4/H.A.C. + 7/R.F will be loaded into Train 'A'
Those of 4/Bedfordshire Regt and 10/R.D.F into Train 'B'.
This cancels the order that blankets were to be carried on the person.

13. Destinations not yet known

[signature] Major.
Brigade Major.

Time issued to Signals 2.30 p.m.

1. 1/Royal Fus"
2. 10/Royal Dublin F"
3. 4/Bedfordshire Regt
4. 1/HAC
5. 190th M.G. Coy
6. 190th T.M.B
7. Signal Section
8. 2/Lieut Stopford 1/Bedf. Regt
9. Staff Captain
10. 14/Bn Worcester Regt
11. Lt Col Hesketh 7/R.F.
12. Lt Col Smith 1/R.F.
13. Capt BASTIN. R.A.L.I.
14. N.4 Coy Div Train
15. 63rd (RN) Division
16. File
17. War Diary (3)

P.S. Para 14 Troops will detrain at ACHEUX and will be met by a Div S.O. who will inform them of the areas in which they will be billeted and the routes thereto.
Horse standings in course of preparation in new areas are not to be used until completed — when application for their use will be made to Bde HQ.

Schedule

Series No 1. (Personnel, Lewis Guns & handcarts)

Train A
Hour of departure 10.30 pm 3/10/16
Probable Hour of arrival. 4.20 am 4/10/16

		Offrs	O.R.
Bde. Hd. Qrs		4	53
attached to Sig Sectn		—	10
" " M.G Coy		1	34
" " T.M. Batty		—	17
1/H.A.C		35	792
7/R.F.		34	892
14/Worcester Regt		6	100

Train B
Hour of departure 12.29 am 4/10/16
Probable Hour of arrival. 5.20 am 4/10/16

		Offrs	O.R.
4/Beds Regt		37	868
10/R.D.F.		33	774
14/Worcester Regt		12	250

Series 1. (Transport etc)

Train "C"
Hour of departure 4.14 am 4/10/16
Probable hour of arrival 9.20 am 4/10/16

	Off.	O.R.	Animals	Transport
Bde Hd Qrs	2	9	8	1 Limber G.S
Sig Sect	1	26	8	1 " "
M.G. Coy	9	130	41	8 " "
Wagons S.A.A. 1 per Bn	—	4	8	4 " "
MESS Carts 1 per Bn	—	4	4	4 Mess Carts
T.M. Batty	4	46	—	8 {Mortars handcarts}
Pack Mules 2 per Coy	—	32	32	—
Cookers 4 per Bn	—	16	32	16 Cookers

In addition the Lewis Guns and detachments of 14/Worcester Regt will entrain in Train "C" in the spare coaches.

SECRET.

Headquarters,
190th Infantry Bde.
24/10/16.

All Units.
14th Worcester Regt. } For units to be
3/ Field Coy. R.N.D.E. } attached to the 190th Inf. Bde.
File.
War Diary.

Memo:

It is notified for information that "Z" day is postponed until the 28th October.

Major.
Brigade Major.

HEADQUARTERS,
190th
INFANTRY BRIGADE.
No. 2527
Date. 24-10-16

SECRET.

Headquarters,
190th Inf. Bde.
29th Oct. 1916.

Ref: Bde. Orders No.29. "2nd day is now postponed till 30th October.

7/Royal Fusiliers
4/Bedfordshire Regt.
10/R.Dublin Fusiliers.
1/M.A.C.
190th M.G.Coy.
190th T.M.Battery
14/Worcester Regt. } for units attached
3rd Field Coy.(R.M.D.E.) } 190th Inf. Bde.
Signal Section.
Staff Capt.
Bde. Bombing Officer.
Bde. Transport Officer.
Bde. Intelligence Officer.
File
War Diary.

Major.

Brigade Major.

HEADQUARTERS,
190th
INFANTRY BRIGADE.
No. 2573
Date 29/10

Headquarters,
190th Infantry Brigade.
28/10/18.

SECRET.

TO ALL UNITS.

Operations postponed a further 48 hours.

E Ives agg
Major.
for Brigade Major.

HEADQUARTERS,
190th
INFANTRY BRIGADE.
No. 2629
Date 28.10.18

On His Majesty's Service.

D.D.S.T.
G.H.Q.
3rd Echelon

HQ 190 September
to 6
November 1916

S E C R E T.

Headquarters, 190th. Inf. Brigade,
30/11/1916 Date.

VOL. VI.

W A R   D I A R Y
of
190th. Infantry Brigade.

From 1st November 1916 (inclusive)
To 30th November 1916 (inclusive)

[signature]

Major.
Brigade Major,
190th. Infantry Brigade.

To:-
A.G. 3rd Echelon

WAR DIARY of 190th Infantry Brigade

INTELLIGENCE SUMMARY. Vol VI

Army Form C. 2118.

Place	Date	Hour	Summary of Events and Information	Remarks and references to Appendices
ENGLEBELMER	1916 Nov 1		Orders received that we were to be relieved by the 188th & 189th Infantry Brigades with a view to the big operation coming off on November 5th.	
"	" 2		Above orders cancelled. Rained heavily during the night and morning, clearing towards evening. Wind veered into the NORTH. Issued orders for internal reliefs.	Appendix 30
"	" 3		Carried out internal Reliefs. Heavy Rain. Operations indefinitely postponed. Large working parties nightly on improvement of trenches and drainage work. Defence Scheme for HAMEL SECTOR entirely built. Heavy rain at night.	Appendix 31
"	" 4			
"	" 5		Decided to carry out a minor operation against the position known as the Mound, and orders sent out. There is an enemy post in the swamps of the R. ANCRE near on the plank of the RIGHT of our front line.	Appendix 32
"	" 6		Informed that to-day is "W" day for the big operation and that the 189th Infantry Brigade was to relieve our RIGHT to-day and the 188th our LEFT to-morrow.	

WAR DIARY
of 1/190th Infantry Brigade
or
INTELLIGENCE SUMMARY.   VOL VI

Place	Date	Hour	Summary of Events and Information	Remarks and references to Appendices
ENGLEBELMER	19th contd		The minor operation was therefore postponed until the night 9th/8th. RIGHT Section relieved, and troops for the minor operation billeted in ENGLEBELMER.	APPENDIX 33
"	" 7th		Evening. Big Operations again postponed. Very heavy explosion to S.W. and fire lasting all night, apparently an ammunition dump on fire about 8 miles away. Very heavy rain during the night and all day. LEFT Section relieved by 188th Infantry Brigade. At 5 p.m. our attacking party left MESNIL for their rendez-vous. At 5:45 p.m. the 51st Division commenced a raid on our LEFT, of which we had not been informed. This news brought a very heavy retaliatory fire all along our line, resulting in the killing of Lieut. Scott Holding Officer of the 2nd Royal Fusiliers and 1 N.C.O., and the wounding of 7 others, all of the attacking party. The remainder go into position and advanced according to	

WAR DIARY or INTELLIGENCE SUMMARY.

Army Form C. 2118.

of 190th Infantry Brigade Vol VI

(Erase heading not required.)

Place	Date	Hour	Summary of Events and Information	Remarks and references to Appendices
ENGLEBELMER	Nov 7		Appendix 31 at 7pm. The rain was torrential and the country almost impassable. The HAMEL-BEAUCOURT road was found to be absolutely impassable and at last one man had to be dug out of it. The party therefore climbed the bank to the N of the road and proceeded along the higher ground having taken 2½ hours to cover about 200 yards. Every where due to the state of the country they were now 150 yards from the enemy trench which discusses was covered with the greatest difficulty in a further ¾ hour. On arrival at the point of entry to the enemy trench it was found that new wire had been placed right across it. This wire was cut, they 4 days ago when Capt. FORSTER reconnoitred the position and actually entered the trench. Proceeding for some distance a dark direction. Capt. FORSTER, Lt. SIMMONS and a Pte of the 11 H.A.C. got into the wood. The former actually getting through — the others however being	

Army Form C. 2118.

WAR DIARY of 190th Infantry Brigade

INTELLIGENCE SUMMARY. VOL VI.

(Erase heading not required.)

Place	Date	Hour	Summary of Events and Information	Remarks and references to Appendices
ENGLEBELMER	1916 Nov 7		badly hung up, he had to come back to release them, which was done with the greatest difficulty. In the meantime the enemy who had been thoroughly taken by surprise by the 51st Division raid opened a heavy fire with a machine gun on the mound and also trained the party, fortunately with no effect, the firing being too high. CAPT FORSTER seeing no chance of getting his men through the wire in the face of this opposition decided to withdraw the party, which was done. The Value of the reconnaissance was remarked on by both Corps and Divisional Commanders, as forming beyond doubt the terrible state of the Country — the fact that there is a M.G. on the "MOUND" and the fact that unless this position is either taken or destroyed it will not be possible to make any advance on our RIGHT flank. This party had about 400 yards to go and were completely	

Army Form C. 2118.

WAR DIARY for 190th Infantry Brigade
or
INTELLIGENCE SUMMARY. VOL VI

(Erase heading not required.)

Place	Date	Hour	Summary of Events and Information	Remarks and references to Appendices
ENGLEBELMER	1916 Nov 7		exhausted. It afterwards transpired that the 51st Division were unable to get even as far as the enemy wire, the state of the ground being so bad.	
PUCHEVILLERS	" 8		The Brigade less the 10/R Dublin Fusiliers were moved to PUCHEVILLERS.	
"	" 9		The whole Brigade assembled at PUCHEVILLERS. The big Operation is indefinitely postponed.	
"	10		Brigade inspected by Maj Gen Schutt, Commanding the 63rd Div. Orders received that the Brig Operation will take place on the 13th inst, on a new plan.	
VARENNES	11		New set of orders got out during night and issued. The Division will now only go so far as BEAUCOURT. Brigade moves to VARENNES and HEDAUVILLE with 1/4 O. & 2/O. at VARENNES. 5 p.m. Brigade Conference. Very thick misty weather.	APPENDIX 27 APPENDIX 35
MESNIL	12		Still misty. During the evening the Brigade moved into its assembly trenches in accordance with the attack orders, and	APPENDIX 37

Army Form C. 2118.

of 190th Inf. Bde.
VOL VI

WAR DIARY
or
INTELLIGENCE SUMMARY.
(Erase heading not required.)

Instructions regarding War Diaries and Intelligence Summaries are contained in F.S. Regs., Part II. and the Staff Manual respectively. Title pages will be prepared in manuscript.

Place	Date	Hour	Summary of Events and Information	Remarks and references to Appendices
MESNIL	1916 Nov.12		Brigade H.Q.rs moved to MESNIL from now to the 15th November the Diary should be read in conjunction with APPENDICES and name of the ANCRE :-	APPENDIX 36 & 37
	13 to 14		The battle opened at 6AM in pitch darkness and a thick fog which continued most of the day. Lightening forbids the entering. An account will be found in APPENDIX 36. There are many incidents which might be recorded, one, the action of the Rev Father THORNTON, who with a party of the Dublin Fusiliers and one or two others of mixed units about 30 or 40 induced a whole German battalion with its lot. 40 strong, to surrender. The whole party was completely covered by a Lbs happened before the enemy were completely covered by the suddenness of our attack and took refuge in their dugouts. Owing to the fog the leading brigades did not sufficiently deal with these and the 190th Infantry Brigade	

WAR DIARY

Army Form C. 2118.

of 190th Infantry Brigade VOL VI

INTELLIGENCE SUMMARY.

(Erase heading not required.)

Place	Date	Hour	Summary of Events and Information	Remarks and references to Appendices
MESNIL	1916 Nov 13th/14th		coming up met the full blast of all the enemy machine guns which in the meantime had been brought into ground. Our Artillery was now excellently and its simultaneous opening of nearly 1000 guns when all hope had been given must have had a most terrifying effect upon the enemy. The ground was absolutely ploughed up and of the communication trenches there was not a sign to be seen, hardly a depression even. The Brigade was withdrawn into Shelters Tents near ENGLEBELMER.	
ENGLEBELMER	15			
	16		There were very hard during the night. Bitterly cold with hardly any covering. The Battle continuing with new troops, but they do not appear to get forward with such speed as in the initial advance.	
	17		The 190th Inf Bde engaged in clearing the battle field. Some hundreds of our dead and new burial and many prisoners brought	

WAR DIARY
INTELLIGENCE SUMMARY.

Army Form C. 2118.

of 190th Infantry Brigade Vol VI

(Erase heading not required.)

Instructions regarding War Diaries and Intelligence Summaries are contained in F. S. Regs., Part II. and the Staff Manual respectively. Title pages will be prepared in manuscript.

Place	Date	Hour	Summary of Events and Information	Remarks and references to Appendices
ENGLEBELMER	1916 Nov 17		in found hiding in dugouts. (K. of all the Division has captured over 2,000 prisoners). Today tons of war material were collected including many machine guns and 5 batteries of heavy trench mortars, besides numerous small ones. Snow and heavy frost in night turning later into rain.	
	18		The Brigade moves to Beauval some 12 miles from where we are to march to RUE near the mouth of the SOMME to rest and reorganise.	APPENDIX 39
	19		Continued our march towards the coast under more favourable conditions.	
	20		The Divisional Commander inspected the Brigade and congratulated them on their fine work. The Brigadier subsequently spoke to them also. Everyone due sees is full of praise for the work of the Division.	

WAR DIARY
or
INTELLIGENCE SUMMARY.

190th Infantry Brigade. Army Form C. 2118.
Vol VII

(Erase heading not required.)

Place	Date	Hour	Summary of Events and Information	Remarks and references to Appendices
OCCOCHES	1916 Nov 21 22 + 23 24		Received march to RUE training area in fine weather. Moved into area except 10/ Royal Dublin Fusiliers for whom there is no room. They will probably have to go under canvas. Dull and slight rain.	APPENDIX 41 42, 7 43 APPENDIX 44
NOUVION				
2	25th Nov. 26th Nov.		10/R.D.Fus. Bn. moved into Camp at NOUVION. Heavy rain. (Sunday.) Brigade rested. Heavy rain - 10/R.D.F moved to NOYELLES - SUR MER.	
	27th Nov 28th Nov 29 Nov 30 Nov		Training commenced. Brigade Route head Steering. Thick fog. Lack of Platoon + Section training +389. huts of training. Condition of the huts Appendix 45.	Appendix 45.

A. Hunter Bolckow
Lieut Col
135th My Bn.
8th November 1916.

63rd Div. No. G.130/22/.

V Corps.

      Forwarded with reference to V Corps No.G.X.8238/2 of 9th instant.

12-11-16.
                                Major General,
                    Comdg. 63rd (R^N) Division.

63rd Div.
G.945/22/3.

V Corps,
———

1. The attached report is forwarded as it is thought that the information obtained may be of some value.

2. I entirely concur with the opinion of G.O.C. 190th Infantry Brigade regarding the wisdom of abandoning the raid when it was found that the enemy's wire was a serious obstacle.

(sd) C.F.ASPINALL,
Lt.Col.,
for Major General,
Comdg. 63rd Div.

8/11/16.

V Corps,
GX.8238.
9/11/16.

Fifth Army,
———

Forwarded. From a previous reconnaissance it appeared possible to cut off the German trench to the east of the Mound with the machine gun which was suspected at G. Had it not been for the heavy rain it should have succeeded, but the enemy probably had suspicions as he had put up fresh wire within the last 2 days.

The report is useful in showing the state of the road; of which a further reconnaissance will be made in accordance with verbal instructions of Army Commander.

(sd) E.A.FANSHAWE,
Lieut. Genl,
Comdg. V Corps.

63rd Div.No.G.945/22/3.

V Corps.

1. The attached report is forwarded as it is thought that the information obtained may be of some value.

2. I entirely concur with the opinion of G.O.C. 190th Infantry Brigade regarding the wisdom of abandoning the raid when it was found that the enemy's wire was a serious obstacle.

8-11-16.

C.D.Shute.
for Major General
Commanding 63rd (RN) Division.

C.E. - For information reference state of Hamel - Beaucourt road. A reconnaissance of this road by an Officer, R.E. 63 Div. has been ordered to be carried out. Please return.
9/11/16

S.D.1593/1918.

1. This letter to be forwarded to some suitable very ? C.I.G.S.

2. I submit it should be sent to the Secretary of the War Office, who may forward it to whichever other department(s) of the War Office that it may concern.

3. I suggest that a copy should also be sent to the Foreign Office.

G. Rideout
Major General
Commanding 65th Army Brigade
Commanders.

REPORT ON PATROL
of 190th Infantry Brigade night of 7/8th Nov.

Ref. Map attached.

Vide 190th Infantry Brigade Order No.32. the patrol left point A at 7.0.pm as ordered. Unfortunately during the march from MESNIL to Point A, when passing along DEVIAL AVE., a chance shell fired by the enemy killed 2nd Lieut. Scott and Lance Corporal McCarthy, both of 7/Royal Fusiliers and wounded 5.0.Rs. 7/Royal Fusiliers and 3 O.Rs. 1/H.A.C.

On leaving point A the patrol moved to B. The mud was found to be so deep on the road from A to B that movement became impossible. Capt.FORSTER therefore lead the patrol to the high ground at C, and followed the high ground to point D. The going was so heavy that it took over two hours to go from A to D. At D. the wire was found very strong. (No wire was up at D. during previous reconnaisances Capt. FORSTER and 2nd Lieut. SPOONER. 7/Royal Fusiliers, together with a man of 1/H.A.C., endeavoured to get through the wire. They were hung up and were bombed and fired at by 3 Germans, luckily without effect. At the same time a machine gun at G opened fire and swept the line from C to D. but all the shots went high and no casualties resulted.

Rockets etc were sent up by the Germans from E and F. Capt FORSTER, seeing the impossibility of getting through the wire without risk of grave losses, decided to withdraw the patrol, which returned along the same route as it had advanced. The working party were all this time waiting under cover in the trench running N.W. from H, and as the patrol returned the Officer in charge of the working party was ordered to withdraw his men. The patrol and working party returned to billets without further adventure.

While the patrol did not succeed in carrying out its role there can be no doubt that valuable information was gained as under:-

  (1) The road is impassable for transport of any kind.

  (2) There is a machine gun at G.

  (3) The line F.D.E. is heavily wired

  (4) That it is imperative to occupy the MOUND before any troops could move along the road in daylight

2.

I am satisfied that all ranks behaved excellently, and I consider that Capt FORSTER 7/Royal Fusiliers commanded the operation well and shewed great common sense and judgement in deciding to withdraw his men when he did.

An officer with less ballast might easily have decided to push the affair through having got as far as he did, and might in consequence have had heavy casualties.

There is some rumour of the 2 of the enemy's scouts being seen on the Eastern side of the railway about point "J" but I can find no real confirmation of this.

Brigadier General.
Coammanding 190th Infantry Brigade.

8/11/16.

SECRET.   Copy No........

War Diary   Appendix 30
17

190th Infantry Brigade Order No.32.
by
Brigadier General.W.G.Heneker.D.S.O.,A.D.C.Commanding 190th Infantry
Brigade.

Headquarters,
190th Infantry Bde.
2nd Nov. 1916.

Ref. Map HAMEL 1/10,000
Sheet 57 D.1/40,000

1. Internal reliefs will be carried out tomorrow (3rd inst) in accordance with attached table.
2. C.Os, Coy. Commanders, Lewis Gun, Bn. Bombing and Scout Officers of ingoing units will visit the line this afternoon and make careful notes of all work etc.which is being carried out in their areas.
3. Billeting parties of outgoing units are to be sent to take over billets by 9.am.
4. The 7/Royal Fusiliers will become the Support Bn. to the RIGHT Section.
   The 4/Bedfordshire Regt. the support Bn. to the LEFT Section.
5. The 190th M.G.Coy. will relieve guns as convenient on the 4th inst.
6. Orders as regards work and salvage are to be most carefully complied with.
   Night fatigue parties will be required from units going out of the trenches; up to 200 in addition to salvage parties.

Time issued to Signals...... 2.45 pm

Major.
Brigade Major

1. 7/Royal Fusiliers.
2. 4/Bedfordshire Regt.
3. 10/R.Dublin Fusiliers.
4. 1/H.A.C.
5. 190th M.G.Coy.
6. 190th T.M.Battery.
7. 1st Field Coy. R.N.D.E.
8. "A" Coy. 14/Worcestershire Regt.
9. "A" Group 63rd Divn. Art.
10. Act. Staff. Capt.
11. Bde. Signal Officer.
12. Bde. Intelligence Officer.
13. Bde. Bombing Officer.
14. Bde. Transport Officer.
15. 63rd Division.
16. Bilo
17. War Diary (3)

MARCH TABLE.

Unit relieving.	Unit relieved.	Subsection.	GUIDES Time	GUIDES Place.	Up Trench.	Down Trench.	Remarks
10/Royal Dublin Fus.	4/Bedfordshire Regt.	LEFT.	8.30am	H.Q.10/RDF ENGLEBELMER	GABION AVENUE	CHARLES AVENUE.	Lewis Guns will precede the Bn. All movement by platoons at 200x distance.
1/Honourable Artillery Company.	7/Royal Fusiliers.	RIGHT.	12.30pm	H.Q.1/H.A.C. MESNIL.	JACOBS LADDER.	CHARLES AVENUE.	ditto.

SECRET.

APPENDIX 31

Defence Scheme for
HAMEL SECTOR
Whilst held by the 190th INF.Bde.
Ref. Map.HAMEL 1/10,000
57D 1/40,000

HEADQUARTERS,
190th
INFANTRY BRIGADE.
No. 2808
Date.............

A DESCRIPTION

1. **BOUNDARIES.**
    on the NORTH :- Q.17.a.45. - SHAFTESBURY AVENUE
        (Q.17.a.35.58..to Q.17.a.00.13) exclusive -
        CONSTITUTION HILL - KNIGHTSBRIDGE - GABION AVENUE
        inclusive.
    on the SOUTH :- The River ANCRE.

2. **SUB-DIVISIONS.**
    RIGHT Section :- Held by No.1. Bn.
    LEFT Section :-   "   " No.2. Bn.
       Dividing line LOUVERCY ST - ROYAL AVENUE inclusive to RIGHT.
    No.3.Bn. is billeted in MESNIL.
     " 4. "   "   "   "   ENGLEBE.MER.

3. **DEFENSIVE SYSTEM :-**
    Consists of
        (a) The Front System of Trenches.
        (b) The WATEAU- SLOAN - VICTORIA ST. LINE.
        (c) PROSPECT ROW and QUEENS ROAD.
        (d) RIDGE TRENCH.
    (a) The Front System:- Consists of a Front Line trench (GORDON TRENCH)
        and an immediate support line (ROBERTS TRENCH). Both these
        running S.E.and some 600 yds from the RIVER ANCRE.
        The RIGHT of the position is held by a series of Posts in the
        swamp on either side of the Railway which runs along the RIGHT
        bank of the river.
    (b) Consists of two badly damaged lines; which form the immediate
        Reserve Line.
    (c) The PROSPECT - QUEENS ROAD line is in a very unfinished state,
        especially the NORTHERN position which is only about 1 to 2 feet
        deep; well sited it would be most useful if fit for occupation.
    (d) The RIDGE TRENCH is also a very neglected trench.
        The Brigade holding the line is not responsible for the upkeep
        of either (C) or (D).

4. **COMMUNICATIONS :-**
    There are three main communication trenches.
        (a) JACOBS LADDER.
        (b) CHARLES AVENUE.
        (c) GABION AVENUE.

B. DISPOSITIONS.

5. **DEFENCE OF FRONT LINE :-**
    The line of Resistance and the line of observation is the front
    line.
    The actual front trench, however, will be lightly held by
    infantry with a large proportion of Lewis Guns ; the main strength
    of the Garrison being in the support line in dugouts so far as
    available.
    Sentries will be posted so as to ensure that the whole front
    is observed.
    Troops in the front and support line are self supporting, and,
    in the event of an enemy lodgement in our trenches, will at once
    counter attack over the open and down communication trenches;
    troops on the flanks attacking inwards.

6. **FRONT LINE BNS.**
    No.1.Bn. with H.Q. at HAMEL holds the RIGHT Section as follows:-
        1 Coy. in GORDON and ROBERTS Trenches.
        1 Coy. in WATEAU-SLOAN ST line.
        1 Coy. holding the river side Posts.
        1 Coy. in HAMEL

No.2.Bn. with H.Q. in KNIGHTSBRIDGE holds the LEFT Section as follows :-
- 2 Coys. less 1 platoon in GORDON and ROBERTS trenches.
- 2 Platoons in VICTORIA and S.JAMES ST.
- 2 Platoons " FORT JACKSON
- 1 Coy. in KNIGHTSBRIDGE.

Lewis Guns. No.1.Bn. has 8 guns in position, 4 of which are in the firing line.
2 guns are kept in Reserve.
No.2.Bn. has 5 guns in position, all in front line or posts; remainder in reserve.

7. SUPPORT BN. (No.3.)
On receipt of an order "MOVE" No.3 Bn. will move into its Battle positions as follows:-
- 1 Coy. will occupy RIDGE trench N. of CHARLES AVE.
- 1 Coy. RIDGE trench S of CHARLES AV. to JACOBS LADDER
- 1 Coy. the continuation of RIDGE trench, SOUTHWARDS from JACOBS LADDER thence the trench along the road to about Q.35.a.1.9.
- 1 Coy. will stand to in MESNIL ready to move as required.
- Lewis guns will be with their Coys, *hold the position as above*

This Bn. will be prepared to counter attack ~~on receipt of orders from Bde. Hd.Qrs. or~~ at the discretion of the Officer Commanding ~~should he consider that circumstances demand such action~~ *and as circumstances demand.*

8. RESERVE BN.
No.4.Bn. will stand to, armed, in ENGLEBELMER ready to either
- (a) Hold the outskirts of this village.
- (b) Aid the other 3 Bns. in holding the enemy E. of the RIDGE Trench until the G.O.C. of the Division is able to organise an efficient counter attack with the aid of artillery and fresh infantry.

9. MACHINE GUNS:- Are posted as in Appendix A.
These positions are not to be altered without reference to Bde. Hd.Qrs.:-
On receipt of the S.O.S. Signal all guns, which will bear, will fire in "No Man's Land" and the enemy front line.
On receipt of the order "MOVE" Reserve guns will move into the positions shown in APPENDIX "A".

10. There are no strong points in the area, which it is possible to garrison and hold.
Forts MOULIN and PROWSE have been partially demolished.

11. Brigade Headquarters in the event of enemy attack, will remain at ENGLEBELMER.

Major.

Brigade Major.

SECRET.   Copy No... 19

190th Infantry Brigade Order No.32.
                            by
Brigadier General W.C.G.Heneker.D.S.O.,A.D.C.Commanding 190th Infantry
                                                              Brigade.
                                        Headquarters,
                                          190th Infantry Brigade.
                                            5th Nov. 1916.

Ref. Map. BEAUMONT (SECRET) 1/10,000.
     Map.A.(attached)

1. Operation.   A minor operation will be carried out by parties
                       from 7/Royal Fusiliers and 1/H.A.C.

2. Object.   To cut the enemy Communications, which join his front
                       trenches across the ANCRE.R. and to occupy the MOUND.

3. Description   From Q.18.c.55.25. the two (2) enemy trenches running
   of position   NORTHWARDS will be occupied and blocked.
   to be taken.   The trench running SOUTH from above point to
                       Q.24.a.7.8. (in future to be known as MOUND TRENCH)
                       will be occupied.
                       The trench running from the latter point across to
                       the SUMMER HOUSE will be blocked.

4. Strength and
   Composition of
   attacking party
      (a) Strength:-
              2 Platoons, 5 bombing Sections and 2 Lewis Guns.
              under Command of Capt.J.FORSTER 7/R.F.

         Composition:-1 platoon, 1 Lewis gun, 3 bombing Sections of the
                       7/Royal Fusiliers.
                      1 platoon, 1 Lewis gun, 2 bombing Sections of
                       the 1/H.A.C.
         Tasks of various parties will be as follows:-
      (I) "A" Bombing Section. 1 N.C.O. 8 Ptes 1/H.A.C. Cpl R.MANSELL
          will hold and block the trench running NORTHWARDS and
          parallel to the RAILWAY front point Q.18.c.55.25. The
          trench being flattened in for a distance of 70^x from
          above point.
     (II) "B" Bombing Section. 1 N.C.O. and 8 ptes 1/H.A.C.
          Cpl S.SUDGEN will hold and block the trench running
          N.W. from Q.18.c.55.25. in a similar manner.
    (III) Liason Party.1 N.C.O. and 3 ptes, 1/H.A.C.
          to Q.18.c.55.25. to keep connection between Bombing Section
          "A" and "B" and the main party as below.
     (IV) Main Party. 1 platoon, 3 bombing sections, and 1 Lewis
          gun 7/R.F.   1 platoon (less Liason party)
          and 1 Lewis gun 1/H.A.C;   will proceed along
          MOUND TRENCH, clear it of the enemy and occupy it.
          This party will also block the trench which runs from
          Q.24.a.7.8. across the R.ANCRE; to SUMMER HOUSE.

5. Forming up
   place.-   The attacking party will assemble in MESNIL on Y/Z night
                       and will be formed up with its head at GIANT'S CAUSEWAY
                       (Q.24.a.3.7.) at 6.45.pm on "Z" day.
                       Note:- This spot will be marked by a notice board and a
                       guide, placed under arrangements to be made by Capt FORSTER
                       7/R.F.

       Order of Forming up:-
              Bombing parties "A" and "B"
              Liason Party.
              Main Party. (as detailed by Capt FORSTER)

6. Advance.-   The party will advance at "Zero" hour moving along the
                       NORTH side of the RAILWAY to point Q.18.c.55.25. where
                       they will enter the enemy trench and proceed as in para 4

7. **Working Party:-** Found from 7/Royal Fusiliers.
Strength and composition to be detailed later.
This party (Lieut.J.S.WILLIAMS.R.M. of R.N.D.E.) under arrangements to be made by the O.C. 1st Field Coy.RNDE, will rendezvous in the prolongation of ROBERTS trench to the S.E. of its junction with PECHE ST; and will link up the end of this trench with the MOUND TRENCH at about point Q.18.c.60.15. and will wire the front of it.
The above assembly trench will be dug under Engineer supervision on the night of the 5/6th Nov.
The party will be formed up by 6.30.pm on "Z" day and will commence work immediately the main party of the attacking force has entered the enemy trenches.
Lieut. WILLIAMS.R.M. will be responsible that the working party does NOT spread across the line of advance of the attack until after the attacking party has passed.
Lt. WILLIAMS will withdraw this party via ROBERTS Trench on completion of their duty, he himself report to the Infantry Liason Officer at KENTISH CAVES.

8. **Artillery.-** During the afternoon of "Z" day 4.5 Howitzer Batteries D/184, D/186, D/223 in conjunction with the Heavy Artillery will fire on enemy trenches and suspected T.M. and M.G. emplacements in Q.18, and also those in the enemy 1st and 2nd line trenches in Q.17.b.
The Heavy T.Ms. will co-operate.
This bombardment will cease by 5.0pm

After 5pm "Barrage" fire will NOT be required until called for by telephone.
An Artillery Liason Officer will be at KENTISH CAVES at 6.0.pm on "Z" day and will be in communication with both the Heavy and Divisional Artillery.
He will remain at this post until 7.am.

Three (3) 18 pdr Batteries A,B and C 223 will open "Barrage" fire, if called for, on enemy trenches Q.18.c.2.9. to Q.18.c.8.9. and the prolongation of this line over the RAILWAY.
Each Barrage as called for will be for 5 minutes, 3 minutes of which will be intense.
Counter Batteries of the Heavy Artillery will open on Enemy Batteries if called for from KENTISH CAVES or by the F.O.O. of these batteries.

9. **Stokes Guns:-** The O.C.190th Light T.M.Battery will arrange to have two (2) Stokes Guns mounted in the cutting SOUTH of ROBERTS TRENCH at about Q.18.c.0.3. on "Z" night. These guns will range during the following day on points in the enemy trenches in Q.18.a. and c, so as to be ready to deal with any counter attack on the night following "Z" night.

10. **Bn.Liason Officer:-** will be Major OSMOND 1/HAC with Hd.Qrs. at KENTISH CAVES.
He will be responsible, on request from the front, for passing Signals to Artillery, sending up working parties, stores etc. and for keeping Brigade Hd.Qrs. informed as to progress.

11. **Future Garrison:-** The future garrision of the captured position will consist of Bombing posts, the number and composition being left to the discretion of Capt. FORSTER 7/R.F.
When these have been placed and the situation is considered satisfactory, the remainder of the attacking party will be withdrawn and an officer appointed to command the post.
The name of this officer will be communicated to Bde. Hd.Qrs. as soon as possible.

3.

12. **Dress etc :-** "Fighting order with Coats".
Each bomber will carry 18 Mills Grenades in a bucket, with the exception of 2 bombers per section who will carry 18 No.23 bombs.
Four (4) bombers of the 7/R.F. in the main party will carry two (2) "P" bombs each.
Each bombing section will carry 2 shovels.
Each bomber will carry 120 rounds of S.A.A. and 4 sandbags.
Each Infantry man will carry 200 rds S.A.A., 4 sandbags, 2 Very Lights, 50% shovels, 10% picks and two (2) bombs.

13. **Watches :-** Watches will be synchronised by Bde. time at 4.0pm on "Z" day by telephone.
The Brigade Signal Officer will be responsible for this.

14. **Telephone Post:-** will be established at KENTISH CAVES, the necessary personnel being found by the Bde. Signal Section.
This post will be established by 4.30.pm on "Z" day and will be relieved by the Bn. holding the RIGHT SECTION at 7.am on the following day.
good → Linesmen to keep the line from TELEPHONE POST to Bn. H.Q. of the RIGHT Bn. will also be found by the Sig. Section

15. "Z" day will be the 6th Nov.
"ZERO" hour 7.pm.

Time issued to Signals... 8 pm

Major.
Brigade Major.

1. 7/Royal Fusiliers.
2. 1/H.A.C.
3. 190th T.M.Battery.
4. 4/Bedfordshire Regt.
5. 10/R.Dublin Fusiliers.
6. 190th M.G.Coy.
7. Bde. Signal Section.
8. Bde Bombing Officer.
9. Bde Intelligence Officer.
10. "A" Group Artillery.
11. 1st Field Coy. R.N.D.E.
12. 116th Inf. Bde.
13. 154th Inf. Bde.
14. 63rd Division
15. C.R.A.   )
16. C.R.E.   ) for information.
17. Corps Heavy Artillery)
18. File.
19. War Diary (3)
20. Spare (3)

SECRET.
Copy No. 25

190th Infantry Brigade Order No.33.
by
Brigadier General.W.C.G.Heneker.D.S.O.,A.D.C.Commanding 190th Inf Bde.

Headquarters,
190th Infantry Bde.
6/11/16.

Ref. Map 57D 1/40,000
Trench Map HAMEL 1/10,000

1. The 190th Infantry Bde will be relieved in the HAMEL SECTOR on the 6th and 7th inst.
   The table for relief on the 6th inst is attached.

2. On completion of relief on the 6th the LEFT Section will be commanded by Brigadier General W.C.G.HENEKER. D.S.O. A.D.C., whose Hd.Qrs. will remain in ENGLEBELMER and the RIGHT by Brigadier General PHILLIPS commanding 189th Inf. Bde. with HD.Qrs. at ENGLEBELMER.

3. The "Hood" Bn. will occupy with a garrison the new trench dug last night from the S.E. end of ROBERT TRENCH to the HAMEL-BEAUCOURT ROAD.

Torries issued to Signals. 2.10 pm

Major.
Brigade Major.

1. 7/Royal Fusiliers.
2. 4/Bedfordshire Regt.
3. 10/R.Dublin Fusiliers.
4. 1/H.A.C.
5. 190th M.G.Coy.
6. 190th T.M.Battery.
7. Hood Bn.
8. Hawke Bn.
9. 189th M.G.Coy.
10. 189th T.M.Battery.
11. Signal Section.
12. Staff Capt.
13. Intelligence Officer.
14. Bombing Officer.
15. Bde Transport Officer.
16. 189th. Inf. Bde.
17. 188th Inf. Bde.
18. 1st Field Coy. R.N.D.E.
19. 14/Worcestershire Regt (Pioneers)
20. 63rd Division.
21. 116th Inf. Bde.
22. 154th Inf. Bde.
23. File.
24. War Diary. (3)

MARCH TABLE for 6th inst.

Unit relieved	Unit relieving	Section	GUIDES No.	GUIDES Place	Time	Remarks
1/H.A.C.	Hood Bn.	RIGHT	1 for H.Q. 1 per platoon 1" Section of Lewis Guns	Hood Bn. H.Q. ENGLEBELMER	5.pm	1/H.A.C. take over billets of Hood Bn. Billeting party to be at ENGLEBELMER by 4.0.pm
7/Royal Fusiliers	Hawke Bn.	SUPPORT	Nil	Nil	Nil	7/R.F. to shelters in ENGLEBELMER. HAWKE Bn. billets in LESNIE. Billeting parties of both Bns to be at above places at 4.0.pm.
Part.189th M.G.Coy.	Part 189th M.G.Coy.	RIGHT	as arranged by O.Cs. concerned.			Relief to be completed by 8.0.pm
Part.189th T.M.B.	Part 189th T.M.B.	- do -	------do------			" " " 8.0.pm 189th M.G.Coy. and 189th T.M.B. move to billets in ENGLEBELMER.

Note.- All movement by platoons at 200X distance.

HEADQUARTERS,
190th
INFANTRY BRIGADE.
No. 2978
Date............

SECRET

Hd. Qrs. 190th Inf. Bde.
6th November 1916

Reference Bde Order No 32. The operation will take place on the 7th inst as laid down for the 6th with the following exceptions:-

The working parties will be found by 1/H.A.C. and NOT by 7/R.F.

The parties are as follows:-

(A) 1 Platoon (about 50) 45% shovels 45% picks and 4 sandbags per man. Parade Bn H.Q. MESNIL at 5 p.m. For opening up communication.

(B) 1 Platoon (about 50) 65% with wire cutters and gloves and 4 sandbags per man. Parade as above at 5.10 p.m. as wiring and carrying party.

The whole under command of LT. WILLIAMS R.M. of 1st Field Coy.

The T.M. and M.G. support will be given by the 189th Inf. Bde. guns.

All other details remain as before.

[signature]
Major
Brigade Major

1. 7/Royal Fusiliers
2. 1/H.A.C.
3. 190th T.M. Battery.
4. 4/The Yorkshire Regt.
5. 10/Royal Dublin Fusiliers
6. 190th M.G. Coy.
7. Bde. Signal Section
8. Bde. Bombing Officer
9. Bde. Intelligence Officer
10. "Y" Group Artillery
11. 1st Field Coy. R.N.D.E.
12. 116th Inf. Bde.
13. 154th "
14. 63rd Division
15. C.R.A.
16. C.R.E.
17. Corps Heavy Artillery
18. File
19. War Diary (3)
20. Spare (3)
21. Staff Captain

} for information.

Secret

APPENDIX. A.

190th Infantry Brigade Defence Scheme
HAMEL SECTOR.
Machine Gun Emplacements

Ref. Map BEAUMONT 1/10,000. SECRET.

S.1. Q.17.c.50.02. Open emplacement of little value as a defensive position. It is however very good for indirect fire by Day or Night. I suggest building a permanent position for this gun in SHOOTERS HILL at Q.17.c.8.2.

S.2. Q.17.c.55.20. It is now a very good emplacement, covered with iron rails and loop holed.
Field of fire good.

S.3. Q.17.c.30.14. A new open emplacement with a good Field of fire on to "No Man's Land" and enemy front line.

S.4. Q.17.c.00.55. A new open emplacement with a good field of fire on "No Man's Land" and enemy front line. If this is to become a permanent defensive position a dugout for team could be easily made under the bank on which gun is placed.

R.1. Q.23.c.62.05. Splinters proof tunnelled position with a good field of fire filled with trench mounting.

R.2. Q.23.c.7.2. Splinter proof emplacement, good field of fire over the ANCRE.

R.3. Q.23.c.5.3. Dugout and gun position combined, good field of fire.

R.4. Q.23.c.25.50. Splinter proof emplacement, good field of fire.

R.5. Q.23.c.14.65. Dugout and gun position combined, lopp holed, has a good field of fire.

R.6. Q.23.c.14.83. New splinter proof emplacement. Good field of fire.

Bde. R.1. Q.35.a.13.90.
Bde. R.2. Q.28.d.97.06.
Bde. R.3. Q.27.d.48.65.
Bde. R.4. Q.27.b.53.30.
Bde. R.5. Q.21.d.3.2.
Bde. R.6. Q.21.d.05.70.
Bde. R.7. Q.21.b.31.31.
Bde. R.8. Q.15.d.05.30.

Dugouts generally are not good, having only one entrance, and are very small.

Major.
Brigade Major.
Hd.Qrs.190th Infantry Bde.

SECRET   Appendix 34.   Copy No: ......

190th Infantry Brigade Order No 35
— by —

Brigadier ~~General~~ W.C.G. HENEKER D.S.O., A.D.C., Comdg. 190th Inf Brigade.

H.Qrs 190th Inf: Bde;
6th Nov: 1916.

Ref Maps 57 D 1/40,000
French Map HAMEL 1/10,000.

1. In continuation of Bde Order No 33 the 188th Inf Bde will take over the LEFT SECTION on the 7th inst., in accordance with attached Table.

2. On completion of Relief the 190th Inf. Brigade will be disposed as follows:-

   Bde H.Qrs   ⎫
   M.G. Coy   ⎬ VARENNES
   T.M. Batty   ⎭

   1/H.A.C. + raiding party of 7/R.Fus. ⎱ ENGLEBELMER Billets.

   7/Royal Fusiliers   ⎫
   4/Bedfordshire Regt   ⎬ HEDAUVILLE
   10/Royal Dublin Fusiliers   ⎭

   (signed) Ormond
   Major
   Brigade Major

Issue to Signals .... 10 for

1. 7th Royal Fusiliers
2. 4/Bedfordshire Regt
3. 10/Royal Dublin Fus.
4. 1/H.A.C.
5. 190th T.M. Batty
6. " M. Gun Coy.
7. Staff Capt
8. Intelligence Officer
9. Signal Officer
10. Bde Bombing Officer
11. Bde Transport Officer
12. No 4 Coy. Div. Train
13. No 1 Field Coy. R.N.D.E.
14. 188th Inf Bde
15. 189th Inf Bde
16. 154th Inf Bde
17. 63rd Div:
18. File
19. War Diary.

March Table

190th Inf Bde only

Unit Relieving	Section	Relief Time	Relief Place	Destination	Time for Holding parties to arrive	Remarks
1st Royal Dublin Fusiliers	LEFT	noon	KNIGHTSBRIDGE DUMP.	HEDAUVILLE	9am	moves astraka retired or not cleaning cross rds. Q25 a.b.7 at 8am
10/Lancashire Fusiliers	RESERVE	"	"	— do —	8am	Clear Q25.a.b.7 at 8am
1/Royal Inn. Fus.	LEFT	"	—	HEDAUVILLE.	8am	
2nd R.G.Gds 166th RGR	LEFT	12½ pm	ENGLEBELMER KNIGHTS BRIDGE	VARENNES	9am	
" T.M.Bn	"	2 pm				
166th Bde H.Q.	"	—	—	VARENNES	10.30am	will move off at 2pm

Note:— Movements E of ENGLEBELMER will be by Platoons at 200x distance

SECRET.

APPENDIX 35

Copy No. 19

190th Infantry Brigade Order No.36.

Ref. Map. FRANCE 1/40,000.
Sheet 57D.

Headquarters, 190th Inf. Bde.
10th November.1916.

1. The 190th Infantry Brigade will move to HEDAUVILLE and VARENNES on the 11th inst according to the attached table.

2. 5 G.S. wagons per Bn. have been asked for. Orders as to sending guides to meet these will be wired later.

3. Orders as to re-filling point later.

4. Units will report their arrival in billets to new Bde. Hd. Qrs.

5. An uniform speed of 2½ miles per hour will be maintained including halts, which will be made from 10 minutes to clock hour to clock hour.

6. An officer from each Unit will be sent to Bde.Hd.Qrs. at 8 am. tomorrow to receive Bde.time.

7. Bde.Hd.Qrs. will close at PUCHEVILLERS at 8 am. and open at VARENNES at noon.

Major.
Brigade Major.

Issued to Signals...... 3.30 pm

1. 7/Royal Fusiliers.
2. 4/Bedfordshire Regt.
3. 10/Royal Dublin Fusiliers.
4. 1/H.A.C.
5. 190th. Bde. M.G.Coy.
6. 190th. T.M.Battery.
7. Signal Section.
8. Staff Captain.
9. Bde. Transport Officer.
10. Bde. Bombing Officer.
11. Bde. Intelligence Officer.
12. No.4 Coy. Div. Train.
13. 1st. Field Coy. R.N.D.E.
14. 14/Worcester Regt.
15. 188th. Inf. Bde.
16. 189th. Inf. Bde.
17. 63rd.Division.
18. File.
19. War Diary (3).

MARCH TABLE.

Unit.	Moves to.	Route.	Starting Point.	Time of passing starting point.	Remarks.
7/Royal Fusiliers.	HEDAUVILLE	TOUTENCOURT - HARPONVILLE - VARENNES.	House at Q of QUENOYE	9 am.	10/Royal Dublin Fusiliers takes precedence for billets.
1/H.A.C.	"	"	"	9.15 am.	
10/Royal Dublin Fusiliers	"	"	"	9.30 am.	To go into billets if available.
Brigade Hd.Qrs.	VARENNES.	TOUTENCOURT - HARPONVILLE.	"	9.40 am.	
4/Bedfordshire Regt.	"	"	"	9.45 am.	
190th.Bde.M.G.Coy.	"	"	"	10. am.	
190th.T.M.Battery.	"	"	"	10.10 am.	

Billeting parties to proceed 2 hours ahead of Units.

H.Q., 63rd (R.N.) Division.

REPORT ON HAMEL BEAUCOURT ROAD FROM

Q.23.d.3.5. - Q.18.c.52.

The road through HAMEL village down as far as DOLLY BRAE DUMP has a good surface.

It is crossed by JACOB'S LADDER TRENCH once, and by DIAVAL TRENCH three times, the road being carried through on light wooden bridges capable of taking light traffic.

Near the DOLLY BRAE DUMP there are a few small shell holes.

After passing the Dump there is a small bomb store built on the road.   It is also crossed by a communication trench leading to LANCASHIRE POST etc.   The parapet of this trench is thrown on the road making a big mound of earth at this place.

The next 150 yards is in a very bad condition being full of shell holes.   It is also crossed by GRANT'S CAUSEWAY TRENCH.

From this point on to near the German Trenches the surface is in good condition.

The road can be used for traffic as far as DOLLY BRAE DUMP.

From near the German Front line onwards the road appears to be quite obliterated and for 600 to 1,000 yards will probably require entire reconstruction and possibly deviation.

Copy to:-
Chief Engineer, V Corps.

Lieutenant-Colonel.,
C. R. E., 63rd (R.N.) Divn.

SECRET.   Copy...23......

190th Infantry Brigade Order No. 37.

                                            Headquarters,
                                              190th Infantry Brigade.
                                               14/11/16.

Ref. Maps (A) HAMEL 1/10,000
         (B) Assembly Trenches.
         (C) Enemy Trenches.
         (D) Tank Routes
         (E) Objectives and lines of
             Demarcation between Bns.

1.   190th Infantry Brigade Order No. 34 is cancelled.

2. Operation.   The Vth Army is to attack the enemy's positions on both sides of the RIVER ANCRE.

3. Task of   To the 63rd Division is allotted the task of capturing
   63rd Division. the RED LINE including the village of BEAUCOURT shown in map (E)

4. Objectives.   The objectives allotted to the Division are shown on map E and are three (3) in number, known as :-
                 (a) GREEN LINE
                 (b) YELLOW LINE.
                 (c) RED   "
                 The capture of these is allotted to the 189th and 188th Infantry Bdes. on the SOUTH and NORTH respectively. The 190th Infantry Bde. will be in reserve; prepared, either to assist in the capture of the RED LINE or to relieve the attacking troops after it has been captured.

5. Date   The day of attack will be known as "Z" day and the hour of attack "ZERO".

6. Preliminary   The attack will be preceded by an intense bombardment
   Bombardment. on "X" and "Y" days, commencing at 5.0.am and becoming intense at 6.0.am.
                 On "Z" day the fire of the Heavy Artillery will commence as usual at 5.am.
                 At "ZERO" the whole of the 18 pdr batteries will open fire simultaneously on the enemy front line and 50^X on this side of it and the attacking troops of the 189th and 188th Inf. Bdes. will at once advance.

7. Order of   The order of battle for the 190th Inf. Bde. will be from
   Battle.   RIGHT to LEFT:-

                 1/Honourable Artillery Company (less 1 Coy.)
                 7/Royal Fusiliers.
                 4/Bedfordshire Regt.
                 10/R.Dublin Fusiliers.
                 190th Bde. M.G.Coy. Headquarters and 2 Sections in rear
                                          of the Brigade (will be in reserve)
                                     1 Section in rear of the RIGHT Bn.
                                     1 "   "   "   "   LEFT Bn.
                 190th Light Trench Mortar Battery, 4 guns in reserve at MESNIL. 4 guns in POTTAGE.

8. Map Reference
   of Hd.Qrs.:-
   In Assembly   Brigade Hd. Qrs....................... Q.28.c.9.9.
   Area.
                 7/Royal Fusiliers..................... Q.23.a.9.6.
                 4/Bedfordshire Regt................... Q.23.a.40.85.
                 10/R.Dublin Fusiliers................. Q.17.c.1.7.
                 1/H.A.C............................... Q.23.b.35.25.
                 190th Bde. M.G.Coy.................... Q.23.a.9.2.
                 190th T.M.Battery..................... Close to Bde.Hd.Qrs

9. Assembly.

The Brigade (less 1 Coy. 1/H.A.C.) will assemble in the assembly lines shown in map "B" on "Y" night and will march from their billets so as to be at the following points at the times mentioned:-
1/H.A.C. (less 1 Coy.) pass MESNIL CHURCH at 6.30.pm and move via HAMEL ROAD.
7/Royal Fusiliers   ditto   at 8.0.pm
190th M.G.Coy. Hd.Qrs. and 3 Sections -ditto- 9.30.pm.
4/Bedfordshire Regt. enter GABION AV. at point Q.16.c.9.2. at 6.30.pm.
10/Royal Dublin Fusiliers ditto at 8.0.pm.
M.G.Coy. 1 section   ditto at 9.30.pm.
Note:- In the case of heavy shelling, the troops moving by the MESNIL - HAMEL ROAD will be diverted into JACOB's LADDER.
As soon as troops are formed up in their assembly areas they will inform Bde. H.Q. by runner or by the code word TRESCO by telephone.
1 Coy. of 1/H.A.C. will be attached to the 189th Inf. Bde. and will join this Bde. without further orders on "Y" day reporting to "Hood" Bn. in MESNIL during the morning, where orders will be received.

10. Attached Units.

2 Sections of No.3.Field Coy. R.N.D.E. and a half Coy. 14/Worcestershire Regt. (Pioneers) are attached to the Brigade and will on Y/Z night form up in HAMEL Village without further orders, with Hd. Qrs. at the Road junction Q.23.d.5.9. They will move into position passing MESNIL CHURCH at 10.0.pm.
They will occupy our front line trench, when evacuated by the 190th Inf. Bde., close to TELEPHONE POST where runners will be kept by them.

11. Tanks.

Three groups of "TANKS" will be working with the 63rd Division namely:-

Groups IV. V. and VI.

Their routes are shown on map "D".

12. Advance of the Brigade.

(a) At ZERO the Brigade in four waves will advance and ~~over~~ occupy GORDON and ROBERTS TRENCHES and their Continuations, so as to cover the whole front, on the evacuation of those trenches by the 188th and 189th Inf. Bdes.
The first two waves will be in GORDON; the third and fourth in ROBERTS TRENCH.
(b) At 2 hours 0' the Brigade will move forward and occupy the GREEN LINE as follows:-
First two waves in GREEN LINE TRENCH, third and fourth waves in trench immediately WEST of STATION ROAD; except 10/R.Dublin Fusiliers who will be disposed:-
First two waves in trench immediately WEST of STATION ROAD.
Third and fourth waves in trench along road immeditely WEST of Q in QUARRY (Map C.)
Machine Guns and Trench Mortars will be close up in rear of Bns. in the most convenient trenches.
Note:-The waves are the most convenient formation for offensive action, but Bn. Commanders should, at any time they consider advisable, adopt artillery formations and subsequently deploy into waves.
(c) The Coy. 1/H.A.C. detached to 189th Inf. Bde. will here rejoin its Bn.
(d) On arrival at the GREEN LINE the Brigade will consolidate.
All trenches approaching our flanks and which are not occupied by our troops are to be blocked.

13. Action of other Brigades.	In the meantime the YELLOWLINE will have been captured by the advanced troops of the 188th and 189th Inf. Bdes. There will be a halt of about 1 hour here and 4 pauses in the barrage, after the fourth of which "C" and "D" Bns. of the above Bdes. will advance and capture the RED LINE. After the capture of the RED LINE Engineers will be sent up by the C.R.E. to assist in putting BEAUCOURT into a state of defence.
14. Future work of 190th Inf. Bde.	The Brigade will either relieve other troops on or assist in the capture of the RED LINE. In either case the procedure will be the same. Rapid consolidation, working first on the important tactical points, or strong points commenced by other troops. Battle patrols, strength about 10 to 12 men each will be pushed well to the front with the double object of gaining ground and breaking up any enemy counter attack before it arrives at the line of defence. Later the posts of the patrols will be linked up and will become our front line. Special attention should be paid to the trench junction at R.1.c.2.8. All available machine and Lewis Guns will at once, be brought up, thus relieving infantry for the work of consolidation, necessary fatigues and ~~finally~~ subsequently rest.
15. Action of M.G.Coy.	On arrival at the GREEN LINE the O.C.190th M.G.Coy. will at once select positions and get two sections into positions in or forward of the GREEN LINE covering the front and flanks of the final objective, and will aid the advanced troops in every way. He will be prepared to move the two sections in reserve up to the YELLOW LINE should more machine guns be required there. When the final objective is taken, he is to be prepared to move all guns forward to assist in holding the line.
16. Action if Troops on flanks are held up.	It must be impressed on all subordinate commanders that they must NOT halt because units on their flanks are held up; they must rather assist those units by advancing and taking the enemy in flank or rear.
17. Communications.	(a) A buried cable will run from Bde. Hd. Qrs. to near our front line trench; the advanced end will be known as "TELEPHONE POST" and be clearly marked as such; its position will be Q.17.d.(Central) mine shaft immediately S.E. of junction of ROBERTS and LOUVERCY TRENCHES. This post must be known to all runners. (b) From this point lines will be run to flank Bns. as they advance.

(c) After Bde. Hd. Qrs. is established at GREEN LINE all these runners behind Bde. Hd. Qrs. will be collected at that place.

The two Bns. on the RIGHT will combine to form a system of runners on the relay system, and a similar procedure will be adopted by the two LEFT Bns. The relay posts should be on the cable line and the runners will carry out with them one shovel per pair of runners to dig themselves in.

(d) One cable detachment from the Hd. Qrs. section Div. Sig. Company will be attached to Bde. Hd. Qrs and will come under the orders of the O.C.Sig. Section.

Following the advance of the infantry this section will run out a line to the proposed advanced Bde. Hd.Qrs. in the GREEN LINE.

An officer from Bde. Hd. Qrs. will accompany this line and chose the site for Hd. Qrs.

(e) When the 190th Inf. Bde. Hd. Qrs. move forward to the GREEN LINE, the despatch riders at MESNIL will move forward as far as HAMEL Q.23.d.40. to which point the Bde runners will carry their messages.

(f) The O.C.Bde. Signal Section will arrange for 10 Bde. runners for use as required in carrying despatches to Division and Brigades.

Three motor cyclists D.R. will be attached to the Bde.

(g) All runners and mounted despatch riders will carry depatches in the LEFT hand breast pocket.

Anyone seeing a dead or wounded D.R. will search him for despatches and hand them in as soon as possible to the nearest runner post or Signal Office.

(h) <u>Pigeons</u>:- Two HEDAUVILLE birds will be issued to each Bn. by the Bde. Signal Officer on "Y" day.

These birds must be used with the greatest discretion. they will only be employed for very important messages and then only when all other means of communication has failed.

Only one bird should be released at a time.

(i) <u>Aeroplanes</u>.- Contact aeroplanes will be employed to fix positions gained by the infantry.

    Flares will be lighted:-
      (1) On gaining each objective.
      (2) Whenever hung up.
      (3) When an aeroplane sounds its "Klaxon Horn".
      (4) Just before dark and in the early morning if an aeroplane is about.

It must be remembered that it is <u>ONLY</u> the most advanced troops which light these flares.

Red Flares only will be used.

(j) "S.O.S" Rockets are "White","Green", "White"

18. Communication Trenches.

    "UP"   JACOBS LADDER.
            McMAHON AV.
            PECHE ST.
            GABION AV.
            LONG SAP.

    "DOWN" LOUVERCY ST.
            ROYAL AV.
            POTTAGE TRENCH.
            CHARLES AV.
            LONG ACRE.
            CONSTITUTION HILL
            KNIGHTSBRIDGE.
            RAILWAY.

19. Equipment.

Troops will attack in battle order and will carry the following:-
4 Sandbags per man (passed through the belt, 2 on each side)
2 Iron Rations.
Unexpired portion of days rations.
Gas Helmet.
1 Flare.
1 Very Light.
Mills Grenades at a rate of 2 per man; and in addition twelve to be carried by each bomber.
In addition to above, each man of the rear wave of the attacking troops will carry two tools,(1 pick to 10 shovels)
Men carrying wire cutters will wear Yellow Armlets.
10 White and 5 Green S.O.S. Rockets and "P" Bombs will be carried under Bn. arrangements.
Runners will be in battle order with two clips of S.A.A. but will NOT carry rifles; they will wear a Blue Armlet with a White Stripe.
Pack will NOT be carried.
Great Coats will be carried to the assembly trenches and then put on.
Coats will be removed at 5.0.am; each section will make a bundle, tied with rope to which will be attached a strong label showing the No. of the section etc.
The bundles will be packed on the RIGHT of each platoon and 2 men per Bn. left in charge.

20. Reports.

Reports will be sent in to Bde. Hd. Qrs. at every clock hour and every half hour, and at other times when necessary.
Skeleton Maps which have been issued to all units will be filled in and sent with reports.

21. Medical Arrangements.

One bearer Sub-Division of No.1 Field Ambulance will work with the Bde.; they will assemble in POTTAGE TRENCH in HAMEL.
Route JACOBS LADDER which will be entered at 10.30pm on Y/Z night.
Bearer Sub-Divisions will clear wounded as follows:-
(a) From present front line to A.D.S. at MESNIL and COOKERS:-
    2 bearer Sub-Divisions of 3rd F.A.
(b) From GREEN LINE to present front line:-
    2 bearer Sub-Divisions of 2nd F.A.
(c) From YELLOW LINE to GREEN LINE:-
    1 bearer Sub-Division of 2nd F.A.
    1   "   "   "   3rd F.A.
(d) From BLUE to YELLOW LINE :-
    2 bearer Sub-Divisions of 1st F.A.
(e) From BROWN to BLUE LINE:-
    1 bearer Sub-Division of 1st F.A.
    (Surgeon WALKER.R.N.)
Bearer and collecting posts will be established as far forward as possible in the above areas and will be marked by sign boards.
Regimental Medical Officers will, as soon as the objective has been reached, select positions for Regtl Aid Posts in the vicinity of Bn. Hd. Qrs. These Posts should be clearly marked with the Red Cross and letter R.A.P.
Reserve stretchers and dressings will be brought up to Regtl. Aid Posts by the bearer Sub-Divisions.
Bearer Sub-Divisions have orders to keep in close touch with Regtl Medical Officers

6.

The Regtl. stretcher bearers are NOT required to assist in the evacuation of the wounded during movement.
When halted, however, and the Regtl. Aid Posts established the REgtl. stretcher bearers will be responsible for clearing the wounded in front of the Regtl. Aid Posts and for taking them to that post.
The bearer Sub-Divisions will collect the wounded from the Regtl. AidPost and from the rear.
Should it be necessary for Regtl. stretcher bearers to assist in the evacuation of wounded from the Regtl.Aid Posts, they will carry only so far as the nearest bearer posts and return to their units.

22. Administrative Orders. are as issued by Staff Capt.

23. A mine will be sprung by us in "No Man's Land" at ZERO hour.

24. Laison. An officer from each Bn. will report to Bde. Hd. Qrs. at 7.0.pm on Y day.

25. Gas. If the wind is favourable gas will be discharged on "Y" day against ~~BEAUCOURT~~ BEAUMONT HAMEL.

26. Time. Time will be synchronised from D.H.Q. at 12.30.pm and 8.30.pm on "Y" day.

27. Zero. "Z" day has been notified to all concerned.
Zero hour will be shortly after daybreak.

28. Brigade Hd.Qrs. will be established at MESNIL Q.28.c.99 at 5.0.pm on "Y" day and will move forward to about the GREEN LINE when this line has been occupied by the 190th Inf.Bde.

29. Appendices. Appendix 1. Barrage Table (to be issued later)
" 2. List of Compass Bearings)
Map.A)
" B) To be detached
" C) from order No.34
" D) and attached here.
" E)
Note:- Map "B" is to be corrected as follows:-
A Red Line showing forming up place for M.G.Coy. to be added, running along CARNALEA-ESAU - E half of POTTAGE and PRINCESS ST.
For 4 guns T.M.B. junction of POTTAGE and ESAU.
(For names see Map A.)
(b)Map C and E are to be corrected as follows:-
Delete all coloured lines except BLUE and YELLOW and add RED Line as on Map"F" attached.

30. Notes. (a)The ground over which the attack is to take place must be carefully studied and bearings taken of any points which may assist commander in keeping direction
(b)Special mopping up parties, detailed from the third wave must be told off to deal with all trenches captured by 190th Infantry Bde.
(c)It must be impressed on all ranks that it is of the utmost importance to the success of the operations that no movement takes place in the assembly area during dawn on "Z" day prior to ZERO hour.
During the night of Y/Z there should be as little noise as possible and no loud talking.
Matches must be carefully screened and every precaution taken to conceal the fact of our assembly for attack.

7.

(d) A proportion of the reserve personnel for Machine and Lewis guns should be left behind and not taken into action.
Officer and N.C.Os. must move IN the ranks of their platoons.
(f) Battalions must have a special carrying party detailed for Verys' Lights in addition to the one carried on the man
(g) No papers etc showing position of Hd. Qrs. dumps, or other important information are to be taken into action.
Maps of enemy trenches NOT giving above information may and should be taken.

[signature]
Major.
Brigade Major.

Time issued to Signals... 9:15 am.

Copies to:-

1. 7/Royal Fusiliers.
2. 4/Bedfordshire Regt.
3. 10/R.Dublin Fusiliers
4. 1/H.A.C.
5. 190th M.G.Coy.
6. 190th T.M.Battery.
7. Staff Capt.
8. Bde. Intelligence Officer.
9. Bde. Bombing Officer.
10. Bde. Transport Officer.
11. No.3 Field Coy.
12. 14/Worcestershire Regt.
13. Signal Section.
14. No.4.Coy. Div. Train.
15. 63rd Division.
16.   ditto.
17. 188th Inf. Bde.
18. 189th   "   "
19. A.D.M.S.
20. Artillery Laison Officer.
21. File.
22. War Diary. (3)
24. Spare.(5)

SECRET.

Amendments to Brigade Order No.37

Headquarters,
190th Infantry Brigade
12/11/16.

Para.12. Sub.para (b)
after (b) insert
"At 0 hours 46' the Brigade moves into the enemy 1st system of trenches.
First two waves into enemy 3rd Trench.
3rd and 4th waves into enemy 2nd Trench.

Para.21 line 15. (d)
For BLUE read RED.

line 17 (e) delete and insert
"In reserve with 190th Inf. Bde.

Para.29. line 1. Copies have been issued to all units of or attached to 190th Inf. Bde.

C.F.Jorram.Major.
Brigade Major.

7/Royal Fusiliers.
4/Bedfordshire Regt.
10/R.Dublin Fusiliers
1/H.A.C.
190th M.G.Coy.
190th T.M.Battery.
Staff Capt.
Bde. Int. Officer.
Bde.Bombing Officer
Bde.Transport Officer.
No.3.Field Coy.
14/Worcestershire. Regt.
Signal Section
No.4.Coy. Div Train
63rd Division
  ditto
188th Inf. Bde.
189th Inf. Bde.
A.D.M.S.
Artillery Laison Officer
File
War Diary.
Spare.

Copy No 93

AMENDED TIME TABLE OF 63rd (RN) DIVISION ATTACK

(to accompany Order No. 68, dated 10th November, 1916.)

Time	Artillery (18-Pdrs).	Infantry
ZERO	All guns open intense barrage, 75% on enemy front line, 25% on No Man's Land, 50 yards in front of it.	Leave trenches and advance.
0.2'	Barrage on No Man's Land lifts to front line.	
0.6'	All guns lift from front line, and move back to DOTTED GREEN LINE at average rate of 100 yards in five minutes; stay there five minutes, and then lifts 100 yards beyond it, where barrage dwells till 0.26'.	Assault enemy front trench.
0.21'		Capture of DOTTED GREEN LINE completed. Troops for advance on GREEN LINE pass straight through and move close up to the barrage.
0.26'	Barrage lifts 100 yards and continues to lift 100 yards every five minutes till it reaches GREEN LINE. It stays an GREEN LINE five minutes and then lifts to 150 yards beyond it, where it dwells (with exception of four pauses of five minutes, see below) till 1.58').	
0.46'		Capture of GREEN LINE completed. Halt 1 hour 10 minutes on GREEN LINE. During this halt infantry for attack of YELLOW LINE move up from enemy front system to GREEN LINE and reserve brigade moves forward to enemy front system.
0.55':1.0') 1.15':1.20') 1.30':1.35') 1.51':1.56')	Pauses in Barrage.	
1.56'	Intense barrage re-opens 150 yards beyond GREEN LINE.	
1.58'	Barrage lifts 100 yards, and continues to lift 100 yards every five minutes till it reaches YELLOW LINE. It stays on YELLOW LINE five minutes and then	Advance towards YELLOW LINE.

lifts/

Time	Artillery (18-Pdrs).	Infantry.
2.43'	lifts to 150 yards beyond it, where it dwells (with the exception of four pauses of five minutes, see below) till 3.45'.	Capture of YELLOW LINE completed. Halt one hour on YELLOW LINE. During this halt troops for capture of RED LINE move up from GREEN LINE to YELLOW LINE, and reserve brigade moves to GREEN LINE.
2.50'-2.55' 3.5'-3.10' 3.20'-3.25' 3.41'-3.46'	Pauses in Barrage.	
3.48'	Intense barrage re-opens 150 yards beyond YELLOW LINE. Barrage lifts 100 yards, and continues lifting 100 yards every five minutes till RED LINE is reached. On the left and left centre, where RED LINE consists of a trench, the barrage will stay on the trench for five minutes and will then lift 150 yards beyond it, where it will dwell for 15 minutes. It will then lift back to a line joining R.1.a.5.0. and R.8.a.8.5. (to be called the DOTTED RED LINE) where it will eventually die down. right — On the right and centre, where the RED LINE is not defined by a trench the barrage will move straight through from the YELLOW to the DOTTED RED LINE by lifts of 100 yards every five minutes, and there will be no pause of 15 minutes in front of the RED LINE. N.B. After the barrage has died down, in the event of a new protective barrage being called for by the infantry, it will, in the absence of more definite orders, be put down on the DOTTED RED LINE.	Advance towards RED LINE
4.18'	the artillery will put down a barrage if their assistance is called for without further particulars being given.	Capture of RED LINE completed. As soon as this line is captured, small patrols will be pushed forward, close under the barrage, towards the line R.1.a.5.0. - R.8.a.8.5. They will not establish themselves within 100 yards on either side of this line, which is the line on which

Appendix 36

Report on the action of 190th Infantry Brigade.
during the 13th and 14th November. 1916.

The Brigade was formed up vide attached diagram on night 12/13 November ready to move forward at Zero hour 5.45am 13th.

5.45am	Barrage opened and brigade moved forward behind 189th and 188th Inf. Brigades and occupied our original front and Support Line trenches. It was too foggy for landmarks to be picked up and 1/H.A.C in particular had to march by compass.
6.46' or 6.51am	Brigade advanced out of our front line system and moved forward as ordered (Barrage table).
6.40am	Informed Division that visibility was about 50 yards and that the enemy had not opened a barrage. This information was received from Brigade advanced report centre (Telephone Post)
7.5.am	Message from Division (verbal) to send forward one platoon per Battalion to the enemy front line trench as it had been reported it was difficult to take enemy's front line on front of left Brigade. The Brigade had already gone forward according to barrage table so this could not be carried out.
7.29.am	39th Division report their left flank half way to 2nd objective their centre held up at R.19.c.3.8.
7.40am	H.A.C. report no news of brigade in front. At this hour three Companies of H.A.C. had reached the German reserve lines and digging in. They report having lost touch with 7/R.Fus. on their left. This is accounted for by the fact that the 7/R.Fus. had got up to the German front line and were there held up by machine gun fire. The same thing was happening on the left and except for small parties which managed to get forward the bulk of the 4/Bedfordshire Regt and 10/R.Dublin Fus. were held up in the enemy's front line.
7.45.am	Wired situation to Division (our B.M.800). This however quickly altered for the H.A.C. were able to push on as above stated.
7.55am	Sent instructions to battalions to take German front lines and that H.A.C. had penetrated to enemy"s 3rd trench on extreme right. Suggested that in rear of H.A.C. would be a good place to push into and spread N.W.
8.0.am	4/Bedfordshire Regt. and 10/R.Dublin Fus. advanced their H.Q. into enemy's lines but as it transpired they became mixed up in the fighting and were cut off from all communication with Brigade. H.Q. except by runner. During the above the Company of the/H.A.C. which had been attached to the 189th Brigade had rushed the MOUND under cover of T.M.B. and Lewis Gun fire. It was temporarily held up by a machine gun situated on the railway. This gun and party were bombed and all obstruction being at an end along the line of the railway the company pushed on and took up a position into the German third line with another company of the same battalion.
8.35.am	Orders to 4 guns T.M.B. to assist infantry on the left. These guns went forward but got stuck in the mud in the German front line and being unable to dig their base plates in, and also owing to the fact that their barrels got choked with mud, took no further part in the action.

2.

Various parties of the R.Dublin Fusiliers had meanwhile pushed well into the German system of trenches. Lt. Col. Smith who had lost all his H.Q. killed or wounded organised various bombing parties One worked up towards the left and relieving the pressure along the front of his left company the latter was able to push on. Another party under 2nd Lieut Cox moved against a strong point in which was a German Hospital. This was occupied after some fighting and the garrison and 2 machine guns captured. 2nd Lieut Cox was subsequently dangerously wounded leading a further attack. At about this time Father Thornton collected some 30 men and advancing towards the left front managed to capture some German Officers and about 350 men who were hiding in a large dugout. These he and his party successfully brought back.
This brings the situation on the left up to about 9.0.am.
Lt. Commdr. Sprange was with this party and as he had no men with him was detained as Adjutant of the 10/R.D.F. where he did excellent work.

At 8.45am   From reports received from 188th and 189th Inf. Bdes. by telephone conversation B.M.803 was sent to all Units as follows:-
"All appears to be going well. Division on our left is in Station Road. 188th and 189th Inf. Bdes. appeared to have captured most of German third line. When enemy third line is evacuated by advanced brigades 190th brigade will occupy enemy third and second trenches as previously ordered.
It will push forward in close support of advanced brigades and must be prepared to assist in capture of YELLOW LINE."

8.52am   Units reported enemy snipers active in front line shell holes and orders were issued to deal with them.

9.5.am   On receipt of G.157 from Division units were informed that our artillery barrage would remain 150 yards on enemy's side YELLOW LINE.

9.25am   B.M.808. sent to Division. This contained result of liaison officer's report from H.A.C. and Royal Fusiliers and stated that H.A.C. had not suffered severely but that estimated casualties of Royal Fusiliers were 11 officers and 350 O.R. and that enemy's first, second and third lines not completely mopped up.

9.50.am   2.Officers Royal Fusiliers were sent up as reinforcements on receipt of request from that battalion.

9.52.   The question of moving forward 190th Inf. Bde. Hd.Qrs. came up with Division and it was pointed out that it was not possible to move into German system until it had been captured.

9.55.am   B.M.811. sent out, that liaison officers 189th Bde. reports that portion of that bde. has pushed forward to YELLOW LINE time 9am This information was sent to Division.

10.8.   B.M.812. to Division asking that 51st Division might be asked to assist the R.Dublin Fusiliers who were being held up by enfilade fire from their left flank. This request was answered by Division in their G.154 received at 10.42.
Word was now received that three companies of H.A.C. had reached GREEN LINE and were digging themselves in.

10.20.   Headquarters H.A.C. moved to GREEN LINE.

3.

Time	Entry

10.30.am   Following message sent out:-
"188th Bde. has occupied YELLOW LINE and ~~destroyed~~ is throwing back its left flank. H.A.C. will at once push forward in close support and will assist in consolidating YELLOW LINE. Royal Fus. to push up and turn enemy's left flank opposite 188th Bde. Troops will take up all the S.A.A. and Bombs they can carry."

10.40   Message received from 4/Bedfordshire Regt. time 5.30 a.m through 188th Bde. advanced report centre.
"As previously reported have been held up all day in enemy's 2nd line with about 20 men. I have made three attempts to get forward but have been stopped each time by sniping and M.G. from my RIGHT flank. losing some men, adjutant and and Signalling Officer killed. I can therefore give no report as to the Bn. but understand that a good proportion have got ~~for~~ forward and will go myself later"

10.45.   First situation map sent to 63rd Division showing advanced position of portion of 189th Bde. and positions of Germans on their 3rd Line.
About this time H.A.C. reported that a message was received from Capt Ellis Commanding "A" Coy. that he was on GREEN LINE. that he had captured 5 officers and good bag of prisoners and 1 M.G.. His casualties were severe.

10.45.   Received message that at 9.10am that our shells were falling short at BEAUCOURT. The artillery liaison officer was informed.

10.50.am   B,M.850. to Units as follows except H.A.C.:-
"Push on at all costs as 188th Bde. has similar instructions. It is imperative that you push on with 188th and join up with Left of 189th.

11.0.am   Orders to H.A.C. and 7/Royal Fusiliers for the former to organise bombing parties to work along the German trenches and take the Germans in flank and so permit the Royal Fusiliers to advance.

11.27.   Informed Division tat 188th and 189th in conversation had reported that GREEN LINE was held by a mixture of all three Bdes.

12.22   Information came from liaison officer that "No Man's Land" was being swept by Machine Gun fire from Across the river South of us. This was reported to Division B.M.819. Wire received G.160 from Division that 39th Division South of ANCRE had been informed.
During the morning the M.G.Coy. had pushed a half section up in support of each battalion. Those supporting the 3 left battalions did good work and attempted in the mist to take on the German Machine Guns. They all lost heavily and were eventually held up. The section on the right following the H.A.C. finally established itself about STATION ROAD. Having one gun knocked out, a captured German gun was brought into action and did good work. This section was handled very well by Lt.Goldingham.
Capt. Bastin during the morning took the remaining two sections in to the German lines, but coming under heavy fire was himself killed and his guns, crew decimated.

12.25.pm   Orders to H.A.C. to move forward to support troops on YELLOW LINE and to cancel the operation for taking the Germans in left flank.
This was the result of an order from Division.
Lt.Col.Freyberg said that he did not require those reinforcements and sent them back.

1.30   Message from O.C.Bedfords that there was great confusion in the deep mud in the German 2nd line but that he and as many men as he could collect were trying to push forward.

2.10.   2nd Situation map sent to Division showing Germans holding practically all 3rd line trenches and about ½ 2nd line trenches that G.O.C. 188th reports he can only just hold his own and that men have run out of bombs.

4.

.15.	H.A.C. request extra officers to be sent up. 5 additional officers were sent up by D.H.Q. About this time the H.A.C. sent an officer to Lt Colo Froyberg commanding "Hood" Bn. on YELLOW LINE, who stated that he was going to stay where he was and required no help except carrying parties. Lt. Gilliland R.N.V.R., who had reported with some 100 men to H.A.C. with a view to rejoining "Hood" Bn undertook this carrying.
3.15.	Informed by Division on Telephone that 10 minutes barrage was about to be put on enemy 3rd line commencing 3.45.pm; all troops must take advantage of this barrage to move forward. On receipt of this B.M.824 and 825 were sent out, warning Bns. of the above orders. Units did not receive this information until after the barrage was over.
.0.pm	On representations of units, who were calling for bombs, ammunition and water, and owing to the fact that, except H.A.C. all units were so involved with the enemy in enemy front line trenches, that it was impossible to collect carrying parties from them, the Division was asked (B.M.826) to collect and send up all details left behind at HEDAUVILLE and send them to Bde. Hd. Qrs. where they would be organised into carrying parties to work between dump and units. In reply to this Q.120 from the Division, timed 6.30.pm, stated that 100 men were on their way up.
25.pm	B.M.828 sent to 4/Bedfordshire Regt. and 10/R.Dublin Fus. as follows:- "You should withdraw your Hd.Qrs. to our original line until enemy first system has been cleared up. The 4/Bedfordshire Regt H.Q. to 2nd Tunnel from our RIGHT, 10/R.D.F. 3rd Tunnel from RIGHT, am laying telephones to these places from TELEPHONE POST. Reorganise your Bns. and collect all those lying about in shell holes etc. The ground won must be held at all costs and when reorganised you must make every endeavour to turn the enemy out of the trenches this side of the GREEN LINE, which he still holds, then get forward to the GREEN LINE. All well on our RIGHT, the YELLOW LINE is held and a fresh Brigade is being sent up to help to consolidate it. LEFT must make every endeavour to get forward to GREEN LINE"
5.10pm	On request from H.A.C. a telephone line was run out to his Hd. Qrs. on GREEN LINE. This was so frequently cut that it was finally abandoned and a forward runner relay post established vide Appendix "C".
6.20.pm	Informed through 189th Inf. Bde. Liaison Officer that 189th and portion of H.A.C. were in BEAUCOURT.
.40.pm	As result of a telephone message from the Division and conversation with 189th Inf. Bde. the following message (BM 829) was sent to H.A.C:- "Engineer and Pioneer Parties are now carrying tools to your Hd.Qrs., keep them for digging. One of the new Bns. it appears, is going to YELLOW the other to GREEN LINE; in the meanwhile 189th wish you to carry on consolidating GREEN and NOT communication trench to YELLOW. As soon as the two new Bns. have come up you will withdraw, reorganise your Bn. and organise parties for sweeping N.W. up the enemy 2nd and 3rd trenches and round up the enemy still holding out in them" About this time Division informed up that TANKS would operate in the morning to deal with enemy's strong points in first enemy system.
9.30.pm	Conforming with verbal orders from 63rd Division that an attack on the RED LINE was to be launched on the 14th inst, the following orders were issued to H.A.C. :- "The 190th Inf. Bde. will take over the GREEN LINE from Q.12a.7.1. to Q.11.d.7.7. tonight with 111th Brigade on their RIGHT and 51st Division on LEFT.

5.

We shall attack tomorrow in conjunction with above. Orders later.
H.A.C. *** occupy GREEN LINE from Q.12.a.7.1. to STATION ALLEY inclusive. Report when in position with whole Bn. and also strength of Bn. Bombs and S.A.A. are being sent up.
Report position of new Bn. Hd. Qrs. in GREEN LINE"
To 7/R.F., 4/Bed., 10/R.D.F.

"O.Cs. to report to G.O.C. 190th Infantry Brigade at H.Q. 188th Inf. Bde. KNIGHTSBRIDGE at once"
I proceeded to KNIGHTSBRIDGE meeting O.C.4/Bedfordshire Regt. and 7/R.F.. Explained what was required with reference to the attack and sent them off at once to collect all the men they could and proceed to the GREEN LINE via advanced Divisional DUMP on the BEAUCOURT where they would replenish bombs and S.A.A. and so proceed to take up position in rear of H.A.C. preparatory to the attack.

12.midnight At 12 midnight 13/14th as O.C.10/R.D.F. had not arrived I returned to MESNIL and sent the following Signal to 10/R.D.F.:-
"Pull all your men out of the line forthwith and report with all you can get at HAMEL to Bde. Hd.Qrs. which is moving to the POTTAGE TRENCH Hd.Qrs. in HAMEL.
Most important you should get them there as soon as possible.
Send an officer in advance to receive orders.
Division was asked on telephone is the Brigade night attack on the RIGHT instead of on the LEFT for the following reasons:-
(1) Because the H.A.C. were in position on the RIGHT of the line.
(2) Because units moving up to get into position for attack would have to pass round the RIGHT of the Line in order to replenish from the advanced Divisional Dump.
(3) As this Division was already occupying the RIGHT of YELLOW LINE it would save a future mixture of Divisions.
This was approved and orders issued accordingly.
The H.A.C. had been ordered to remain on the RIGHT of the line pending further orders.

14th Nov. 1916. am Order No. 70 received from Division at   am on which Bde. Order No.37 was written and a copy of this was forwarded to D.H.Q.
This was received by H.A.C. at 3.45.am and by other Bns. as they passed through Bde. Hd. Qrs. on their way to the forming up place.

2.25am Bde. Hd. Qrs. established in HAMEL and report sent to D.H.Q

4.32.am G.187 received from Division reporting one Bn. of 111th Bde. in position on YELLOW LINE and giving directions re Barrage, which were passed to artillery liaison officer.

5.5.am B.M.836 (morning report) sent to Division:-
"Wind light a.t.s, Very misty, but not quite so bad as yesterday. Situation 189th and 111th Bde. hold RIGHT of YELLOW LINE, GREEN LINE held by us.
Portions of enemy 1st 2nd and 3rd Line partly held by us and partly by enemy. 190th Bde. getting into position as follows, H.A.C. on RIGHT of GREEN LINE numbers not known, in rear 7/R.F. about 70, 4/Bedfordshire Regt about 40. 10/R.D.F. about 50. In rear of these attached Engineers and Pioneers".

6.0am In effect the attack of the 190th Inf. Bde. was carried out by about the following numbers:-
1/H.A.C. ~~about 400~~ in front about 400.
7/R.F. in support about 80.
The 10/R.D.F. about 18. and 4/Bedfordshire Regt about 53 did not arrive in time to advance at ZERO hour, but followed shortly after and turned themselves into carrying parties.

Time	
8.25.am	B.M.839 sent to Division stating that Tanks had captured about 200 prisoners in enemy front system and that the two Medical ~~offic~~ Officers in HAMEL had been killed.

The attack was launched and proceeded up to the line of the "Hood" Trench this side of YELLOW LINE where the RIGHT (H.A.C. and 7/R.F. came under heavy M.G.fire and was for a short time held up. Capt ELLIS showed great gallantry here in organising his men and was very severely wounded. The LEFT of the H.A.C. advanced by crawling by sections and taking the Germans on the YELLOW LINE in flank relieved the pressure in the front and the whole line charged in and captured it. |
| 8.50am | The H.A.C. now pushed through BEAUCOURT and occupied the RED LINE about 8.50am from the ANCRE along the EASTERN outskirts of BEAUCOURT with the 7/R.F. on their LEFT and the K.R.R. again on their LEFT with their LEFT flank thrown back towards thr YELLOW LINE.
The Engineers (attached 190th Bde.) were now employed in making a strong point at R.7.d.6.5., the half Coy. Pioneers having lost both their Officers, Sgt CHERRY took command and under orders issued by Capt MONTAGUE of "Hood"Bn. dug a fire trench from about R.7.a.9.0. to R.7.a.5.3., under a considerable enemy fire. This work was continued until 5pm when the K.R.R. occupied the trench and the Pioneers withdrawn into HAMEL. |
| 10.30.am | Reported to Division "BEAUCOURT surrendered with entire garrison" |
| 10.45.am | 4/Bedfordshire Regt and 10/R.Dublin Fus. ordered to withdraw to the RIGHT of our original front lines except those actually in action in RED LINE, collect together and reorganise as Bns. Food and water sent to this place.
Reported this to Division in B.M.846. |
11.4.am	Received from Division by G.213 position of 51st Division on our LEFT.
1.45.pm	Informed H.A.C. of proposed attack on MUCK TRENCH on his LEFT by /11th Inf. Bde..
4.35.pm	On orders from Division instructed H.A.C. to form a post at Railway Bridge. at R.8.c.4.6.
4.40.pm	Having received notification of disposition of troops and in view of the fact that 190th Bde. was receiving orders from Division as to defence of BEAUCOURT and organisation of BEAUCOURT district, whilst 189th Bde. Hd. Qrs. had been ordered to move to an advanced position in GREEN LINE, sent following wire as there seemed a likelihood of confusion of command arising:-
"B.M.855. Instructions requested as to who is responsible for the line held by 63rd Division and attached Bde..At present I have remains of one Bn. and the ~~12th~~ 111th has 3 Bns. holding front line. 189th has two Bns holding YELLOW LINE in immediate suppo rt of BEAUCOURT. I suggest 111th Bde. takes over command of whole sector as, at present, defence of the important post of BEAUCOURT does not devolve on one Brigadier."
This was answered by the Division that we were to be withdrawn from the line.
6.35.pm	Instructions as to the reorganisation of the sector received from Division and ordering the relief of the troops of the 63rd Division by the 63rd Inf. Bde.

15th Nov.1916

4.30.am   This relief was completed and 190th Inf. Bde. withdrawn to our original First line system by 4.30.am.
As the enemy had placed an heavy artillery barrage on the BEAUCOURT, Artillery Liaison Officer was asked to arrange for counter batteries to deal with it during relief.
This effectually stopped enemy fire and the relief was carried out without a casualty

In concluding the above report I should like to say that while a great many of the difficulties which arose in the handling of the battalions was due to the fact that a thorough organisation did not exist in some of the units, still individual gallantry was conspicuous. This led to a great loss in officers. The 1/H.A.C. on the RIGHT worked excellently by companies and retained to a great extent their organisation and this battalion was ably commanded by Lt.Col.Boyle.
The 10/R.D.Fus and 4/Bedfordshire pushed into the enemy's lines and in the fog soon lost direction and cohesion. The C.Os. of these units gallantly followed their commands into the confusion with the idea of straightening things out. They thus lost touch with Bde. Hd. Qrs. and would have done better to have remained further back.
The 7/Royal Fusiliers in like manner became almost at once heavily involved in the fight and confusion and all these three battalions by the evening of 13th were so mixed up and committed that it was impossible to withdraw them when necessary for the fresh offensive on 14th.
The going was too heavy for the T.M.B.
The M.G.Coy. had little scope. They advanced with the object of rendering what aid they could but became involved in the mist, and confusion, and while the Germans guns trained to sweep areas of ground in defence were effective even in the fog, our machine guns found it difficult to locate the target.
I have nothing but praise for the Engineers and Pioneers who worked splendidly.
Both during the preparation for and in the actual operations, the signallers and runners showed exceptional staunchness and carried out their duties under sometimes very heavy fire.
I am greatly indebted to all the members of my staff for their work, this especially applies to my Brigade Major who has a capacity for work and whose advice was of the greatest assistance

20/11/16.

Brigadier General
Commanding the 190th Infantry Brigade.

APPENDIX
A

Position of 190th Inf. Bde at Zero hour 13th inst.

ROUGH DIAGRAM NOT TO SCALE.

| 10/Royal Dublin Fusiliers. | 4/Bedfordshire Regt. | 7/Royal Fusiliers. | 1/M.A.C. | D Co, 1/M.A.C. attached to 190th Inf. Bde. |

X Hd Qrs
10/R.D.F.

X Hd Qrs 4/Beds.Regt.   Hd Qrs 7/R.F.

X Hd Qrs H.A.C.

2 Sec. M.G.   1 Sec. M.G.

1 Sec. T.M.B.   1 Sec. T.M.B.

2 Secs. M.G.

Hd Qrs
M.G.Coy. X   ⊕ HAMEL
Brigade H.Q. opened
here 2.25 a.m. 14th
inst.

Brigade H.Q. night of 12/13
until 2.25 a.m.14th inst.
⊕ MESNIL
2 Sec. T.M.B.
and Hd Qrs

APPENDIX B.

190th Bde Communications, at Zero.

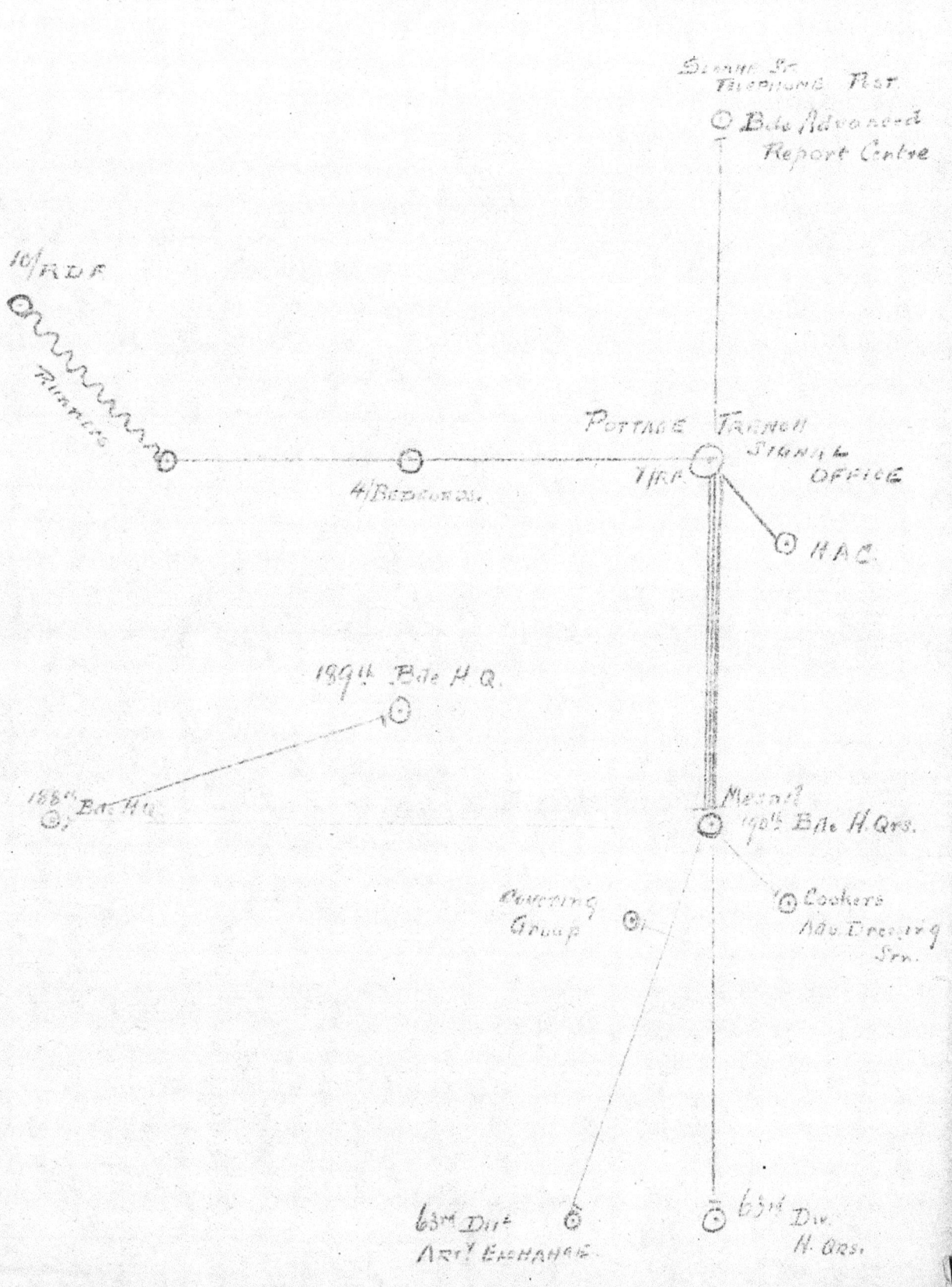

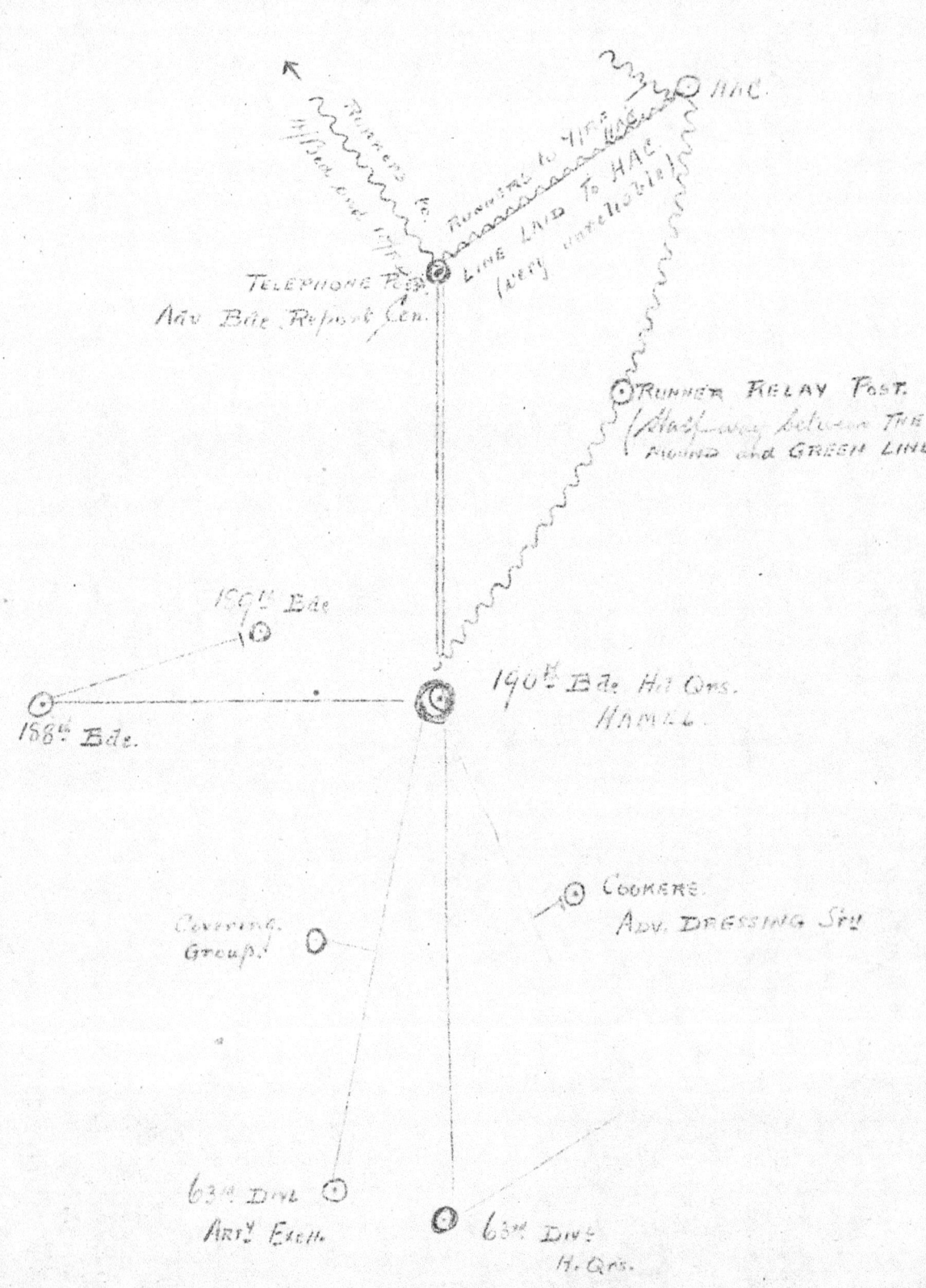

APPENDIX D.

LIAISON OFFICERS.

ARTILLERY,	Lieut-Col. T.A.HIGGINBOTHAM.
do Signals	Lieut. C.J.ROBERTSON.
7/ROYAL FUSILIERS	" A.R.WILSON.
4/BEDFORDSHIRE REGT	" A.J.CLARKE.
10/ROYAL DUBLIN FUSILIERS	" C.ALLGOOD.
1/H.A.C.	" A.R.MALM.
190TH TRENCH MORTAR BATTERY	" R.J.HOLROYD.
189th BRIGADE	CAPT. P.P.COTTON.
188th "	S/Lieut. H.V.HOWARD.

SIGNAL RUNNERS.

The following runners were employed by Brigade Hd Qrs with the Signal Section:-

12 permanent Signal Orderlies	12
2 men per Bn. who reported Y night	8
6 Brigade Scouts	6
TOTAL	26

D TANKS.

Scale: 1/16,000.

EACH GROUP = 2 MACHINES

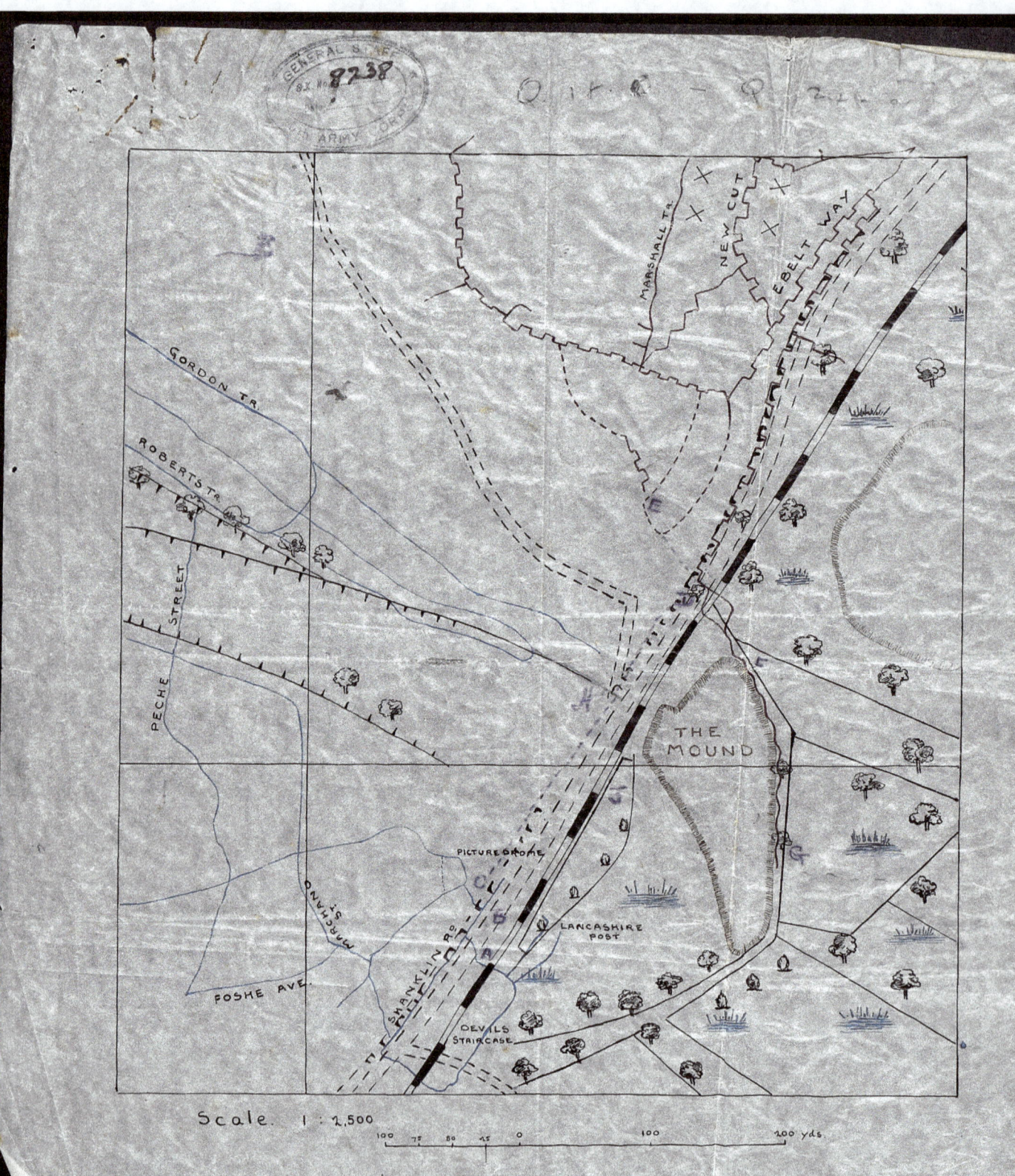

Appendix 36.

Report on the action of 190th Infantry Brigade
during the 13th and 14th November. 1916.
****

The Brigade was formed up vide attached diagram on night 12/13 November ready to move forward at Zero hour 5.45am 13th.

5.45am	Barrage opened and brigade moved forward behind 189th and 188th Inf. Brigades and occupied our original front and Support Line trenches. It was too foggy for landmarks to be picked up and 1/H.A.C in particular had to march by compass.
6.46' or 6.31am	Brigade advanced out of our front line system and moved forward as ordered (Barrage table).
6.40am	Informed Division that visibility was about 50 yards and that the enemy had not opened a barrage. This information was received from Brigade advanced report centre (Telephone Post)
7.5.am	Message from Division (verbal) to send forward one platoon per Battalion to the enemy front line trench as it had been reported it was difficult to take enemy's front line on front of left Brigade. The Brigade had already gone forward according to barrage table so this could not be carried out.
7.29.am	39th Division report their left flank half way to 2nd objective, their centre held up at R.19.c.3.8.
7.40am	H.A.C. report no news of brigade in front. At this hour three Companies of H.A.C. had reached the German reserve lines and digging in. They report having lost touch with 7/R.Fus, on their left. This is accounted for by the fact that the 7/R.Fus. had got up to the German front line and were there held up by machine gun fire. The same thing was happening on the left and except for small parties which managed to get forward the bulk of the 4/Bedfordshire Regt and 10/R.Dublin Fus. were held up in the enemy's front line.
7.45.am	Wired situation to Division (our B.M.800). This however quickly altered, for the H.A.C. were able to push on as above stated.
7.55am	Sent instructions to battalions to take German front lines and that H.A.C. had penetrated to enemy"s 3rd trench on extreme right. Suggested that in rear of H.A.C. would be a good place to push into and spread N.W.
8.0.am	4/Bedfordshire Regt. and 10/R.Dublin Fus. advanced their H.Q. into enemy's lines but as it transpired they became mixed up in the fighting and were cut off from all communication with Brigade. H.Q. except by runner. During the above the Company of the 1/H.A.C. which had been attached to the 189th Brigade had rushed the MOUND under cover of T.M.B. and Lewis Gun fire. It was temporarily held up by a machine gun situated on the railway. This gun and party were bombed and all obstruction being at an end along the line of the railway the company pushed on and took up a position into the German third line with another company of the same battalion.
8.35.am	Orders to 4 guns T.M.B. to assist infantry on the left. These guns went forward but got stuck in the mud in the German front line and being unable to dig their base plates in, and also owing to the fact that their barrels got choked with mud, took no further part in the action.

Various parties of the R.Dublin Fusiliers had meanwhile pushed well into the German system of trenches. Lt. Col. Smith who had lost all his H.Q. killed or wounded organised various bombing parties One worked up towards the left and relieving the pressure along the front of his left company the latter was able to push on. Another party under 2nd Lieut Cox moved against a strong point in which was a German Hospital. This was occupied after some fighting and the garrison and 2 machine guns captured. 2nd Lieut Cox was subsequently dangerously wounded leading a further attack. At about this time Father Thornton collected some 30 men and advancing towards the left front managed to capture some German Officers and about 350 men who were hiding in a large dugout. These he and his party successfully brought back.
This brings the situation on the left up to about 9.0.am.
Lt. Commdr. Sprange was with this party and as he had no men with him was detained as Adjutant of the 10/R.D.F. where he did excellent work.

At 8.45am — From reports received from 188th and 189th Inf. Bdes. by telephone conversation B.M.803 was sent to all Units as follows:-
"All appears to be going well. Division on our left is in Station Road. 188th and 189th Inf. Bdes. appeared to have captured most of German third line. When enemy third line is evacuated by Advanced brigades 190th brigade will occupy enemy third and second trenches as previously ordered.
It will push forward in close support of advanced brigades and must be prepared to assist in capture of YELLOW LINE."

8.52am — Units reported enemy snipers active in front line shell holes and orders were issued to deal with them.

9.5.am — On receipt of G.157 from Division units were informed that our artillery barrage would remain 150 yards on enemy's side YELLOW LINE.

9.25am — B.M.808. sent to Division. This contained result of liaison officer's report from H.A.C. and Royal Fusiliers and stated that H.A.C. had not suffered severely but that estimated casualties of Royal Fusiliers were 11 officers and 350 O.R. and that enemy's first, second and third lines not completely mopped up.

9.50.am — 2.Officers Royal Fusiliers were sent up as reinforcements on receipt of request from that battalion.

9.52. — The question of moving forward 190th Inf. Bde. Hd.Qrs. came up with Division and it was pointed out that it was not possible to move into German system until it had been captured.

9.55.am — B.M.811. sent out, that liaison officers 189th Bde. reports that portion of that bde. has pushed forward to YELLOW LINE time 9am This information was sent to Division.

10.8. — B.M.812. to Division asking that 51st Division might be asked to assist the R.Dublin Fusiliers who were being held up by enfilade fire from their left flank. This request was answered by Division in their G.154 received at 10.42.
Word was now received that three companies of H.A.C. had reached GREEN LINE and were digging themselves in.

10.20. — Headquarters H.A.C. moved to GREEN LINE.

3.

Time	
10.30.am	Following message sent out:- "189th Bde. has occupied YELLOW LINE and ~~destroyed~~ is throwing back its left flank. H.A.C. will at once push forward in close support and will assist in consolidating YELLOW LINE. Royal Fus. to push up and turn enemy's left flank opposite 188th Bde. Troops will take up all the S.A.A. and Bombs they can carry."
10.40	Message received from 4/Bedfordshire Regt. time 5.30.a. through 188th Bde. advanced report centre. "As previously reported have been held up all day in enemy's 2nd line with about 20 men. I have made three attempts to get forward but have been stopped each time by sniping and M.G. from my RIGHT. flank. losing some men, adjutant and and Signalling Officer killed. I can therefore give no report as to the Bn. but understand that a good proportion have got ~~for~~ forward and will go myself later"
10.45.	First situation map sent to 63rd Division showing advanced position of portion of 189th Bde. and positions of Germans on their 3rd Line. About this time H.A.C. reported that a message was received from Capt Ellis Commanding "A" Coy. that he was on GREEN LINE that he had captured 5 officers and good bag of prisoners and 1 M.G.. His casualties were severe.
10.45.	Received message that at 9.10am that our shells were falling short at BEAUCOURT. The artillery liaison officer was informed.
10.50.am	B,M.850. to Units as follows except H.A.C.:- "Push on at all costs as 188th Bde. has similar instructions. It is imperative that you push on with 188th and join up with Left of 189th.
11.0.am	Orders to H.A.C. and 7/Royal Fusiliers for the former to organise bombing parties to work along the German trenches and take the Germans in flank and so permit the Royal Fusiliers to advance.
11.27.	Informed Division that 188th and 189th in conversation had reported that GREEN LINE was held by a mixture of all three Bdes.
12.22	Information came from liaison officer that "No Man's Land" was being swept by Machine Gun fire from across the river South of us. This was reported to Division B.M.819. Wire received G.160 from Division that 39th Division South of ANCRE had been informed. During the morning the M.G.Coy. had pushed a half section up in support of each battalion. Those supporting the 3 left battalions did good work and attempted in the mist to take on the German Machine Guns. They all lost heavily and were eventually held up. The section on the right following the H.A.C. finally established itself about STATION ROAD. Having one gun knocked out, a captured German gun was brought into action and did good work. This section was handled very well by Lt.Goldingham. Capt. Bastin during the morning took the remaining two sections well in to the German lines, but coming under heavy fire was himself killed and his guns, crew decimated.
12.25.pm	Orders to H.A.C. to move forward to support troops on YELLOW LINE and to cancel the operation for taking the Germans in left flank. This was the result of an order from Division. Lt.Col.Freyberg said that he did not require these reinforcements and sent them back.
1.30	Message from O.C.Bedfords that there was great confusion in the deep mud in the German 2nd line but that he and as many men as he could collect were trying to push forward.
2.10.	2nd Situation map sent to Division showing Germans holding practically all 3rd line trenches and about ½-2nd line trenches that G.O.C. 188th reports he can only just hold his own and that men have run out of bombs.

4.

.15.   H.A.C. request extra officers to be sent up.
5 additional officers were sent up by D.H.Q. About this time the
H.A.C. sent an officer to Lt Col. Freyberg commanding "Hood" Bn.
on YELLOW LINE, who stated that he was going to stay where he was
and required no help except carrying parties.
Lt. Gilliland R.N.V.R., who had reported with some 100 men to
H.A.C. with a view to rejoining "Hood" Bn undertook this carrying.

3.15. Informed by Division on Telephone that 10 minutes barrage was
about to be put on enemy 3rd line commencing 3.45.pm; all troops
must take advantage of this barrage to move forward.
On receipt of this B.M.824 and 825 were sent out, warning Bns.
of the above orders.
Units did not receive this information until after the barrage was
over.

.0.pm On representations of units, who were calling for bombs, ammunition
and water, and owing to the fact that, except H.A.C. all units were
so involved with the enemy in enemy front line trenches, that it
was impossible to collect carrying parties from them, the
Division was asked (B.M.826) to collect and send up all details
left behind at HEDAUVILLE and send them to Bde. Hd. Qrs. where they
would be organised into carrying parties to work between dump and
units. In reply to this Q.120 from the Division, timed 6.30.pm,
stated that 100 men were on their way up.

25.pm B.M.828 sent to 4/Bedfordshire Regt. and 10/R.Dublin Fus. as
follows:-
"You should withdraw your Hd.Qrs. to our original line until
enemy first system has been cleared up. The 4/Bedfordshire
Regt H.Q. to 2nd Tunnel from our RIGHT, 10/R.D.F. 3rd Tunnel
from RIGHT, am laying telephones to those places from TELEPHONE
POST. Reorganise your Bns. and collect all those lying about in
shell holes etc. The ground won must be held at all costs and when
reorganised you must make every endeavour to turn the enemy out
of the trenches this side of the GREEN LINE, which he still holds,
then get forward to the GREEN LINE.
All well on our RIGHT, the YELLOW LINE is held and a fresh Brigade
is being sent up to help to consolidate it. LEFT must make every
endeavour to get forward to GREEN LINE"

.10pm On request from H.A.C. a telephone line was run out to his Hd.
Qrs. on GREEN LINE. This was so frequently cut that it was finally
abandoned and a forward runner relay post established vide Appendix
"C".

.20.pm Informed through 189th Inf. Bde. Liaison Officer that 189th and
portion of H.A.C. were in BEAUCOURT.

.40.pm As usual result of a telephone message from the Division and
conversation with 189th Inf. Bde. the following message (BM 829)
was sent to H.A.C:-
"Engineer and Pioneer Parties are now carrying tools to your
Hd.Qrs., keep them for digging.
One of the new Bns. it appears, is going to YELLOW the other to
GREEN LINE; in the meanwhile 189th wish you to carry on consolidating GREEN and NOT communication trench to YELLOW.
As soon as the two new Bns. have come up you will withdraw,
reorganise your Bn. and organise parties for sweeping N.W. up the
enemy 2nd and 3rd trenches and round up the enmy still holding
out in them"
About this time Division informed up that TANKS would operate in
the morning to deal with enemy's strong points in first enemy
system.

.30.pm Conforming with verbal orders from 63rd Division that an attack
on the RED LINE was to be launched on the 14th inst, the following
orders were issued to H.A.C. :-
"The 190th Inf. Bde.will take over the GREEN LINE from
Q.12a.7.1. to Q.11.d.7.7. tonight with 111th Brigade on their
RIGHT and 51st Division on LEFT.

5.

We shall attack tomorrow in conjunction with above. Orders later.
H.A.C. will occupy GREEN LINE from Q.12.a.7.1. to STATION ALLEY
inclusive. Report when in position with whole Bn. and also strength
of Bn. Bombs and S.A.A. are being sent up.
Report position of new Bn. Hd. Qrs. in GREEN LINE"
To 7/R.F.,4/Bed., 10/R.D.F.
    "O.Cs. to report to G.O.C. 190th Infantry Brigade at H.Q.
188th Inf. Bde. KNIGHTSBRIDGE at once"
I proceeded to KNIGHTSBRIDGE meeting O.C.4/Bedfordshire Regt.
and 7/R.F.. Explained what was required with reference to the
attack and sent them off at once to collect all the men they
could and proceed to the GREEN LINE via advanced Divisional
DUMP on the BEAUCOURT where they would replenish bombs and S.A.A.
and so proceed to take up position in rear of H.A.C. preparatory
to the attack.

12.midnight   At 12 midnight 13/14th as O.C.10/R.D.F. had not arrived I returned
to MESNIL and sent the following Signal to 10/R.D.F.:-
    "Pull all your men out of the line forthwith and report with
all you can get at HAMEL to Bde. Hd.Qrs. which is moving to the
POTTAGE TRENCH Hd.Qrs. in HAMEL.
Most important you should get them there as soon as possible.
Send an officer in advance to receive orders.
Division was asked on telephone is the Brigade night attack on
the RIGHT instead of on the LEFT for the following reasons:-
    (1) Because the H.A.C. were in position on the RIGHT of the
line.
    (2) Because units moving up to get into position for attack
would have to pass round the RIGHT of the Line in order to
replenish from the advanced Divisional Dump.
    (3) As this Division was already occupying the RIGHT of
YELLOW LINE it would save a future mixture of Divisions.
This was approved and orders issued accordingly.
The H.A.C. had been ordered to remain on the RIGHT of the line
pending further orders.

14th Nov.
1916.
12.30am   Order No. 70 received from Division at 12.30am on which Bde.
            Order No.37 was written and a copy of this was forwarded to
            D.H.Q.
            This was received by H.A.C. at 3.45.am and by other Bns. as they
            passed through Bde. Hd. Qrs. on their way to the forming up
            place.

2.25am   Bde. Hd. Qrs. established in HAMEL and report sent to D.H.Q

4.32.am   G.187 received from Division reporting one Bn. of 111th Bde. in
            position on YELLOW LINE and giving directions re barrage, which
            were passed to artillery liaison officer.

5.5.am   B.M.836 (morning report) sent to Division:-
            "Wind light airs, Very misty, but not quite so bad as yesterday.
            Situation 189th and 111th Bde. hold RIGHT of YELLOW LINE,
            GREEN LINE held by us.
            Portions of enemy 1st 2nd and 3rd Line partly held by us
            and partly by enemy. 190th Bde. getting into position as
            follows, H.A.C. on RIGHT of GREEN LINE numbers not known, in
            rear 7/R.F. about 70, 4/Bedfordshire Regt about 40. 10/R.D.F.
            about 50. In rear of these attached Engineers and Pioneers".

6.0am In effect the attack of the 190th Inf. Bde. was carried out by about
      the following numbers:-
            1/H.A.C.   in front about 400.
            7/R.F.   in support about 80.
      The 10/R.D.F. about 18. and 4/Bedfordshire Regt about 53
did not arrive in time to advance at ZERO hour, but followed
shortly after and turned themselves into carrying parties.

8.25.am	B.M.839 sent to Division stating that Tanks had captured about 200 prisoners in enemy front system and that the two Medical Officers in HAMEL had been killed.
	The attack was launched and proceeded up to the line of the "Hood" Trench this side of YELLOW LINE where the RIGHT (H.A.C. and 7/R.F.) came under heavy L.G. fire and was for a short time held up. Capt ELLIS showed great gallantry here in organising his men and was very severely wounded. The LEFT of the H.A.C. advanced by crawling by sections and taking the Germans on the YELLOW LINE in flank relieved the pressure in the front and the whole line charged in and captured it.
8.50am	The H.A.C. now pushed through BEAUCOURT and occupied the RED LINE about 8.50am from the ANCRE along the EASTERN outskirts of BEAUCOURT with the 7/R.F. on their LEFT and the K.R.R. again on their LEFT with their LEFT flank thrown back towards thr YELLOW LINE.
	The Engineers (attached 190th Bde.) were now employed in making a strong point at R.7.d.8.5., the half Coy. Pioneers having lost both their Officers, Sgt CHERRY took command and under orders issued by Capt MONTAGUE of "Hood" Bn. dug a fire trench from about R.7.a.9.0. to R.7.a.5.3., under a considerable enemy fire. This work was continued until 5pm when the K.R.R. occupied the trench and the Pioneers withdrawn into HAMEL.
10.30.am	Reported to Division "BEAUCOURT surrendered with entire garrison"
10.45.am	4/Bedfordshire Regt and 10/R.Dublin Fus. ordered to withdraw to the RIGHT of our original front lines except those actually in action in RED LINE, collect together and reorganise as Bns. Food and water sent to this place.
	Reported this to Division in B.M.846.
11.4.am	Received from Division by G.213 position of 51st Division on our LEFT.
1.45.pm	Informed H.A.C. of proposed attack on MUCK TRENCH on his LEFT by /11th Inf. Bde..
4.35.pm	On orders from Division instructed H.A.C. to form a post at Railway Bridge at R.8.c.4.6.
4.40.pm	Having received notification of disposition of troops and in view of the fact that 190th Bde. was receiving orders from Division as to defence of BEAUCOURT and organisation of BEAUCOURT district, whilst 189th Bde. Hd. Qrs. had been ordered to move to an advanced position in GREEN LINE, sent following wire as there seemed a likelihood of confusion of command arising:-
	"B.M.855. Instructions requested as to who is responsible for the line held by 63rd Division and attached Bde.. At present I have remains of one Bn. and the 111th has 3 Bns. holding front line. 189th has two Bns holding YELLOW LINE in immediate support of BEAUCOURT. I suggest 111th Bde. takes over command of whole sector as, at present, defence of the important post of BEAUCOURT does not devolve on one Brigadier."
	This was answered by the Division that we were to be withdrawn from the line.
6.35.pm	Instructions as to the reorganisation of the sector received from Division and ordering the relief of the troops of the 63rd Division by the 63rd Inf. Bde.

15th Nov.1916

4.30.am   This relief was completed and 190th Inf. Bde. withdrawn to our original First line system by 4.30.am.
As the enemy had placed an heavy artillery barrage on the BEAUCOURT, Artillery Liaison Officer was asked to arrange for counter batteries to deal with it during relief.
This effectually stopped enemy fire and the relief was carried out without a casualty

In concluding the above report I should like to say that while a great many of the difficulties which arose in the handling of the battalions was due to the fact that a thorough organisation did not exist in some of the units, still individual gallantry was conspicuous. This led to a great loss in officers. The 1/H.A.C. on the RIGHT worked excellently by companies and retained to a great extent their organisation and this battalion was ably commanded by Lt.Col.Boyle.
The 10/R.D.Fus and 4/Bedfordshire pushed into the enemy's lines and in the fog soon lost direction and cohesion. The C.Os. of these units gallantly followed their commands into the confusion with the idea of straightening things out. They thus lost touch with Bde. Hd. Qrs. and would have done better to have remained further back.
The 7/Royal Fusiliers in like manner became almost at once heavily involved in the fight and confusion and all these three battalions by the evening of 13th were so mixed up and committed that it was impossible to withdraw them when necessary for the fresh offensive on 14th.
The going was too heavy for the T.M.B.
The M.G.Coy. had little scope. They advanced with the object of rendering what aid they could but became involved in the mist, and confusion, and while the Germans guns trained to sweep areas of ground in defence were effective even in the fog, our machine guns found it difficult to locate the target.
I have nothing but praise for the Engineers and Pioneers who worked splendidly.
Both during the preparation for and in the actual operations, the signallers and runners showed exceptional staunchness and carried out their duties under sometimes very heavy fire.
I am greatly indebted to all the members of my staff for their work, this especially applies to my Brigade Major who has a capacity for work and whose advice was of the greatest assistance

Brigadier General
Commanding the 190th Infantry Brigade.

20/11/16.

APPENDIX

A.

Position of 100th Inf. Bde. at Zero Hour 13th inst.

NON: LINGHAM ROAD TO EWALD.

10/Royal Dublin   2/Hertford-   7/Royal   1 A.A.C.   A Coy. 1/A.A.C. attached to
Fusiliers.   shire Regt.   Fusiliers.   13th Inf. Bde.

✗ Hd Qrs
  10/R.D.F.

                          ─── ─── ─── ───
                          ─── ─── ─── ───
                          ─── ─── ─── ───
                          ─── ─── ─── ───

                                    ✗ Hd Qrs M.A.C.

1 Sec. M.G.   Hd Qrs 2/Beds.Regt   Hd Qrs 7/R.F.   1 Sec. M.G.
      ●   ●

1 Sec. T.M.B.   1 Sec. T.M.B.
      ●   ●

              2 Secs. M.G.   Hd Qrs   ⊕ H.A.N.B.
                   ●   M.G.Coy. ✗   Brigade H.Q. night of 12/13
                                                                   until 2.25 a.m. 14th inst.
                                                               ⊕ MESNIL
                                                     2 Sec. T.M.B.   Brigade H.Q. opened
                                                     and Hd Qrs   here 2.25 a.m. 14th
                                                                     inst.

APPENDIX B.

190th Bde Communications at Zero.

Sloan St.
Trenchers Post
◎ Bde Advanced
Report Centre

10/RDF
◎ ⌇⌇⌇⌇⌇
Runners

POTTAGE TRENCH
────────◎────────◎──── 7/RF ◎ SIGNAL OFFICE
4/Bedfords
◎ H.A.C.

189th Bde H.Q.
◎

188th Bde H.Q.
◎

Mesnil
◎ 190th Bde H.Qrs.

Covering
Group ◎

◎ Cookers
Advd Dressing
Stn.

62nd Div ◎
Artl Exchange

◎ 63rd Div
H. Qrs.

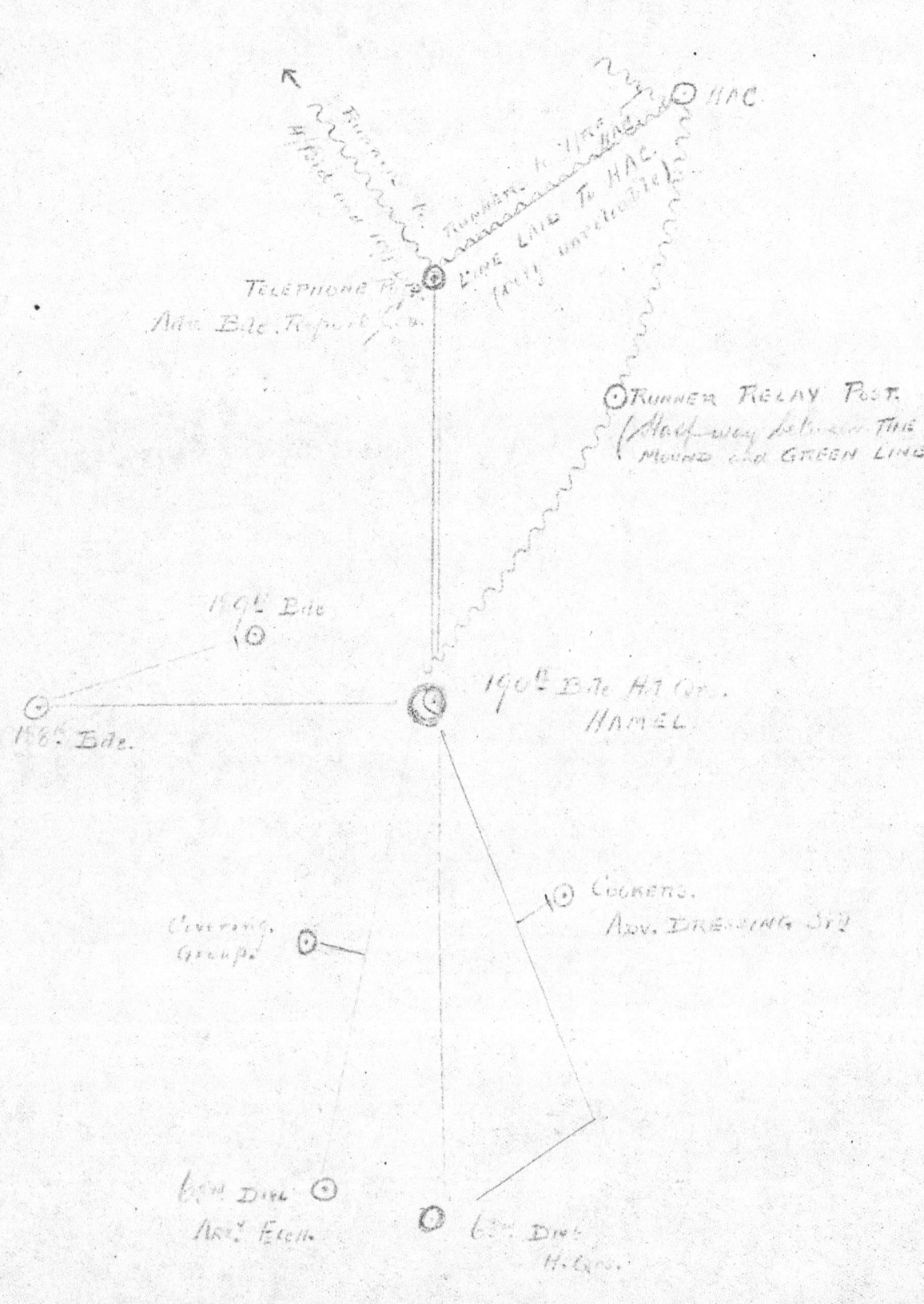

APPENDIX D.

LIAISON OFFICERS.

ARTILLERY,	Lieut-Col. T.A.HIGGINBOTHAM.
do Signals	Lieut. C.J.ROBERTSON.
7/ROYAL FUSILIERS	" A.H.WILSON.
4/BEDFORDSHIRE REGT	" A.J.CLARKE.
10/ROYAL DUBLIN FUSILIERS	" C.ALLGOOD.
1/H.A.C.	" H.N.HALL.
190TH TRENCH MORTAR BATTERY	" R.E.HOLROYD.
189th BRIGADE	CAPT. P.P.COTTON.
188th "	S/Lieut. H.V.HOWARD.

SIGNAL RUNNERS.

The following runners were employed by Brigade Hd Qrs with the Signal Section:-

12 permanent Signal Orderlies	12
2 men per Bn. who reported Y night	8
6 Brigade Scouts	6
TOTAL	26

HAMEL–BEAUCOURT ROAD

DIAGRAM SKETCH FROM Q.23.d.35 TO Q.18.c.52.

NO SCALE

Copy Appendix 87

190th Infantry Brigade Order No.38.

14/11/16

Ref: Maps as for Order No.37.

1. Advance on RED LINE will be continued to day.

2. ZERO. 6.0.am.

3. 111th Inf. Bde. will be on LEFT.
   190th " " on RIGHT.
   189th and 189th will support 111th and 190th respectively.

4. Objectives:—

Brigade.	YELLOW LINE	RED LINE.
111th	Q.6.c.9.3. to R.7.a.1.3.	From junction of MUCK TRENCH and LEAVE ALLY to R 7.a.5.4.
190th	R.7.a.1.3. to junction RAILWAY AV. and BEAUCOURT TR. inclusive.	R.7.a.5.4. to a line drawn round EASTERN outskirts of BEAUCOURT.

5. For advance beyond YELLOW LINE 190th Inf. Bde. will be assisted by HOOD BN and other units of 189th Inf. Bde. holding and supporting YELLOW LINE.
The BN. of the 111th Bde. now in YELLOW LINE will rejoin its Bde. on that line being captured.

6. As soon as RED LINE has been captured, Battle Patrols will be sent out as previously ordered.

7. 1/H.A.C. will occupy frontage allotted to 190th Inf. Bde. Remaining Infantry of 190th Inf. Bde will form up in STATION ROAD in rear of 1/H.A.C.
   7/Royal Fus. on RIGHT.
   4/Bedfordshire
        Regt. in..CENTRE.
   10/R.Dublin
        Fus...on LEFT.
Engineers and Pioneers immediately in rear of Brigade.

8. At ZERO hour H.A.C. in 4 waves will advance followed in close support by remainder.

9. Barrage Table attached.

10. O.C.190th M.G.Coy will collect guns and send them up to RED LINE in rear of bde.

11. The H.A.C. will detail 3rd wave for mopping up BEAUCOURT TRENCH.

12. Units other than H.A.C. will carry up all available tools and bombs.

13. Engineers will at once assist in putting BEAUCOURT in a state of defence.

14. Brigade Hd. Qrs. will be at "POTTAGE Hd. Qrs. at HAMEL.

C.F.Jerram Major.
Brigade Major.

7/Royal Fusiliers   1/H.A.C.
4/Bedfordshire Regt.   HOOD Bn.
10/R.Dublin Fus.   Engineers)
                         Pioneers) 63rd Div.
                         63rd Div.
                         Retained
                         111th Bde.
                         M.G.Coy.

BARRAGE TABLE.

Time	Artillery	Infantry.
6. am	Barrage opens 150 yards in front of GREEN LINE.	Leave GREEN LINE
6.2.am	Barrage lift 100x and continues to lift 100x every 5 minutes till YELLOW LINE is reached.	
6.47 am		Complete capture of YELLOW LINE.
6.47 to 7.40am	Barrage remains 150x in front YELLOW LINE.	Halt 1 hour.
7.40. to 7.45am	Pause 5 minutes.	
7.45.	Intense barrage reopens	
7.47.	Barrage lifts 100x and continues lifting 100x every 5 minutes till RED LINE is captured.	Advance from YELLOW LINE.

Then as for Order No.37, except that RED LINE is reached at 8.12.am instead of at 4 hours 12 minutes.

(Copy) APPENDIX 88

190th Infantry Brigade Order No.39.

Headquarters,
190th Infantry Brigade
14th November 1916.

Ref. A.&C.
of Order No.37:

1. All details of and attached to the 190th Infantry Bde will be relieved in the captured enemy positions tonight by 63rd Infantry Brigade.

2. On relief units will withdraw and take up positions as follows in our original trench system:-

   From RIGHT to LOUVERCY ST. exclusive 1/H.A.C.
   LOUVERCY ST. inclusive to
       WORCESTER ST. exclusive.........7/Royal Fusiliers
   From WORCESTER ST inclusive to
       POUND ST exclusive............4/Bedfordshire Rgt.
   POUND ST inclusive to
       SHAFTESBURY LANE exclusive....10/R.Dublin Fus.
   190th M.G.Company in HAMEL.
   190th T.M.Battery at MESNIL for tonight.
   Engineers and Pioneers to HAMEL.

3. Units will be reorganised by Companies; so far as possible, 1 Company behind the other in 4 different lines. Rear of the Brigade will be forward of a line POTTAGE ST-KNIGHTSBRIDGE DUMP.

4. Units will select their own Hd.Qrs. reporting at once Map reference to Bde. Hd. Qrs.

5. Great Coats will be collected by Units.
Food will be arranged for by Bde. H.Q. on receipt of Map Ref. of unit Hd. Qrs. Men must be given all possible rest. Position need not be made a defensive one and the/only sentries required are Gas Sentries on dug-outs.

6. Bde. Hd. Qrs. will remain at POTTAGE ST.

7. Arrangements must be made for giving men all possible rest, reorganisation commencing in morning.

                              C.F.Jerram. Major.
                              Brigade Major.

7/Royal Fusiliers.
4/Bedfordshire Regt.
10/R.Dublin Fusiliers.
1/H.A.C.
190th M.G.Coy.
190th T.M.Battery.
Engineers)
Pioneers)
63rd Division.
188th Inf Bde.
189th Inf. Bde.
111th Inf. Bde.

Copy Appendix 39

190th Infantry Brigade Order No.41.

Headquarters,
190th Infantry Brigade.
18/11/16.

Ref. Map LENS. 1/100,000

1. 190th Infantry Brigade Group will move tomorrow in accordance with attached table.

2. Billeting parties will be sent in advance by all units.

3. Should the loading of blankets etc. ordered to be sent to station not have been finished, the necessary personnel will be left behind to deal with this and will rejoin their units later.

4. Lorries will be available as under :-
   at AUTHIEULE CHURCH at 8.30.am
      1. for Bde. Hd. Qrs.
      1. for 10/R.Dublin Fusiliers.
      1. for 1/H.A.C.
   at BEAUVAL CHURCH at 9.0.am
      1 for 7/Royal Fusiliers.
   at LONGUEVILLETTE CHURCH at 9.15.am
      1. for 4/Bedfordshire Regt.
      1. between M.G.Coy. and T.M.B.
   Units will send guides to these places.

5. Immediately on arrival at new destination, units will send map reference of Headquarters and Transport to new Bde. Hd. Qrs.

6. Senior unit commander in each village will detail a mounted officer to control traffic of this Bde. whilst leaving the town.

7. 3rd Field Coy. will arrive at OCCOCHES tomorrow and will join Bde Group.

8. Bde. Hd.Qrs. will open at OCCOCHES at 4.0.pm

C.F.Jerram, Major.
Brigade Major.

7/Royal Fusiliers
4/Bedfordshire Regt
10/R.Dublin Fusiliers.
1/H.A.C.
190th M.G.Coy.
190th T.M.Battery.
3rd Field Ambulance.
No.4.Coy Div Train.
63rd Division.
Staff Capt.
File
War Diary.

MARCH TABLE.

Unit.	Destination.	Time of Start.	Route.
Bde. Hd. Qrs.	COCQUREL.	1.30.pm	Road NORTH of River.
10/R.Dublin Fus.	OUTREBOIS.	12.30.pm	Road SOUTH of River through HEM.
1/R.M.F.C.	LE MEILLARD.	8.30.am	Road NORTH of River through L'ETOILE. (must be WEST of BOUILLENS Stn. by 9.30.am
4/Bedfordshire Regt.	HEUZECOURT.	10.30.am	FIENVILLERS - BERNAVILLE.
190th M.G.Coy.	OUTREBOIS.	10.30.am	MONPLAISIR.
190th T.M.B.	ditto.	10.45.am	ditto.
7/Royal Fusiliers.	BOISBERGUES.	10.30.am	CANDAS - FIENVILLERS.
3rd Field Ambulance	HEUZECOURT.	9.30.am	CANDAS - BERNAVILLE.
No.4.Coy. Train.	BOISBERGUES-LE QUESNEL Fm.	10.45.am	FIENVILLERS.

War Diary APPENDIX 40

190th Infantry Brigade Order No. 42.   Copy No......

Headquarters,
190th Infantry Brigade.
20/11/16.

Ref. Map LENS 1/100,000

1. The 190th Inf. Bde. Group (less Artillery) will continue its march tomorrow in accordance with attached table.

2. All Units will be WEST of FROHEN-LE-PETIT - HEUZECOURT - BERNAVILLE by noon.

3. An interval of 200 yds. will be maintained between Coys. and 500 yds. between units.

4. Motor lorries will report to Units as follows :-

   1. to 7/Royal Fusiliers.
   1. to 4/Bedfordshire Regt.
   1. to 10/R. Dublin Fusiliers.
   1. to 1/H.A.C.
   1. to Bde. Hd. Qrs.
   1. to M.G. Coy. and T.M. Batt.

   These lorries will complete the move of the unit mentioned and will then report to the new Bde. Hd. Qrs. for orders. The N.C.O. in charge reporting personally to the Staff Capt. Other units requiring the services of lorries will inform Bde. Hd. Qrs. as soon as possible.

5. On arrival in billets units will report the map reference of their Hd. Qrs. and Transport Lines on map LENS 1/100,000 as accurately as possible.

6. The senior Officer in each village will detail a mounted officer to see that units clear the village in the proper order.

7. Bde. Hd. Qrs. will open at PROUVILLE at 3 p.m.

Time issued to Signals... 9.15 pm

Major.

1. 7/Royal Fusiliers.   (BOISBERGUES)   Brigade Major.
2. 4/Bedfordshire Regt   (HEUZECOURT)
3. 10/R. Dublin Fus.   (OUTREBOIS)
4. 1/H.A.C.   (LE MEILLARD)
5. 14/Worcestershire Regt   (AUTHEUX.)
6. 3rd Field Coy.   (LE MEILLARD)
7. 3rd Field Ambulance   (HEUZECOURT)
8. No. 4. Coy. Div. Train.   (BOISBERGUES)
9. 190th M.G. Coy.   (OUTREBOIS)
10. 190th T.M. Battery.   (-do-)
11. Staff Capt.
12. 63rd Division.
File.
    War Diary (3)

TABLE.

Unit.	From	To.	Time of start	Route.
Bde.Hd.Qrs.	OCCOCHES.	PROUVILLE	9.0.am	MÉZEROLES – LE MEILLARD – BERNAVILLE.
No.4.Coy. Train	BOISLEAGUES.	LONGVILLERS.	8.10.am	BERNAVILLE – BEAUMETZ.
7/Royal Fusiliers	--do--	BEAUMETZ.	8.30.am	BERNAVILLE.
4/Bedfordshire Regt	HEUZECOURT	DOMLEGER.	8.10.am	PROUVILLE.
3rd Field Ambulance	HEUZECOURT	AGENVILLE.	8.30.am	--do--
10/R.Dublin Fus.	OUTREBOIS.	BEAUMETZ.	8.15.am	LE MEILLARD.
190th M.G.Coy.	--do--	PROUVILLE.	8.35.am	--do--
190th T.M.B.	--do--	--do--	8.45.am	--do--
1/H.A.C.	LE MEILLARD.	MONTIGNY.	8.10.am	HEUZECOURT (Transport will probably have to go via S.ACHEUL. The short cut should be previously reconnoitred.)
3rd Field Coy.	--do--	BEAUMETZ.	8.30.am	direct.
14/Worcestershire Regt.	AUTHEUX.	PROUVILLE.	9.0.am	5.C (Central) and BERNAVILLE.

Note:- Billeting parties to be sent in advance.
Speed of all units 2¼ miles per hour including usual halts.

APPENDIX 41

Copy No. 18

190th Infantry Brigade Order No.43.

Headquarters,
190th Infantry Brigade.
21/11/16.

Ref. Maps LENS and
ABBEVILLE. 1/100,000

1. The 190th Infantry Brigade will resume its march tomorrow according to the attached table.

2. O.C.No.4.Coy Div. Train will detail motor lorries as follows to be at their respective unit Hd. Qrs 1½ hours before the time unit starts.

        1 to 7/Royal Fusiliers.
        1 to 4/Bedfordshire Regt.
        1 tp 10/R.Dublin Fusiliers.
        1 tp 1/H.A.C.
        1 tp M.G.Coy. (For T.M.B. as well)
        1 to 3rd Field Coy.
        1 to Bde. Hd. Qrs.

Motor lorries will return to No.4. Coy. Div. Train on completion of duty.

3. An interval of 200^X is to be kept between Companies and 200^X between rear company and transport.

4. Rear parties are <u>always</u> to be left to clear up billots. These should consist of men from each Coy. and from Hd. Qrs. all under an officer. On completion of their duty they will follow their Bn. as a formed body under command of the officer.

5. All officers and men are to be in marching order. Great Coats are NEVER to be worn on the march.

6. Units requiring the attendance of an Ambulance will inform the 3rd Field Ambulance as soon as possible.
The O.C. 3rd F.A. will so far as is possible, comply with these requests.

7. The Senior Officer in each village will detail a mounted Officer to see that units clear the village in the proper order.

8. Bde. Hd. Qrs. will open at MAISON-PONTHIEU at 2 pm

Time issued to Signals.. 8.15 pm

Major.
Brigade Major.

1. 7/Royal Fusiliers.
2. 4/Bedfordshire Regt.
3. 10/R.Dublin Fusiliers.
4. 1/H.A.C.
5. 14/Worcestershire Regt.
6. 3rd Field Coy.
7. 3rd Field Ambulance.
8. No.4.Coy. Div. Train.
9. 190th M.G.Coy.
10. 190th T.M.Battery.
11. G.O.C.
12. Staff Capt.
13. 63rd Division.
14. File.
15. War Diary. (3)
16. Sig Section.

MARCH TABLE.

Unit.	From.	To.	Time of start.	Route.
Bde. Hd. Qrs.	PROUVILLE.	MAISON-PONTHIEU.	10.30am	AGENVILLE - CONTEVILLE
No.4.Coy.Train.	--do--	MAISON-PONTHIEU.	10.45.am	AGENVILLE - CONTEVILLE.
14/Worcestershire Regt.	--do--	HEIRMONT.	11.30.am	AGENVILLE - CONTEVILLE and X roads 1 mile S.W. of HIERMONT.
190th M.G.Coy.	--do--	BERNATRE.	12.30.pm	AGENVILLE - CONTEVILLE.
190th T.M.B.	--do--	--do--	12.45.pm	--do--
7/Royal Fusiliers.	BEAUMETZ.	MAISON - PONTHIEU.	11.0.am	--do-- (Picking up 2 Coys on route)
10/R.Dublin Fus.	--do--	CONTEVILLE.	1.15.pm.	AGENVILLE.
3rd Field Ambulance.	AGENVILLE.	NOYELLES.	10.45.am	CONTEVILLE.
3rd Field Coy.	--do--	--do--	11.0.am	--do--
4/Bedfordshire Regt.	DOMLEGER.	--do--	11.05.am	AGENVILLE - CONTEVILLE.
1/H.A.C.	LOUTIGNY.	NEUILLY-LE-DIEU.	10.45.am	AGENVILLE-CONTEVILLE-MAISON

Note:- Starting Point for Transport Troops at PROUVILLE and BEAUMETZ is X roads on AGENVILLE Rd. on a line cutting up in PROUVILLE and S in LONGVILLERS. This point will be marked by a mounted policeman.
(2) billeting parties to be sent on in advance.

APPENDIX 42

190th Infantry Brigade Order No. 44.   Copy No......

Headquarters,
190th Infantry Brigade.
22/11/16.

Ref. Map LENS and
ABBEVILLE 1/100,000.

1. The 190th Infantry Brigade will resume its march tomorrow according to the attached table.

2. The O.C. No. 4 Coy. Div. Train will detail lorries as in Bde. Order No. 43.

3. Paras 3, 4, 5, and 6 of Bde. Order No. 43 are to be observed.

4. 500x distance is to be maintained between units.

5. Units must carefully work out their times for arriving at starting point. It must be remembered that it is just as bad to be too early, as too late.

6. The O.C. 3rd Field Ambulance will detail one motor ambulance to be at X roads CONTEVILLE at 9.0.am.
    This ambulance will follow the Trench Mortar Battery and will pick up any sick who may fall out and are considered too ill to walk.

7. Bde. Hd. Qrs. will open at LAMOTTE - BULEUX at 3.0.pm.

Time issued to Signals........5-30 pm

                                                            . Major.
                                                       Brigade Major.

1. 7/Royal Fusiliers.
2. 4/Bedfordshire Regt.
3. 10/R.Dublin Fusiliers
4. 1/H.A.C.
5. 14/Worcestershire Regt.
6. 3rd Field Coy.
7. 3rd Field Ambulance.
8. No. 4 Coy. Divl Train.
9. 190th M.G.Coy.
10. 190th T.M. Battery.
11. G.O.C.
12. Staff Capt.
13. 63rd Division.
14. File.
15. War Diary. (3)
16. Signal Section.

TABLE.

Unit.	From.	To.	Time for head to pass starting pt.	Route.
4/Bedfordshire Rgt.	NOYELLES	LAMOTTE – BULEUX	9.0.am	BRAILLY – X roads 900x N.E. of FROYELLES Church – CANCHY – N of NEUILLY.
3/Field Coy.	–do–	–do–	9.20.am	–do–
3/Field Ambulance.	–do–	–do–	9.35.am	–do–,,,
No.4.Coy. Train.	MAISON-PONTHIEU.CANCHY		9.45.am 8.30.	
7/Royal Fusiliers.	–do–	CANCHY.	10.0.am	NOYELLES – Then as above.
1/H.A.C.	NEUILLY – LE DIEU.	CANCHY.	10.20.am	MAISON PONTHIEU – Then as above.
Bde. H.Q.	MAISON – PONTHIEU.	LAMOTTE-BULEUX.	10.45.am	–do–
1st/Worcestershire Regt.	HIERMONT.	NEUILLY L'HOPITAL.	10.50.am	NOYELLES – Then as for 4/Bedfordshire Rgt.
10/R.Dublin Fusiliers.	COMTEVILLE.	–do–	11.10.am	–do–
M.G.Coy.	BERNATRE.	CANCHY.	11.30.am	COMTEVILLE – Then as above.
Train.	–do–	–do–	11.45.am	–do–

1. Halts to be made from 10 minutes to clock hour to clock hour.
2. Billeting parties will be sent in advance.
3. Brigade starting point is at Fork roads 600x N. of 2nd L in NOYELLE – EN – CHAUSEE

APPENDIX 43

190th Infantry Brigade Order No.45.   Copy No. 16

Headquarters,
190th Infantry Brigade
23/11/16.

Ref. Map. ABBEVILLE.
1/100000

1. The 190th Infantry Brigade will move into the Training Area tomorrow according to the attached table.

2. Units will have complete, the 200^X between Coys. not being required.

3. Orders for the 10/R.Dublin Fusiliers and 3rd Field Coy. will be issued when it is known where they can go; in the meantime they will stay in present billets.

4. Billeting parties of the 3rd Field Ambulance, 190th M.G.Coy. and 190th T.M.Battery will meet the Staff Capt. or a person deputed by him at the X roads in the Centre of HOLETTES at 10.0am tomorrow when they will be shown their areas. Billeting parties of other units, except as in para.3, will proceed at the same time to the villages alloted to them, and will meet their advanced parties, in each case at the MAIRIE at 10.0am.

5. No troops other than billeting parties of the 190th Inf. Bde. will cross or be on the main ABBEVILLE - NOUVION road until after 11.0.am.

6. O.C.No. 4. Coy Divl. Train will detail motor lorries as for today's march.

7. The O.C. 3rd Field Ambulance will detail one ambulance wagon to follow in rear of troops proceeding to HOLETTES and one in rear of those proceeding to NOUVION.

Major.
Brigade Major

Time issued to Signals..........

1. 7/Royal Fusiliers
2. 4/Bedfordshire Regt.
3. 10/R.Dublin Fusliers.
4. 1/H.A.C.
5. 14/Worcestershire Regt.
6. 3rd Field Coy.
7. 3rd Field Ambulance.
8. No.4.Coy.Div Train.
9. 190th M.G.Coy.
10. 190th T.M.Battery.
11. G.O.C.
12. Staff Capt. (MARTINRUISE NOUVION-EN
13. 63rd Division   PONTHIEU)
14. Bde. Transport Officer. (U 3.)
15. File.
16. War Diary.
17. Signal Section.

TABLE.

Unit.	From	To.	Time of start.	Route.
4/Bedfordshire Regt	LAMOTTE-BULEUX	NOUVION-EN-PONTHIEU (EAST)	12.30.pm	Direct.
1/H.A.C.	CANCHY.	--do-- (WEST)	12.30.pm	X roads 700x N. of 2nd C in CANCHY - LAMOTTE-BULEUX.
Bde. Hd. Qrs.	--do--	--do--	12.45.pm	--do--
7/Royal Fusiliers	--do--	SAILLY-BRAY.	1.0.pm	LAMOTTE-LE TITRE-SAILLY LE SEC (CHAU)
5/Fld. Ambulance.	LAMOTTE-BULEUX	NOLETTE	12.45.pm	LE TITRE - SAILLY LE SEC (CHURCH)
190th M.G.Coy	CANCHY.	--do--	1.15.pm	LAMOTTA - LE TITRE- SAILLY LE SEC.
190th T.M.B.	--do--	--do--	1.25.pm	--do--
No.4.Coy. Train	CANCHY.	~~NOUVELLES-SUR-MER~~ NOUVION-EN-PONTHIEU	7.30.am	LA MOTTE - Jam

Note:- This Coy. must on no account join any troops of 189th Bde. in crossing main ABBEVILLE road, however long it may have to wait.

Headquarters,
190th Infantry Bde.
23/11/16.

Ref. Order No.45.
10/Royal Dublin Fusiliers will move at 2.0.pm to LAMOTTE-BULEUX.

Major.
Brigade Major.

10/R Dublin Fus
7/Royal Fusiliers.
4/Bedfordshire Regt.
1/H.A.C.
14/Worcestershire Regt.
3rd Field Coy.
3rd Field Ambulance.
No.4.Coy Div Train.
190th M.G.Coy.
190th T.M.Battery.
G.O.C.
Staff Capt.
63rd Division.
File.
Bde. Transport Officer.
War Diary (3)
Signal Section.

APPENDIX 44

190th Infantry Brigade Order No.46.   Copy......

Ref. Map. ABBEVILLE.   24/11/16
     1/100,000

1.   The 10/R.Dublin Fusiliers will move to Camp in NOUVION
        -EN-PONTHIEU tomorrow, starting at 1.0.pm.
        The Camp will be pitched by the time they arrive by other
        troops.
        Advanced party will meet Staff Capt. at NOUVION Church at
        1.0.pm.
        The Bn. will move on the next day to NOYELLES-SUR-MER
        starting at 9.30.am.
        Billeting party to proceed two hours ahead.
        The officer of the billeting party will report for orders
        to the Staff Capt., tomorrow evening.

2.   The 3rd Field Coy. R.N.D.E. will move to NOUVION-EN-PONTHIEU
        tomorrow starting at 9.30.am.
        Billeting party to report to Staff Capt. at 8.0.am

        Time issued to Signals......7pm   Major.
                                              Brigade Major.

    1. 7/Royal Fusiliers.
    2. 4/Bedfordshire Regt.
    3. 10/R.Dublin Fusiliers.
    4. 1/H.A.C.
    5. 190th M.G.Coy.
    6. 190th T.M.Battery.
    7. 3rd Field Coy.
    8. 3rd Field Ambulance.
    9. No.4.Coy. Divl. Train.
    10. G.O.C.
    11. Staff Capt.
    12. 63rd Division.
    13. Bde. Transport Officer.
    14. Signal Section.
    15. File.
    16. War Diary.

CASUALTIES FOR NOVEMBER.   Appendix. 45.

Unit.	Killed		Wounded		Missing.		Total.	
	Off.	O.R.	Off.	O.R.	Off.	O.R.	Off.	O.R.
7/Royal Fusiliers	5	41	11	147	0	159	16	347.
4/Bedfordshire Regt	8	50	7	97	0	44	15	191
10/R.Dublin Fusiliers	6	56	9	148	0	54	15	238
1/H.A.C.	2.	40	13	180	1	31	16	251
190th M.G.Coy.	2	9	3	24	0	22	5	55
190th T.M.Battery.	1	3	0	0	0	0	1	3.
TOTAL.	24	179	43	596	1	310	68	1085

Including for Battle of the ANCRE.

Unit	Killed		Wounded		Missing		Total	
7/Royal Fus.	4	37	11	131	-	159	15	327.
4/Bedfordshire Regt.	8	47	7	87	-	44	15	178
10/R.Dublin Fus..	6	32	9	137	-	54	15	223
1/H.A.C.	2	37	13	164	1	31	16	232
190th M.G.Coy.	2	9	3	24	-	22	5	55.
190th T.M.Battery.	1	3	-	-	-	-	-	3.
TOTAL.	23	165	43	543	1	310	67	1018

H.Q.190th Inf. Bde.
30/11/16.

On His Majesty's Service.

190/83

Officer i/c
My office
Base

SECRET
190th Bde

HEADQUARTERS,
190th
INFANTRY BRIGADE.
No.
Date.

December
1916

SECRET.

Headquarters, 190th. Inf. Brigade,
2nd Jan 1917. Date.

Vol 7

VOL. VII.

WAR DIARY
of
190th. Infantry Brigade.

From Dec 1st 1917
To Dec 31st 1917

9/16

Major.

Brigade Major,
190th. Infantry Brigade.

To:- A.G's Office
    Base
    (through DAD 63rd Dvn)

WAR DIARY of 190th Infantry Brigade.

INTELLIGENCE SUMMARY.

VOL VII

Place	Date	Hour	Summary of Events and Information	Remarks and references to Appendices
NOUVION	Dec 1.		Training - fine frosty weather.	
	Dec 4.		On the 4th a Brigade Souvenir 'Open Trophy' was carried out.	
	Dec 5.		Theos and Rum - Commanding Officers & subalterns taking part attacking own.	
	Dec 6.		Training.	
	Dec 7.			
	Dec 8.		Brig. Gen. HENEKER D.S.O. A.D.C. (promoted) to Temp Maj General & appointed to Command the 8th Division. 190th Inf Bde. Lt Col E.P.C. BOYLE 1/HAC assumed Command pending arrival of Gen FINCH.	
	Dec 9.		Training	
	Dec 11.			
	Dec 12.		Lt Col HESKETH 7/Royal Fusiliers on return from leave assumed command of Brigade vice BOYLE.	
NOYELLES -SUR-MER	Dec 13.		Bde. to Qrs moved to NOYELLES.	
	Dec 14		Training.	
	Dec 17		Brig. Gen. H.W.E. FINCH joined and took over Command of the Brigade.	
	Dec 18.		Training, chiefly in Trench warfare.	
	Dec 19			
	Dec 31			Hermann Bde Maj 190th Inf Bde

Vol. 8.

Headquarters,
190th Inf. Bde.
(63rd Div.)

January
1917

HEADQUARTERS,
190th
INFANTRY BRIGADE.

No. 8/9
Date.................

SECRET.

Headquarters,190th.Inf.Brigade,
1-2-17 ....Date.

W A R   D I A R Y

of

190th. Infantry Brigade.

From 1-1-17
To 31-1-17

E.V.B.Tagg

Captain
Major.

Brigade Major,
190th.Infantry Brigade.

To:- A.G's Office
Base.
(through DAG)

SECRET.

Army Form C. 2118.

WAR DIARY
or
INTELLIGENCE SUMMARY.
(Erase heading not required.)

VOL VIII

January 1917

Instructions regarding War Diaries and Intelligence Summaries are contained in F. S. Regs., Part II. and the Staff Manual respectively. Title pages will be prepared in manuscript.

Place	Date	Hour	Summary of Events and Information	Remarks and references to Appendices
Jan	1st – 12th		Training in NOUVION area.	
	13th – 20th		Moved to FORCEVILLE. Fine weather with some snow during the whole period.	APP { A. B. C. D.
	21st		Major C.F. JERRAM (Bde Major) D.S.O. R.M.L.I. left to take up appointment of G.S.O.2 to 31st Div.	
	22nd		Working parties.	
	23rd		Relief orders received to relieve 189th Bde. G.S.O. Div Order No. 81.	APP. E
	24th		10th R.D.F. moved to ARQUEVES. 4th Bedfordshire Regt moved to FORCEVILLE	} E
	26th		Went in to the line BAHA Qu. 7th R.F. and 4th Bedfordshire Regt and relieved two front line Battns. of 189th Inf Bde. The relief took place without incident.	
	27th		10th R.D.F. and 1st H.A.C. relieved the support and reserve Batts. of 189th Inf Bde respectively. Weather continues	

Army Form C. 2118.

WAR DIARY
or
INTELLIGENCE SUMMARY.
(Erase heading not required.)

VOL VIII page 2. January 1917

Place	Date	Hour	Summary of Events and Information	Remarks and references to Appendices
	28th		Cold and dry. Ground very hard. Our artillery active during the day especially against PUSIEUX TRENCH and RIVER TRENCH. Some hostile retaliation, but little damage done.	
	29th		The usual daily artillery activity. BEAUCOURT, THE QUARRY and SUVLA TRENCH receiving attention. Support and Reserve Batts engaged in constant carrying and digging fatigues.	
	30th		Carried out internal relief. The 1/H.A.C. taking over the RIGHT Sub-section from 7th R.F. The 10th R.D.F. taking over the LEFT from 4th Bedfordshire Regt. No unusual occurrence.	APP. F.
	31st		On the early morning of 31st inst. the enemy after an intense bombardment raided No 3 post occupied by 1/H.A.C. The enemy appeared to be about 30 strong. They entered the post and returned with the garrison	

Army Form C. 2118.

Vol VIII page 3

WAR DIARY
or
INTELLIGENCE SUMMARY.
(Erase heading not required.)

January 1917.

Place	Date	Hour	Summary of Events and Information	Remarks and references to Appendices

and one Jeiso Sepoy with the exception of two men, one of whom was found dead and the other unconscious. One dead Sentry was found in the post. At dusk took a wire from the post returned to our lines. Support and Reserve Bath's out most of the night on carrying parties.

Order (Div No 53) not being relied by 169th Iny Bde on nights of 1st & 2nd and 2nd & 3rd received.

E. MSTagg
Capt R.M.L.
3/2/17

Army Form C. 2118.

WAR DIARY
or
INTELLIGENCE SUMMARY.
(Erase heading not required.)

Summary of Casualties for JANUARY 1917.

	KILLED		WOUNDED		MISSING		Remarks
	Off.	O.R.	Off.	O.R.	Off.	O.R.	
Attached Bde Hd Qrs. (L/Berks. Regt.)	-	1	-	1	-	1	
7th R.F.	-	3	-	*28	-	1	*Including 1 attached Bde Hd Qrs. 1 S.I. and 3 shell shock.
4th Bedfords Regt.	-	4	-	#12	-	1	#Including 1 shell shock.
10th R.D.F.	x1	-	-	%6	-	1	x Asphyxiation %incl. 3 Accidental
1 H.A.C.	-	2	@1	6	-	-	@ shell shock.
190th M.G. Coy	-	-	-	1	-	-	
190th T.M.B	-	-	-	-	-	-	
	1	10	1	53.	-	8	
	1	1			1	8	

APPENDIX. A.

SECRET.   Copy.No...3....

190th Infantry Brigade Warning Order No.47.

Headquarters,
190 Infantry Brigade.
1st Jany. 1917.

Ref. Map. Sheets. ABBEVILLE.
and LENS.
1/100,000

1. The 63rd (R.N.) Division less Artillery will leave its present area on route for the front area on the 13th Jan.

2. The various stages of the march, detailed orders for which will be issued later will be as follows:-

Date.			To.
13th Jany.	...	...	BUIGNY Area
14th "	...	...	DRAILLY "
15th "	...	...	LEMNAVILLE "
16th "	...	...	HALT.
17th "	...	...	HARIEUX "
18/20 "	...	...	IV Corps "

3. Acknowledge.

Time issued to Signals....6p.....

E.J.B.Tagg.
Captain.
Acting Brigade Major.

1. File.
2. (4) War Diary.
3. Brigadier.
4. Staff Capt.
5. Bde. Bombing Officer.
6. 7/Royal Fusiliers.
7. 10/R. Dublin Fusiliers.
8. 4/Bedfordshire Regt.
9. 1/H.A.C.
10. 190th M.G.Coy.
11. 190th T.M.Battery.
12. No.3.Field Amb.
13. No.4.Coy. Div. Train.
14. 92nd Field Coy. (for information)
15. Town Major. MOYELLES.
16.   "   "   NOUVION.
17. 63rd (R.N.) Division.
18. Signals.
19. Bde. Intelligence Officer.
20. Bde. Transport Officer.

APPENDIX. B.

190th Infantry Brigade Order. No.48   Copy No 14

Headquarters,
190th Infantry Bde.
8th Jany. 1917

Ref.Maps ABBEVILLE and
LENS: 1/100,000

1. The 190th Infantry Brigade Group less Artillery, Engineers and Light T.M.B. will move on the 13th, 14th and 15th inst. according to the attached March Table.

2. All ranks comprising the Salvage Company will rejoin their units before noon on Jany. 12th.

3. 200x will be maintained between Companies and a minimum of 500x between units; Bn. Transport being reckoned as a Coy.
Transport will NOT be brigaded owing to units moving by different roads; all Transport will therefore be with units.

4. Attention is called to the notes on March Discipline previously issued.
The rear unit will always provide a rear party, immediately in rear of which will march an ambulance wagon provided by 3rd Field Ambulance. (When moving by different routes, the available ambulances will be distributed amongst the units, which have furthest to go.)

5. Orders as to the allotment of motor lorries will be issued later.

6. On arrival in billets units will report the map reference of their Hd. Qrs. and Transport lines.

7. On resuming a march the senior officer in each village will detail a mounted officer to ensure that units clear the village in the right order.

8. The Bde. Police will ride at the head of the column and give notice of approaching troops, blocks etc. and will mark all doubtful turnings.
When moving by different routes, a mounted policeman will be allotted to the leading unit in each column.

9. Rear parties are always to be left to clear up billots. These should consist of men from each Company and from Hd. Qrs., all under command of an officer. On completion of duty they will follow their Bn. as a formed unit under command of the officer.

10. All dismounted officers and men are to be in Marching Order, with caps. Steel helmets will be carried on the back of the pack kept in position by the supporting straps.
Drivers will wear their equipment less packs, which may be placed in the wagons.
All Drivers and Brakesmen of G.S.wagons will wear their leather jerkins; the jerkins of dismounted men will be carried by the transport.
Wagons must be properly packed and nothing is to be allowed outside the cover.
The packs of Lewis Gunners may be carried on the handcarts but nothing else.

11. Times of arrival at starting points must be carefully worked out; it must be remembered that it is just as bad to be too early as too late.

12. Billeting parties will always proceed at least two hours ahead of their units and should be mounted on horses or bicycles.

13. Units will, so far as possible occupy the same billets as during the march to Training Area.

14. Units will observe the usual halts - 10 minutes to clock hour to clock hour.

15. No unit will pass another of this Brigade on the march unless the unit in front is halted <u>for a meal</u>; units halting for such a purpose must clear right off the road.
Units may, if they wish, halt for meals but if they do so, must post a sentry 500^x in rear of their rear party to warn units coming up behind; This sentry must know where the head of his unit is and the exact time the unit is continuing its march.

Time issued to Signals......9pm..........   Major.
                                                Brigade Major.

Copies to:-

1. 7/Royal Fusiliers.
2. 4/Bedfordshire Regt.
3. 10/R.Dublin Fusiliers
4. 1/H.A.C.
5. 190th M.G.Company.
6. No.4.Coy. Train.
7. 3rd Field Ambulance.
8. 63rd Division.
9. 188th Inf. Bde.
10. 189th Inf. Bde.
11. Staff Captain.
12. Bde Transport Officer.
13. File.
14. War Diary. (3)

MARCH TABLE. Continued.

Date.	Unit.	From.	To.	Time of start.	Starting point	Route.
15th Jan.	10/R.Dublin Fus.	CONTEVILLE.	LONGUEVILLETTE.	11.45.am	X roads 500x N.W. of AGENVILLE Church.	AGENVILLE-PROUVILLE; BERNAVILLE-FIENVILLERS
		Absolute punctuality is essential. The head of the column must pass the starting point at the exact hour given and not before or after it. The Bn. will march on this day closed up to normal intervals instead of the usual 300x				
	No.4.Coy.Train.	BERNAVRE.	GEZAINCOURT.	as convenient but must not be in the way of other units.		AUXI-LE-CH.TRAUX-WAMIN: REZEROLLES-HEM.
	1/H.A.C.	NEUILLY-LE-DIEU.	GEZAINCOURT.	8.0.am	AOQUET X roads.	-- ditto --
	3rd Field Ambulance.	HIERMONT.	GEZAINCOURT.	8.5.am	HIERMONT Church.	-- ditto --
	M.G.Coy.	CONTEVILLE.	GEZAINCOURT.	8.0.am	CONTEVILLE Church.	BERNAVTRE, thence as above.
	7/Royal Fus.	MAISON PONTHIEU	GEZAINCOURT.	8.5.am	MAISON PONTHIEU Church.	HIERMONT, thence as for Train.
	4/Bedfordshire Regt.	GUESCHART	GEZAINCOURT.	8.0.am	GUESCHART Church.	VILLEROY-SUR-AUTHIE-VITZ VILLEROY-LE POMMEL thence as for Train
	Bde.Hd.Qrs.	MAISON-PONTHIEU.	GEZAINCOURT.	9.0.am	MAISON-PONTHIEU Church.	as for 7/Royal Fus.

Note:- (1) On this day Billeting Parties will meet the Staff Capt. at GEZAINCOURT Church at 10.am and will be shown their billeting areas.

(2) The above, from 1/H.A.C. to Bde. Hd. Qrs. shows the order of march, and units must be careful, when entering a road along which another unit is marching, that they do not break into or pass in front of the unit they should be following. The times are arranged for an average speed of 3 miles per hour.

MARCH TABLE

Date.	Unit.	From.	To.	Time of start.	Starting point.	Route
13th Jany.	10/R.Dublin Fus.	NOYELLES	NEUILLY-L'HOPITAL	9.0.am	Road junction N.E. end of NOYELLES.	SAILLY-LE-SEC-LE TITRE-LAMOTTE BULEUX. Follow 10/R.Dublin Fus at 500x
	190th M.G.Coy.	NOLETTES	NEUILLY-L'HOPITAL.	9.10.am		Follow 10/R.Dublin Fus at 500x
	3rd Field Amb.	SAILLY BRAY	LAMOTTE-BULEUX.	8.15.am	As the M.A.C. Horl.roads ¾ mile S of 2nd M in NOUVION.	
	1/R.A.C.	NOUVION	CANCHY.	9.0.am		LE TITRE — LAMOTTE BULEUX.
	7/Royal Fus.	SAILLY BRAY	CANCHY.	9.0.am	SAILLY BRAY X roads.	LE TITRE-LAMOTTE BULEUX
	Bde. Hd. Qrs.	NOYELLES.	CANCHY.	9.30.am	NOYELLES.	SAILLY-LE-SEC— LE TITRE -LAMOTTE BULEUX
	4/Bedfordshire Regt.	NOUVION	LAMOTTE-BULEUX.	9.10.am	as for H.A.C.	Direct
	No.4.Coy.Train.	NOUVION.	CANCHY.	as convenient must be clear of NOUVION by 11.am		LAMOTTE BULEUX.
14th Jany.	10/R.Dublin Fus	NEUILLY-L'HOPITAL.	COUTEVILLE.	9.am	X roads at E. end of NEUILLY-L'HOPITAL.	ARGENVILLERS-GAPENNES
						YVRENCH-BOIS CARRE (in rear of 7/Royal Fus.)
	190th M.G.Coy.	do.	do.	9.10.am	do	Follow 10/R.Dublin Fus.
	7/Royal Fus.	CANCHY.	MAISON FORTHIEU	9.0.am	First L of NOUVLENT.	ARGENVILLERS-GAPENNES-YVRENCH.
	Bde. Hd. Qrs.	CANCHY.	MAISON FORTHIEU.	9.45.am	do	do
	1/H.A.C.	CANCHY.	NEUILLY-L'HOPITAL (if required)	9.0.am	X roads ¼ mile N.E. of Last house in CANCHY.	DOMV.ST-BR.ILLY-NOYELLE- X. NEUILLY
	4/Bedfordshire Regt.	LAMOTTE-BULEUX	GUESCHART	9.0.am	Point where railway crosses the CANCHY road.	CANCHY-DOMV.-ST-BR.ILLY Pt. BELINV-L.
	Garfield Amb.	LAMOTTE-BULEUX.	NEUILLY-L'HOPT.	9.10.am	do	CANCHY-ARGENVILLERS-B.CARRE.
	No.4.Coy.Train.	CANCHY.	CANCHY.	as convenient but must be clear of ARGENVILLERS by 11.am		ARGENVILLERS-ARGENVILLE, COUTEVILLE

APPENDIX C

Copy No. 16

190th Infantry Brigade Order. No.49.

Headquarters,
190th Infantry Brigade
12th Jany. 1917.

Ref. Map. LENS. 1/100,000.

1. The 190th Infantry Brigade Group will resume its march to the forward area as in attached March Table.

2. Paras. 3, 4, 6, 7, 8, 9, 10, 11, 12, 14 and 15. of Bde. Order No.48. are to be observed.

3. Units will send an orderly to Bde. Hd. Qrs. daily at 4.pm, commencing 12th inst. to obtain the time for the next day from the Bde. Signal Officer. Bde. Signals must therefore alter the time at 4.pm during the march instead of at 9.am as usual.

Time issued to Signals...... 6:30pm

Major.
Brigade Major.

Copies to:-

1. 7/Royal Fusiliers.
2. 4/Bedfordshire Regt.
3. 10/R.Dublin Fusiliers.
4. 1/H.A.C.
5. 190th M.G.Coy.
6. No.4.Coy. Div. Train.
7. 3rd Field Ambulance.
8. 63rd Division.
9. 188th Inf. Bde.
10. 189th Inf. Bde.
11. Staff Captain.
12. Bde. Transport Officer.
13. File.
14. War Diary. (3)
15. Sig Siatu.

MARCH TABLE.

Date.	Unit.	From.	To.	Time of Start.	Starting Point.	Route.
17th Jan.	7/Royal Fusiliers	GEZAINCOURT.	PUCHEVILLERS.	9.15.am.	X Roads on GEZAINCOURT—BEAUVAL road, 1 mile SOUTH of GEZAINCOURT Church.	Road junction 200x S.W. of BEAUVAL STN
	4/Bedfordshire Regt.	---do---	---do---	9.32.am.	---do---	Road junction 100x S. of BEAUQUESNE STN
	1/H.A.C.	---do---	---do---	9.49.am.	---do---	X roads 200x N.E. of 3rd E in BEAUQUESNE
	Bde. Hd. Qrs.	---do---	---do---	10.05.am	---do---	PUCHEVILLERS.
	3rd Field Ambulance.	---do---	---do---	10.10.am	---do---	
	10/R.Dublin Fus.	LONGUEVILLETTE	---do---	10.20.am.	---do---	
	No.4.Coy. Train.	GEZAINCOURT.	---do---	As convenient.	---do---	

Note:— (1) All troops to be clear of BEAUQUESNE by 12.30.pm.
(2) The Staff Capt. will meet billeting parties of all units at PUCHEVILLERS Church at 10.am.

Date.	Unit.	From.	To.	Time of start.	Starting point.	Route.
20th Jan.	No.4.Coy. Train.	PUCHEVILLERS	FORCEVILLE.	as convenient.		
	7/Royal Fusiliers	--do--	--do--	9.15.am	QUESNOY.	TOUTENCOURT HARPONVILLE VARENNES.
	10/R.Dublin Fus.	--do--	--do--	9.32.am	--do--	--do--
	Bde. Hd. Qrs.	--do--	--do--	9.49.am	--do--	--do--
	3rd Field ambulance.	--do--	CLAIRFAYE.	10.0.am	--do--	TOUTENCOURT HARPONVILLE.
	1/H.A.C.	--do--	LEALVILLERS.	10.10.am	--do--	TOUTENCOURT.
	4/Bedfordshire Regt.	--do--	ARQUEVES.	9.15.am	X Roads N. end of PUCHEVILLERS.	RAINCHEVAL.

Note:- 1.Billeting parties of units proceeding to FORCEVILLE will meet Staff Captain at FORCEVILLE Church at 10.0.am.
2. 3rd Field ambulance.will relieve 34th Field Ambulance.
3. A.D.M.S. & A.D.V.S. will be at ENGLEBELMER. D.A.D.O.S. at FORCEVILLE.

SECRET.   Copy No. 3

APPENDIX D

190th Infantry Brigade Operation Order No. 50.

Ref. Map 57D   Headquarters, 190th Inf. Bde.
1/40,000.   23rd Jany. 1917.

1. The 4th Bn. Bedfordshire Regt. will move to FORCEVILLE and 10th Bn. Royal Dublin Fusiliers to ARQUEVES tomorrow 24th instant in accordance with attached March Table.

2. Billeting parties are to be sent on 1 hour in advance to make all arrangements.
Each unit will leave behind 1 Officer per Bn. and 1 N.C.O. per Coy. to hand over billets to incoming Bn.

3. 8 G.S. waggons will report at 10th Royal Dublin Fusiliers Hd. Qrs. at 8.am and be sent independently as a convoy to ARQUEVES, unload and return to FORCEVILLE with 4th Bedfordshire Regt's Stores. On completion of this duty, waggons are to return to No.4.Coy. Div. Train.

4. 1st Line Transport will accompany units.

5. Acknowledge.

                                                                              E.J.B.Tagg.   Captain.

Time issued to Signals .... 9pm ......   Acting Brigade Major.

1. Brigadier.
2.)
3.) War Diary.
4.)
5.) 63rd Division.
6.)
7. 4/Bedfordshire Regt.
8. 10/R.Dublin Fusiliers.
9. 7/Royal Fusiliers.
10. 1/H.A.C.
11. 190th M.G.Company.
12. 190th T.M.Battery.
13. No.4.Coy. Train.
14. Signal Section.
15. File.
16. 188th Infantry Brigade.) For information.
17. 189th Infantry Brigade.)
18. *Bde. Transport Officer.*

MARCH TABLE.

Time.	From.	To.	Starting Point.	Time.	Route	Remarks.
10/1 Dublin Fus.	FORCEVILLE	ARQUEVES	X Roads P.21.a.5.1.	9.30.am.	"ACHEUX" – "LEALVILLERS"	Not to enter LEALVILLERS before 10.30.am.
4/Northants. Regt.	ARQUEVES	FORCEVILLE	Rd. Junction O.8.c.6.3.	9.0.am.	LEALVILLERS – VARENNES.	To be clear of LEALVILLERS by 10.30.am.

SECRET. 190th Infantry Brigade Order No.51. Copy No. 1

[Stamp: HEADQUARTERS, 190th INFANTRY BRIGADE. No...... Date......]

APPENDIX E

Headquarters,
190th Infantry Brigade.
25th January, 1917.

Ref. map 57D 1/40,000.

1. The 190th Infantry Brigade will relieve the 189th Infantry Brigade on the 26th and 27th instant and will move in accordance with attached March Table.

2. Relief will be carried out as follows :-

   Jany. 26th. 190th Infantry Brigade Hd. Qrs.
   7th Royal Fusiliers.
   4th Bedfordshire Regt.
   190th T.M.Battery.

   Jany. 27th 1st H.A.C.
   10th R.Dublin Fusiliers.
   190th M.G.Company.

   Relief of Field Coys. will be made under mutual arrangements of Officers Commanding and will be completed on the 28th instant.

3. Signals will be taken over on the 26th Jany. under mutual arrangements of Signal Officers concerned.

4. Bde. Stores etc. will be taken over under arrangements between Staff Captains.

5. Instructions for taking over trenches vide part 1. of Trench Standing Orders as far as they apply to the present situation will be strictly carried out.

6. All movement along the HAMEL-BEAUCOURT Road in daytime is to be reduced to a minimum and such parties as use this road are not to be larger than 1 Section.
The junction of Station Road and the HAMEL-BEAUCOURT Road is to be avoided as dangerous.

7. Details as to relief of working parties will be issued as soon as possible.

8. 1st Line Transport will proceed to ENGLEBELMER independently on the 26th and 27th instants to destinations already issued.
Cookers, water carts and lewis gun limbers will accompany Bns. to Bde. Dump.

9. Administrative instructions will be issued later.

10. The completion of the relief of each Bn. will be notified to Bde. Hd. Qrs. by code word "LINK".

11. 190th Bde, Hd. Qrs. will close at FORCEVILLE at 2.pm and reopen at Q.18.a. at 5.pm.

12. Acknowledge.

Time issued to Signals... 11 /m

E. V. B. Tagg
Captain.
Acting Brigade Major.

2.

1.)
2.) WarDiary.
3.)
4.) File.
5.)
6. Brigadier.
7. Brigade Major.
8. Staff Captain.
9. Signals.
10. 63rd Division.G.
11. 63rd   "   Q.
12. C.R.A.
13. C.R.E.
14. 7/Royal Fusiliers.
15. 4/Bedfordshire Regt.
16. 10/R.Dublin Fusiliers.
17. 1/H.A.C.
18. 190th M.G.Coy.
19. 190th T.M.Battery.
20. 3rd Field Coy.
21. A.D.M.S.
22. S.S.O.
23. No.4.Coy. Train.
24. Town Major. ENGLEBELMER.
25. Brigade Transport. Officer.
26. 189th Infantry Brigade.

M A R C H   T A B L E. to accompany 190th Infantry Brigade Order No.51.

26th January, 1917.

Units relieving.	Unit relieved.	Starting point.	Time.	Destination.	Route.	GUIDES Time.	GUIDES Place.	GUIDES No.	Remarks.
1/Bedfordshire Regt.	Hawke Bn.	P.27.B.6.0.	12.00am	Left Subsection	HEDAUVILLE-BOUZINCOURT-AVELUY WOOD-HAMEL.	5.pm	RE Dump HaML	1 per platoon 1 per Hd.Qrs. Coy.	1. 1 hrs halt will be made for dinner 2. Units will send on an officer to reconnoitre suitable place for dinner halt. 3. Units will march with 200ˣ interval between Coys. & 500ˣ between Bns. 4. Units will not proceed beyond AVELUY WOOD before 4.45.pm.
7/Royal Fus.	Howe Bn.	-ditto-	12.30pm	Right Subsection	-ditto-	do	do	do	
190th T.M.Bty.	189th T.M.B.	-ditto-	12.56pm	---	-ditto-	do	do	do	

M A R C H   T A B L E. to accompany 190th Infantry Brigade Order. No.51.

27th January, 1917.

Unit relieving.	Unit relieved.	Starting point.	Time.	Destination.	Route.	GUIDES Time.	GUIDES Place.	GUIDES No.	Remarks
1/H.A.C.	Drake Bn.	X Roads O.23.D.2.4.	11.am	Reserve Line	LEALVILLERS HEDAUVILLE BOUZINCOURT AVELUY HAMEL	5.pm	RE DUMP HAMEL	1 per platoon 1 per Hd.Qrs. Coy.	1. The Left will be made for dinner, ½ hr for tea. 2. Units will send on an officer to reconnoitre a suitable place for a dinner halt. 3. Units will march with 200X interval between Coys. and 500X between Bns. 4. Units will not proceed beyond AVELUY WOOD before 4.45pm. 5. 10/R.Dublin Fus. not to enter LEALVILLERS before 11.20am
190th M.G.Coy.	189th M.G.Coy.	ditto.	11.20am		-ditto-	do	do	1 per L.Gun.	
10/R.Dublin Fus.	Nelson Bn.	Rd.junction O.8.d.6.3.	11.am	Support Line.	ditto.	do	do	1 per platoon 1 per H.Q.Co.	

190th Infantry Brigade Administrative Instructions
issued with reference to 190th Infantry Brigade Order No. 51.

1. **Supplies.** On 26/1/17 supplies for consumption on the 27th will be delivered under Div. Train arrangements for Bde. Hd. Qrs. 7/Royal Fusiliers, 4/Bedfordshire Regt. and 190th T.M.Battery. at their new Q.M.Stores at ENGLEBELMER. Remainder of 190th Infantry Brigade will continue to draw by 1st Line Transport from FORCEVILLE Dump on 26th instant.

    From 27th January and onwards rations will be delivered to whole of Bde. by Div. Train. Rations are taken by limber to the cookers at Bde. Dump thence by Light Railway to a point just N. of Station Road and from here by carrying parties to Units.

    Hot food containers are trench stores and will be turned over on relief. Should units require more, application should be made to Bde.Hd.Qrs.. Containers fit on a man's back like a Vermorel Sprayer and for a short carry 1 man to each container when filled.

2. **Transport.** Baggage wagons for units moving on the 26th will report on the 25th inst, for units moving on the 27th on the 26th inst.

    Waggons on completion of their duty will return to No.4. Coy. Train Q.25.c. at ENGLEBELMER.

    Arrangements have been made with 189th Infantry Brigade to pool transport and waggons coming to FORCEVILLE, LEALVILLERS and ARQUEVES with Stores of 189th Infantry Brigade should return to ENGLEBELMER filled with Stores of 190th Infantry Brigade and vice versa.

3. **Water.** 1 Watercart will supply water for the BN.Cookers as thought fit.

    Water is got from spring about 100^X S. of Cookers. There is a good well in BEAUCOURT for water for front line.

    All water has to be carried to trenches in petrol tins. Owing to their scarcity units requiring additional ones indent on Bde. Hd. Qrs.

4. **Cookers** are at present concentrated by the Bde Dump. It is proposed to bring them further forward when positions have been prepared.

5. **Blankets.** Arrangements are to be made to store blankets at FORCEVILLE under a guard of Bn. Pioneers who will work under Staff Captain 189th Infantry Brigade in the bunking of billets of Reserve Brigade area.

6. **R.E.material.** R.E.material will be drawn from Bde. Dump on the BEAUCOURT-HAMEL Road. Indents for same from Bns. must reach Bde. Hd. Qrs. by 10.am daily. Bde. Transport Officer will arrange to draw same from LANCASHIRE DUMP and convey to Bde. Dump by 4.pm daily. Carrying parties will be provided from Reserve and Support Bns. to carry material forward to front line Units.

7. **Bde. Dump.** Bde. Dump is under the Brigade Bombing Officer and contains material and Ammunition of all kinds. Units will indent on Bde.Hd.Qrs. for their requirements and draw from Bde. Dump. 2 Bombing Sections from the Reserve Bn. will report daily to O.C. Bde. Dump at 7.30.am as a ration carrying party for Bde. Hd. Qrs. and on return will work as detailed by O.C.Dump.

8. **Reserve Dump.** A reserve Dump which is only to be touched in case of emergency is in the process of being established in the small valley 100^X N. of Station Road on the BEAUCOURT-HAMEL Road.

9. **Tools.** Picks and Shovels can be drawn from Bde. Dump and every effort should be made to collect all tools lying about into the Coy. Tool Dumps and so save unnecessary fatigue.

10. Salvage. A great lot of salvage work can be done in this area and no man should come down from the trenches to the Bde Dump without bringing some article with him to put into the salvage dump. The organization of the Bde. Area into 4 salvage areas under a salvage officer will be issued later.

11. Tramways. A tramway exists along the BEAUCOURT-HAMEL Road and is being repaired as quickly as possible.

12. Drying Rooms. A gum-boot drying room under O.C. Bde. Dump has been established close to the Bde. Dump. Socks can be sent down to be dried and it is hoped shortly to be able to issue dry socks for wet ones.

13. Detached Parties. The following parties will relieve those of the 189th Infantry Brigade as below:-

Number.	Unit.	Work.	Remarks.
1.N.C.O.& 3.O.Rs. 3.O.Rs.	7/Royal Fus. 4/Bedfords.	Gum Boots Store.	(Work under O.C. (Bde Dump.
1.N.C.O.3.O.Rs.	1/H.A.C.	Tramway maintenance party.	
1.N.C.O.3.O.Rs.	10/R.Dublin Fus.	Bde. Dump.	2.O.Rs. to be Bombers.

E.J.B.Tagg. Captain.
Staff Captain.

26/1/17.   H.Q.190th Infantry Bde.

1.)
2.) War Diary.
3.)
4.) File.
5.)
6. Brigadier
7. Brigade Major.
8. Staff Captain.
9. Signals.
10. 63rd Division. G.
11. 63rd   do   Q.
12. C.R.A.
13. C.R.E.
14. 7/Royal Fusiliers.
15. 4/Bedfordshire Regt.
16. 10/R.Dublin Fusiliers.
17. 1/H.A.C.
18. 190th M.G.Coy.
19. 190th T.M.Battery.
20. 3rd Field Coy.
21. A.D.M.S.
22. S.S.O.
23. No.4.Coy, Train.
24. Town Major, ENGLEBELMER.
25. Bde. Transport Officer.
26. 189th Infantry Brigade.

SECRET. 190th Infantry Brigade Order No. 51.   Copy No. 3

APPENDIX F

Headquarters,
190th Infantry Brigade.
Ref. Map BEAUMONT 1/10000.   29th Jan 1917.

1. The following internal reliefs will be carried out on Tuesday, 30th January.
   (a) The 10/Royal Dublin Fusiliers will relieve the 4/Bn. Bedfordshire Regt.
   (b) The 1/H.A.C. will relieve the 7/Royal Fusiliers. Lewis Guns will be relieved by their Companies.

2. All detail of relief will be arranged by Commanding Officers concerned, the 10/Royal Dublin Fusiliers relieving 4/Bedfordshire Regt by REDOUBT ALLEY, 1/H.A.C. relieving 7/Royal Fusiliers by RAILWAY ALLEY and ENGINE TRENCH.

3. No Units are to relieve before dark.

4. After relief the 7/Royal Fusiliers will be in Brigade Reserve, 4/Bedfordshire Regt in Bde support.

5. 190th M.G.Coy will carry out internal reliefs taking care not to interfere with Battalion reliefs.

6. The evening situation report will be rendered by Bns. now in the line who will hand over the summary of previous 24 hours information to relieving Bns.

7. 63rd (R.N) Div. Standing Orders are to be strictly carried out and lists of Trench Stores taken over, sent to Bde Hd Qrs after relief.

8. Bns. going into the line will hand over any permanent working parties furnished by them.

9. Code word for relief LEGS.

10. Acknowledge.

E. B. Tagg.

Time issued to Signals 12.30 am

Captain,
Acting Brigade Major.

1. File
2.)
3.) War Diary.
4.)
5. 7/Royal Fusiliers.
6. 4/Bedfordshire Regt.
7. 10/Royal Dublin Fusiliers.
8. 1/H.A.C.
9. 63rd Division "G"
10. 63rd   "   "Q"
11. 190th M.G.Coy.
12. 190th T.M.Battery.
13. Signals.
14. 188th Inf. Bde.
15. 189th Inf. Bde.
16. Bde Transport Officer
17. Brigadier.
18. Bde. Major.
19. Staff Captain,
20. C.R.A.
21. C.R.E.
22. No 3 Coy R.E.
23. 175th Tunnelling Co
24. A.D.M.S.

SECRET.   190th Infantry Brigade Order No. 5.   Copy No 4

                                                    Headquarters,
                                                    190th Infantry Brigade.
Ref. Map BEAUMONT 1/10000.   29th Jan 1917.

1. The following internal reliefs will be carried out on Tuesday, 30th January.
    (a) The 10/Royal Dublin Fusiliers will relieve the 4/Bn. Bedfordshire Regt.
    (b) The 1/H.A.C. will relieve the 7/Royal Fusiliers. Lewis Guns will be relieved by their Companies.

2. All details of relief will be arranged by Commanding Officers concerned, the 10/Royal Dublin Fusiliers relieving 4/Bedfordshire Regt by REDOUBT ALLEY, 1/H.A.C. relieving 7/Royal Fusiliers by RAILWAY ALLEY and ENGINE TRENCH.

3. No Units are to relieve before dark.

4. After relief the 7/Royal Fusiliers will be in Brigade Reserve, 4/Bedfordshire Regt in Bde support.

5. 190th M.G.Coy will carry out internal reliefs taking care not to interfere with Battalion reliefs.

6. The evening situation report will be rendered by Bns. now in the line who will hand over the summary of previous 24 hours information to relieving Bns

7. 63rd (R.N) Div. Standing Orders are to be strictly carried out and lists of Trench Stores taken over, sent to Bde Hd Qrs after relief.

8. Bns. going into the line will hand over any permanent working parties furnished by them.

9. Code word for relief LEGS.

10. Acknowledge.

                                    E. B. Tagg

Time issued to Signals... 12.30 am
                                                    Captain,
                                                    Acting Brigade Major.

1. File
2.)
3.) War Diary.
4.)
5.) 7/Royal Fusiliers.
6. 4/Bedfordshire Regt.   14. 188th Inf. Bde.
7. 10/Royal Dublin Fusiliers.   15. 97th Inf. Bde.
8. 1/H.A.C.   16. Bde Transport Officer
9. 63rd Division "G"   17. Brigadier.
10. 63rd   "   "Q"   18. Bde Major.
11. 190th M.G.Coy.   19. Staff Captain,
12. 190th T.M.Battery.   20. C.R.A.
13. Signals.   21. C.R.E.
                                 22. No 3 Coy R.E.
                                 23. 175th Tunnelling Co
                                 24. A.D.M.S.

Any Answer to this Letter must be Prepaid.

On His Majesty's Service.

Historical Section
C.I.D. Military Branch
2 Cavendish Square
W.C.

WAR OFFICE.

If undelivered, to be returned to the Officer Commanding at the place shown in the post mark of origin.

Vol. 2.

Headquarters
190th Inf. Bde.
(63rd Div.)
February 1919

Original

VOLUME IX

SECRET.

Headquarters, 190th. Inf. Brigade,
28th Feb 1917 ....Date.

HEADQUARTERS,
190th
INFANTRY BRIGADE.
No. G146
Date. 1.3.17

Vol 9

WAR DIARY

of

190th. Infantry Brigade.

From.... 1-2-17
To...... 28-2-17

C H Dowden
~~Captain~~
Major.

Brigade Major,
190th. Infantry Brigade.

To:- The A.G's Office
Base
(through DHQ 63rd Div).

Army Form C. 2118.

WAR DIARY
of
INTELLIGENCE SUMMARY.
(Erase heading not required.)

Instructions regarding War Diaries and Intelligence Summaries are contained in F. S. Regs., Part II. and the Staff Manual respectively. Title pages will be prepared in manuscript.

Place	Date	Hour	Summary of Events and Information	Remarks and references to Appendices
	1/2/17.		Brigade was relieved in the line by the 189th.Inf.Bde. 1/H.A.C. and 10/Royal Dublin Fusiliers marched out to FORCEVILLE. 190th.Bde.Hd.Qrs. to FORCEVILLE. 4/Beds.Regt remained in support with 7/Royal Fusiliers in Reserve. (App.1). Relief complete about 10 pm. Captain C.M.Dowden,D.S.O.,M.C.,K.R.R.C. joined the Brigade and took over the duties of Brigade Major.	
	2/2/17.		1/H.A.C. moved to LEALVILLERS. 4/Bedfordshire Regt to FORCEVILLE. 7/Royal Fusiliers to ENGLEBELMER.	
	3/2/17.		7/R.F. moved up to old German Front line system as a reserve to 189th.Brigade who are carrying out a minor operation tonight. Zero for this operation is 11.30 pm. 4/Beds Regt. from FORCEVILLE to ENGLEBELMER to replace 7/R.F. 1/H.A.C. from LEALVILLERS to FORCEVILLE. 4/Beds. Regt. ordered to stand by during the night, in the event of them being required they will move up to old german system.	
	4/2/17.		4/Beds Regt.moved up to old german front line system in order to be able to assist 189th Brigade if required. 10/Royal Dublin Fusiliers moved forward to ENGLEBELMER at 10.30 am. 1/H.A.C. 190th.T.M.Battery and Bde.Hd.Qrs.stand by to move forward. Bde.Major to trenches with 189th.Bde. to keep in touch with the situation.	

Army Form C. 2118.

WAR DIARY
or
INTELLIGENCE SUMMARY.
(Erase heading not required.)

Instructions regarding War Diaries and Intelligence Summaries are contained in F. S. Regs., Part II. and the Staff Manual respectively. Title pages will be prepared in manuscript.

Place	Date	Hour	Summary of Events and Information	Remarks and references to Appendices
	5/2/17.		Orders received at 4.0 am. that the Brigade would commence to relieve the 189th.Brigade at at once and would be completed tonight. 10/Royal Dublin Fusiliers move to Reserve trenches at once. Bde.Hd.Qrs., 1/H.A.C. and T.M.B.move to ENGLEBELMER at once and on to trenches tonight. A difficult relief completed at 12.20 am. 6/2/17.	
	6/2/17.		Quiet night. 3 Bns.holding front line i.e. 1/H.A.C.,10/R.D.F.,4/Beds.Regt. 7/R.Fusiliers in Support. Working parties engaged in joining up shell holes, and putting out wire.	
	7/2/17.		Orders at 2.pm. that right of the line would be advanced at once in order to come up with 185th.Bde.South of the river. 1/H.A.C. carried out this advance most successful. Zerp at 11 pm. 80 prisoners taken. 3 Counter attacks beaten off. 1 Coy.7/R.F. pushed up to assist 1/H.A.C. (App.11)	
	8/2/17.		Lieut.Col.E.C.P.Boyle,1/H.A.C. killed. Heavy shelling of new line by enemy. Congratulations from Divisional and Corps Commanders to 1/H.A.C. on most successful operation.	
	9/2/17.		Usual trench warfare with fairly heavy shelling during the day. C.O's from 189th.Bde. came to look over the line previous to taking over.	
	10/2/17.		Uneventful day on our front. The Brigade on our left carried out a minor operation and	

Army Form C. 2118.

WAR DIARY
or
INTELLIGENCE SUMMARY.
(Erase heading not required.)

Instructions regarding War Diaries and Intelligence Summaries are contained in F. S. Regs., Part II. and the Staff Manual respectively. Title pages will be prepared in manuscript.

Place	Date	Hour	Summary of Events and Information	Remarks and references to Appendices
	11/2/17.		advanced their line to TEN TREE ALLEY. Orders received to advance our left Posts to come up with Brigade on our left.	
	12/2/17.		Fairly quiet during the day. 4/Bedfordshire Regt. carried out a minor operation to advance the left of our line, this was only partially successful owing to wire which had not been previously located. Bad reconnaissance on their part. About 70 casualties. (App.111). Enemy shelled with Gas during the evening and caught ½ Coy. of 7/R.F. They suffered about 50 casualties before they were able to adjust their respirators owing to shells bursting amongst them suddenly. 4/Beds.Regt attempted to push post line forward but with little success. Orders received for relief on night 14/15th.	
	13/2/17.		Fairly quiet on our front. Enemy counter attacked left Brigade about 8 am. but without success. A few more Gas Shells in the evening but no casualties. 4/Beds Regt.advanced Post Line during the night. Capt.E.J.B.Tagg, Royal Marines, Staff Captain, 190th.Bde, left to take up appointment of D.A.Q.M.G. XIXth.Corps.	
	14/2/17.		Nothing of interest during the day. 188th.Bde.relieved the 190th.Bde. in the line. Relief	

Army Form C. 2118.

WAR DIARY
INTELLIGENCE SUMMARY.
(Erase heading not required.)

Instructions regarding War Diaries and Intelligence Summaries are contained in F. S. Regs., Part II. and the Staff Manual respectively. Title pages will be prepared in manuscript.

Place	Date	Hour	Summary of Events and Information	Remarks and references to Appendices
	15/2/17.		completed 2.55 am. 15/2/17. 300 yards of front transferred to 62nd.Division. Bde.Hd.Qrs. to FORCEVILLE on relief (App.IV).	
	16/2/17.		General clean up, Baths etc and working parties.	
	17/2/17.		Brigade find 1400 men for working parties. Lecture by Divisional Commander to officers of his Brigade. Conference of C.O's at Hd.Qrs.of 1/H.A.C. 7/Royal Fusiliers ordered from MARTINSART to old german line to assist 188th.Brigade in their operation if required (4.30 pm) (App.V). All men of Brigade employed on working parties.	
	18/2/17.		7/Royal Fusiliers returned to MARTINSART at 3.40 am. Remainder of Brigade employed on working parties. C.S.M.Chapman, Army Gymnasium Staff, attached to Brigade.	
	19/2/17.		Brigade Hd.Qrs. moved from FORCEVILLE to HEDAUVILLE (App.VI). G.O.C. visited all Bns. All men working.	
	20/2/17.		Orders received to relieve 188th.Brigade in the line on 21/22nd. All men working.	
	21/2/17.		Brigade relieved the 188th.Brigade in the line. 7/R.F. and 4/Beds.Regt in the front line, the 1/H.A.C. in support with 10/R.D.F. in reserve. Drake Bn. placed at disposal of Brigade for carrying work. Bde.H.Q. Q.18.a. Relief completed 6.30 am.22/2/17 (App.VII).	

Army Form C. 2118.

WAR DIARY
of
INTELLIGENCE SUMMARY.
(Erase heading not required.)

Instructions regarding War Diaries and Intelligence Summaries are contained in F. S. Regs., Part II. and the Staff Manual respectively. Title pages will be prepared in manuscript.

Place	Date	Hour	Summary of Events and Information	Remarks and references to Appendices
	22/2/17.		Rather more artillery activity than usual. Labour Coy. to Old German Line.	
	23/2/17.		Very quiet day.	
	24/2/17.		Patrols pushed forward to MIRAUMONT, which they found evacuated. Outpost line established immediately West of MIRAUMONT (App.VII).	
	25/2/17.		Brigade ordered to advance and occupy the line of the Eastern edge of Miraumont to DOVECOTE (App.IX). Advanced in Artillery formation 10/R.D.F. on right, 7/R.F. centre, 1/H.A.C. on the left, with 4/Bedfordshire Regt. in support, Drake Bn. was pushed up in Reserve. The line was occupied with little resistance, enemy retired about 700 yards to GUDGEON trench. Touch was gained of both flanks.	
	26/2/17.		Reconnaissance pushed forward and enemy found in strength with Machine Guns in GUDGEON trench, guns turn on and later trench occupied by 1/H.A.C. and 10/Royal Dublin Fusiliers.(App.X).	
	26/2/17.		Relief completed 6.30 am. 27/2/17.	
	27/2/17.		Brigade Headquarters to Paisley Dump Dugouts Thiepval. 1/H.A.C. to Camp near MESNIL. 7/R.F. to THIEPVAL DUGOUTS. 4/Bedfordshire Regt. to Huts in MARTINSART WOOD. 10/R.D.F. to THIEPVAL DUGOUTS.	
	28/2/17.		Quiet day. Cleaning up. Working parties.	

signature
Brigade Major.

Captain.

SUMMARY OF CASUALTIES - FEBRUARY 1917.

190th Infantry Brigade.

	KILLED. Off.	KILLED. O.R.	WOUNDED. Off.	WOUNDED. O.R.	MISSING. Off.	MISSING. O.R.
7th Royal Fusiliers	-	*21	*4	*167	-	23
4th Bedfordshire Regt	3	51	9	115	-	53
10th R. Dublin Fus.	2	22	1	88	1	20
1st H.A.C.	2	26	5	88	-	5
190th Machine Gun Co.	-	4	2	15	-	1
190th Trench Mortar Batty	-	-	-	4	-	-
TOTAL	7	124	21	477	1	102

	KILLED Off.	KILLED O.R.	WOUNDED Off.	WOUNDED O.R.
* Includes	-	2	1	50 (caused by gas shells)

28th February 1917.

Appendix I

SECRET.   190th Infantry Brigade Order No. 53.   Copy No ....

Ref Map 57D/1/40,000.

                                        Headquarters,
                                        190th Infantry Bde.
                                        31/1/17.

1. The 190th Inf. Bde will be relieved by the 189th Infantry Brigade on the nights of Feb. 1/2 and Feb. 2/3.

2. The relief will be carried out as follows:-

    Feb. 1st.   190th Inf. Bde Hd. Qrs.
                 190th T.M.Battery.
                 1/H.A.C.
                 10/R.Dublin Fusiliers.

    Feb. 2nd.   7/Royal Fusiliers.
                 4/Bedfordshire Regt.

    Relief of Field Coy. will be made under mutual arrangement of Officers Commanding same.

3. Units will move to their billets in accordance with attached table, on completion of relief.

4. All details of relief will be arranged mutually between Commanding Officers.

5. Signal Section will be relieved on Feb. 1st under mutual arrangement of Signal Officers concerned.

6. Brigade Dumps, Stores etc will be handed over under mutual arrangements between Staff Captains.

7. Instructions for handing over trenches, contained in 63rd (R.N) Divn. Standing Orders are to be strictly carried out. Particular care must be taken in handing over Posts.
Receipts for trench stores etc handed over are to be forwarded on A.F.W.3405 to Bde. Hd. Qrs by 12 noon, 3rd Feb.

8. Movement along the HAMEL - BEAUCOURT Road must be in small parties with 50^x interval.

9. Details as to relief of working parties are attached.

10. Brigade Transport Officer will make all arrangements re moving of Battalion Q.M.Stores. First Line Transport will move independantly to their respective billets.

11. The command of the Brigade section will pass the G.O.C., 189th Inf. Bde. on completion of relief of front line Battalions.

12. Billeting parties will be sent in advance to make all arrangements.

13. Baggage Wagons are being sent tonight as follows:-
2 to 10/R.D.F. 2 to 1/H.A.C. 1 to Bde.Hd.Qrs.
Tomorrow 1st Feb. 2 to 7/R.F., 2 to 4/Bedfords. Regt.
Bde. Hd. Qrs, 10/R.D.F. & 1/H.A.C. will draw their rations by First Line Transport on the 2/2/17 from FORCEVILLE DUMP.

14. O.C. Units will arrange Rendezvous to the S. of Cross Roads Q.35.b.0.2. as it is essential that units march as formed bodies, 100x between Companies and 200x between units.

15. Code word for relief "STICK IT"
16. Acknowledge.

E.J.B.Tagg
Captain,
Acting Brigade Major.

Time issued to Signals ......

1.)
2.) War Diary.
3.)
4.) File.
5.)
6. Brigadier.
7. Brigade Major.
8. Staff Captain.
9. Signals.
10. 63rd Division "G"
11. "   "   "Q"
12. C.R.A.
13. C.R.E.
14. 7/Royal Fusiliers.
15. 4/Bedfordshire Regt.
16. 10/R. Dublin Fusiliers.
17. 1/H.A.C.
18. 190th M.G.Co.
19. 190th T.M.Battery.
20. 3rd Field Co.,
21. A.D.M.S.
22. S.S.O.
23. No. 4 Rey. Train.
24. Town Major, ENGLEBELMER,
25. Brigade Transport Officer.
26. 189th Inf. Bde.
27. Town Major, FORCEVILLE.
28. 188th Inf. Bde.
29. 97th Inf. Bde.

MARCH TABLE to accompany 190th Infantry Bde Order No. 53.
****

Date.	Unit.	From.	To.	Relieving Unit.	Route.	Remarks.
Feb. 1st.	190th Inf. Bde Hd. Qrs.	Q.18.a.	FORCEVILLE	189th Inf. Bde. Hd. Qrs.	HAMEL - MESNIL - MARTINSART - ENGLEBELMER.	(a) 1 Guide per platoon, 1 per H.Q.Coy will rendezvous under an Officer of each unit at R.E. Dump HAMEL at 5 p.m.
ditto	190th T.M. Battery	HAMEL	ditto	189th T.M. Battery	BOUZENCOURT - HEDAUVILLE	
ditto	10/R.Dublin Fusiliers.	Front line	ditto	notified later.	HAMEL -BOUZENCOURT HEDAUVILLE	
ditto	1/H.A.C.	ditto	ditto	ditto	ditto	
Feb. 2nd.	7/Royal Fusiliers.	Reserve Line	LEAVILLERS	notified later.	HAMEL -BOUZENCOURT HEDAUVILLE - VARENNES.	(b) Baggage wagons of units will report at Q.M. Stores, ENGLEBELMER, 9 a.m. tomorrow Feb. 1st.
ditto	4/Bedfords. Regt.	Support Line	ENGLEBELMER	ditto	HAMEL - MESNIL - MARTINSART.	

WORKING PARTY RELIEFS.
****

Ref. 190th Inf. Bde. Order No. 53, the following will be arrangements for relief of working parties on 1st & 2nd February.

(a) Party of 2 platoons working on MILL ROAD supplied by 7/Royal Fusiliers will be detailed for Feb. 1st only, afterwards by 188th Inf. Bde.

(b) Party of 20 O.Rs at LANCASHIRE DUMP will be provided by 7/Royal Fusiliers on 1st & 2nd Feb. afterwards by 189th Inf. Bde.

(c) Platoon at PAISLEY DUMP provided by 7/Royal Fusiliers will be relieved as above in "b".

(d) 50 O.Rs working on roads rendezvous CLAIRFAYE X Roads reporting to O.C. "A" Coy, 9th.Labour Bn. at 8 am at present supplied by 189th.Inf.Bde., will be detailed by 1/H.A.C. onwards from the 3rd.inst inclusive.

(e) 100 O.R's reporting at No.91 FORCEVILLE to O.C. "A" Coy. 9th.Labour Bn. at 8 am.daily, at present supplied by 189th.Inf.Bde., will be detailed by 10/R.D.F. onwards from 3rd.inst.inclusive.

(f) 1 Platoon for No.11 C.C.S. VARENNES supplied by 189th. Inf.Bde., will be relieved by 1/H.A.C. by 12 noon 2nd.February.

H.Q.190th.Inf.Bde.
31/1/17.

sd) E.J.B.Tagg. Captain.
Acting Brigade Major.

SECRET.   190th Infantry Brigade Order No.54.   Copy No. 21

APPENDIX II

Headquarters,
190th Infantry Brigade.
7th February. 1917.

Reference BEAUMONT Map 1/10,000.

1. The 190th Infantry Brigade will establish themselves around the Eastern outskirts of GRANDCOURT from R.9.b.3.7. to the Cemetery today.

2. The 1/H.A.C. will attack and capture the line of the SUNKEN ROAD from MIRAUMONT ALLEY in the North to BAILLESCOURT FARM in the South and thence Eastward to the North Eastern corner of the outbuildings of BAILLESCOURT FARM thence South to the River ANCRE.
The company of 7/Royal Fusiliers accommodated in SUVLA TRENCH and the QUARRY is placed at the disposal of the O.C. 1/H.A.C. for this operation. If this company is advanced it will be replaced by a company in BEAUCOURT TRENCH.

3. The attack will be carried out by 2 companies organised each in three waves with a distance of 20 yards between first and second wave and 70 yards between second and third.

4. The O.C.190th T.M.Battery will select a position for one mortar in RIVER TRENCH from which he can bombard the SUNKEN ROAD 50 yards North of MIRAUMONT ALLEY and also MIRAUMONT ALLEY 50 yards East of the SUNKEN ROAD.

5. O.C.190th M.G.Company will arrange that the road North of MIRAUMONT ALLEY is kept under fire, also that a barrage is placed on (a) MIRAUMONT BEAUCOURT ROAD (b) MIRAUMONT ALLEY (c) SWAN TRENCH.
After the position is taken he will send up one M.G. to each of the following strong points :-

    (a) R.3.c.1.5.
    (b) Junction of MIRAUMONT ROAD and the SUNKEN ROAD.
    (c) Eastern side of BAILLESCOURT FARM.

6. At ZERO (a) the artillery will place a standing barrage on the line of the objective to be captured, (b) a creeping barrage on a line 150 yards West of the objective. (c) first wave of the infantry will advance, followed by the other waves.
At ZERO plus 3 minutes the creeping barrage will jump back 50 yards to a line 100 yards West of the objective.
At ZERO plus 6 minutes creeping barrage will jump on to the line of the objective.
At ZERO plus 9 minutes all guns North of MIRAUMONT BEAUCOURT ROAD lift 150 yards and infantry assault line of SUNKEN ROAD from MIRAUMONT ALLEY to the MIRAUMONT BEAUCOURT ROAD.
The infantry South of the MIRAUMONT BEAUCOURT ROAD will advance to the line SUNKEN ROAD to bridge over the ANCRE R.9.a.9.5.
At ZERO plus 14 minutes all guns will lift 150 yards and infantry will assault the objective South of the MIRAUMONT BEAUCOURT ROAD.
A protective barrage will remain 200 yards East of the objective for one hour to facilitate consolidation.

7. A defensive flank will be established along MIRAUMONT ALLEY between RIVER TRENCH and the SUNKEN ROAD.

2.

8. Strong points will be constructed at:-

    1. R.3.c.1.5.
    2. R.3.c.40.65.
    3. Junction of MIRAUMONT ROAD and SUNKEN ROAD.
    4. Eastern side of BAILLESCOURT FARM.

9. Liaison Posts will be established by 1/H.A.C. at the following places:-

    (a) R.9.b.3.7.
    (b) Bridge over ANCRE. at R.9.a.6.9.
    (c) R.9.a.2.1.

Posts of 188th Brigade will also be established at above points.

10. ZERO hour will be notified later.

11. Acknowledge.

Time issued to Signals................ C.H.Dowden
                                                                Captain.
                                                              Brigade Major

1.&2.	File.
3.	Brigadier.
4.	Brigade Major.
5.	Staff Captain.
6.	63rd Division "G"
7.	63rd Division "Q"
8.	7/Royal Fusiliers.
9.	4/Bedfordshire Regt.
10.	10/Royal Dublin Fusiliers.
11.	1/H.A.C.
12.	190th M.G.Company.
13.	190th T.M.Battery.
13a.	"G" Group Division Artillery.
14.	C.R.E.
15.	188th Infantry Brigade.
16.	189th Infantry Brigade.
17.	97th Infantry Brigade.
18.	Signals.
19.)	
20.)	War Diary.
21.)	
22.	A.D.M.S.
23.	3rd Field Coy.

HEADQUARTERS,
190th
INFANTRY BRIGADE.
No. 960
Date 7-2-17

SECRET.
Headquarters,
190th Infantry Brigade
7th February, 1917.

Reference 190th Infantry Brigade Order No.54.

ZERO hour will be 11-0pm on 7-2-17

C H Dowden
Captain.
Brigade Major.

```
1 & 2.   File.
3.       Brigadier.
4.       Brigade Major.
5.       Staff Captain.
6.       63rd Division."G"
7.       63rd Division"Q"
8.       7/Royal Fusiliers.
9.       4/Bedfordshire Regt.
10.      10/Royal Dublin Fusiliers.
11.      1/H.A.C.
12.      190th M.G.Company.
13.      190th T.M.Battery.
13a.     "G"Group Division. Artillery.
14.      B.R.E.
15.      188th Infantry Brigade.
16.      189th Infantry Brigade.
17.       97th Infantry Brigade.
18.      Signals.
19.)
20.)     War Diary.
21.)
22.      A.D.M.S.
23.      3rd Field Coy.
24.      Nelson Bn.
25.      Drake Bn.
```

Appendix III

SECRET.   Copy No........

                    22

190th Infantry Brigade Order No.55.

                        Headquarters.
                          190th Infantry Brigade.
                            11th February. 1917.

Reference BEAUMONT Map 1/10,000.

1. The 97th Infantry Bde. advanced their right on the night of the 10/11th inst. to a point about L.31.d.3.1.

2. On the night of the 11/12th inst. the 4th Bedfordshire Regt. will advance its left Company and join up with the new line occupied by the 97th Brigade.

3. This forward move will be carried out by 2 companies, organised in two waves. A distance of 25 yards will be observed between the waves. The movement will be preceded by an artillery barrage.

4. AT ZERO minus 5 minutes the leading wave of infantry will be formed up on a tape line approximately from about 20 yards in rear of B.2. Post (R.1.b.6.4.) to a point 220 yards South of ARTILLERY ALLEY about R.2.a.5.2. with the second wave 25 yards in rear.
   Remainder of 4th Bedfordshire Regt. will be located as under:-

       2.platoons as a carrying party about the junction
            of PUISIEUX ROAD and ARTILLERY ALLEY.
       1.Company in ARTILLERY ALLEY and supporting post line.
       2 platoons post line about R.2.c.1.9.

5. At ZERO (a) the Artillery will place a barrage approximately on the line R.1.b.50.65. to R.2.a.4.6. (b) the infantry will advance.
   At ZERO plus 1 minute the barrage will lift 50 yards and will continue to lift in jumps of 50 yards at the rate 100 yards every 3 minutes until it reaches the approximate line L.31.d.45.25. to L.32.c.55.20.
   A protective barrage will remain on this line until ZERO plus 1 hour.

6. The infantry will halt on the line approximately R.1.b.5.9. through R.1.b.9.9. to join ARTILLERY ALLEY about R.2.a.6.6. and establish a chain of posts on this line.

7. The O.C.190th T.M.Battery. will instal two mortars in ARTILLERY ALLEY about R.2.a.8.6. and will bombard PUISIEUX and RIVER TRENCHES from ZERO onwards.
   The O.C.190th M.G.Company will arrange for two guns to be installed near ARTILLERY ALLEY about R.2.a.8.6. to keep the RIVER and PUISIEUX TRENCHES North of ARTILLERY ALLEY under fire.
   As soon as the infantry have arrived on the new line Machine Guns will be placed in position as under:-

       1. At the left of the new line at its junction with
            the PUISIEUX ROAD.
       2. In ARTILLERY ALLEY about R.2.a.6.6.

8. Howitzers will engage PUISIEUX ALLEY and the PUISIEUX and RIVER Trench SYSTEM North of ARTILLERY ALLEY, from ZERO to ZERO plus 1 hour and longer if required.
   The guns will not fire further South than the line R.2.b.0.9. - R.2.b.2.9.

9. When the infantry arrive on their new front line the supporting company from ARTILLERY ALLEY and supporting post line will move forward to the present front post line and remain in support.
The carrying platoons will move forward to new front line with tools, wire, sandbags etc., to assist in consolidation. Wire will be put out at once.

10. At the conclusion of this operation the 4th Bedfordshire Regt. will be distributed as under :-

   1 company in new post line and the Eastern end of ARTILLERY ALLEY.
   1 company in support in present front post line and ARTILLERY ALLEY.
   1 company in present supporting post line and ARTILLERY ALLEY.
   1 company in SUVLA TRENCH.

11. ZERO will be 9.0pm

12. Acknowledge.

Time issued to Signals..........

C H Dowden
Captain.
Brigade Major.

1 & 2 File.
3. Brigadier
4. Brigade Major.
5. Staff Captain.
6. 63rd Division "G"
7. ditto "Q"
8. 7th Royal Fusiliers.
9. 4th Bedfordshire Regt.
10. 10th R. Dublin Fusiliers.
11. 1st H.A.C.
12. 190th M.G. Company.
13. 190th T.M. Battery.
14. "G" Group Div. Artillery.
15. C.R.E.
16. 188th Inf. Bde.
17. 189th Inf. Bde.
18. 97th Infantry Bde.
19. Signals.
20.)
21.) War Diary
22.)
23. A.D.M.S.
24. 3rd Field Coy.
25. 2nd Field Amb.
26.) HAWKE Bn.
27.) HOOD Bn.

Appendix IV

SECRET. Copy No. 2

190th Infantry Brigade Order No. 57.

Headquarters,
190th Infantry Brigade.
13th Feby. 1917.

Reference BEAUMONT Map 1/10,000.
      " 57D. " 1/40,000.

1. The 190th Infantry Brigade will be relieved by the 188th Infantry Brigade on the night of 14/15th inst.

2. The relief will be carried out in accordance with attached table, and units will move direct to billets on completion of relief.
Relief of Field Coy. R.E. will be carried out under arrangements made by O.C. Companies concerned.
The 190th M.G.Coy. will relieve the 189th M.G.Coy. on the night of 13th inst.
The 189th M.G.Coy. will proceed to MARTINSART on relief.
The 188th M.G.Coy. will relieve the 190th M.G.Coy. under arrangements made between O.C. Companies. The 190th M.G.Coy. will remain in the line.
The 190th T.M.Battery will be relieved by the 188th T.M.B. on the 14th inst.
All outgoing units will move out via STATION ROAD and MILL TRACK.

3. All further details of relief will be arranged by O.C. units concerned.

4. One guide per platoon and one to each Lewis Gun in addition to the guides of relieving units which are at present in the line will be sent to Brigade Dump.
The Right platoons will come in first, except in the case of the 4/Bedfordshire Regt. when the left platoons will lead.
Guides must be arranged accordingly.

5. Instructions regarding the handing over of trenches as laid down in "63rd (R.N.) Division Trench Standing Orders" will be strictly adhered to.

6. All movement along the HAMEL-BEAUCOURT ROAD will be by parties not larger than one platoon at 50 yards distance.

7. All plans, photographs, Defence Schemes etc. will be handed over to incoming units and receipts obtained. These receipts will be forwarded to Brigade Hd.Qrs. by 6.0.pm. on 15th inst.

8. Every care must be exercised when handing over posts, the outgoing garrison should not leave until the incoming one is installed and the Officer or N.C.O. i/c has satisfied himself regarding the situation.

9. Brigade Dumps and all stores etc. will be handed over under arrangements between Staff Captains concerned.

2.

10. Brigade Transport Officer will arrange the moving of
    A.L.Stores and 1 st Line Transport of battalions.

11. O.C.Units will arrange rendezvous immediately South
    of LESNIL.
    Units will march as formed bodies from this point with
    a distance of 100 yards. between companies or similar
    units and 500 yards between battalions.

12. The Command of the Section will pass to the G.O.C. 188th
    Brigade on completion of relief of front line. Units
    will report relief complete by wiring the word "GOODNIGHT".

13. Billeting parties will be sent on in advance to arrange
    billets before unit arrives.

14. Headquarters will close at Q.18.a. on completion of relief
    and open at FORCEVILLE on arrival.

15. Acknowledge by wire.

                                            A.H.Dowden
                                              Captain.
                                            Brigade Major.

Time issued to Signals........

1.)
2.) War Diary.
3.)
4.) File.
5.)
6. Brigadier.
7. Brigade Major.
8. Staff Captain.
9. Signals.
10. 63rd Division."G"
11.   ditto   "A"
12. C.R.A.
13. C.R.E.
14. 7th Royal Fusiliers.
15. 4th Bedfordshire Regt.
16. 10th R.Dublin Fusiliers.
17. 1st H.A.C.
18. 190th M.G.Company.
19. 190th T.M.Battery.
20. 3rd Field Coy.
21. A.D.M.S.
22. S.S.O.
23. No.4.Coy. Train.
24. Town Major. ENGLEBELMER.
25. Brigade Transport Officer.
26. 189th Inf. Bde.
27. Town Major. FORCEVILLE.
28. 188th Inf. Bde.
29. 97th Inf. Bde.
30. 54th "   "
31. 55th "   "

MARCH TABLE (to accompany Bde. Order No.57.)

Unit.	From.	To.	Route.	Relieved by.	
H.Q. 190th Inf. Bde.	Q.18.a.	FONCEVILLE	—	H.Q. 188th Inf. Bde.	Guides to Bde. Dump at 5.0.pm.
4/Bedfordshire Regt.	Trenches (Left)	MARTINSART	HAMEL - MESNIL.	2nd Marine Bn.	Guides to Bde. Dump at 6.0.pm.
1/H.A.C.	Trenches (Right)	ENGLEBELMER.	HAMEL - MESNIL MARTINSART.	Anson Battn.	Guides to Bde. Dump at 7.0.pm.
7/R.Gyal Fusiliers.	Support Trenches.	MARTINSART.	HAMEL - MESNIL.	Hood Bn.	Guides to Bde. Dump at 8.0.pm.
10/R.Dublin Fusiliers.	Trenches (Centre)	ENGLEBELMER.	HAMEL - MESNIL MARTINSART.	1st Marine Bn.	
190th T.M.Battery.	Trenches	MARTINSART.	HAMEL - MESNIL.	188th T.M.Battery.	Guides will be arranged by O.C.Comar.Inf.

Warden

Headquarters,
190th Infantry Brigade.
13th February. 1917.

Reference 190th Infantry Brigade Order No.57. para. 2
last line. For "HILL TRACK" read "MULE TRACK".

                                        Captain.
                                   Brigade Major.

To whom B.O.57. was issued.

SECRET.   *Appendix [?]*   Copy No. 1

190th Infantry Brigade Order No. 58.

Headquarters,
190th Infantry Brigade.
17th Feby. 1917.

Ref. BEAUMONT Map 1/10,000.

1. The 7/Royal Fusiliers will move from MARTINSART to the Old German Front System at once. On arrival they will be at the disposal of G.O.C. 188th Brigade after reference to Div Hd. Qrs. and will be ready to move at 20 minutes notice.

2. Detached working parties will not be withdrawn. Parties reporting daily will be taken with Battalion.

3. Acknowledge.

Time issued to Signals........ 4.45 p

C.H. Powell
Captain.
Brigade Major.

1.2.3. War Diary.
4. File.
5. Brigadier.
6. Brigade Major.
7. Staff Captain.
8. Signals.
9. 63rd Division "G"
10. "   "   "Q"
11. C.R.A.
12. C.R.E.
13. 7th Royal Fusiliers.
14. 4th Bedfordshire Regt.
15. 10th R.Dublin Fusiliers.
16. 1st H.A.C.
17. 190th M.G. Coy.
18. 190th T.M. Battery.
19. 3rd Field Coy. R.E.
20. A.D.M.S.
21. S.S.O.
22. No.4. Coy. Div Train.
23. Bde Transport Officer.
24. 189th Bde.
25. 188th Bde.

SECRET.   *Appendix VI*   Copy No. 1

190th. Infantry Brigade Order No.59.
****

Hd.Qrs., 190th.Inf.Bde.
18th. Feb.1917.

Reference 57d 1/40,000.

1. All Units of the Brigade now billetted in FORCEVILLE will move to HEDAUVILLE on the 19th.inst. To be clear of FORCEVILLE by 10 am.

2. Brigade Headquarters will close at FORCEVILLE at 9 am. and will open at HEDAUVILLE at 10.30 am.

3. 7/Royal Fusiliers returned to MARTINSART from old German front line this morning.

4. Acknowledge.

Issued to Signals......10.30 am   W.H.Lowden
                                          Captain.
                                       Brigade Major.

1.2.3. War Diary.
   4. File.
   5. Brigadier.
   6. B.e.Major.
   7. Staff Captain.
   8. Signals.
   9. 63rd.Div "G".
  10.   "   "Q".
  11. C.R.A.
  12. C.R.E.
  13. 7/Royal Fusiliers.
  14. 4/Bedfordshire Regt.
  15. 10/Royal Dublin Fusiliers.
  16. 1/H.A.C.
  17. 190th.M.G.Coy.
  18. "   T.M.Battery.
  19. 3rd.Field Coy.
  20. A.D.M.S.
  21. S.S.O.
  22. No.4 Coy.Div.Train.
  23. Bde.Transport Offr.
  24. 189th.Inf.Bde.
  25. 188th.Inf.Bde.

SECRET. *Appendix VII* Copy No. 3

190th Infantry Brigade Order No. 60.

Headquarters,
190th Infantry Brigade.
20th Feby. 1917.

Reference BEAUMONT Map 1/10,000.
57D " 1/40,000.

1. The 190th Infantry Brigade will relieve the 188th Inf.Bde. in the line on the night of 21/22nd. February.

2. The relief will be carried out in accordance with attached March Table.
The 189th Machine Gun Company is placed under the orders of the 190th Infantry Brigade and will relieve the 188th Machine Gun Company in the line on the night of the 22nd inst.
The relief of Trench Mortar Batteries will be carried out on 21st instant under arrangement of O.C.Batteries concerned.
Relief of Field Companies will be arranged by Officers Commanding Companies, and arrangements reported to Brigade Hd.Qrs. early as possible.
One Battalion of 189th Brigade will be at the disposal of 190th Brigade for carrying purposes and will be located in old German Front Line System.
The 190th Labour Company will be attached to the battalion in Reserve from 22nd instant for accommodation and will be located in old German Front Line System. Guides for this Company on the morning of the 22nd instant will be arranged by O.C.Reserve battalion

3. All further details of relief will be arranged by Commanding Officers concerned.

4. One guide per platoon and one per Lewis Gun will meet units at Cooker Dump at times shown in March Table.

5. The usual distance of 100 yards between Companies or similar units and 500 yards between battalions will be observed on the march. All movement forward of MESNIL will be by parties not larger than one platoon at 100 yards distance.

6. Instructions regarding the handing over of trenches as laid down in "63rd (R.N.) Division Trench Standing Orders" will be strictly adhered to.

7. Box Respirators will be worn in the "Alert" position during the relief.

8. Bombing sections of units going forward into front and supporting lines will carry a supply of bombs detonated ready for use.
The Brigade Bombing Officer will arrange with units for the issue of these bombs from the HAMEL DUMP.
The Rifle Grenade Cup attachments will be taken over from relieved units.

9. All photographs, plans, defence schemes etc will be taken over and receipt given.

10. A statement of work in hand, current Intelligence Summary and work report, will be taken over from relieved units.

11. Brigade Dumps and all stores will be taken over under arrangements of Staff Captains.

2.

12. Arrangements for the issue of gum-boots will be made later.

13. Guards on water points etc., will be taken over by incoming units.

14. Arrangements for relief of working parties are attached as Appendix "A".

15. Command of Section will pass to G.O.C. 190th Bde. on completion of relief of front line.

16. Relief complete will be reported to Brigade Headquarters by wiring the word "DOWN".

17. Headquarters will close at HEDAUVILLE at 1.30.pm. and open at Q.18.a. on arrival there.

18. ACKNOWLEDGE.

C.H.Dowden
Captain.
Brigade Major.

Time issued to Signals. 4.32p.

```
1.2.3.  War Diary.
    4.  File.
    5.  Brigadier.
    6.  Brigade Major.
    7.  Staff Captain.
    8.  Signals.
    9.  63rd Div. "G"
   10.  63rd Div. "Q"
   11.  C.R.A.
   12.  C.R.E.
   13.  7/Royal Fusiliers.
   14.  4/Bedfordshire Regt.
   15.  10/R.Dublin Fusiliers.
   16.  1/H.A.C.
   17.  190th M.G.Coy.
   18.  190th T.M.Battery.
   19.  3rd Field Coy.
   20.  A.D.M.S.
   21.  S.S.O.
   22.  No.4.Coy.Div.Train.
   23.  Bde.Transport Officers.
   24.  189th Inf. Bde.
   25.  188th Inf. Bde.
```

MARCH TABLE TO ACCOMPANY 190th INFANTRY BRIGADE ORDER No. 60.

Unit.	From.	To.	Route.	In relief of	Guides at Jocker Dump at	Remarks
10/R.Dublin Fus.	ENGLEBELMER.	Reserve Line.	MESNIL-HAMEL	1st Bn. Marines	2.0.pm.	All movement East of the Western end of MESNIL to be by platoons at 100 yards distance.
*7/Royal Fusiliers	MARTINSART.	Front Line (Left.)	MESNIL-HAMEL.	2nd Bn. Marines.	5.0.pm.	
4/Bedfordshire Regt.	MARTINSART.	Front Line (Right.)	MESNIL-HAMEL.	Anson Bn.	6.0.pm.	
1/H.A.C.	ENGLEBELMER.	Support Lines	MESNIL-HAMEL.	Howe Bn.	6.45.pm.	
190th Bde. Labour Coy.	MESNIL.	Reserve Lines.	HAMEL.	------	8.am. on 22-2-17.	All movement to be by platoons at 100 yards distance.

APPENDIX "A"

Arrangements for Relief of Working Parties.

Reference to moves ordered in 190th Infantry Brigade Order No.60.

The following alterations in working parties will take place:-

(a) Party No.18 will be supplied by 1/H.A.C. on 21st inst and cancelled on the 22nd.
Found by 188th Bde. on 23rd.

(b) Party No.19. will be supplied by the 10/R.Dublin Fusiliers on 21st and 22nd inclusive and by 189th Bde on 23rd.

(c) Party No.21. will be supplied by 10/R.Dublin Fusiliers on 21st and 22nd inst. and by 188th Brigade on 23rd inst.

(d) Party No.29 will be reduced to 30 men and supplied by 10/R.Dublin Fusiliers on 21st, it will be cancelled for 22nd inst and taken over by the 188th Brigade on 23rd inst.

(e) Party No.42. will be cancelled on the 21st and 22nd inst. and taken over by 188th Bde. on 23rd inst.

(f) Party No.43. will be cancelled on 21st and supplied by 189th Brigade on 22nd inst.

(g) Parties Nos. 22, 23 and 58 will be taken over by 189th Brigade on 21st instant.

Parties not mentioned hereon will remain employed as at present.

Headquarters,
190th Infantry Brigade.
21st February, 1917.

Amendment to March Table issued with 190th Brigade Order No.60.

(a) Guides for 1/H.A.C. will be at COOKER DUMP at 5.30.pm.

(b) Guides for 4th Bedfordshire Regt. will be at COOKER DUMP at 5.45.pm

To all whom Bde.Order No.60. was sent.

Captain.
Bde Major.

SECRET Appendix VIII   Copy No. 77

190th Infantry Brigade Order No.62.

                                            Headquarters,
                                              190th Inf. Bde.
                                              24/2/17.

Reference 57D N.E. 1/20,000
     "   57D S.E. 1/20,000
     "   SERRE SHEET 1/10,000.

1. The enemy has evidently withdrawn his troops to the
    Western edge of MIRAUMONT.

2. The 18th Division have established themselves on the line
    of SOUTH MIRAUMONT TRENCH.
    Patrols have now reached the following points:-

        R.11.b.4.9.- R.5.Central.- R.4.d.4.0.

    and are now pushing forward to R.5.a.Central and to
    the MILL at R.4.d.4.7. (MILL is reported occupied at
    present).

3. At 3.30.pm today strong patrols will be pushed forward
    as below.-

    (a) 4th Bedfords. Patrol along the BEAUCOURT - MIRAUMONT
        ROAD to 100 yards East of the Road Junction
        R.4.a.5.1. and establish themselves at that point
        and get touch with the 18th Division on the right
        flank.

    (b) 4th Bedfordshire Regt. push out strong patrol along
        the trench running East from MIRAUMONT ALLEY at
        R.3.c.6.9. to the road at R.4.a.4.3. and establish
        themselves there.

    (c) 4th Bedfordshire Regt push out strong patrol along
        MIRAUMONT ALLEY to the SUNKEN ROAD and establish
        themselves at R.3.b.6.7..

    (d) The 7th Royal Fus, will push out a strong patrol
        along SWAN TRENCH to the SUNKEN ROAD at R.3.b.4.8.
        and establish themselves in HINDENBURG TRENCH about
        R.3.b.5.9.

4. (a) The 7th Royal Fus will then establish themselves on the
        line of SWAN TRENCH facing North to join up with the
        present Northern Post Line at about R.2.b.9.9.

    (b) The 4th Bedfordshire Regt will then establish posts at
        about R.4.a.7.1. R.4.a.5.3.   R.4.a.4.5. R.4.a.5.7.
        R.3.b.9.7. R.3.b.8.8. The latter three in MIRAUMONT
        ALLEY R.3.b.7.8.

5. The 4th Bedfordshire Regt. will then push forward patrols
    to the Western edge of MIRAUMONT and ascertain if the
    Trench running North and South through R.4.b. is occupied

6. Frequent reports as to the progress of this movement must be sent to Brigade Headquarters (at least every half an hour from 4.pm. inclusive.)

7. Acknowledge by wire.

Tinme issued to Signals...... 245/-   C.H.Dowden
                                                                          Captain.

                                        Brigade Major.

1. File.
2. Brigadier
3. Brigade Major.
4. Staff Captain.
5. 63rd Div. "G" (6 copies)
6. 63rd Div "Q"
7. 7th Royal Fus.
8. 4th Bedfordshire Regt.
9. 10th Royal Dublin Fus.
10. 1st H.A.C.
11. 190th M.G.Co.
12. 190th T.M.Battery.
13. "G" Group R.A.
14. 188th Infantry Bde.
15. 189th Inf. Bde.
16. 187th Inf. Bde.
19. 55th Inf. Bde.
20. 54th Inf. Bde.
21. 53rd Inf. Bde.
22. S.R.E.
23. Signals.
24. Drake.
25. A.D.M.S.
26. 3rd Field Coy.
27. Spare. 189 M.G.C
28. 190 Labour Co
29. Spare

SECRET. Copy No......

Addendum No.1. to 190th Brigade Order No.62.

Headquarters,
190th Infantry Brigade.
24/2/17.

1. O.C.189th M.G.Coy. will   , reconnoitre positions
   and establish guns at the following points:-

   1 Gun at Cross Roads R.4.a.5.1.
   1. " " Bend of Road about R.4.a.4.5.
   1. " ". Junction of HINDENBURG TRENCH and Road
            about R.4.a.3.8.
   1. " " in SWAN TRENCH about R.3.a.7.8.
   1 "   near SUNKEN ROAD about R.3.a.1.7.
   1 "   in SWAN TRENCH about R.2.b.4.7
   1. "   in ARTILLERY ALLEY about R.2.a.8.6.
   1. "   about R.2.a.6.7.
   1. "   "   R.3.a.9.5.
   1. "   "   on Northern end of QUARRY about
                 R.3.b.98.18.
   1. "   at Cross Roads North of BAILLESCOURT FARM
   4 guns along PUISIEUX TRENCH
   4. "   (190th M.G.Coy.) BEAUCOURT RIDGE.
   Headquarters M.G.Coy. SUNKEN ROAD.

2. O.C.190th T.M.Battery will establish guns as under:-

   3 Guns now in SUNKEN ROAD will be established at:-
   (a) QUARRY in R.4.a.
   (b) Road Junction about R.4.a.5.2.
   (c) Junction of HINDENBURG TRENCH and the SUNKEN ROAD
       R.3.b.3.7.
   Other guns will remain in present positions.

   Headquarters 190th T.M.B. SUNKEN ROAD.

3. On completion of move the dispositions of troops will be
   as under:-

   (a) 4th BEDFORDSHIRE REGT Hd.Qrs. QUARRY R.4.a.

       3 Companies. In new post line East of road in
                    R.4.a. - R.3.b.
       1 Company. In QUARRY R.4.a.

   (b) 7th Royal Fusiliers Hd.Qrs. SUNKEN ROAD R.3.a.2.5.

       3 Companies. In new post line on Northern Front.
       1 Company.   MIRAUMONT ALLEY in R.3.b.

   (c) 10th R.Dublin Fusiliers Hd.Qrs. In dugout at present
              occupied as Hd.Qrs. 4th Bedfordshire Regt.
              about R.8.b.8.4.
       1.Company. In Trench running East from MIRAUMONT ALLEY
                  in R.3.d.a.B.
       1.Company. In Southern End of the SUNKEN ROAD and
                  BAILLESCOURT FARM.
       1.Company. In PUISIEUX TRENCH (South)
       1.Company. In ANCRE TRENCH. in R.8.b.

2.

(d) 1st H.A.C.Hd.Qrs. SUVLA DUGOUT.

   1.Company. In SUNKEN ROAD about the PIMPLE. R3a.2.5
   1.Company. In PUISIEUX TRENCH. (North)
   1.Company. In post line North of BOIS D' HOLLANDE.
   1.Company. In PUISIEUX ROAD.

(f) Drake Bn. Hd.Qrs. In BEAUCOURT TRENCH Loft (now occupied
                           by 1st H.A.C.)
   2.Companies. In BEAUCOURT TRENCH.
   1.Company.   In QUARRY in R.8.b. and SUVLA TRENCH East.
   1.Company.   In BEAUCOURT CAVES.

(g) Labour Coy. In RAVINE in R.12.d.

4. The above moves will take place immediately on receipt of the Code Word "GO".

5. Completion of move will be reported by the Code Word "MOVED".

6. Acknowledge by wire.

Time issued to Signals. 5.45/p

C.H.Bowden.
Captain.
Brigade Major.

To all whom B.O.O. was issued.

R138

Headquarters
180th Inf. Brig.
7th May, 1917.

Field Orders No. 1. to 180th Inf. Bde. Order No. 49.

Par. 1. line 6. for R.4.4.B.D. road R.4.5.B.
Par. 2. subpara. (c) line 4. for R.N.b.d. read R.N.b.8.
Par. 3. subpara. (c) for N.19d. read N.19d.
Par. 5. subpara. (c) for N.19d. read N.19d.

By order H.O.Smedle, 2nd Lieut.

Captain

Brigade Major

SECRET.   Copy No...... 29

Addendum No.2. to 190th Brigade Order No.62.

                                        24/2/17.

1. The 1/H.A.C. will push forward a strong patrol Northward
   along the PUISIEUX and RIVER TRENCH System to its
   junction with PUISIEUX ALLEY and establish themselves
   there and got in touch with 187th Brigade who are
   working up PUISIEUX ALLEY.
   They will also push a patrol up the SUNKEN ROAD to
   continuation of PUISIEUX ALLEY thence North-Eastward
   to the WUNDT WERK at L.32.b.5.6. and establish themselves
   there and keep touch with posts at junction of PUISIEUX
   TRENCH and PUISIEUX ALLEY.

2. The 7th Royal Fusiliers will push a strong patrol North-
   Westward along the road from the junction of HINDENBURG
   TRENCH, thence up SAFETY TRENCH to the WUNDT WERK about
   L.32.b.9.6., and got in touch with 1/H.A.C.

3. The 4th Bedfordshire Regt. will push on and establish
   themselves in the trench at the Western End of MIRAUMONT
   in R.4.a.b and d, and get in touch with the 7th Royal Fus
   in Hindenburg TRENCH and 18th Division on Right.

4. The 7th Royal Fus. will push on Eastwards along HINDENBURG
   TRENCH and got touch with the 4th Bedfordshire Regt there.

5. ACKNOWLEDGE.

                                              Captain.
Time issued to Signals........ 6.50 pm   Brigade Major.

To all whom B.O.62 was issued.

SECRET

Appendix IX

Copy N°........

190th Infantry Brigade Order No. 63.

Headquarters,
190th Inf. Bde.
25/2/17.

Reference PENDANT COPSE 1/5000.
          MIRAUMONT   1/5000.
          57D N.E.   1/20,000.
          57D S.E.   1/20,000.

1. All information tends to show that enemy has evacuated his defences in front of PYS as well as the village of MIRAUMONT.

2. The II.Corps is moving forward on the line M.9.b.7 5.- BEAUREGARD DOVECOTE

3. Boundary between 63rd and 18th Divisions is the GRANDCOURT - MIRAUMONT RAILWAY.
Boundary between 63rd Division and Fifth Corps is line R.2.b.8.6 to L.29.a.5.5.

4. The Drake Bn is placed at the disposal of G.O.C.190th Inf. Bde. for these operations.

5. At 7.30.am on 25th the 190th Infantry Brigade will advance and occupy the line L.35.Central - BEAUREGARD DOVECOTE.

6. The advance will be carried out by 3 battalions with one battalion in support and one battalion in reserve. The 10/R.Dublin Fusiliers will be on the Right, the 7th Royal Fus. in the Centre with the 1st H.A.C. on the Left. The 4th Bedfordshire Regt. will be in support with the Drake Bn. in Reserve.

7. At 7.30 am the 10th R.Dublin Fus. will be formed up in artillery formation on the line of the SUNKEN ROAD in R.2.a. and c. and at 7.30.am will advance in this formation with scouts, pushed forward The Right of the battalion will be on the BEAUCOURT- MIRAUMONT ROAD.
They will advance to the Eastern outskirts of MIRAUMONT and establish themselves on the line L.35.Central to L.35.a.0.3. and push forward a strong patrol to occupy the brickfield in L.75.a.
The 10/R.Dublin Fus. should be disposed as under on the completion of this move.-

    <u>Two Companies</u> in an outpost line on the Eastern edge of MIRAUMONT and in the brickfield.
    <u>One Company</u> on the line L.35.c.6.0. to L.34.d.8.9.
    <u>One Company</u> on the line R.5.a.0.5. to L.34.d.3.0.
    Headquarters at L.34.d.3.0.

8. The 1st H.A.C. will be formed up in artillery formation on the SUNKEN ROAD in L.35.d. and R.2.b. with its Right on SWAN TRENCH. At 7.30.am. they will advance in this formation with scouts pushed well forward, and a strong flank guard of two companies on their left.
Their objective will be the BEAUREGARD DOVECOTE which is on a bearing of 64 magnetic from junction of SWAN TRENCH and the SUNKEN ROAD.
They will establish themselves at BEAUREGARD DOVECOTE and form a defensive flank along BEAUREGARD ALLEY in L.33.b.
On the completion of this operation they will be distributed as under.
    <u>One Company</u> at BEAUREGARD DOVECOTE with its Right on L.28.d.1.1 and its Left on L.28.c.6.5.
    <u>One Company</u> in Trench from L.34.a.6.9. to L.28.c.8.0.
    <u>One Company</u> in BEAUREGARD ALLEY from L.28.c.8.0. to L.33.b.8.5
    <u>One Company</u> in VALLEY from L.33.b.5.5. to L.34.a.3.2.
    Headquarters about L.34.a.3.2.

2.

The 7th Royal Fus. will be formed up in artillery formation on the line of the road from R.3.b.5.6. to R.3.a.9.9.
About 8 a.m., or when the two flank battalions arrive in line with position of assembly of this battalion it will advance with those battalions in artillery formation with scouts pushed well forward and keep in touch with their flanks until it arrives at the Eastern edge of the village of MIRAUMONT when it will establish itself on the line L.35.a.0.3. to L.28.d.1.1.
On completion of this operation the battalion will be disposed as under:-
  Two Companies in outpost line on Eastern edge of MIRAUMONT
  One Company in Road from L.34.d.5.9. to L.34.b.3.8.
  One Company in Valley from L.34.c.7.6. to L.34.d.3.6.
  Headquarters L.34.d.3.6.

10. As soon as the three battalions above have gone forward the 4th Bedfordshire Regt. will establish themselves in the HINDENBURG Trench from R.4.b.2.2. to R.3.b.8.9.
Headquarters in QUARRY about R.4.a.1.1.

11. At 8 a.m. the Drake Bn. will move forward from present position and occupy the SUNKEN ROAD from R.3.c.6.2. to R.3.a.1.7.
Headquarters about R.3.c.3.6.

12. A report centre has been established in SUNKEN ROAD about R.3.c.3.6.
Frequent information as to progress must be sent back to Bde. Headquarters.
All units must send back at least two runners to report when they are established.
Telephonic communication will be established as soon as possible.

13. O.C. 189th M.G.Coy. will arrange to send forward 4 guns with 1st M.G. and 2 guns with each of other two battalions.
An officer of the M.G.Coy. will be sent forward with each Bn. to select position for these guns.
Four guns will be established on the line of the track from about R.34.central. to R.33.b.2.2.
Remaining 8 guns will be brought forward to SUNKEN ROAD with the Reserve Battalion and held ready to move forward at once when required.

14. O.C.190th T.M.Battery will proceed with all mortars to the Cross Roads at R.4.b.8.7. and await further orders.

15. ACKNOWLEDGE.

Time issued to Signals...... 3 am

C.H. Dowden
Captain.
Brigade Major.

1. File.
2. Brigadier.
3. Brigade Major.
4. Staff Captain.
5. 63rd Div. "G" (3 copies)
6. 63rd Div. "Q"
7. 7th Royal Fusiliers.
8. 4th Bedfordshire Regt.
9. 10th Royal Dublin Fusiliers.
10. 1st M.G.
11. 189th M.G.Coy.
12. 190th T.M.Battery.
13. "G" Group R.A.
14. 188th Inf. Bde.
15. 189th Inf. Bde.
16. 187th Inf. Bde.
17. 55th Inf. Bde.
18. 54th Inf. Bde.
19. 53rd Inf. Bde.
20. C.R.E.
21. Signals.
22. Drake Bn.
23. A.D.M.S.
24. 3rd Field Coy.
25. 189th M.G.Coy.
26. 190th Bde. Labour Co.
27. Spare.

SECRET   Appendix X   Copy No......

190th Infantry Brigade Order No.64.

25/2/17.

Reference ACHIET Sheet. 1/10,000.

1. The Left of the 18th Division is now established about L.30.Central.

2. The Brigade will at once push forward and occupy the trench line from L.30.c.2.9. to L.28.a.9.1.

3. The 10th R.Dublin Fusiliers will push forward a strong patrol of 1 Officer and 30 men with two Lewis Guns and occupy the trench from L.30.c.2.9. to old gun pits about L.29.b.2.1. and get touch with troops of 18th Division on the Right.
   They will also push forward and occupy the Northern edge of the trench system from L.29.d.4.1. to L.29.c.5.1. with a similar party.
   The Company at present on the line L.5.a.0.0. to L.34.d.5.0. will be pushed forward to fill the gap made by the movement of above troops.

4. The 7th Royal Fusiliers will push forward a patrol of similar strength and occupy the trench line from old gun pits L.29.b.2.1. to gun pits about L.29.a.0.1. and get touch with 10th R.Dublin Fus. on the Right.
   They will also push forward a post to about L.28.d.9.0.

5. The 1/H.A.C. will push forward a similar party to occupy trench from the Left of the 7th Royal Fus. about L.29.b.2.1. to the road at L.28.a.9.1. and get in touch with troops of 32nd Division on the Left and 7th Royal Fus. on the Right.

6. The above movements will take place at once and reports sent back when established.

7. ACKNOWLEDGE.

                                               [signature]
                                               Captain.
                                          Brigade Major.

1. File.
2. Brigadier.
3. Brigade Major.
4. Staff Captain.
5. 63rd Div "G" (6 copies)
6. 63rd Div "Q"
7. 7th Royal Fusiliers.
8. 4th Bedfordshire Regt.
9. 10th Royal Dublin Fus.
10. 1st H.A.C.
11. 190th M.G.Coy.
12. 190th T.M.Battery.
13. "G" Group R.A.
14. 188th Inf. Bde.
15. 189th Inf. Bde.
16. 187th Inf. Bde.
17. 55th Inf. Bde.
18. 54th Inf. Bde.
19. 53rd Inf. Bde.
20. C.R.E.
21. Signals.
22. Drake Bn.
23. A.D.M.S.
24. 3rd Field Coy.
25. 189th M.G.Coy.
26. 190th Bde. Labour Co.
27. Spare.

Appendix XI

SECRET.   Copy No........

190th. Infantry Brigade Order No.65.

26/2/17.

Reference 57D 1/40,000.
"   ACHIET   1/10,000.
"   BEAUMONT 1/10,000.
"   MIRAUMONT 1/5,000.

1.   The 185th.Inf.Bde.will relieve the 190th.Inf.Bde. in the line tonight, 26/27th.inst.

2.   The relief will be carried out in accordance with attached March Table.
        The 4 Machine Guns of the 190th.M.G.Coy.will be withdrawn tonight and will rejoin 190th M.G.Coy.
        The 189th.M.G.Coy.will be relieved on the night 27/28th. inst.under arrangements made between O.C.Coys.concerned.
        The relief of T.M.Battery will be carried out tonight under arrangements made between Officers Commanding Batteries.
        The relief of 3rd.Field Coy.will be carried out under arrangements made with O.C.relieving Coy.

3.   Further details of relief will be arranged by O.C.Units concerned.

4.   One guide per Platoon and one per Lewis Gun will meet incoming units as under.
        (a) Guides from 1/H.A.C. to meet units of 2/5 W.Yorks Regt. at the Quarry in R.4.a.3.2. at 6 pm.

        (b) Guides from 10/R.D.F. to meet units of 2/8 W.Yorks Regt. at Quarry in R.4.a.3.2. at 6.45 pm.

        (c) Guides from 7/Royal Fusiliers to meet units of 2/7 W. Yorks Regt.at the Junction of the SUNKEN ROAD North of BAILLESCOURT FARM at 7.pm.

        (d) Guides from 4/Bedfordshire Regt.to meet units of 2/6th W.Yorks Regt. at Junction of PUISIEUX and MIRAUMONT ROAD at 7.30 pm.

        (e) The Brigade Signalling Officer will send "Runners" to the Brigade Dump at Q.24.a.3.9. as below.

            1. One runner to meet the 2/5 W.Yorks at 4.30 pm. and conduct them to meet guides at Quarry in R.4.a.3.2.
            2. One runner to meet 2/8 W.Yorks at 5.15 pm. and conduct them to meet guides at Quarry in R.4.a.3.2.
            3. One runner to meet 2/7 W.Yorks at 6 pm.and conduct them to meet guides at Road Junction North of BAILLESCOURT FARM.
            4. One runner to meet 2/6 W.Yorks at 6.30 pm.and conduct them to meet guides at Junction of PUISIEUX and MIRAUMONT ROAD.

5.   O.C.Units will leave one N.C.O. from each Platoon with the relieving Unit for 24 hours, and one runner from Bn.Hd.Qrs. for a similar period. Two runners from Bde.Hd.Qrs.will be left with the relieving Brigade for 24 hours.

6. Instructions regarding the handing over of trenches as laid down in "63rd(RN)Division Trench Standing Orders" will be strictly adhered to.

7. All photographs, plans, Defence Schemes etc, will be handed over to relieving units.

8. On relief, Units will proceed direct to Billets etc. The usual distance of 100 yards between Platoons will be strictly observed on the MIRAUMONT ROAD. West of HAMEL 100 yards will be observed between Coys.and 500 yards between Battalions.

9. Gum boots will be collected under arrangements made by the Staff Captain. Units are responsible that they hand over the same number that were issued to them on proceeding to the trenches.

10. Command of Section will pass to G.O.C. 185th.Inf.Bde. on relief of Brigade (less M.G.Coy.).

11. Relief will be reported by the words "WELL DONE".

12. Hd.Qrs.will close at Q.18.a. on completion of relief and open at PAISLEY DUMP on arrival there.

13. Drake Bn.will return to 189th.Inf.Bde. under orders issued by that Brigade.

14. ACKNOWLEDGE.

Issied to Signals.....3.5/

                                                Captain.
                                 Brigade Major.

1. File.
2. G.O.C.
3. Bde.Major.
4. Staff Capt.
5. 33rd.Div."G" (6 copies).
6. " " "Q"
7. 7/Royal Fusiliers.
8. 4/Bedfordshire.Regt.
9. 10/R.D.F.
10. 1/H.A.C.
11. 190th.M.G.Coy.
12. 190th.T.M.B.
13. "G" Group R.A.
14. 188th.Inf.Bde.
15. 189th. " "
16. 187th. " "
17. 55th. " "
18. 54th. " "
19. 53rd. " "
20. C.R.E.
21. Signals.
22. Drake Bn.
23. A.D.M.S.
24. 3rd.Field Coy.R.E.
25. 189th.M.G.Coy.
26. 190th.Bde.Labour Coy.
27. Spare.

SECRET.   Copy No......

Addendum No.1 to 199th.Inf.Bde.Order No.64.

                                                        25/2/17.

Reference BEAUCOURT Map 1/10,000.
    "   ACHIET   "   "
    "   MIRAUMONT   "   1/5,000.

1.   On the conclusion of the movement ordered in Order
        No.64 the Brigade will be organised with two Bns. in
        the front line, one in support and one in Reserve. The
        10/R.D.F. will be on the RIGHT front and the 1/H.A.C.
        on the LEFT front. The 7/R.F. will be in support with
        the 4/Bedfordshire Regt. in reserve.

2.   Battalions etc, will be located as under:-
   (a) 10/R.D.F. (Right front).
        1 Company in trench from the Railway at L.30.c.2.9.
            to L.29.a.8.1. and the Trench System
            from L.29.d.3.1. - L.29.c.5.1.

        Two Companies in Outpost Line from L.35 central to
            L.34.b.7.7.

        One Company on line L.35.c.8.0. to L.34.d.8.9.
        Headquarters Dugout R.4.b.6.8.

   (b) 1/H.A.C. (Left Front).
        One Company in trench from L.29.a.8.1. to L.28.a.9.1.
            with Post about L.28.d.98.60.

        One Company in outpost line from L.34b.7.7. to L.28.
            c.6.5.

        One Company in PIGEON LANE from L.34.a.9.6. to
            L.34.a.3.8.

        One Company in VALLEY from L.34.c.4.9. to L.34.d.3.6.
        Headquarters SUNKEN ROAD L.34.c.7.2.

   (c) 7/Royal Fusiliers (Support).
        Two Companies about the SUNKEN ROAD in R.4.a. and
            R.3.b.

        Two Companies in Quarry in R.4.a. and c and vicinity.
        Headquarters in Quarry in R.4.c.

   (d) 4/Bedfordshire Regt. (Reserve)
        One Company in Southern end of SUNKEN ROAD in
            R.3.c. and BAILLESCOURT FARM.

        Two Companies in PUISIEUX Trench (South).

        One Company in ANCRE Trench in R.8.b. and Quarry in
            R.8.b.9.5.
        Headquarters in ANCRE Trench about R.8.b.2.5.

   (e) Drake Bn.
        Two Companies in BEAUCOURT Trench.
        One Company   in BEAUCOURT CAVES.
        One Company   in Quarry R.8.a.2.1.
        Headquarters   BEAUCOURT Trench (Left) R.7.a.3.2.

2.

(f) Machine Guns.
Two Guns about BEAUREGARD DOVECOTE.
One Gun about L.34.b.3.8.
Two Guns in Brickfield L.35.a.
One Gun about L.35.central.
Four Guns on SPUR L.34.c. - L.33.d.
Four Guns on SPUR R.3.a. & b.
Two Guns in reserve in Northern end of SUNKEN ROAD.
Headquarters in SUNKEN ROAD about R.3.c.3.6.

The O.C.189th.Machine Gun Company will arrange to reconnoitre positions for Guns as above.

(g) Trench Mortars
One L.T.M. in BEAUREGARD DOVECOTE.
One L.T.M. about L.34.b.3.8.
One L.T.M. in Brickfield L.35.a.
One L.T.M. about L.35.c.8.6.
Two L.T.M's in HINDENBERG Trench R.4.a.& b.
Two L.T.M's in Reserve in SUNKEN ROAD about R.3.c.4.4.
Headquarters in SUNKEN ROAD about R.3.c.3.6.

3. The above moves will take place as soon as possible after move ordered in Order No.64 is completed.
All details of necessary reliefs will be arranged between Units concerned.

4. Units will move on receipt of the code word "WHISKY".
Completion of move will be reported by the code word "WATER".

5. Acknowledge.

Issued to Signals....4.55.am.   C.H.Dowden
                                                  Captain.
                                              Brigade Major.

1. File.
2. Brigadier.
3. Brigade Major.
4. Staff Captain.
5. 63rd.Div. "G". (6 copies).
6. "   "   "Q".
7. 7/Royal Fusiliers.
8. 4/Beds Regt.
9. 10/R.D.F.
10. 1/H.A.C.
11. 190th.M.G.Coy.
12. 190th.T.M.B.
13. "G" Group R.A.
14. 188th.Inf.Bde.
15. 189th.Inf.Bde.
16. 187th.Inf.Bde.
17. 55th. Inf.Bde.
18. 54th. Inf.Bde.
19. 53rd. Inf.Bde.
20. C.R.E.
21. Signals.
22. Drake Bn.
23. A.D.M.S.
24. 3rd.Field Coy.R.E.
25. 189th.M.G.Coy.
26. 190th.Bde.Labour Coy.
27. Spare.

MARCH TABLE TO ACCOMPANY 190th INFANTRY BRIGADE ORDER NO.65.

Unit.	From.	To.	Route.	Relieved by.	Remarks.
1/H.A.C.	Front Line Left.	Tents MESNIL.	BEAUCOURT - HAMEL.	2/5 W.Yorks.	
10/R.D.F.	Front Line Right.	Huts THIEPVAL WOOD.		2/8 W.Yorks.	
7/Royal Fusiliers	Support Lines.	THIEPVAL.		2/7 W.Yorks.	
4/Bedfordshire Regt.	Reserve.	MARTINSART.	HAMEL - MESNIL.	2/6 W.Yorks.	

On His Majesty's Service.

Historical Section
Committee of Imperial Defence.
2 Cavendish Sq
W. 1.

WAR OFFICE.

Vol. 10.

Headquarters
190th Inf. Bde.
(63rd Div.)
March 1919.

Original

VOLUMN X

Vol 10

S E C R E T.

Headquarters, 190th. Inf. Brigade,
1st April 17 ....Date.

W A R   D I A R Y

of

190th. Infantry Brigade.

From........ 1 - 3 - 17.
To.......... 31 - 3 - 17.

C A Dowden Capt
Major.
Brigade Major,
190th. Infantry Brigade.

To :- The A.G's office
3rd Echelon
(through D.H.Q.)

Army Form C. 2118.

WAR DIARY
or
INTELLIGENCE SUMMARY.
(Erase heading not required.)

MARCH 1917
VOLUME X

Instructions regarding War Diaries and Intelligence Summaries are contained in F. S. Regs., Part II. and the Staff Manual respectively. Title pages will be prepared in manuscript.

Place	Date	Hour	Summary of Events and Information	Remarks and references to Appendices
	1/3/17		Working parties for roadmaking remainder general clean up and Arm, clothing etc. inspections — Divisional headquarters moved HEDAUVILLE	AAA
	2/3/17		Brigade moved to Martinsart Area as in Appendix I Headquarters opened at Martinsart Chateau at 10/40 p.m.	AAA
	3/3/17		Training Specialists and working parties on roads	AAA
	4/3/17		Training Specialists and working parties	AAA
	5/3/17		Training Specialists and working parties	AAA
	6/3/17		Working parties only	AAA
	7/3/17		Working parties only	AAA
	8/3/17		Divisional Commander inspected Machine Gun Company and Trench Mortar battery. He expressed satisfaction at their turnout Remainder of Brigade working parties	AAA
	9/3/17		Working parties and Specialist training with available men	AAA
	10/3/17		Working parties and Specialist training with available men CRS taken	AAA

Army Form C. 2118.

WAR DIARY
or
INTELLIGENCE SUMMARY.
(Erase heading not required.)

Instructions regarding War Diaries and Intelligence Summaries are contained in F. S. Regs., Part II. and the Staff Manual respectively. Title pages will be prepared in manuscript.

Place	Date	Hour	Summary of Events and Information	Remarks and references to Appendices
	11/3/17		Working Parties as usual. Church Parades	C.W.D
	12/3/17		Working Parties and Training of Specialists. Brigade Lewis Gun Course Commenced	C.W.D
	13/3/17		Working Parties as usual. Enemy has left the Achiet le petit — Serpent Line and is being followed by 2nd Corps	C.W.D
	14/3/17		All available men working on roads and railways etc. Lieut Watts 4/Bedford Regt (Staff Learner) proceeded to Divison to commence course of Staff Duties after himself of attachment to a Brigade. Went to Vimy MC/VIMC attached to Brigade as staff learner	C.W.D
	15/3/17		All men on Working Parties	C.W.D
	16/3/17		Usual working parties. Transport of the Brigade was inspected by the Divisional Commander who expressed satisfaction at their turnout	C.W.D
	17/3/17		Working Parties as usual	C.W.D

WAR DIARY
or
INTELLIGENCE SUMMARY.
(Erase heading not required.)

Army Form C. 2118.

Place	Date	Hour	Summary of Events and Information	Remarks and references to Appendices
	18/3/17		Preparations for move from 5th to 1st Army	G.S.O
	19/3/17		Brigade marched to Conteay area (APPENDIX II)	G.S.O
	20/3/17		Brigade marched to Beauval area (APPENDIX III)	G.S.O
	21/3/17		Brigade marched to Beauval Bonniers area (APPENDIX IV)	G.S.O
	22/3/17		Brigade marched to Blangermont area (APPENDIX V)	G.S.O
	23/3/17		Halted in Blangermont area	
	24/3/17		Marched to Pernes area (APPENDIX VI)	G.S.O
	25/3/17		Brigade marched to Laires area (APPENDIX VII)	G.S.O
	26/3/17		Brigade Marched to Boues area (APPENDIX VIII)	G.S.O
			14th (Reserve) Norcestn. Regt and 247 Field Coy attached to Brigade Group from 188 Brigade Group	G.S.O
	27/3/17		General clean up and rearrangement of Billets	
			M.G.Coy moved to ROBECQ — L'ECLEME road	G.S.O
	28/3/17		All units commence individual training, country very flat and cultivated, ground for training almost impossible to obtain.	G.S.O

Army Form C. 2118.

WAR DIARY
or
INTELLIGENCE SUMMARY.
(Erase heading not required.)

Place	Date	Hour	Summary of Events and Information	Remarks and references to Appendices
	29/3/17		Individual training continued (very wet)	BM D
	30/3/17		Individual Training. Brigadier and Commanding Officers reconnoitred the front of Canadian Corps from Arras to Souchez River	BM D
	31/3/17		1/4 MMGC and 4/1 Bedfords carried out annual tactical scheme as an appendix. IX Corps every lesson learned. Remainder of Brigade Individual Training	BM D

W A St John
Captain
Brigade Major
for GOC 190 Inf Bde

APPENDIX I

SECRET.   Copy No........

190th. Infantry Brigade Order No. 66.

Hd.Qrs.190th.Inf.Bde,
1/3/17.

Reference ALBERT Combined Sheet 1/40,000.

1.   The 190th.Inf.Bde. (less 4/Bedfordshire Regt.) will move from present dugouts and Camps etc, to Hutted Camps in the MARTINSART Area and billets in MARTINSART on the 2nd.inst in accordance with attached March Table.

2.   Advance parties to take over Camps and billets will be sent forward to arrive at destination at 9 am.
        Representatives of 54th.Inf.Bde.Hd.Qrs.; 12th.Bn.Middlesex Regt. and 8th.Northampton Regt. will arrive at Headquarters of 190th.Inf.Bde., 7/Royal Fusiliers and 10/Royal Dublin Fusiliers respectively at 9 am.

3.   All Dugouts, Camps, Billets etc, must be left scrupulously clean.

4.   The usual distance of 100 yards between Companies and 500 yards between Battalions must be observed on the march. Units must move strictly in accordance with March Table to avoid conjestion on the roads.

5.   Brigade Headquarters will close at PAISLEY DUMP at 9.30 am and open at the CHATEAU at MARTINSART on arrival there.

6.   ACKNOWLEDGE.

                                                                    signature
                                                                    Captain.
Issued to Signals........   Brigade Major.

        1-3 War Diary.
        4. File.
        5. Brigadier.
        6. Bde.Major.
        7. Staff Captain.
        8. Signals.
        9. 63rd.Div."G".
        10. "   "Q".
        11. 7/Royal Fusiliers.
        12. 4/Bedfordshire Regt.
        13. 10/R.D.F.
        14. 1/H.A.C.
        15. 190th.M.G.Coy.
        16. 190th.T.M.Battery.
        17. S.S.O.
        18. 4 Coy.Div.Train.
        19. Bde.Transport Officer.
        20. 188th.Inf.Bde.
        21. 189th. " "Bde.
        22. Town Major MARTINSART.
        23. 54th Inf. Bde.
        24. 190th Labour Coy.

MARCH TABLE TO ACCOMPANY 190th.INFANTRY BRIGADE ORDER NO.66.

Unit.	From.	To.	Time.	Starting Point.	Route.	Remarks.
190th.Inf.Bde.H.Q.	PAISLEY DUMP.	MARTINSART.	10.am.	PAISLEY DUMP.	AVELUY WOOD.	-
1/A.M.C.	Camp Q.35.a.	MONMOUTH HUTS. W.16.A.8.6.	10.15 am.	Cross Roads Q.35.d.2.9.	AVELUY WOOD.	-
7/Royal Fusiliers.	THIEPVAL.	DOGSLEG HUTS. W.9.d.5.2.	-	THIEPVAL.	AUTHUILLE - Road East of the River - AVELUY.	To be clear of AUTHUILLE by 10 am.
10/R.D.F.	THIEPVAL WOOD.	GRESTAND HUTS. W.10.c.8.2.	-	THIEPVAL WOOD.	AUTHUILLE - Cross Roads Q.35.d.2.9. - AVELUY WOOD.	Not to enter AUTHUILLE before 11 am.
190th.T.M.Battery.	Camp Q.35.a.	MARTINSART.	9 am.	Q.35.a.	MESNIL	-
190th.M.G.Coy.	HEDAUVILLE.	MARTINSART.	9 am.	HEDAUVILLE	BOUZINCOURT.	-

APPENDIX II

SECRET.

Copy No........ 20

190th. Infantry Brigade Order No.67.

18th. March 1917.

Reference LENS Sheet 1/100,000.
"   57d   "   1/40,000.

1. The 63rd (RN) Division is being transferred from 2nd. Corps, Vth. Army, to 13th. Corps, 1st. Army.

2. The 190th. Infantry Brigade Group will march to the CONTAY Area on the 19th. inst., and continue the march to the BEAUVAL Area on the 20th. inst., in accordance with attached march table.
   Table for the 20th. inst. will be issued later.

3. Headquarters Divisional Train and the Mobile Veterinary Section are attached to the 190th. Infantry Brigade for the move.
   These Units will move with No.4 Company Divisional Train.
   The three above mentioned Units will come under the orders of Headquarters Divisional Train.

4. Normal halts will be observed, i.e., 10 minutes before each clock hour until the hour.
   A distance of 200 yards between companies and transport and 500 yards between other units will be observed on the march.

5. The strictest attention must be paid to March Discipline both on the march and during halts.
   This applies equally to Transport and others.

6. Baggage wagons will accompany units. Supply wagons move with the Train Company.

7. Special attention must be paid to the turnout of transport throughout the move. Covers of Limbers, etc., must be neatly fastened, and Cookers must be kept as clean as possible.
   G.R.O's referring to riding on wagons or leaving animals unattended must be strictly observed. Attention is directed to General Routine Orders of 1/1/17, Appendix 11.

8. Billetting Parties from each Unit under an Officer must be sent forward each day to arrange billets with Town Majors before the arrival of the Units. These parties must be marched by the Officer.
   An Officer will be detailed each day to obtain from Town Majors after the Unit has left, a certificate to the effect that billets have been left in a satisfactory condition, and that there are no claims against the unit.
   of any description

9. Extra transport will be notified as soon as possible.

10. Brigade Headquarters will close at MARTINSART at 9 am. on the 19th. and open at CONTAY on arrival there.

11. Acknowledge by wire.

C. H. Dowden
Captain.
Brigade Major.

Issued to Signals...... 1.15 pm

1. 63rd.Div. "G"
2.   "   "   "Q"
3. 7/Royal Fusiliers.
4. 1/H.A.C.
5. 4/Bedfordshire Regt.
6. 10/R.D.F.
7. 190th.M.G.Coy.
8. 190th.T.M.Battery.
9. H.Q.Div.Train.
10. No.4 Coy.Div.Train.
11. 3rd.Field Ambulance.
12. 249th.Field Coy.R.E.
13. 188th.Inf.Bde.
14. 189th.Inf.Bde.
15. Staff Captain.
16. Brigade Transport Officer.
17. Mobile Vet Sec.
18. File.
19. War Diary (3)
20. O/C Sig.

MARCH TABLE TO ACCOMPANY 190th.INF.BDE.ORDER NO.67.

Order of march.	Unit.	From	To	Starting point	Time	Route	Remarks.
1.	H.Q.Div.Train. No.4 Coy.Div.Train. M.V.Section.	BOUZINCOURT.	CONTAY Area.	BOUZINCOURT W.7.c.4.0.	10.5am	SENLIS - WARLOY.	
2.	249 Field Coy.R.E.	MESNIL	"		9.5 am	MARTINSART - ROAD JUNCTION W.3.d.-BOUZIN-COURT - SENLIS - WARLOY.	To enter BOUZINCOURT at 10.10am.
3.	4/Beds.Regt.	Martinsart Wood.	"	MARTINSART WOOD	9.45am	BOUZINCOURT - SENLIS - WARLOY.	To follow 249 Field Coy.R.E. from MAR-TINSART WOOD.
4.	10/K.D.F.	CABSTAND HUTS	"	On Road W.9.d.9.1.	10.0am	Cross Roads V.15.b. - BOUZINCOURT - SENLIS - WARLOY	
5.	7/R.F.	DOGSLEG HUTS	"	W.9.d.9.4.	10.25am	-as above-	
6.	1/H.A.C.	MONMOUTH HUTS	"	W.10.d.3.0.	10.30am	-as above-	
7.	Bde.H.Q.	MARTINSART	"	MARTINSART.	10.55am	BOUZINCOURT - SENLIS - WARLOY	To follow 1/H.A.C. from BOUZINCOURT.
8.	M.G.Coy.	MARTINSART WOOD	"	MARTINSART WOOD	11.10am	"	To follow Bde.H.Q.
9.	T.M.Battery.	MACKENZIE HUTS.	"	Cross Roads V.3.d.	11.10am	"	To follow M.G.Coy.& to be clear of BOUZINCOURT by 12 noon.
10.	No.3 Field Amblce.						Stand fast at CLAIRFAYE until 20th.inst.

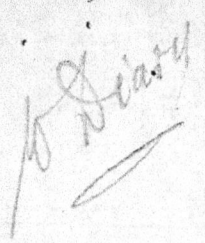

Headquarters,
190th Infantry Brigade.
18th March. 1917.

To Recipients of 190th Inf. Bde. Order No. 67.

1. Reference para.2. of Brigade Order No. 67 dated 18.3.17.
Units of the 190th Infantry Brigade Group will be distributed as follows in the CONTAY AREA for the night 19th/20th March.1917:-

190th Inf. Bde. Hd. Qrs.	at	CONTAY
1st Bn. H.A.C.	"	"
7th Bn. Royal Fusiliers	"	"
4th Bn. Bedfordshire Regt.	"	VAL DE MAISON.
10th R. Dublin Fusiliers	"	HARPONVILLE.
190th M.G. Coy.	"	CONTAY.
190th T.M. Battery.	"	CONTAY.
249th Field Coy.	"	VADENCOURT.
No.4. Coy. Train.	"	HARPONVILLE.
Hd.Qrs. Div. Train.	"	"
Mob. Vet. Section.	"	"
No. 3. Field Amb. remains	"	CLAIRFAYE.

Lieutenant. R.N.V.R.
Staff Captain.

APPENDIX III

SECRET.   Copy No........

Addendum No.1. to 190th Inf.Bde. Order No.67.

1. The Brigade Group will continue the march on the 20th instant in accordance with attached March Table.

2. There will be a halt of about $\frac{3}{4}$ hours when the head of the column reaches a point about M.27.d.2.0.
   The March will be continued by all units at 12.noon.

3. Distribution of units for the night of the 19th inst. is attached.

4. Acknowledge by wire.

Time issued to Signals.........   C.H. Dowden
                                              Captain.
                                           Brigade Major.

1. 63rd Div. "G"
2. 63rd Div. "Q"
3. 7th Royal Fusiliers.
4. 4th Bedfordshire Regt.
5. 1st H.A.C.
6. 10th R.Dublin Fus.
7. 190th M.G.Coy.
8. 190th T.M.Battery.
9. H.Q.Div. Train.
10. No.4.Coy.Div. Train.
11. 3rd Field Amb.
12. 249th Field Coy. R.E.
13. 188th Inf. Bde.
14. 189th Inf. Bde.
15. Staff Captain.
16. Brigade Transport Officer
17. Mobile Vet. Section.
18. File.
19. War Diary.
20. O.C.Signals.

MARCH TABLE.

Order of March.	Unit.	From.	To.	Starting Point.	Time.	Route.	Remarks.
1.	H.Q.Div.Train. No.4.Coy. A.V.Section.	HARPONVILLE.	BEAUVAL AREA.	Road Junction U.4.d.3.7.	7.40am.	TOUTENCOURT PUCHEVILLERS- VAL DE MASON- FMES DU ROSEL- CROSS RDS.A.9.a.8.3.	Not to pass Cross Rds. A.9.a.3.3. before 12.5pm.
2.	249. Coy.R.E.	VADENCOURT	BEAUVAL AREA.	Road Junction U.21.a.8.2.	8.0am.	--ditto--	To follow Train Group from TOUTENCOURT.
3.	10/K.D.F.	HARPONVILLE.	BEAUVAL AREA.	Road Junction U.4.d.3.7.	8.10am.	--ditto--	To follow R.E. Coy.from TOUTENCOURT.
4.	7/R.F.	CONTAY.	BEAUVAL AREA	Road Junction U.21.a.8.2.	8.20am.	--ditto--	
5.	1/H.A.C.	CONTAY.	BEAUVAL	--as above--	8.35am.	--ditto--	
6.	190th.M.G.Coy.	CONTAY.	BEAUVAL	--as above--	9.0am.	--ditto--	
7.	Bde.H.Q. & T.M.Battery.	CONTAY.	BEAUVAL	--as above--	9.10am.	--ditto--	
8.	3rd.Field Amb.	CLAIRFAYE	BEAUVAL.	CLAIRFAYE		HARPONVILLE- TOUTENCOURT- PUCHEVILLERS- VAL DE MASON- FMES DU ROSEL- Cross Roads A.9.a.8.3.	To enter TOUTEN- CCURT at 10.0am and to be clear of same by 10.15am. To follow Bde.H.Q. from TOUTENCOURT.
9.	4/Beds.Regt.	VAL DE MASON.	BEAUVAL.	VAL DE MASON.	12.40pm	FMES DU ROSEL - Cross Roads A.9.a.8.3.	To follow No.3 Field Amb.

SECRET.   Copy No.......

Amendment No.1. to 190th Infantry Brigade Order No.67.
-

1. The 3rd Field Ambulance will march via LEALVILLERS -
   ARQUEVES - RAINCHEVAL - BEAUQUESNES and not as shown
   in March Table issued with Addendum No.1 to Brigade
   Order No.67.

2. Hour of start 12.noon.

3. Acknowledge by wire.

Issued to Signals....11.30/   [signature] Captain.
                                         Brigade Major.

To all Whom Brigade Order No.67
was issued.

Appendix IV

SECRET.   Copy No.............

190th Infantry Brigade Order No. 69.

Reference LENS Sheet. 1/100,000.   20th March. 1917.

1. 190th Infantry Brigade Order No. 38 is cancelled.

2. The Brigade Group will continue the march on the 21st instant in accordance with attached March Table. Distance about 12½ miles.

3. A distance of 300 yards only will be observed between battalions and 100 yards between companies and other units. Transport must be kept closed up throughout the march. Care must be exercised that the distances as above are not exceeded.

4. There is not sufficient water for animals either at BONNIERES or BOUQUE MAISON. The nearest watering points are the River CANCHE and the River AUTHIE respectively. Buckets must be taken.

5. Brigade Headquarters will close at BEAUVAL at 11.0.am and open at BONNIERES on arrival there.

6. Please acknowledge by wire.

Time issued to Signals.......5.50 pm   C.H.Lowden
                                                                                Captain.
                                                                          Brigade Major.

1. 63rd Div. "G"
2. 63rd Div. "Q"
3. 7th Royal Fus.
4. 4th Bedfordshire Regt.
5. 1st H.A.C.
6. 10th R.Dublin Fus.
7. 190th M.G.Coy.
8. H.Q.Div. Train.
9. No.4.Coy. Div. Train.
10. 3rd Field Amb.
11. 249th Field Coy. R.E.
12. 188th Inf. Bde.
13. 189th Inf. Bde.
14. Staff Captain.
15. Brigade Transport Officer.
16. Mobile Vet. Section.
17. File.
18. War Diary.
19. O.C.Signals.

March Table to accompany 190th Infantry Brigade Order No.69
****

Order.	Unit.	From.	To.	Starting Point.	Time.	Route.	Remarks.
1.	H.Q.Div.Train. No.4.Coy.Train. L.V.Section.	BEAUVAL.	BONNIERES	Railway Crossing on the DOULLENS Road immediately North of BEAUVAL.	10.30.am.	DOULLENS-BOUQUE MAISON-Cross Roads MON LELLOND.	Head not to pass BOUQUE MAISON - FROHEN Road before 1.15.pm.
2.	249th Coy. R.E.	"	"	"	10.35am.	"	
3.	7th Royal Fus.	"	"	"	10.45am.	"	
4.	C 1st H.A.C.	"	"	"	11.5.am.	"	
5.	4th Beds.Regt.	"	BOUQUEMAISON	"	11.15.am.	DOULLENS Direct.	
6.	10th R.Dublin Fus.	"	"	"	11.25.am.	"	
7.	190th M.G.Coy.	"	BONNIERES.	"	11.35.am.	As in No.1.	
8.	Bde. H.Q.	"	"	"	11.40.am.	"	
9.	No.? Field Amb.	"	"	"	11.45.am.	"	

SECRET.   Copy No. 18

190th Infantry Brigade Order No.70.

APPENDIX V

Headquarters,
190th Inf. Bde.
20th March. 1917.

Reference LENS Sheet 1/100,000.

1. The march will be continued on the 22nd instant in accordance with attached March Table. Distance about 9 miles.

2. There is a scarcity of water for animals in all the villages. The nearest Rivers are the TERNOISE and CANCHE. There are springs at PRONAY. Buckets must be taken in each case.

3. Distances of 300 yards between battalions and 100 between companies must be most strictly observed. Transport must not be allowed to straggle and must halt at 10 minutes to clock hour, the same as the infantry.

4. There will most probably be a halt on the 23rd instant.

5. Brigade Headquarters will close at BONNIERES at 10.am. and open at BLANGERMONT on arrival there.

6. Please acknowledge.

Time issued to Signals......

C. H. Dowden
Captain.
Brigade Major.

1. 63rd Div. "G"
2. 63rd Div. "Q"
3. 7th Royal Fus.
4. 4th Bedfordshire Regt.
5. 1st H.A.C.
6. 10th R.Dublin Fusiliers.
7. 190th M.G.Coy.
8. H.Q. Div. Train.
9. No.4. Coy. Train.
10. 3rd Field Amb.
11. 249th Field Coy. R.E.
12. 188th Inf. Bde.
13. 189th Inf. Bde.
14. Staff Captain.
15. Brigade Transport Officer.
16. Mobile Vet. Section.
17. File.
18. War Diary.
19. O.C.Signals.

March Table to accompany 190th Infantry Brigade Order No.70.

Order of March.	Unit.	From.	To.	Starting Point.	Time.	Route.	Remarks.
1.	H.Q.Div.Train. No.4.Coy. M.V.Section.	BONNIERES	HERLIN LE SEC.	Road Junction ½ mile N.E. of BONNIERES on the FREVENT Road.	9.45.am.	FREVENT-NUNCQ	
2.	249th Field Coy. R.E.	"	BLANGERMONT	"	10.am.	FREVENT-NUNCQ-HAUTE COTE - FLERS.	
3.	1/H.A.C.	"	BLANGERVAL	"	10.5am.	"	
4.	4/Leas Regt.	BOUQUEMAISON	FRAMECOURT and PT MOUVIN.	Road Junction S. of ABBES N.N.W. of BOUQUEMAISON.	9.25.am.	FREVENT-NUNCQ.	To follow 1/H.A.C. from FREVENT.
5.	10/R.Dublin F.	"	HERICOURT.	"	9.35.am.	FREVENT-NUNCQ -F of FRAME-COURT - Cross Roads S.E. end of CROISETTE.	To be clear of BOUQUEMAISON by 9.50am.
6.	7/Royal Fus.	BONNIERES.	HAUTE COTE.	Road Junction ½ mile N.E. of BONNIERES on the FREVENT Road.	10.35.am.	FREVENT-NUNCQ.	To follow 10/RDF from FREVENT.
7.	BDE. H.Q.	"	BLANGERMONT	"	10.45am.	FREVENT-NUNCQ- HAUTE COTE - FLERS.	
8.	190th M.G.Co.	"	"	"	11.0am.	"	
9.	No.3.Field Amb	"	"	"	11.10am.	"	

(APPENDIX VI)

SECRET. Copy No. 2.

190th Infantry Brigade Order No. 71.

23/3/17.

Reference LENS Map 1/100,000.
Hazebrouck 5 a 1/100,000

1. The march will be continued on the 24th. inst., in accordance with attached March Table. Distance about 13 miles.

2. Billeting Lists for 25th & 26th. inst. are attached.

3. Brigade Headquarters will close at BLANGERMONT at 8.0 am. and open at PERNES on arrival.

4. ACKNOWLEDGE.

C.H. Dowdie
Captain.
Brigade Major.

Issued to Signals...... 5/1m

1. 63rd Div. "G"
2. " "Q"
3. 1/H.A.C.
4. 7/Royal Fusiliers.
5. 4/Bedfordshire Regt.
6. 10/R.D.F.
7. 190th M.G.Coy.
8. H.Q.Div.Train.
9. No.4 Coy. Div. Train.
10. 3rd.Field Amb.
11. 249th.Field Coy.R.E.
12. 188th.Inf.Bde.
13. 189th. " "
14. Staff Captain.
15. Bde.Transport Officer.
16. Mobile Vet. Section.
17. File.
18. War Diary.
19. O.C.Signals.

MARCH TABLE TO ACCOMPANY 190th.INF.BDE.ORDER NO.71.

Unit.	From.	To.	Starting Point.	Time.	Route.	Remarks.
249th.Field Coy. R.E.	LIANGERMONT.	EPS and HERLEVAL.	Cross Roads N.W. end of LIANGERMONT.	8.am.	LINZEEL - OEUF - LEAUVOIS - PIERREMONT - WAVRANS - HESTRUS.	
190th.M.G.Coy.	"	PERNES.	"	8.5am	LINZEUL - OEUF - LEAUVOIS - PIERREMONT - WAVRANS - HESTRUS - TANGRY.	
B/H.A.C.	LIANGERVAL.	TANGRY.	"	8.10am	"	
3rd Field Amb.	LIANGERMONT.	GUERNONVAL & HESTRUS.	"	8.25am	LINZEUL - OEUF - LEAUVOIS - PIERREMONT - WAVRANS - HESTRUS.	
H.Q.Div.Train. No.4 Coy. M.V.Section.	HERLIN LE SEC.	PERNES.	Cross Roads N of HERLIN LE SEC.	10.am.	St.POL direct route.	
4/Leeds Regt.	FRAMECOURT and Pt.HOUVIN.	PERNES.	Cross Roads N of Pt.HOUVIN.	9.am.	"	
10/K.D.F.	HERICOURT.	PERNES.	CROISETTE Church.	9.30am.	Q in RAMECOURT - St.POL direct.	
7/R.B.	HAUTE COTE	PRESSY.LES PERNES.	Cross Roads S.W. of first N in HUMCQ.	9.am.	St.POL direct Road.	
2do.H.Q.	LIANGERMONT.	PERNES.	LIANGERMONT.	8.30am	FLEAS - U in HERLINCOURT - St.POL direct.	

BILLETING LIST FOR 25th.Inst.

Brigade Headquarters. 1/H.A.S. 190th.M.G.Coy.	LAIRES. " "
7/Royal Fusiliers. 10/Royal Dublin Fusiliers.	FLECHIN. "
4/Bedfordshire Regt.	FELVIN PALFART.
249th.Field Coy. R.E. H.Q.Div.Train. No.4 Coy. Div.Train. M.V.Section.	ESTREE BLANCHE. " " "
No.3 Field Ambulance.	LIVOSSART.

BILLETING LIST FOR 26th.inst.

Brigade Headquarters.	L'ECLEME.
1/H.A.C.	--"--
4/Bedfordshire Regt.	LUSMETTES.
7/Royal Fusiliers.	PT.BERNECHON.
10/Royal Dublin Fusiliers.	--"--
190th.M.G.Coy.	MARQUEVILLE.
249th.Field Coy.R.E.	--"--
M.V.Section.	ROBECQ - L'ECLEME road.
190th.T.M.Battery.	--------"--------
3rd.Field Ambulance.	LA MIQUELLERIE.
H.Q.Div.Train.	BUSNES.
No.4 Coy.Div.Train.	--"--
* 14th (Pioneer) Worcester Regt.	--"--
* 247th.Field Coy. R.E.	LA PIERRIERE

    * March under orders of 188th.Inf.Bde. until evening of 26th.inst.

SECRET.   Copy No ......

190th Inf. Brigade Order No. 72.

Reference LENS sheet 1/100,000.
HAZEBROUCK 5a. 1/100,000.

HEADQUARTERS,
190th
INFANTRY BRIGADE.

No. ......
Date 25/5/

1. The Brigade Group will continue the march on the 25th and 26th inst. in accordance with attached march tables.

2. A distance of 500 yards will be observed between Battalions and 100 yards between Companies and other Units - Transport must be kept closed up - Normal halts must be strictly observed by all Units and Transport.

3. All M.T. must move as under :-

    (a) On 25th inst. by route PERNES - LILLERS - ST. HILAIRE.
    (b) On 26th inst. by route ST. HILAIRE - LILLERS.

4. Railheads will be :-

    25th March .... LILLERS.
    26th March .... BETHUNE.

5. The 14th (Pioneer) Worcester Regt. and the 247th Field Co., R.E., will be attached to the 190th Brigade Group on completion of the march on the 26th inst. They will be billeted as shown in Brigade Order No. 71.

6. Headquarters, (a) will close at PERNES at 7.30 a.m. on 25th inst. and open at LAIRES on arrival, (b) will close at LAIRES at 8.0 a.m. on 26th inst. and open at L'ECLEME on arrival.

7. Please ACKNOWLEDGE.

Capt. in,
Brigade Major.

Time issued to Signals ....

Copies to:-

1. 63rd Division "G".
2. 63rd Division "Q".
3. 1/H.A.C.
4. 7/Royal Fusiliers.
5. 4/Bedfords. Regt.
6. 10/R. Dublin Fus.
7. 190th M.G.Co.,
8. H.Q., Divnl. Train.
9. No. 4 Coy., Divnl Train.
10. 3rd Field Amb.
11. 249th Field Co. R.E.
12. 188th Inf. Bde.
13. 189th Inf. Bde.
14. Staff Captain,
15. Bde Transport Officer.
16. Mob. Vet. Section.
17. File.
18. War Diary
19. O.C., Signals.
20. 14th Worc Regt
21. 247th Field Coy RE

Unit.	From	To	Starting Point.	Time.	Route.	Remarks.
249th.Coy.R.E.	EPS.	ESTREE BLANCHE.	EPS.	8.30am	SAINS LES PERNES - FIEFS - FEBVIN - FLECHIN - CUHEM - FLECHIMELLE.	Not to reach FIEFS before 10.10am.
d.C.Div.Train. No.4 Coy. L.V.Section	PERNES.	"	Road Junction W of the Southern end of PERNES.	8.40am	"	To follow 249th Coy.R.E. from FIEFS.
3rd.Field Amb.	NESTRUS.	LIVOSSART.	Cross roads S.W. end of NESTRUS.	8.30am	NPS - BOYAVAL - MEUCHIN - FONTAINE les BOULERS - PALFART	
190th.M.G.Coy.	PERNES.	LAIRES.	Road Junction W of the Southern end of PERNES.	8.45 am	SAINS - FIEFS - PALFART	To follow Train Group.
Bde.H.Q.	PERNES.	LAIRES.	"	9.0am	"	
1/F.A.C.	TANGRY.	LAIRES.	Road Junction N.E.margard of	10.0 A.M.	"	
10/R.D.F.	do	FLECHIN	H in BLARINGHEM	10.0 a.m.	AUMERVAL - FLEXIN PALFART	
7/Royal Fus.	PRESSY les PERNES	do	do	10.10 a.m.	do	To follow 10/ R.D.F. from PERNES
4th Bedford.Rgt	PERNES	FEBVIN PALFART	do	10.30 a.m.	do	

March Table.

Unit	From	To	Starting Point.	Time	Route	Remarks.
No.1 Div.Train. No.4 Coy.	ESTREE BLANCHE	BUSNES	Road junction N.W. of B in BLANCHE	9.5 am	Cross Roads N.of AUCHY-AU-LOIS - ST.HILAIRE - LILLERS.	Not to enter ST. HILAIRE before 11.0am.
M.V.Section.	—"—	ROBECQ - L'CLEME.	—"—	9.8 am	Cross Roads N.of AUCHY-AU-BOIS - ST.HILAIRE - LILLERS - L'CLEME.	
249 Field Co. R.E.	—"—	NANQUEVILLE	Road junction N.W. of B in BLANCHE.	9.15 am	Cross Roads N of AUCHY-AU-BOIS - ST.HILAIRE - HAM.	
190th A.T. Coy.	LAIRES.	—"—	Cross roads ½ mile S of L in LAIRES.	8.5 am	PALFART - WESTRELEN - ST.HILAIRE - HAM.	To follow 249 Coy. R.E. through St. Hilaire.
1/A.A.C.	—"—	L'CLEME	—"—	8.10am	PALFART - WESTREMEN - ST.HILAIRE - LILLERS.	
4/Leeds.Regt.	FEBVIN.	BUSNETTES.	Cross roads S of L in FEBVIN	9.45am	WESTREMEN - ST.HILAIRE - LILLERS - BAS RIEUX.	
10/K.L.R.	FLECHIN	MT.BERNECHON.	Road junction ¼ mile S of F in FLECHIN.	10.5am.	FEBVIN - WESTREMEN - ST.HILAIRE - LILLERS - L'CLEME.	
7/A.S.R.	—"—	—"—	—"—	10.20am	—"—	
R.C.H.Q.	LAIRES.	S'CLEME	Cross roads ½ mile S of L in LAIRES.	8.40am	PALFART - WESTREMEN - ST.HILAIRE - LILLERS.	
3rd.Field Amb.	LIVOSSART.	LA NIQUELMERIE LIVOSSART.		9.0am	—"—	

Appendix IX

GENERAL IDEA.

Reference HAZEBROUCK Map 1/100,000.
    "   36a   " 1/40,000.

1. A state of War exists between "Northland" and "Southland".

2. The Southern Army, after its defeat on the BELGIAN-FRENCH Border, about BAILLEUL, retired in a Southwesterly direction and is reported to be holding the high ground South West of LILLERS with outposts on the line AIRE - BETHUNE.

3. There is no Cavalry with either Army.

4. The Northern Army who have lost touch, are advancing in a Southwesterly direction with the object of completing the defeat of the Southern Army before it has time to reform.

5. The 4/Bedfordshire Regt. will represent the Northern Army and the 1/H.A.C. the Southern Army.

Issued to:-
    1. Brigadier.
    2. Brigade Major.
    3.4.5. War Diary.
    6. 1/H.A.C.
    7. 4/Beds Regt.
    8. M.G.Coy.
    9) Spare.
    10)

SPECIAL IDEA NORTH.

Reference HAZEBROUCK Map 1/100,000.
    "   36a.   " 1/40,000.

1.   The Central Division of the Northern Army is marching Southward in three columns. The 290th. Brigade is advancing along the MERVILLE - ST. VENANT - LILLERS Road.

2.   The Advance Guard consisting of the 4/Bedfordshire Regt. arrives at the North Eastern outskirts of ST. VENANT at 11.30 am, when it receives orders to push forward and reconnoitre the crossings over the AIRE - LA BASSEE Canal between the LILLERS - HAZEBROUCK Railway and the River CLARENCE, and, without attracting the attention of the enemy, get as many men as possible in position with a view to rushing the crossings at a given signal.

Frequent information must be sent in from all reconnoitring parties.

Every endeavour must be made to conceal our approach from the enemy.

3.   For the purpose of this exercise the 4/Bedfordshire Regt. will march out via BUSNES to ST. VENANT and will take Cookers and have dinner North of the Canal on completion of the operation.

It will be considered as an Advanced Guard throughout the march.

4.   Brigade Headquarters (imaginary) will be at ST. VENANT during the reconnaissance.

Issued to :-
1. Brigadier.
2. Brigade Major.
3.4.5 War Diary.
6. 4/Bedfordshire Regt.
7.8. Spare.

SPECIAL IDEA SOUTH.

Reference HAZEBROUCK Map 1/100,000.
"   36a   "   1/40,000.

1.   The Southern Army has retired to the high ground behind the line AIRE – LILLERS – BETHUNE where it intends to reform and establish itself.

2.   The 790th.Brigade is detailed to hold the crossing of the AIRE – LA BASSEE Canal between the LILLERS – HAZEBROUCK Railway and the HINGES – MERVILLE road.

3.   The 10/Blankshire Regt. (imaginary) will hold the line from the right (Eastern) boundary to the river Clarence (exclusive).

        The 1/H.A.C. will hold the line Clarence river (inclusive) to the LILLERS – HAZEBROUCK Railway (inclusive).

        The 7/Royal Fusiliers (imaginary) will be in support at GONNEHEM with the 71/Buffs (imaginary) at LILLERS.

        Brigade Headquarters (imaginary) will be at LILLERS.

4.   The crossings over the Canal are to be held at all costs until the Army in rear is established and ready to give battle.

5.   Two sections of 190th.M.G.Company are placed at the disposal of O.C.1/H.A.C. for this exercise. All orders for M.Guns will be issued to O.C.190th.M.G.Coy. by O.C.1/H.A.C. direct.

6   For the purpose of this exercise the 1/H.A.C. will move into position via LILLERS and BUSNES and will not be North or East of BUSNES before 10.30 am.

7   Cookers will be taken and dinners issued <u>during the operation</u>

Issued to:-
    1.Brigadier.
    2.Brigade Major.
    3.4.5.War Diary.
    6.1/H.A.C.
    7.190th.M.G.Coy.
    8.9.Spare.

On His Majesty's Service.

The Director,
Historical Section (Military Branch),
Committee of Imperial Defence,
2 Cavendish Square,
W.

May 1917
(63rd Div.)
XI

April 1917.

ORIGINAL.

HEADQUARTERS,
190th
INFANTRY BRIGADE.
No. 9664
Date. 1-5-17

S E C R E T.

Headquarters, 190th. Inf. Brigade,
30th April '17 Date.

VOLUME XI

W A R   D I A R Y

of

190th. Infantry Brigade.

From 1-4-17
To 30-4-17

Dowden
Captain ~~Major~~
Brigade Major,
190th. Infantry Brigade.

To:- The A.G's Office
Base
(through D.A.G.)

Army Form C. 2118.

WAR DIARY
or
INTELLIGENCE SUMMARY.

(Erase heading not required.)

APRIL 1917
VOLUME XI

Instructions regarding War Diaries and Intelligence Summaries are contained in F. S. Regs., Part II. and the Staff Manual respectively. Title pages will be prepared in manuscript.

Place	Date	Hour	Summary of Events and Information	Remarks and references to Appendices
	1/4/17		Sunday A Brigade church parade was held at which the Divisional Commander presented of Medals and decorations to N.C.O.s and men as in Appendix I	G.R.O. I
	2/4/17		Monday 4/RF and 10/RDF carried out Route March combined with Tactical Scheme as in Appendix II Remainder of Brigade Individual Training	G.R.O.
	3/4/17		Tuesday Heavy Snow Individual Training	G.R.O.
	4/4/17		Wednesday Individual Training - Divisional Staff made Aeroplane Contact Patrol Scheme (Appendix III)	G.R.O.
	5/4/17		Thursday Individual Training	G.R.O.
	6/4/17		Friday Company Training. Communication Scheme as in Appendix IV	G.R.O.
	7/4/17		Saturday Company Training	G.R.O.
	8/4/17		Sunday Brigade marched to Bruay area Appendix V Details to remain behind whose units go into a line and train reinforcement Concentrated under 13th Corps at ROBECQ	G.R.O.

Army Form C. 2118.

WAR DIARY
or
INTELLIGENCE SUMMARY.
(Erase heading not required.)

Instructions regarding War Diaries and Intelligence Summaries are contained in F. S. Regs., Part II. and the Staff Manual respectively. Title pages will be prepared in manuscript.

Place	Date	Hour	Summary of Events and Information	Remarks and references to Appendices
	9/4/17		Brigade concentrated as in Appendix V awaiting to move forward at Shoneratres - Canadian Corps captured Vimy Ridge - 11 Corps made good progress	A.A.D
	10/4/17		Brigade concentrated in Bray area	B.A.D
	11/4/17		Brigade Group marched to BAJAS area. Appendix VI. Some training carried out (Weather very bad)	E.A.D
	12/4/17			C.A.D
	13/4/17		Moved to Arras Sector and took over the line as in Appendix VII	E.A.D
	14/4/17		Bedfords and Dublins pushed on 1,000 yards and got touch with enemy at GAVRELLE - Patrols got into Oppy line but had to withdraw owing to short shelling - Casualties occurred in coming back.	M.A.D
	15/4/17		Brigade took over front of 2nd Division front as in Appendix VIII	C.M.D
	16/4/17		Patrol sent to reconnoitre OPPY line and if only lightly held HAC and 7/RF were to occupy same - (Appendix IX)	

T2134. Wt. W708—778. 500000. 4/15. Sir J. C. & S.

WAR DIARY
or
INTELLIGENCE SUMMARY.
(Erase heading not required.)

Army Form C. 2118.

Place	Date	Hour	Summary of Events and Information	Remarks and references to Appendices
		Continued		
	16/4/17		The line was found very strong - 9/RF dug in about 300x from the line 19/RF returned to starting point	
	17/4/17		HAC and 9/RF advanced under cover of darkness and dug in 300x from enemy line (Enemy guns are very active)	
	18/4/17		Enemy guns very busy on our front, troops and rest milk dug in - Digging of new front line continued - Enemy very active - Bright very dark and wet	
	19/4/17		Much shelling of our lines, we have very little shelter and suffer casualties 4/Bedfords aroint. to front to attack to dig new trench	
	20/4/17		Enemy shelled front and support very severely 10/RDF relieved 9/RF in night sector as in appendix x very heavy shelling during relay & by bombing of 10/RDF all many other shell casualties	

WAR DIARY
or
INTELLIGENCE SUMMARY.
(Erase heading not required.)

Army Form C. 2118.

Place	Date	Hour	Summary of Events and Information	Remarks and references to Appendices
	21/4/17		**Continued** 1/HAC relieved in the line by 1st S. Staffs Regt 6th Infy Brigade on readjustment of line taking place as in Appendix XI	App D
	22/4/17		Prep for attack as per App XII	App D App D
	22/4/17		Move to assembly positions	Appendix XII
	22/23/4/17		Preparations for operations as per Appendix XII	Appendix XIIa
	23/4/17		Operations as in Appendix XII. Zero hour was 4.45 am Weather fine light just right everyone got off well left of 4/R.F. came on Turin salient and were diverted to 16 the South suffering heavy in so doing — Bayards went astray though the village and Consolidated on N of Roeux outskirts The line of the railway was not actually consolidated, it being too flat and open — four counter attacks were delivered none of which succeeded	

WAR DIARY or INTELLIGENCE SUMMARY

Place	Date	Hour	Summary of Events and Information	Remarks and references to Appendices
	23/4/17		The 1/R Fus were withdrawn during the night 23/24 and replaced by 1/N.F., two companies of whom had been pushed to reinforce them earlier in the day — The captured position was very heavily shelled which greatly interfered with consolidation.	Maps X III and X IV
	24/4/17		All positions gained were held in spite of the many counterattacks, such by way of bombing attacks down the old german front line and across the open. The 1.8.5 Brigade was relieved by the 1/8th Brigade as in appendix XV relief was completed until 6.0 am 25th. Units located as in appendix XV. The 1/R.D.F. is at the call of G.O.C. 185 Bde in case of necessity. Other units reorganising	
	25/4/17			

WAR DIARY or INTELLIGENCE SUMMARY.

Place	Date	Hour	Summary of Events and Information	Remarks and references to Appendices
	26/4/17	—	1/HAC found party of 100 men to carry up T.M. ammunition. Remainder re-organising. 1/12 Battn. working on roads carrying for 168th Bde. 1 Battn. employed carrying for 168th Bde.	S.A.O.
	27/4/17		168th Brigade assisted in the attack on the OPPY line. 1/HAC and 1/R.D.F. were at the disposal of 168th Brigade. 1/HAC in support to 1/R.D.F. carrying. 4/Bedfords moved up in support to Bank line at 10.0 a.m. — 1/HAC engaged in the capture of enemy strong point which they captured with 240 prisoners. A Composite Battalion formed from 4/Bedford Regt. and 1/R.F. moved into assembly position to take part in fresh attack on the OPPY line in accordance with Appendix XVII	Appendix XVI
	28/4/17			

WAR DIARY
or
INTELLIGENCE SUMMARY.

(Erase heading not required.)

Army Form C. 2118.

Place	Date	Hour	Summary of Events and Information	Remarks and references to Appendices
	29/4/17		7/Royal Fusiliers and 4/Bedfords took part in an attack on the OPPY line as in Appendix XVII. The attack commenced at ZERO which was 4.25am and reached the objective but owing to enemy wire did not all get in — Enemy counter-attacked and drove them out but were in turn counterattacked by NFC who were already in the trench to their flank — The trench changed hands several times during the day but enemy were eventually cleared and we remained masters of the situation. We were relieved by a Brigade of 31st Division and withdrew to Bivt areas as shown in Appendix XVIII.	B40 XVIII
	30/4/17		Moved to Camps as shown in Appendix XIX	XIX

L.O. Gowlen
Capt.
for Lieut. Col. 190 Inf Bde.

HQ Appendix I

Headquarters,
190th Inf. Bde.,
31/3/17.

Headquarters,

    63rd R.N.Division (for information)
    1/H.A.C.
    7/Royal Fusiliers,
    4/Bedfordshire Regt.
    10/Royal Dublin Fusiliers,
    190th M.G.Company,
    190th T.M.Batty.

1.   There will be a Brigade Church Parade in the Chateau grounds at Divisional Headquarters near BUSNES at 9.30 a.m on SUNDAY, 1/4/17.
    The O.C., 7/Royal Fusiliers has kindly consented to loan the band of the Battalion for this service.

2.   The 1/H.A.C., 7/Royal Fusiliers and 4/Bedfordshire Regt will each detail one composite Company consisting of one section from each Platoon in the Battalion to attend.
    The 10/Royal Dublin Fusiliers will send a party of the strength of one Company who would normally attend C. of E. service.
    The O.C. 190th M.G.Company will detail one section.
    The 190th T.M.Battery will attend this parade.
    Units will be drawn up on 3 sides of a square, 7/R.F. on the right, 4/Bedfords and 1/H.A.C. on the rear face, 10/R.D.F., 190th M.G.Coy and 190th T.M.Battery on the left face.
    Dress for the parade will be drill order and caps.
    An Officer from each unit with Markers will meet the Brigade Major on the ground at 9.10 a.m. These Officers should know the frontage required by their companies or parties.

3.   The Divisional Commander will present the ribbons of decorations and medals to Officers, W.Os, N.C.Os and men of the Brigade which have been notified as awarded since 18/2/17 at 10 a.m. after the Church Service.
    Officers and other ranks who are to be decorated will be formed up in front of the rear face immediately after the Church Service.

Captain,
Brigade Major,

190th. Infantry Brigade.

PRESENTATION OF RIBBONS BY G.O.C. DIVISION.

on 1st. April 1917.

ORDER OF PRESENTATION.

OFFICERS.

2/Lt.P.F.Finch 1/H.A.C.   -   MILITARY CROSS.

For bravery and dash in clearing a strong point of the enemy on the night of Feb.7th/8th.

2/Lt.N.Baines 1/H.A.C.   -   MILITARY CROSS.

For patrol work, which led to the capture of GUDGEON Trench.

2/Lt.R.W.Taylor 7/Royal Fusiliers - MILITARY CROSS.

Between 2nd Feb and 27th.Feb.1917, North of River ANCRE - For conspicuous gallantry and devotion to duty while duty with No.2 Echelon Pack Train. On one occasion when a man of the 10/R.D.F. was seriously wounded, he showed the utmost coolness and presence of mind in getting the man to cover, and although there were many degrees of frost took off his own tunic to cover over the man.

Throughout, by his own cheerfulness and fine example, he kept the men under him in excellent spirits and so got the utmost out of them under very difficult circumstances.

2/LT R.L.Higgins 10D royal Dublin Fusiliers MILITARY CROSS.

On the morning 26th.Feb 1917, after the occupation of MIRAUMONT he was sent forward with a strong patrol to occupy GUDGEON Trench. When within 50 yards of his objective, the enemy opened a heavy fire from Machine Guns. He showed great initiative in handling his men, and withdrawing the patrol in broad daylight when surrounded on 3 sides and under fire from Machine Guns and snipers. He volunteered for this operation although this was his first tour in the line.

N.C.O's

1715 Sergt.J.A.M.Rumbold, 1/H.A.C. - MEDAILLE MILITAIRE.

For invaluable in tending wounded under exhausting conditions, during the operations in the YPRES SALIENT in September 1915.

1682 Sergt.F.Mighell, 1/H.A.C.   - MILITARY MEDAL.

For the splendid management of the Pack Train during the operations 5/25th Feb. 1917, under exhausting and difficult conditions.

N.C.Os (continued)

3042. A/Sergt C. Freter, 1/H.A.C.   -   MILITARY MEDAL.

For excellent patrol work which led to the subsequent capture of GRANDCOURT.

S/7253. Corporal A. Dunn, 7/Royal Fusiliers   -   MILITARY MEDAL.

Between the 2nd and 15th February 1917, N. of River ANCRE – For conspicious gallantry and devotion to duty while employed with No. 2 Echelon Pack Train.
On one occasion when a loaded pack animal had fallen into a hole, he worked for ¾ hour under heavy shell fire trying to extricate it, showing absolute disregard for his own personal safety. On another occasion in broad daylight and under heavy shell fire, he volunteered to go about 200 yards to put out of its pain an injured pack animal. Throughout, this N.C.O. showed great coolness and courage, and through his good example and cheerfulness, he inspired great confidence in the men under him.

10177. Corporal G. Oakley, 4/Bedfords. Regt - MILITARY MEDAL.

During the period that rations were being brought up by pack transport this Corporal did extremely good work, leading the pack transport over a bad track which was heavily shelled nearly every night. By his example and good leading the rations were delivered satisfactorily under difficult circumstances.

1788. L/Cpl S.L.Squires, 1/H.A.C.   -   MILITARY MEDAL.

For courage and determination, in spite of wounds, in controlling the parties of the Pack Animal Train under his command.

Other Ranks.

5094 Pte. C.H.Perry 1/H.A.C.   -   BAR TO MILITARY MEDAL

For capturing and bringing in unaided on night of Feb.7th/8th 15 German Prisoners.

3550 Pte.J.G.Hoodless 1/H.A.C.   -   MILITARY MEDAL.

Gallantry and determination under heavy shell fire and M.G.Fire in carrying messages to and from the front trenches, after the capture of BEAUREGARD DOVECOTE.

26708 Pte.W.J.Smith 4/Bedfords.   -   MILITARY MEDAL.

Near MIRAUMONT - when employed as a runner, this man did consistent good work and unaccompanied carried messages between Coy. and Bn. Hd.Qrs. under shell fire. Though sick he refused to

leave the Coy. and continued to volunteer to carry messages until the Coy. was relieved.

Other Ranks (Continued).

10722 Pte.W.Redmond 10/Royal Dublin Fusiliers. - MILITARY MEDAL

On the morning of 26th.Feb 1917, when a strong Officers patrol had been sent out from MIRAUMONT to occupy GEDGEON Trench and had been forced to withdraw, he, although not a Lewis Gunner seeing that the Lewis Gunner had been Killed ran forward and rscued the the Lewis Gun. He brought it back and establishing himself in a position opened fire on the enemy who thraatened to surround the party, covering the withdrawal of the patrol. He brought the gun safely back. His action very materially assisted the withdrawal of the patrol when other Lewis Guns has been put out of action.

25970 Pte.T.Mulrennan, 10/Royal Dublin Fusiliers.-MILITARY MEDAL.

On the 25th/and 26th.Feb 1917, after the occupation of MIRAUMONT, he showed conspicuous bravery and devotion to duty. He repeatedly carried messages through heavy shell fore. He went out with a strong patrol which occupied the BRICKFIRLE Trench System and brought back important medsages in daylight under Machine Gun fibe and fire from snipers. He was left with the relieving unit for 24 hours, whose Company Commander has brought to my notice, the excellent work he did during the period, under similar circumstances.

Appendix II

GENERAL IDEA.

Reference HAZEBROUCK Map 1/100,000.
           36a   "   1/40,000.

1. A state of War exists between "Northland" and "Southland".

2. The Southern Army after its defeat on the BELGIAN-FRENCH Border, about BAILLEUL, retired in a Southwesterly direction and is reported to be holding the high ground South West of LILLERS with outposts on the line AIRE - BETHUNE.

3. There is no Cavalry with either Army.

4. The Northern Army who have lost touch, are advancing in a Southwesterly direction with the object of completing the defeat of the Southern Army before it has time to reform.

5. The 10/R.D.F will represent the Northern Army and the 7/R.F. the Southern Army.

Issued to :-
    1 Brigadier.
    2.Brigade Major.
    3.4.5.War Diary.
    6.7/R.F.
    7.10/R.D.F.
    8.M.G.Coy.
    9.10.Spare.

SPECIAL IDEA SOUTH.

Reference HAZEBROUCK Map 1/100,000.
" 36a " 1/40,000.

1. The Southern Army has retired to the high ground behind the line AIRE - LILLERS - BETHUNE where it intends to reform and establish itself.

2. The 790th.Brigade is detailed to hold the crossing of the AIRE - La BASSEE Canal between the LILLERS - HAZEBROUCK Railway and the HINGES - MERVILLE Road.

3. The 10/Blankshire Regt.(imaginary) will hold the line from the right (Eastern) boundary to the river Clarence (exclusive).

    The 7/Royal Fusiliers will hold the line Clarence river (inclusive) to the LILLERS - HAZEBROUCK Railway (inclusive).

    The 1/H.A.C. (imaginary) will be in support at GONNEHEM with the 71/Buffs (imaginary) at Lillers.

    Brigade Headquarters (imaginary) will be at LILLERS.

4. The crossings over the canal are to be held at all costs until the Army in rear is established and ready to give battle.

5. Two sections of 190th.M.G.Company are placed at the disposal of O.C.7/R.F. for this exercise. All orders for M.Guns will be issued to O.C.190th.M.G.Coy. by O.C.7/R.F. direct.

6. For the purpose of this exercise the 7/R.F. will move into position via E'ECLEME LILLERS and BUSNES and will not be North or East of BUSNES before 10.30am

7. Cookers will be taken and dinners issued <u>during the operation</u>

Issued to :-
    1.Brigadier.
    2.Brigade Major.
    345 War Diary.
    6 7/R.F.
    7.190th.M.G.Coy.
    89 Spare.

SPECIAL IDEA NORTH.

Reference HAZEBROUCK map 1/100,000.
" 36a " 1/40,000.

1. The Central Division of the Northern Army is marching Southward in three columns. The 290th. Brigade is advancing along the MERVILLE - ST.VENANT - LILLERS Road.

2. The Advance Guard consisting of the 10/Royal Dublin Fusiliers arrives at the North Eastern outskirts of ST.VENANT at 11.30am, when it receives orders to push forward and reconnoitre the crossings over the AIRE - LA BASSEE Canal between the LILLERS - HAZEBROUCK Railway and the River CLARENCE, and, without attracting the attention of the enemy, get as many men as possible in position with a view to rushing the crossings at a given signal.

Frequent information must be sent in from all reconnoitring parties.

Every endeavour must be made to conceal our approach from the enemy.

3. For the purpose of this exercise the 10/Royal Dublin Fusiliers will march out via BUSNES to ST.VENANT and will take Cookers and have dinner North of the Canal on completion of the operation.

It will be considered as an advanced guard throughout the march.

Brigade Headquarters (imaginary) will be at ST.VENANT during the reconnaissance.

Issued to :-
    1. Brigadier.
    2. Brigade Major
    3.4.5. War Diary.
    6. 10/R.D.F.
    7.8. Spare.

HEADQUARTERS,
190th
INFANTRY BRIGADE.
G/400/2.
No.
Date 3-4-17

War Diary
Appendix III

Communication between

AEROPLANES AND INFANTRY.

Reference 36a 1/40,000.

GENERAL IDEA.

1. The 190th.Inf.Bde. has been ordered to occupy the town of BUSNES and to push on and secure the crossings of the River NAVE South of that town.

2. Brigade Headquarters (imaginary) are located at BUSNES after that place has been cleared.

3. On arriving at the village of L'ECLEME it is found to be very strongly held and the whole of the Brigade became engaged in the endeavour to reach the river.

4. A very heavy barrage is placed between L'ECLEME and BUSNES and it has not been possible either to communicate with, or reinforce troops of the Brigade.

5. The G.O.C. is anxious to learn the present dispositions of his Brigade. A contact aeroplane is sent out to reconnoitre the position and report dispositions of troops as far as possible.

6. For the purpose of this exercise troops will be in position as already detailed by 3 pm.

Captain.
Brigade Major.

Copies to:-
63rd Div."G"
No.5 Squadron.R.F.C.
1/H.A.C.
7/Royal Fusiliers.
4/Bedfordshire Regt.
10/Royal Dublin Fusiliers.
Brigade Signal Officer.
War Diary.

War Diary G.400
Appendix III

Hd.Qrs. 190th.Inf.Bde.
2/4/17.

Headquarters,
   1/H.A.C.
   7/Royal Fusiliers.
   4/Bedfordshire Regt.
   10/Royal Dublin Fusiliers.
   Brigade Signal Officer.

Reference 36a 1/40,000.

1. In order to practice communication between Infantry and Aircraft, the following small scheme will be carried out at 3.0pm on Wednesday 4/4/17.

2. (a) Five men under the Brigade Signalling Officer will represent Brigade Headquarters and will be located at the corner of the road in P.33.c.

   (b) Party of similar strength from 4/Bedfordshire Regt. will be located at "Cantraimne Farm Buildings" V.7.b.2.9. and along bye road S.E. to Main Road.

   (c) Similar party from 7/Royal Fusiliers will be about the bridge over the stream about V.8.7.7.

   (d) Similar party from 1/H.A.C. will be located about the road junction in V.5.d.

   (e) Similar party from 10/Royal Dublin Fusiliers will be located about the buildings at V.2.b.6.7.

3. The above parties will be in position by 3.0 pm. Flares will be lighted when it is considered that the Aeroplane is in a position to see them.
The observer can best see signals etc, from the ground when he is at an angle. Flares should not be lighted when he is overhead.

4. Parties will light Flares at about 3 minutes interval from the time the aeroplane is in position to read.
No other means of communication is to be adopted.

5. Please acknowledge.

6. 10 Flares will be allotted to each party.

sd) C.H.Dowden. Capt.
Brigade Major.

BRIGADE COMMUNICATION SCHEME.

Reference 36. 1/40,000.

Appendix IV

GENERAL IDEA.

1. The Division has bivouaced for the day in the BUSNES area.

2. The 190th Brigade is ordered to find the outposts.

3. The outpost line is divided into four sectors and one sector allotted to each unit which has three companies in the outpost line and one in support.

4. Hd.Qrs. of Battalions and Companies etc., are located as under :-

    1/H.A.C. Bn.Hd.Qrs. — CHATEAU DU QUESNOY V.2.b.
          No.1 Outpost Coy. — Road junction V.9.b.9.9.
          " 2 " — On Road P34.d.9.0.
          " 3 " — Drawbridge P.29.c.
          Support Coy. — On bend of track P33.d.1.9.

    7/R.F. Bn.Hd.Qrs. — Northern end of Cemetary P.25.d.
          No.4 Outpost Coy. — LABIETTE FARM P.27.b.7.0.
          No.5 " " — Buildings on Rd.P27.a.7.7.
          " 6 " " — On Road P20.d.0.9.
          Support Coy. — P26.b.4.3.

    10/R.D.F. Bn.Hd.Qrs. — Buildings on Road P.19.c.6.4.
          No.7 Outpost Coy. — Near foot bridge P20.a.
          " 8 " " — Point where Railway crosses the Canal P.13.a.
          " 9 " " — Point where railway crosses road O.18.9.
          Support Coy. — Cross Roads LA PIERRIERE.

    4/Bds. Bn.Hd.Qrs. — Buildings O.24.d.1.2.
          No.10 Outpost Coy. — Level crossing O.17.d.
          " 11 " " — Road junction O28.b.9.9.
          " 12 " " — Cross Roads in O.34.b.
          Support Coy. — Bend of road in O.29.d.

    190th M.G. Coy. Hd.Qrs. — Point 21, P.32.a.9.1.
          One Section M.G's — P.28.d.5.6.

Bde.Headquarters are at P.31.a.8.8.

5. For the purpose of this exercise, Brigade, Battalions and Companies will all be represented by the signallers of those units and communications will be established both from front to rear and laterally.

6. Officers Commanding units will arrange messages for this scheme which will be forwarded to the Brigade Signalling Officer together with abstracts on the conclusion of the exercise.

7. Telephonic communication will NOT be established.

Runners must be employed equally with visual signalling. Service messages only will be used.

8. Flags must not be exposed to the front where there would be any chance of them being read by the enemy.

9. In order to ascertain if flags are being exposed, scouts will be detailed to reconnoitre from the front and to report on any party of signallers observed. Signallers will in turn keep a look out for these scouts and report by a "Priority" message any scouts observed.
Scouts of the 1/H.A.C. will reconnoitre the front held by 7/R.F. and vice versa.
Scouts of 4/Bedfords will reconnoitre front of 10/R.D.F. and vice versa.
Scouts will wear white cap bands.

10. Signallers etc., will be in position by 9.30 am at which hour all scouts will be at least one mile in front of the outpost line. Scouts will move into position through their own Battalion Sectors.

11. The Brigade Signalling Officer will superintend the exercise.

12. Brigade Signal Section will be under the orders of the senior N.C.O. for this scheme.

12. The exercise will be terminated by Signal from Brigade Headquarters.

Copies to :-
   1/H.A.C.
   7/R.F.
   4/Beds.
   10/R.D.F.
   M.G.Coy.
   Bde.Sig.Off.
   Bde.Sig.Sec.
   G.O.C.
   War Diary.

SECRET. *War Diary* Copy No. 6

190th. Infantry Brigade Order No. 72.

Appendix V 6/4/17.

Reference HAZEBROUCK Sheet 1/100,000.
　"　　　 LENS　　 "　　"

1. The Brigade Group will march to BRUAY Area on the 8th.inst in accordance with attached March Table.

2. Distance of 500 yards will be maintained between Battalions. Normal distance between all other units.

3. Normal halts i.e., 10 minutes before each clock hour until the clock hour will be observed throughout the march.

4. Units must march strictly in accordance with the March Table. Special attention must be paid to March Discipline both on the March and during halts.
   Transport must be kept closed up.

5. The S.A.A.Section of the D.A.C. will come under the orders of the G.O.C.,190th.Brigade on its arrival at HOUDAIN.

6. Billetting parties, from each Unit, under an Officer will be marched on in advance and arrage billets with the Town Majors.
   These parties will observe the same March Discipline as they would if marching with their units, and will, if possible keep clear of other units on the march.
   There are Town Majors at BRUAY; HOUDAIN and HALLICOURT.

7. The 14th (Pioneer) Worcester Regt.,247th.Field Coy. R.E. and 53rd.M.V.Section ceases to form part of 190th.Brigade Group.
   The 247th.Field Coy. R.E. and 53rd.M.V.Section will march under orders of 14th.Bn.(Pioneers) Worcester Regt. to whom orders have been issued direct.
   The 247th.Field Coy.R.E. will come under orders of 189th.Brigade on arrival at HOUCHIN.

8. Brigade Headquarters will close at BUSNES at 8.0am on the 8th.inst. and open at BRUAY on arrival there.

9. Please ACKNOWLEDGE.

　　　　　　　　　　　　　　　　　　　　　　　C.H.Dowden
　　　　　　　　　　　　　　　　　　　　　　　　　　　　Captain.
Issued to Signals.........　　　　　　　　　Brigade Major.

1. G.O.C.
2. Bde.Major.
3. Staff Capt.
4.5.6. War Diary.
7 - 12 Division.
13. A.P.M.
14. 1/H.A.C.
15. 7/R.F.
16. 4/Beds.Regt.
17. 10/R.D.F.
18. 190th.M.G.Coy.
19. 190th.T.M.Battery.
20. 249th.Coy.R.E.
21. 247th.Coy.R.E.
22. H.Q.Div.Train.
23. No.4 Coy. Train.
24. 14/Worcs.Regt.
25. S.A.A.Sec.D.A.C.
26. 53rd.Mobile Vet. Sec.
27. Supply Officer.
28. No.3 Field Ambulance.
29. O.C.Sig.Section.
30. 188th.Inf.Bde.
31. 189th.Inf.Bde.
32. A.D.M.S.
33. A.D.V.S.
34. 63rd.Div.Artillery.
35. D.A.D.O.S.
36. Military Police.
37. Bde. Transport Officer.

SECRET   Copy No. 4

War Diary

Amendment No.1 to 190th.Inf.Bde.Order No.72.

7/4/17.

1.   At end of para 1, add :-

     "The Brigade Group will be prepared to march from its concentration area at 4 hours notice after Zero hour on "Z" day."

2.   The 247th.Field Coy.R.E., will continue to form part of 190th.Brigade Group and will march in accordance with attached March Table.

3.   MESNIL LE RUITZ is under Town Major of BARLIN.

4.   Cancel March Table issued with Brigade Order No.72 and substitute one attached hereto.

5.   ACKNOWLEDGE.

                                                   Captain.
                                             Brigade Major.

Issued to Signals 1.30 pm.

To all recipients of Brigade Order No.72.

MARCH TABLE TO ACCOMPANY AMENDMENTS NO. 1 TO THE ORDER NO.72.

Order of March	Unit	From	To.	Starting Point.	Time.	Route.	Remarks.
1.	H.Q. Train. No.4 Coy. Tent Sub Div No.3 F.Amb.	BUSNES. LE CORGET BOURDOIS.	BRUAY.	BUSNES CHURCH.	10.0am	L'ECLEME - BUSNETTES - BAS RIEUX - HAUTRIEUX - LOZINGHEM - MARLES LES MINES.	Not to enter BRUAY before 1.30 pm.
2.	249th Field Coy.R.E.	BUSNETTES.	BRUAY.	Rd. junction ¼ mile S of U in BUSNETTES	10.45am	BAS RIEUX - HAUTRIEUX - LOZINGHEM - MARLES LES MINES.	
3.	247th Field Coy.R.E.	ST.FERMECHON	LESNIL LE RUITZ.	GONNEHEM CHURCH.	10.20am	L'ECLEME - BUSNETTES - BAS RIEUX - HAUTRIEUX - LOZINGHEM - MARLES LES MINES - BRUAY-RUITZ.	
4.	Bde.H.Q.	BUSNES.	BRUAY.	Rd. junction last E in LA MIQUELLERIE.	10.5 am	BUSNES - L'ECLEME - BUSNETTES - BAS RIEUX - HAUTRIEUX - LOZINGHEM - MARLES LES MINES.	
5.	190th T.M.B.	BUSNES.	BRUAY.	-do-	10.3 am	-do-	
6.	1/H.A.C.	L'ECLEME.	HALLICOURT.	1st.L in L'ECLEME.	10.40am	BUSNETTES - BAS RIEUX - HAUTRIEUX - LOZINGHEM - MARLES LES MINES	
7.	7/R.F.	BUSNES.	-do-	BUSNES CHURCH.	10.30am	L'ECLEME - BUSNETTES - BAS RIEUX - HAUTRIEUX - LOZINGHEM - MARLES LES MINES.	
8.	10/K.R.R.	La PIERRIERE.	BRUAY.	Cross roads LA PIERRIERE.	10.20am	BUSNES - L'ECLEME - BUSNETTES - BAS RIEUX - HAUTRIEUX - LOZINGHEM - MARLES LES MINES.	
9.	4/Beds.	MANQUEVILLE.	LESNIL le RUITZ.	Railway bridge S.E. of last E in MANQUEVILLE.	11.30am	LILLERS - HAUTRIEUX - LOZINGHEM - MARLES LES MINES - BRUAY - RUITZ.	
10.	196th M.G. Coy.	L'ECLEME.	BRUAY.	1st.L in L'ECLEME.	11.25am	BUSNETTES - BAS RIEUX - HAUTRIEUX - LOZINGHEM - MARLES LES MINES.	
11.	No.3 field Ambulance.	LE CORGET BOURDOIS.	BRUAY.	Rd.junction N of C in CORNET.	10.30am	BUSNES - L'ECLEME - BUSNETTES - BAS RIEUX - HAUTRIEUX - LOZINGHEM - MARLES LES MINES.	To be clear of the LILLERS - CHOCQUES - BETHUNE Rd.by 12.30pm.

for Brigade Major.

> HEADQUARTERS,
> 190th
> INFANTRY BRIGADE.
> No. G45c
> Date 9.4.18

Hd.Qrs.190th.Inf.Bde.
9/4/17.

ALL UNITS OF BRIGADE GROUP.

State of readiness ordered in para 1 of Amendment No.1 to Brigade Order No.72 is now in force.

Units will be prepared to move at 3 hours notice.

Acknowledge.

Lieut.R.N.V.R.
~~Captain~~.
Staff Captain.
for Brigade Major.

Appendix VI

SECRET.   Copy No. 5

190th Infantry Brigade Order No. 73.

Reference LENS Map. 1/100,000
" HAZEBROUCK " "   11/4/17.

1. The Brigade Group will march to the BEUGIN-MAGNICOURT Area today in accordance with attached March Table.

2. Distance of 500 yards will be maintained between battalions. Normal distances between all other units. Normal halts will be observed.

3. Units must be prepared to move from new area at 2 hours notice.

4. Billeting parties must be sent on at once to arrange billets.

5. Each man will carry one blanket. The second one will be carried on G.S. wagons of D.A.C. which are being sent to units on following scale:-

    Each battalion   .... 2.
    M.G. Company.   .... 1.
    T.M.B.   .... 1.
    Bde. H.Q.   .... 2.

    Wagons on completion of march will rejoin their section at MAGNICOURT.
    They will not do more than one journey. Blankets will be off loaded immediately they arrive.

6. Brigade Headquarters will close at BRUAY at 8.30.a.m. and open in new area on arrival there.

7. Please acknowledge.

Time issued to Signals. 8.40 a.m.   R. Goude
                                              Captain.
                                           Brigade Major.

1. G.O.C.
2. Brigade Major.
3. Staff Captain.
4-5-6 War Diary.
7 to 12. 63rd Divn.
13. A.P.M.
14. H.A.C.
15. Royal Fus.
16. Beds Regt.
17. R.D.F.
18. M.G. Coy.
19. T.M.B.
20. 249 Field Coy.
21. H.Q. DIV. Train.
22. No. 4. Coy. "
23. S.A.A. Sect. D.A.C.
24. Supply Officer.
25. No. 3 Field Amb.
26. Signals.
27. 188th Bde.
28. 189th Bde.
29. D.A.D.O.S.
30 Military Police.
31. Bde. Transport Off.
32. M.V. Section.

MARCH TABLE.

Order of March	Unit.	From.	To.	Starting Point.	Time to pass starting point	Route	Remarks
1.	4/5 do.	MESNIL	HERLIN	MESNIL	9.45.am.	REBREVE – HERMAIN Road	To be clear of MESNIL by 10.am.
2.	249 Coy.R.E.	BRUAY	ROCOURT	BRUAY Theatre, Entrance to HOUDAIN Road.	9.40.am	HOUDAIN direct Rd.	
3.	H.Q.Div. Train No.4.Coy. " Tnt Sub Div. No.3.Fd.Amb. L.ob.V.S ct.	BRUAY	LA COMTE	"	9.45.am.	"	To march under orders O.C.Div.Train
4.	190th M.G.Coy.	BRUAY.	HOUVELIN	"	10.0.am.	"	
5.	Bd .H.Q.	BRUAY	BAJUS.	"	10.3.am.	"	
6.	T.M.Batty.	BRUAY	BAJUS	"	10.5.	"	
7.	10/R.D.F.	BRUAY	MAGNICOURT	"	10.10.am	"	
8.	7/R.F.	HALLICOURT	LA COMTE	Cross Roads ½ mile North of R in RUITZ	10.15.am	HOUDAIN	
9.	H.A.C.	do	BEUGIN	"	10.25.am.	"	
10.	S.A.A.S ct. D.A.C.	do	MAGNICOURT	"	10.35.am.	"	
11.	No.3.Fd.Amb. (less Tnt Sub Div.)	BRUAY	HERLIN FARM near BAJUS	BRUAY Theatre	10.45.am.	HOUDAIN direct Route	To be South of HALLICOURT– PRUAY lin– by 11.am.

SECRET.
                                    Headquarters,
                                       190th Infantry Brigade.
                                         12th April.1917.

1. Warning Order issued under my G.493 of today is
   cancelled.

2. Dismounted units will most probably go forward by
   bus and lorry on the 14th instant.
   Other units by march route.

3. Further orders later.

                                    C H Lowden
                                         Captain.
                                    Brigade Major.
                                    ****

To ALL UNITS of Brigade Group.

SECRET. Appendix VII Copy No......

190th. Infantry Brigade Order No. 74.

Reference LENS Sheet 1/100,000.   13/4/17.
    "   51b.N.W. 1/20,000.

1. The Division (less Artillery and detached Troops) will relieve the 34th. Division in the line on the night of the 14/15th inst.

2. The Brigade will move forward and take over the line in accordance with attached tables. Transport will proceed by Route March. Dismounted Troops and Infantry will proceed to ARRAS by Bus and march forward from this point.
    Commanding Officers have reconnoitred the line and the approach thereto today.

3. Transport Lines for the Brigade Group are located at ST. CATHERINE G.9.d. and G.15.b.

4. Officers Commanding Battalions and M.G. Company will meet their Units at the De-Bussing Point in ARRAS.
    Units will move out from ARRAS immediately to their transport lines at ST. CATHERINE G.9.d. - G.15.b. where packs will be dumped after which they will proceed via ST. NICHOLAS along the BAILLEUL - ARRAS Road halting if necessary clear of the road West of the Factory in G.16.b.
    Greatcoats will be taken forward.

5. Units proceeding to the front line must take up with them a supply of bombs ready detonated. These will be drawn from the Divisional Dump at B.25.d.9.9. and issued to all Bombers whilst they are in the BLACK Line.

6. All Lewis Guns and drums filled will be taken into the Busses and carried forward by the Gunners from ARRAS.

7. All Troops moving East of ARRAS will do so by Platoons at 100 yards distance.

8. 63rd. Division Trench Standing Orders will be strictly observed so far as they effect the relief.

9. The 249th. Field Coy. R.E. will proceed to G.9.b.25.75. (North of ST. CATHERINE).
    The 3rd. Field Ambulance will proceed to ST. CATHERINE.
    Relief of Medical Units will be arranged by the A.D.M.S.

10. Officers and Other Ranks detailed to remain with transport in case of attack will go forward with their units into the line and will be sent back when ordered.

11. Everyone should take Haversack Rations as there will be very little chance of getting either food or water forward until very late at night.

12. A lorry will be allotted to the Trench Mortar Battery to carry Guns, Handcarts and Blankets.
    On arrival at ARRAS the Battery will proceed direct to the line.

13. All details of relief not arranged herein will be arranged between units concerned. Relief must be completed before daybreak on 15th. inst.
    Command of the Sector will pass to G.O.C. 190th. Brigade on completion of relief.

2.

14. Brigade Headquarters will close at BAJUS at 8.0 am and open in the BLACK Line on arrival there.

15. Please acknowledge.

                                                         C.H.Dowden
                                                                Captain.

Issued to Signals........ 1.40 am 14-4-17.   Brigade Major.

1. G.O.C.
2. Brigade Major.
3. Staff Captain.
4,5,6. War Diary.
7 - 8 63rd.Division G.
9. A.P.M.
10. H.A.C.
11. R.F.
12. Beds Regt.
13. R.D.F.
14. M.G.Coy.
15. T.M.B.
16. 249 Field Coy.
17. H.Q.Div.Train.
18. No. 4 Coy. Train.
19. S.A.A.Section D.A.C.
20. Supply Officer.
21. No.3 Field Ambulance.
22. Signals.
23. 188th.Inf.Bde.
24. 189th. "   "
25. D.A.D.O.S.
26. Military Police.
27. Bde.Transport Officer.
28. M.V.Section.
29. 102.Inf.Bde.
30. 63rdDiv. Q.

BUS TABLE TO ACCOMPANY 190TH. INFANTRY BRIGADE ORDER NO. 74.

Unit.	No. of Busses.	Starting Point.	Time.	Route.	De-Bussing at.	Remarks.
Bde.H.Q.	3	BAJUS	10.0am	TINQUES - Main ST. POL ARRAS Road.	G.21.b.5.7. ARRAS OCTROI.	
10/R.D.F.	20	MAGNICOURT	10.am	---do---	---do---	
7/R.F.	25	LA COMTE.	10.15 am.	---do---	---do---	
4/Bods.	32	HERMIN	10.30 am	---do---	---do---	
1/H.A.C.	24	BEUGIN	10.35 am.	---do---	---do---	
190th.M.G.Co	6	HOUVELIN	10.40 am	---do---	---do---	
190th. T.M.B.	2	BAJUS	10.0 am.	---do---	---do---	
249th. Field Co. R.E.	6	ROCOURT	11.0 am	---do---	---do---	
3rd.F.A. Bearer Sec.	5	BAJUS	11.15 am	---do---	---do---	
No.3 Field Amb.	2	LA COMTE	11.15 am	---do---	---do---	

MARCH TABLE FOR TRANSPORT AND MOUNTED MEN, TO ACCOMPANY 190TH& INFANTRY BRIGADE ORDER NO.74.

Order of March.	Unit.	From	To	Starting Point	Time to pass	Route.	Remarks.
1.	190th.M.G.Coy.	HOUVELIN	ARRAS	Road junction (3 roads) 1 mile South West of MAGNICOURT EN COMTE	6.30 am	CHELERS - TINQUES - ARRAS Main Rd.	O.C., M.G.Coy. will arrange for a guide to meet transport of Coy. coming into ARRAS.
2.	4/Beds.Regt.	HERMIN	ARRAS	Junction of FREVILLERS - CHELERS Road.	6.30am	---do---	
3.	10/R.D.F.	MAGNICOURT	ARRAS	Road junction (3 roads) 1 mile South West of MAGNICOURT EN COMTE.	6.35 am	---do---	
4.	7/R.F.	LA COMTE	ARRAS	---do---	6.40am	---do---	
5.	1/H.A.C.	BEUGIN	ARRAS	---do---	6.45 am	---do---	
6.	Bde.H.Q.	BAJUS	ARRAS	---do---	7.0am	---do---	
7.	249 Field Coy.R.E.	ROCOURT	ARRAS	---do---	7.2 am	---do---	
8.	No.3 F.AMB. (less Tent Sub.Div)	BAJUS	ARRAS	---do---	7.8 am	---do---	
9.	S.A.A.Sec. D.A.C. 53rd.H.V.Sec.	MAGNICOURT & LA COMTE	ARRAS	---do---	7.14am	---do---	March under orders of O.C. S.A.A. Sec.D.A.C.
10.	No.4 Coy.Train Tent Sub.Div No 3 F Amb	LA COMTE	ARRAS	---do---	7.20am	---do---	

RELIEF TABLE TO ACCOMPANY 190TH. INFANTRY BRIGADE ORDER NO.74.

Unit.	From.	To.	In Relief of.	To pass Factory in G.16.c.c. (51b.N.W.)	Guides at Div. Dump (B25.d.9.0) at	Remarks.
10/R.D.F.	ARRAS	Front Line (Right) (Brown & Green)	26th.Bn.N.F. & part of 23rd.N.F.	3. pm.	7.15 pm.	Not to pass Black line before 6.45 pm.
7/R.F.	ARRAS	Support line (Blue)	21st.N.F.	3.20 pm.		
4/Beds.Regt.	ARRAS	Front line (left) (Brown & Green)	22nd.N.F. & part of 23rd N.F.	3.40 pm.	7.30 pm.	Not to pass the Black line before 7.0 pm.
1/H.A.C.	ARRAS	Reserve Line (Black)	20th.Bn.N.F.	3.50 pm.		
190th.M.G. (by.)	ARRAS.	Front & Support lines	102 M.G.Coy.	3.58 pm.	7.10 pm.	Not to pass the Black line before 6.40 pm.
190th.T.M.B.	ARRAS.	Line.	102 T.M.B.		As arranged by O.C.,T.M.B.	

SECRET

Appendix VIII copy No...

190th Inf Bde. Order No 76.

15-4-17.

Reference 51 B NW 1/20,000.

1. The 190 Infantry Brigade will "Slide Up" to the North tonight and take over a part of the line now held by the Second Division.

    The frontage of the Brigade will be from about B.23.c.5.9 in the North to B.29.a.9.7. in the South.

2. The 1/Royal Fusiliers will be on the right and will take over the line from 22/Royal Fusiliers from B.23 central to B.29.a.6.8. with two companies in the front line, one in Support and one in Reserve.

    Hd Qrs at B.28.a.6.8.

    The 1/HAC will be on the left and will take over the line from the 1/Royal Berks from B.23.a.8.9. to B.23 central with two companies in the front line, one in Support and one in Reserve.

    Hd Qrs at B.21.a.8.6.

3. The OC 190 Machine Gun Coy will arrange with OC 99 MG Coy as to relief of MGuns.

    This must be carried out tonight

(2)

4. The 10/R Dublin Fusiliers and 4/Bedfords will be relieved by units of the 189 Brigade tonight. On completion of relief the 4/Bedfords will move into the Brown and Green lines which were originally held by them and the R.D.F.

The 10/R.D.F on completion of relief will be located in the Blue line from B25 b.5.2 - South to the Railway and trenches in this vicinity.

5. Troops in the front line will light flares about 7.0 am tomorrow when called for by Contact Aeroplane.

6. Relief completed will be reported by the word "AGAIN"

7. Please acknowledge

C H Dowden Capt
Brigade Major
190 Bde

Issued at -

To
No 1 7/RF   10/ 189 Bde
   2 1/HAC   11 99 Bde
   3 4/Bedfords   12
   4 10/RDF
   5 M G Coy
   6 Division
   8 War Diary
   9 Brigade

SECRET.   Copy No ....
                    Appendix   IV
190 Inf. Bde. Order No 78.

                                              16-4-17.
Reference 57 B. N.W. 1/20,000.

1. At an hour to be notified tonight each Bn. in the front line will push out two reconnoitring patrols, each of a strength of one section to the OPPY - GAVRELLE line.

   The 1/4 Wilts will go to about B.24 b.
   The 1/R.F. to about B.24 c + d.

   These patrols should move out in skirmishing order with scouts in front.

2. Should they find that the line is not held, (which is expected) they will send back this information to their Battalions, who will then push forward strong patrols, consisting of the remainder of the two companies of each Battalion from which the reconnoitring patrols were drawn.

3. The Brigades on our right and left are both pushing forward patrols with the same object in view.

   Troops on occupying the OPPY line must endeavour to gain touch with troops or patrols of Brigades on either flank as well as with each other.

   Should it be impossible, owing

2.

to the presence of the enemy, to gain touch with the Brigades on our flanks, each Bn. will form a block on its outer flank, the 1/HAC to the North, the 4/R.F. to the South.

The greatest care must be exercised to avoid Bombing patrols of the other Brigades or our own troops.

4. When the two companies of each Bn. are established in the OPPY line the remainder of the Brigade will be advanced to the following places on the signal being given from Bde. Hd. Qrs.

Two Companies of 1/HAC and 2 Companies of 4/R.F. to a position about on the line running between B.23 and B.24.

The 4/Bedfords will move to the lines taken over by the 4/R.F. from 22/R.F. last night in the Southern portion of squares B.22d and B.23c.

The 10/R.F. will move into the Brown lines in relief of 4/Bedfords.

The O.C. M.G. Coy will push up 4 guns to the OPPY line, and 4 guns to the present front line.

The signal for the reconnoitring patrols to start will be ON "Z" fire.

The signal for the remainder of the Brigade to go forward "ANCHOR UP."

2.

5. Supplies of Flares, Bombs, Rifle Grenades, S.A.A. Tools and Wirecutters will be taken forward by the front Battalions.

6. Should it be impossible to occupy the OPPY line owing to it being strongly held by the enemy, the 1/11 AC and 1/RF will advance and dig a trench 300 yards West of the OPPY line which they will hold with 2 companies from each Bn.

Their support and reserve coys would then be brought up to the present front line where they would consolidate.

Other troops would not be brought forward.

7. Infantry Battalions and M.G. Coy please acknowledge.

Captain
Bde. Major.

Copies to:-
1 HAC
2 11RF
3 Howe
4 RDF
5 M.G.Coy
6 190 Bde
7 5th "
8 189 "
9 Left Group RFA
10 63 DiV
11 Diary
12 Spare

SECRET.

Appendix X

Copy No. 2

190th Infantry Brigade Order No. 78.

19.4.17.

Reference 51.B. N.W.

1. The 10/Royal Dublin Fusiliers will relieve the 7/Royal Fusiliers in the Right (Southern) Sector of the Brigade front on the night of the 20th instant.

2. On relief the 7/R.F. will proceed to the Brown and Green Lines in B.27. evacuated by 4/Bedfordshire Regt.

3. The 4/Bedfords will move from the Brown and Green Lines to the Blue Line evacuated by the 10/R.D.F.

4. The 190th T.M.Battery will move in to the Brown Line (West) in B.27.a. (Northern end)

5. Relief must be completed before 2.am. 20/21st instant.

6. Parties will not move in larger bodies than one platoon at 100 yards distance.

7. All details of relief will be made by Commanding Officer concerned.

8. Relief complete will be notified to Brigade Headquarters by wiring the word "HOPPY"

9. Please acknowledge by wire.

Time issued to Signals......

R.H. Dowden
Captain,
Brigade Major.

Copies to:-
1. G.O.C.
2. Brigade Major.
3. Staff Captain.
4. 1/H.A.C.
5. Royal Fusiliers.
6. Bedfordshire Regt.
7. Royal Dublin Fusiliers.
8. M.G.Company.
9. T.M.Battery.
10. 189th Inf. Bde.
11. 6th Bde.
12. 63rd Div. "Q"
13. 63rd Div. "G"
14. Loft Group.
15. C.R.A.
16. Bde. Transport Officer.

Appendix XI

SECRET.   Copy No......

190th. Infantry Brigade Order No.81.

21/4/17.

Reference OPPY Map 1/10,000.
"   51 B. N.W. 1/20,000.

1. 190th.Inf.Bde.Order No.80 is cancelled.

2. The 1/H.A.C. will be relieved in the line tonight by 1/5 Staffs Regt. (6th.Brigade).
   The Northern Boundary of the Brigade will then be the BAILLEUL - GAVRELLE Railway from where it crosses the road in B.23.a. Eastward.

3. The 10/Royal Dublin Fusiliers will hand over any trench they may have North of this Railway.

4. All details of relief will be arranged by Commanding Officers concerned.

5. On relief the 1/H.A.C. will proceed to the old "Black" line in G.6.

6. Movement will be by parties not larger than one Platoon at 100 yards distance.

7. Completion of relief will be wired to Brigade Headquarters by the code word "CURED".

8. Please ACKNOWLEDGE.

                                              C.H.Dowden
                                                       Captain.
Issued to Signals........   Brigade Major,

    Copies to :-

    1. 63rd.Division.
    2. G.O.C.
    3. Brigade Major.
    4. Staff Captain.
    5.6.7.War Diary.
    8. H.A.C.
    9. Royal Fusiliers.
    10. Bedfordshire Regt.
    11. Royal Dublin Fusiliers.
    12. 190th.M.G.Company.
    13. 190th.T.M.Battery.
    14. 189th.Inf.Bde.
    15. 6th.   "   "
    16. Bde.Transport Officer.
    17. Left Group R.F.A.
    18.19. Spare.

SECRET.   *War Diary Appendix XII*   Copy No. 10

190th. Infantry Brigade Order No.82.

22/4/17.

Reference OPPY Map 1/10,000.
"   51 B. N.W. 1/20,000.

1. The 63rd. Division will, at an early date, attack and capture the village of GAVRELLE and consolidate and form a defensive flank along the railway running East and West to the North of that village.

2. The following troops will assist in the operation:-

   (a) The Second Division on our left will put down a Barrage on enemy lines and make a feint attack.

   (b) 24 Machine Guns of the 31st. Division will bring enfilade fire on the enemy's positions on our front.

   (c) 24 Machine Guns from Brigades of the Division will put down a barrage 300 yards in front of Artillery Barrage.

   (d) The Divisional Artillery will be supported by 6 Field Artillery Brigades in addition to Corps and Army Heavy Artillery.

3. The Division will attack on a front of two Brigades. The 189th. Infantry Brigade will be on the right (South) with the 190th. Infantry Brigade on the left (North). The 188th. Infantry Brigade will be in Reserve.

4. The Northern Boundary (between the Second and 63rd. Divisions) will be "The BAILLEUL - GAVRELLE Railway from the Level Crossing in B.23.a. Eastward".
   The Southern Boundary (between the 37th. and 63rd. Divisions) will be "A line from H.6.a.5.6, to the Southern End of the trench running from B.30.d.5.0. to H.6.b.9.6., thence to the S.W. corner of Square Wood.

5. The dividing line between the 190th. Infantry Brigade in the North and the 189th. Infantry Brigade in the South will be :-
   The ARRAS - GAVRELLE Road from a point where it enters the German wire, through the village of GAVRELLE to point C.25.a.4.6. (Road inclusive to 190th. Infantry Brigade): thence to a point on the Railway Line about C.19.d.0.0.

6. The following objectives have been allotted to the Division :-

   (a) The BLUE LINE.
       The German Support line in the OPPY - GAVRELLE SYSTEM, from the Railway line in the North to a point about B.30.c.70.35, thence along the German front line trench to the Southern Divisional Boundary.

   (b) The YELLOW LINE.
       The Communication trench which leaves the German Support trench at B.24.d.02.09. running to about B.30.b.7.7., thence down the road North and South through the Western End of the village of GAVRELLE to FRIGID Trench at B.30.d.3.2., thence to the Southern end of trench at H.6.b.9.6.

(c) The GREEN LINE.
The Railway Line from B.24.d.1.7. to C.19.d.0.0., thence round the Eastern Outskirts of GAVRELLE to the Cemetary, thence down the Sunken Road to the junction with the left flank of the 37th.Division in I.1.b.

7. The attack, within the Brigade, will be carried out by two Battalions in the front line, one in Support and one in Reserve.

The Reserve Battalion will be used to provide carrying parties.

The 4/Bedfordshire Regt.will attack on the right, the 7/Royal Fusiliers on the left, the 1/H.A.C. will be in Support, with 10/Royal Dublin Fusiliers in Reserve.

Four Machine Guns from 190th.M.G.Company will go forward in rear of the fourth wave of each Battalion.

Two of these guns will go on to the "Green line" with each Battalion and the other two remain in the old German system in Support.

Two Stokes Mortars will go forward in rear of the fourth wave of each Battalion and on reaching the German front line will push on to the Support line to engage any suitable target that may appear.

The attack will be carried out in accordance with the Divisional Standard System of Attack, each front Battalion being organised in four waves.

The frontage allotted to each Battalion will be :-

(a) 4/Bedfordshire Regt.
From dividing line between Brigades (the GAVRELLE - ARRAS Road through the village inclusive to 4/Bedfordshire Regt.) to FOXY Communication trench running S.E. from German Support line(inclusive to 4/Bedfordshire Regt) frontage about 600 yards.

(b) 7/Royal Fusiliers.
From Northern Boundary of 4/Bedfordshire Regt. to Railway line (inclusive).
Frontage about 400 yards.

8. All troops of the Brigade will be in their positions of assembly by 2.0 am.on Y/Z night as below :-

(a) Assaulting Battalions.
The first wave will be formed up on a tape line approximately 90 yards in front of our present front line trench with their Lewis Gun Sections immediately in rear of each Platoon.

The second wave will be formed up on a tape line about 30 yards in rear of the first wave.

The mopping up party for the German front line, consisting of one Section from each Platoon of the fourth wave will be formed up 5 yards in rear of the right of each Platoon in the second wave.

The third and fourth waves will be formed up in the present front line trench.

The 8 Machine Guns of 190th.M.G.Company allotted to the Brigade will be formed up 10 yards in rear of the fourth wave, 4 guns in rear of each Battalion.

The four Stokes Mortars to take part in the attack, with their carrying parties will form up in the same line of the M.G.Company - 2 guns in rear of each flank.

The Support Battalion will be assembled, by Companies West of the Sunken Road inE.28.b.

The Reserve Battalion will be assembled in the "Green" line, and the "Brown" line (East) in B.27.

The Two Sections, 249th Field Coy. R.E., will assemble in the "Brown" line (West) in B.27.

The Four Stokes Mortars not taking part in the advance will remain in the "Brown" line (West).

The two Section, Field Coy. R.E. will remain in assembly position until ordered to move. The Senior Officer will be at Brigade Headquarters.

Completion of assembly will be reported to Brigade Headquarters by the word "HERE".

It must be impressed upon all ranks that absolute silence must be maintained during the assembly and until ZERO hour.

9. Headquarters of Units will be located as under :-

Brigade Headquarters near Railway Bridge about B.27.a.0.4.

Advanced Report Centre in old Gun Pits about B.28.a.5.7.

Right Assaulting Battalion, in old Gun Pits about B.23.3.5.6.

Left Assaulting Battalion, in old Gun Pits about B.23.c.5.6.

Support Battalion in old Gun Pits about B.28.a.5.7.

Reserve Battalion, in Railway Cutting about B.27.a.1.4.

Machine Gun Company about B.27.b.3.8.

10. Plan of attack. At ZERO the artillery will place a barrage on enemy front and support lines and the first wave of the attacking battalions will advance, followed by other waves at their recognised distance.

At ZERO plus 8 minutes, barrage will lift from German front line and the first two waves of Infantry will assault the trench, and pass straight over leaving the mopping up party who are following the second wave to mop up the trench until the arrival of the third and fourth waves who will enter the trench, complete the mopping up and commence to consolidate.

The four Machine Guns detailed to remain in the first German line trench will select and consolidate defensive positions for use in case of a counter-attack.

The remaining Machine Guns will enter the trench and prepare for a further advance.

The four Stokes Mortars will push forward to the German Support line and take up position to engage any available target.

At ZERO plus 12 minutes the artillery barrage will lift off the "Blue" line which the two leading waves of infantry will assault, mop up and consolidate.

From ZERO plus 18 to plus 32 minutes a protective barrage will remain 200 yards in front of the "Blue" line to permit of mopping up and consolidating and preparing for the next bound.

At ZERO plus 32 the barrage will commence to lift at the rate of 100 yards every four minutes and the assaulting waves of the 4/Bedfordshire Regt. only will advance following close up to the barrage until the YELLOW line is reached.

This will entail a swinging movement on the part of the 4/Bedfordshire Regt.

The left of the two first waves will not move from their position at the junction of FOXY trench with the support line, the remainder of these two waves will swing lefthanded and occupy FOXY trench to its junction with the road running North and South through the Eastern end of the village, thence Southward down this road to the junction at B.30.b.8.4.

Care must be taken that the right Company clears the road running East and West to this point, and the Building etc to the North of this road.

The right on the road must be kept in advance of the "swing".

The third and fourth waves must conform to the movements of the first and second waves and halt about 60 yards behind them.

The two machine guns will move with the third and fourth waves.

The Trench Mortars will remain in the German second line unless required to engage targets farther forward, when they will be brought up by signal from the front.

From ZERO plus 56 minutes to plus 1 hour 12 the protective barrage will remain 200 yards in front of the YELLOW line to permit of mopping up and consolidation of this line.

Up to this time the 7/Royal Fusiliers will have thrown a defensive flank along the Railway facing North between the German front and support line and have pushed it as far Eastward along the Railway as possible.

The two Stokes Mortars with the left Battalion will have come into action near the junction of German Support line and the Railway.

One of the two Machine Guns to accompany this Battalion will come into action about this point to protect the Northern flank.

From ZERO plus 1 hour 12 minutes, to plus 1 hour 16. There will be a pause in the barrage.

At ZERO plus 1 hour 16 minutes barrage re-opens, and Infantry will move forward as close up to it as possible.

At ZERO plus 1 hour 20 minutes the barrage commences to lift at the rate of 100 yards every four minutes and the Infantry of both Battalions commence to advance again.

4/Bedfordshire Regt, keeping their right flank on the road running East and West through the village will move diagonally to the Railway line, their left flank striking the level crossing at C.19.c.55.15. and their right about C.25.b.4.9.

The O.C.4/Bedfordshire Regt.will detail two Platoons to go straight on and capture the Windmill about C.19.c.9.4. and hold it as a strong point in front of the defensive flank.

The remainder of the 4/Bedfordshire Regt.will advance to

5.

the line of the Railway, after clearing the village North of and including the road, and consolidate there and push out Battle Patrols to where they can see down the Northern and Eastern slopes of the ground to their front.

The 7/Royal Fusiliers will execute a swinging movement keeping the left flank of their first two waves stationary on the Railway. They will swing round lefthanded and cross the communication trench running diagonally through B.24.d., square on, and continue the advance to the Railway line where their right flank should rest on the left of the 4/Bedfordshire Regt.at about C.19.c.55.15., and consolidate here.

The third and fourth waves will conform to their movements but will not proceed beyond the communication trench in B.24.d. but will halt and consolidate there.

Battle Patrols will then be pushed forward where the best view of the ground can be obtained.

11. Strong points in the defensive flank will be constructed as under :-

4/Bedfordshire Regt.
(a) On Railway at point of junction with 189th.Infantry Bde. or the most suitable spot in the vicinity.

(b) About Railway crossing of road at C.19.c.55.15.

by 7/Royal Fusiliers.
at junction of German support line and the Railway.
The O.C.7/Royal Fusiliers will also be responsible that touch is maintained with the second Division on his left.

12. All officers and other ranks will be dressed and equipped as laid down in S.135 chapter XXXI and in addition each man of the bombing sections will carry one smoke bomb for use if required.

All men of rifle sections will carry entrenching tools in the proportion of 5 shovels to 1 pick. They will be carried as laid down in above document.

Great coats will not be worn but will be dumped in rear of the Green line and a small guard of men who normally would go to the transport line will be left in charge.

13. Dumps of S.A.A., bombs, tools, R.E. material etc. have been made as follows :-

Pack Dump.   B.25.d.9.1.
"B" Dump.   B.22.d.8.9.
Forward Dump.   B.23.c.7.5.

Units in and behind the present Green line will draw their requirements from the Pack Dump.
The Forward Dump will not be used until after ZERO hour.

Material from these Dumps will be transferred by carrying parties provided by the Reserve Battalion to the German Support line near the BAILLEUL - GAVRELLE Road as soon as possible after the final objective has been reached.

14. All Battalion Headquarters are linked up by telephone to the advance Report Centre which is similarly linked to Brigade.

In addition visual signalling will be established between the two assaulting Battalions and the report centre. Power Buzzers are also working in this line.

A line of runner posts will be established between Brigade Headquarters and Battalions.

Battalions must adopt similar methods between their Headquarters and their Companies to ensure constant information.

The importance of communication must be impressed upon all Commanders, and constant reports even of a negative nature must be forwarded to Brigade Headquarters.

15. Medical Posts have been established as under :-

   (a) <u>Collecting Posts.</u> In Sunken Road at B.28.a.1.8. and H.4.c.6.4.

   (b) <u>Bearer Relay Posts.</u> About B.26.b.4.0. and H.7.b.5.5.

   (c) <u>Advanced Dressing Station.</u> H.1.c.3.8.

   (d) <u>Walking Wounded.</u> will be directed to the Advanced Dressing Station at H.1.c.3.8. (on the main BAILLEUL - ARRAS Road).

   (e) <u>Main Dressing Station.</u> ST. CATHERINE.

Each Regimental Aid Post will be reinforced by 6 and each Machine Gun Company by 2 Stretcher Bearers.

Fighting men must not be permitted to assist wounded men back from the fighting area.

Lightly wounded men must bring back their arms and equipment to the dressing station.

Disciplinary action must be taken in all cases of non-compliance with this order.

16. All ranks taking part in the assault are forbidden to carry any letters, papers, orders or sketches which, in the event of their capture, would be likely to give information to the enemy.
The B.A.B. Code should be carried by Company Commanders.
Notes as to "corrections" must not appear in the book.

17. Contact aeroplanes will fly over the lines at 6.0 am. and 7.0 am.
Flares will be shewn by the advanced troops at these hours when aeroplane calls on them to do so by sounding a Klaxon Horn or firing white lights.
Flares will also be shown at other times when called for by a Contact Aeroplane.
They must not be lighted unless asked for.

18. All prisoners captured will be passed back to Brigade Headquarters as early as possible.
Escorts should not exceed 5 % and slightly wounded men should be employed on this duty.

19. "Z" day and ZERO hour will be notified to all concerned.

20. Watches will be synchronised from Brigade Headquarters at 1.0 pm., 5.0 pm and 9.0 pm. on "Y" day.

21.   Notes (a) All Commanders must be impressed with the necessity of maintaining their direction and advancing straight to their objective, ground must be studied beforehand when possible, and compass bearings taken. In cases where the final objective is undefined on the ground officers must be careful that they consolidate in the most favourable tactical position

available.

(b) Troops must on no account halt because Units on their flanks are held up. The best way to assist on such occasions is to continue the advance.

22. Please acknowledge by wire.

C.H. Dowden
Captain.
Brigade Major.

Issued to Signals... 12.45 pm

Copies to :-

1. G.O.C.
2. Brigade Major.
3. Staff Captain.
4.- 9 63rd.Division.
10.- 12. War Diary.
13. 6th.Brigade.
14. 189th.Brigade.
15. 1/H.A.C.
16. 7/Royal Fusiliers.
17. 4/Bedfordshire Regt.
18. 10/Royal Dublin Fusiliers.
19. 190th.M.G.Company.
20. 190th.T.M.Battery.
21. 249th.Coy. R.E.
22. No. 3 Field Ambulance.
23. Bde.Transport Officer.
24. Bde. Signals.
25. A.P.M.
26,27,28.(left Group R.F.A.
29. C.R.A.
30. Artillery Liaison Officer.
31. Capt.Knight.
32. Lieut.Viney.
33. Lieut Harriott.
34. Lieut.Ladd.
35 - 40 spare.

Appendix XIIa

Headquarters,
190th Infantry Brigade,
28th April 1917.

Headquarters,
    63rd (RN) Division.

Reference OPPY Map 1/10,000.
    "   51B.N.W. 1/20,000.

    Report on operations carried out by 190th Infantry Brigade in conjunction with 189th Infantry Brigade on 23rd/24th April 1917.

1.   The operation consisted of the capture of the village of GAVRELLE and the forming of a defensive flank on the line of the BAILLEUL – GAVRELLE Railway facing N.N.E.

2.   The Task allotted to the Brigade was the capture of the Northern part of the village as far South and including the main road running East and West through that village, and the forming of a defensive flank, mentioned above.

3.   On the four nights preceding the operation preparations were being made to attack this village and the OPPY line as far North as the Southern end of the village of OPPY.
    Assembly trenches were in course of construction about 300 yards from the enemy wire.

4.   On the night preceding the operations it was found that the Canadian Corps who were to have operated farther North were not in a position to do so, consequently it was decided to operate on a shorter front.
    This necessitated handing over all the line North of the BAILLEUL – GAVRELLE Railway, and the taking over by this Brigade of part of the front held by the 189th Brigade.
    The Assembly Trench in this area was far from complete.

5.   It was decided that the attack was to be carried out by two Battalions (7/Royal Fusiliers on the Left and 4/Bedfordshire Regt. on the Right) in four waves.

6.   In order to facilitate the forming up of these waves the Engineers made out one line of pegs about 90 yards in front of our assembly trench, or the site of same where it did not exist and another line of pegs in 50 yards in rear of the first, as it was decided to form up the two leading waves on tape line as above with the two rear waves in the assembly trench.
    The tape was laid on the line of these pegs a few hours before the attack took place.

7.   All Units were in their position of assembly by 3.30 am. The 4/Bedfordshire Regt. and 7/Royal Fusiliers forming four waves as above with 8 Machine Guns and four Stokes Mortars which were to accompany the attack in a fifth wave.
    The 1/H.A.C. in Support about 1,000 yards in rear.
    The 10/Royal Dublin Fusiliers who were to supply the carrying parties were in trenches still further behind.
    The Field Company were assembled with the Carrying Battalion to await orders.
    Remainder of Stokes Mortars were held in Reserve here.
    Remainder of Machine Guns were employed under Corps arrangements to form a barrage in front of Artillery.

8. The troops were fortunate to get into their assembly position and remain there until ZERO undetected by the enemy, although the 4 waves lay in the open within 250 yards of the enemy front line.
   They were not once disturbed.

9. ZERO was at 4.45.am. The morning was fine and rather light. As the ZERO hour approached it became very doubtful as to whether this hour had not been too far delayed, but events proved that the light was perfect and the ZERO hour correct.

10. At Zero the Artillery barrage commenced and our Infantry left their assembly position.
    It soon became evident that the enemy were on the alert as this barrage commenced just half a minute after our own.

11. The 4/Bedfordshire Regt. followed the barrage and entered the enemy front line and reached the first objective which was the enemy support line with little opposition and few casualties.
    The 7/R.F. on the left were not so fortunate, the wire on their left was very little damaged and they could not get through.
    An enemy machine gun was brought to fire on them as they endeavoured to force their way through which caused many casualties and also caused them to divert to the South and enter enemy front line where wire had been cut. They were also bombed by the enemy from behind the wire.
    During this time they had suffered about 30% casualties including almost all their officers.
    The front on which the R.F. should have entered the trenches was still in enemy hands, and he at once commenced bombing down his front and support line worrying the troops who had got in lower down.

12. The 4/Bedfordshire Regt. had now gone on to the second objective (the YELLOW LINE) and had captured same.

13. One Company of 1/H.A.C. had now been pushed forward to enemy front line in support of 7/R.F. and in conjunction with that battalion commenced to bomb up that part of the objective still occupied by the enemy.

14. The 4/Bedfords. left their second objective at the scheduled time and commenced to move to the third objective, which was the North Eastern outskirts of the village and the line of the railway.
    On clearing the village and debouching from the cover of the buildings they were met by very heavy machine gun fire from about the Windmill (N.E. of the village) and were held up on the line of the Northern and North Eastern outskirts of the village.
    The ground between the village and the line of the railway was quite flat, and impossible to cross in daylight under machine gun and rifle fire so they decided to consolidate the line gained and push on under cover of darkness if possible.

15. The 7/R.F. on the left were still engaged with the enemy in his front and support lines, consequently they could not advance to their final objective on the line of the railway.
    They therefore decided to join up with the 4/Bedfords. on the line of FOXY TRENCH and consolidate there, thus a defensive flank North of the village was established.

16. For about 3 hours no news was received from either battalions, owing to the greater number of the officers becoming casualties.

17. As soon as the situation became more clear the second company of the 1/H.A.C. were pushed up in support of the first.

18. These two companies, together with details of 7/R.F. and assisted very much by the Stokes ejected the enemy, yard by yard from his front and support trenches, and by late in the afternoon a post was established in the support line at its junction with the railway.
   The enemy still held a strong point about 50 yards South of the Railway in his front. line.

19. This was the state of affairs at dusk on the 23rd.

20. During the night posts were pushed forward all along the line that had been consolidated earlier to within about 90 yards of the Railway, and also to join up across what was "No Man's Land" before the fight with the next Division.

21. Two sections of Engineers were pushed up during the night and constructed strong points at :-

   (a) Cross Roads in C.19.a.
   (b) In Support Line about B.24.d.3.5.

22. At daybreak on the 24th it was found that the enemy had got into a position from which he could command the post established on the railway. This post was reduced from 21 to 4 by enemy snipers and rifle grenadiers. It was then decided to abandon this position and to withdraw to the junction of FOLLY and FLURRY and construct blocks to defend the remainder of the trench gained.

23. During the 23rd four fairly heavy counter attacks were launched by the enemy, they were all broken up by our artillery before they came within rifle range.
   On the afternoon of the 24th a much heavier attack was delivered at the N.E.corner of the village.
   This reached to within about 800 yards of our defence and came under artillery, machine gun and rifle fire where it was broken.

24. The Brigade was relieved by the 188th Brigade on the night of 24/25th instants, the relief was completed at 6.am. on the 25th inst.
   Three battalions remained in the trenches in the back area.
   Brigade Headquarters and one battalion to ST CATHERINE.

25. The barrage from the field guns was very good but considering the condition of the ground 100 yards in 4 minutes was too slow and many men,in their excitement, advanced into the barrage and suffered casualties.
   The Howitzer barrage on the village was very slow and always in rear of the field gun barrage causing many casualties to our troops.
   It is thought that 600 yards in 5 minutes is a good pace for the creeping barrage when the going is at all good.
   Howitzer barrage ought to be rather in advance of field gun barrage

26. In order to form a defensive flank across the enemy line of defence, this line must be made untenable to him before the attack commences, and must be destroyed to such an extent that it is impossible for him to occupy same until a defensive line is established across same.
   This was not done, consequently he reinforced his attack down the trench by this means.

Brigadier General.
Commanding 190th Infantry Brigade.

SECRET.   Copy No........

190th. Infantry Brigade Order No. 83.

23/4/17.

Reference Map OPPY 1/10,000.
"   51 B   N.W. 1/20,000.

1. The 1/H.A.C. will relieve the 7/Royal Fusiliers tonight and will take over the front from the German front line to the South - Eastern end of FOGGY Trench at D.24.d.98.00. or the Railway line on this front if it has now been captured.

2. The front line must be held as lightly as possible, chiefly by Lewis Gun Posts but remainder of men must be within striking distance to repel counter attacks.
   The 1/H.A.C. must get touch with 6th. Brigade on their left and report that this is done.

3. The 7/Royal Fusiliers will withdraw to the GREEN line on relief by 1/H.A.C.

4. The 10/Royal Dublin Fusiliers will move forward to the position evacuated by the two rear Companies of the 1/H.A.C. and will be in Reserve there.

5. The 4/Bedfordshire Regt. will continue to hold the front from the right of the 1/H.A.C. to the Eastern end of the village where they will join up with the 189th. Infantry Brigade and will advance their line on to the Railway should an opportunity occur.

6. The defensive flank must be held at all costs.

7. All moves to be completed as soon after dark as possible, and report to Bde. Hd. Qrs. when complete.

8. Please ACKNOWLEDGE.

Issued to Signals..... 4.55 pm

                                                                    Captain.
                                                                    Brigade Major.

Copies to :-

   1. G.O.C.
   2. Brigade Major.
   3. Staff Captain
   4.5. 63rd. Division.
   6.- 8 War Diary.
   9. 6th. Brigade.
   10. 188th. Inf. Bde.
   11. 189th. "   "
   12. 1/H.A.C.   25. C.R.A.
   13. 7/R.F.   26. Art. Liaison Off.
   14. 4/Beds. Regt.   27.28. Spare.
   15. 10/R.D.F.
   16. M.G. Coy.
   17. T.M.B.
   18. 249th. Field Coy.
   19. 3rd. Field Amb.
   20. Bde. Transport Off.
   21. Bde. Signals.
   22.23.24. Left Group R.F.A.

SECRET. GOC Copy No..1...

190th. Infantry Brigade Order No. 84.

Appendix XIV
23/4/17.

Reference OPPY Map 1/10,000.
" 51B.N.W. 1/20,000.

1. The defensive flank on the line of the Railway will be consolidated tonight and as much wire as possible put out after dusk under cover of posts pushed out in front.
   Construction of Strong Points as laid down in para 13 of Brigade Order No. 82 will be proceeded with.

2. The 7/Royal Fusiliers will dig a trench to join up the present left of the Brigade (which rests in the front German line South of the Railway) the right of the 6th. Brigade.
   This trench will be on the line of the Railway if possible.

3. The 4/Bedfordshire Regt. will if possible get in touch with 189th. Brigade on their right.

4. The two Sections of 249th. Field Company R.E. will proceed to construct Strong Points as detailed above.
   1 Section will be allotted to 1/H.A.C.
   1 Section to 4/Bedfordshire Regt.

5. On completion of this consolidation the line will be thinned, and the position held mainly by Lewis and Machine Guns.
   Troops in support will be withdrawn to best cover available so long as they are within striking distance in case of counter attack.

6. The S.O.S. Barrage will be on a line 250 yards North of Railway.

7. Please ACKNOWLEDGE.

                                       Captain.
                                    Brigade Major.

Issued to Signals....9.5 p—

Copies to :-

1. G.O.C.
2. Brigade Major.
3. Staff Captain.
4,5. 63rd. Division.
6-8 War Diary.
9. 6th. Brigade.
10. 188th. Inf. Bde.
11. 189th.   "   "
12. 1/H.A.C.
13. 7/R.F.
14. 4/Beds. Regt.
15. 10/R.D.F.
16. M.G.Coy.
17. T.M.B.
18. 249th. Field Coy.
19. 3rd. Field Amb.
20. Bde. Transport Offr.
21. Bde. Signals.
22.23.24. Left Group R.F.A.
25. O.R.A.
26. Artillery Liaison Offr.
27.28. Spare.

War Diary, Appendix XV

SECRET.   Copy No......

190th. Infantry Brigade Order No. 85.

24/4/17.

Reference 51B.N.W. 1/20,000.
          OPPY   1/10,000.

1. The 1/H.A.C. and 4/Bedfordshire Regt. will be relieved tonight by the 2nd.Bn. Royal Marine L.I. from 188th.Brigade.
   3 Companies will take over the front line from where it joins the 189th.Brigade at the Cross Roads at C.19.c.3.1. to where it joins the 6th.Brigade about B.24.d.7.9.

2. The boundaries between these companies will be approximately :-
   (a) A point immediately South of the Railway at C.19.c.0.3.
   (b) Junction of FLURRY - FOGGY and FAMINE trench.

3. The fourth company will be in close support in FALTER and FILLY trenches in B.30.a.
   Battalion Headquarters in FALTER.

4. O.C.Battalions in the line will arrange for a guide to meet each Platoon of the relieving company at the point where the BAILLEUL - GAVRELLE road enters the front German line to guide them to their respective positions.
   In addition, the 4/Bedfordshire Regt. will send 3 guides to the Headquarters of 2/R.M. in the BROWN Line in B.27.a. and c ____ at 7.30 pm tonight to guide 2 companies and Headquarters forward.
   The 1/H.A.C. will send two guides as above to guide the two remaining companies forward.

5. The relief will be completed by 2.0 am on the night of 24th/25th.inst.

6. The 190th.M.G.Company (less one section) will be relieved by the 188th.M.G.Company on the night of the 25th/26th.inst.under arrangements to be made between O.C. Companies concerned.

7. The 190th.T.M.Battery will be relieved by the 188th. T.M.Battery on the night of 25th/26th.inst.
   The four guns in the line will remain, Personnel only being relieved.
   Four Guns from 188th.T.M.Battery now at ST.CATHERINE will be taken over by 190th.T.M.Battery on relief.

8. On relief being completed, units will be located as follows :-

   Brigade Headquarters.   ST.CATHERINE.
   4/Bedfords.   "
   1/H.A.C.   In the BLACK line in "G" 6 c and d
                             (take over from 2/R.M.).
   7/Royal Fusiliers.   In the BLUE line in B.25.c and d (
                             (take over from 1st.R.M.).
   10/R.D.F.   Trenches in H.1.c.
   190th.M.G.Company.)
   190th.T.M.Battery. }   Notified later.

9. Units will send Company Representatives to reconnoitre and arrange accommodation as early as possible.

10. The two front line Battalions will move back on relief.
7/Royal Fusiliers will move back after 4.0 pm today.
10/Royal Dublin Fusiliers will move back at 9.0 pm tonight.

11. Divisional Trench Standing Orders will be adhered to so far as they affect the relief.

12. Units will move in parties of not more than one Platoon at 100 yards distance.

13. Trench Stores, including water tins, will be collected at Battalion Headquarters and handed over to incoming units.
A receipt for these will be obtained and forwarded to Brigade Headquarters within 12 hours of relief.
Special attention must be paid to the collecting of water tins which are becoming very scarce.

14. The relief completed must be reported to Brigade Headquarters as early as possible by the word "NEXT".

15. Command will pass to G.O.C. 188th.Brigade on completion of relief.

16. Brigade Headquarters close at E.27.a.0.4. at 6 pm and re-opn at ST.CATHERINE on arrival there.

17. Please acknowledge.

C.H.Dowden
Captain.
Brigade Major.

Issued to Signals......2.40 pm

Copies to :-
1. G.O.C.
2. Brigade Major.
3. Staff Captain.
4.)
5.) 63rd.Division "G".
6. " " "Q".
7 - 9 War Diary.
10. 6th.Brigade.
11. 188th.Inf.Bde.
12. 189th. " "
13. 2/R.M.
14. 1/H.A.C.
15. 7/R.F.
16. 4/Beds.Regt.
17. 10/R.D.F.
18. M.G.Coy.
19. T.M.B.
20. 249th.Field Coy.
21. 3rd.Field Amb.
22. Bde.Transport Officer.
23. Bde.Sig.Offr.
24. 23.24 Left.Group R.F.A.
25. C.R.A.
26. Artillery Liaison Offr.
27.28. Spare.

Secret

Addendum to
190th Infantry Brigade Order No 85.

Copy No....

24-4-17

1. The 10/R.D.F. will be located in trenches in H1. (West of BOIS DE LA MAISON BLANC) and will be at the call of the G.O.C. 188th Brigade.

   The 190th M.G. Coy will leave one section at the disposal of G.O.C. 188th Brigade.

   Remainder will be located at ST. CATHERINE on relief.

   The 190th T.M.B. will move to ST. CATHERINE on relief.

2. Please acknowledge.

A.H. Dowden
Captain
Bde. Major

Issued to Sigs. at 550 p.m.

Copies to all recipients of B.O. 85.

War Diary Appendix XVI
10

SECRET.
Copy No......

190th. Infantry Brigade Order No. 86.

Reference 51B N.W. 1/20,000.
" OPPY 1/10,000.

27/4/17.

1. The 63rd. Division will assist in the attack on the OPPY Line at an early date.

2. The attack will be carried out by the 188th. Brigade. Two Battalions of the 190th. Brigade will be placed at the disposal of the 188th. Brigade.
The 1/H.A.C. as Supporting Battalion and the 10/Royal Dublin Fusiliers as carrying Battalion.
These two Battalions come under orders of G.O.C. 188th. Brigade for this operation.

3. 10 Machine Guns of the 190th. M.G. Company will form a Barrage at ZERO Hour 300 yards in front of the Artillery Barrage supporting "A" attack, each gun being given a frontage of 50 yards.
These guns will come under the orders of G.O.C. 188th. Brigade for this operation.
O.C. 190th. Machine Gun Company will submit his proposals for this barrage to G.O.C. 188th. Brigade for approval.
The Guns will be located near Hill 80.

4. All troops taking part in the operation will be equipped as laid down in S.S.135 Section XXXI.

5. Special attention is directed to S.S.135 Section XXX. These officers and other ranks will not be taken into action.

6. Greatcoats and Packs will not be worn but will be left in present trenches under a Guard of men who will normally be left out of the fight.

7. All troops must be in positions of assembly by 2.0 am on night of 27th/28th. inst.

8. Please acknowledge by wire.

E.H. Dowden
Captain.

Issued to Signals. .... Brigade Major.

Copies to :-
1. G.O.C.
2. Brigade Major.
3. Staff Captain.
4 - 9 63rd. Division.
10 - 12 War Diary.
13. 189th. Brigade.
14. 188th. "
15. 1/H.A.C.
16. 7/R.F.

17. 4/Beds. Regt.
18. 10/R.D.F.
19. 190th. M.G.Coy.
20. " T.M.B.
21. 249th. Coy. R.E.
22. 3rd. Field Amb.
23. Bde. Transport Off.
24. Bde. Signals.

SECRET.　　　　　　*Appendix XVII*　　　Copy No......

190th. Infantry Brigade Order No. 88.

28/4/17.

Reference OPPY Sheet 1/10,000.
"　　51B N.W." 1/20,000.

1. The 63rd and 2nd. Divisions have been ordered to attack and capture the enemy front and support lines on the front B.12.b.5.0. in the North to FOLLY Trench in the South and consolidate on this line.
   The attack will take place at 4 am on the 29th. inst.
   All troops must be in their assembly position by 2 am.

2. The boundary between the 63rd and 2nd. Divisions will be the Level Crossing at B.23.a.9.8. to B.24.b.6.8.

3. This operation will be carried out by a composite Battalion of the 190th. Infantry Brigade consisting of the 7/Royal Fusiliers and the 4/Bedfordshire Regt. under Lieut. Colonel Collings-Wells.
   Each of the above Battalions will be organised into two Companies for this operation.
   The Composite Battalion will be under the orders of G.O.C., 188th. Inf. Bde.

4. The frontage allotted to the Battalion will be from the Northern Divisional Boundary to FOLLY Trench. About 550 yards.

5. The attack will be carried out in four waves in accordance with Divisional Scheme of attack.
   One Company of Bedfordshire Regt. will be on the left of 1st and 2nd. wave, with one Company of 7/R.F. on the right.
   One Company of 4/Bedfordshire Regt. will form 3rd. wave with one Company of 7/R.F. as 4th. wave.

6. The leading wave of Infantry will form up about 85 yards in front of assembly trench with the 2nd. wave about 25 yards behind it.
   The 3rd and 4th. waves will form up in the assembly trench.

7. Plan of attack. At ZERO Artillery Barrage opens on front line trench and Infantry advance.
   At ZERO plus 6 minutes the barrage lifts to support trench and the two leading waves of Infantry assault front trench followed by 3rd and 4th. waves.
   The two leading waves will pass straight over the front trench and follow the barrage to support trench.
   At ZERO plus 10 minutes the barrage lifts from the support trench and two leading waves of Infantry assault and capture the support trench and consolidate.
   The 3rd and 4th. waves consolidate the front line trench.

8. Close touch must be maintained with the Brigade operating on our left both at the position of assembly and during the attack.

9. Constant information must be sent back to Brigade Headquarters.

2.

10. Brigade Headquarters are at H.3.d.4.7.
Battalion Headquarters will be at B.17.c.6.2. (in dugout in bank).

11. Dress and equipment will be as laid down in S.135 Section XXXI.
Every rifleman will carry an entrenching tool in the proportion of 5 shovels to 1 pick.
Greatcoats will not be worn.

12. Flares will be lighted when called for by Contact Aeroplane.

13. An Officer of 7/Royal Fusiliers (not one of the Composite Battalion) will proceed to Brigade Headquarters 99th.Inf.Bde. at B.21.a.8.8. and will then accompany the right Battalion of that Brigade to its forming up place, afterwards returning to the left flank of his own unit to ensure that there is no gap. Similar precautions are being taken by the 99th.Inf.Bde., who will attach an officer to the troops of the 63rd.Division.

14. ACKNOWLEDGE.

CH Dowlen
Captain.
Brigade Major.

Issued to Signals. 9/pm

Copies to :-

1 G.O.C.
2 B.M.
3 S.S.
4. 63rd.Div. G
5 " Q
6 War Diary.
7. H.A.C.
8 7/R.F.
9. 4/Beds.Regt.
10. 10/R.D.F.
11. M.G.Coy.
12. T.M.B.
13. 249 Coy. R.E.
14. 3rd.F.A.
15. Bdo.Transport Officer.
16. Bde. Sig.Sec.
17. 99th.Inf.Bde.

SECRET.   Appendix XVIII   Copy No. 9

190th. Infantry Brigade Order No. 89.
(Cancelling Brigade Order No. 87).

29/4/17.

Reference LENS Sheet 1/10,000.
"   51B N.W. 1/20,000.

1.   The Division is being relieved by the 31st. Division on the 30th. April 1917.

2.   The Brigade will move back in accordance with attached March Table.

3.   A distance of 300 yards will be maintained between Units on the march.

4.   Transport of Units will remain where they are.

5.   Billetting parties will be sent on as early as possible to arrange accommodation.

6.   Machine Gun Companies of the Division will concentrate at ANZIN on the 1st. May 1917, on relief by 31st. Division.

7.   Completion of move will be reported to Brigade Headquarters as early as possible by the code word "DOME".

8.   Brigade Headquarters will close at ST. CATHERINE at 9.30 am and open at MAROEUIL on arrival there.

9.   Cookers, Watercarts and empty transport for Lewis Guns of 1/H.A.C. to be at PONT DU JOUR at dusk.
        Rations for 7/Royal Fusiliers and 10/Royal Dublin Fusiliers to come up as usual to the BLUE Line and H.L.C. respectively.
        Rations, Cookers and watercarts for 4/Bedfordshire Regt to go to the BLACK Line.

10.   Please acknowledge by wire.

Issued to Signals

                                                        2/Lieut.
                                                    for Brigade Major.

        Copies to :-
            1. G.O.C.
            2. B.M.
            3. S.C.
            4.- 5 63rd. Div. G.   17. 190th. M.G. Coy.
            6. 63rd. Div. Q.   18. 190th. T.M.B.
            7.8.9. War Diary.   19. Bde. Transport Offr.
            10. 188th. Bde.   20. Bde. Signal Sec.
            11. 189th. Bde.   21. No.4 Coy. Train.
            12. 99th. Bde.   22. Supply Officer.
            13. 1/H.A.C.   23. A.P.M.
            14. 7/R.F.   24
            15. 4/Beds. Regt.   25
            16. 10/R.D.F.   26
                                             27
                                             28

March Table to accompany 190th.Inf.Bde. Order No. 89.

Date.	Unit.	From.	To.	Starting Point.	Time.	Route.	Remarks.
29/4/17.	4/Beds.Regt.	Trenches	Dugouts in G.6.	Trenches	Will start on completion of relief.	Direct	
"	1/H.A.C.	"	Dugouts in G.10.b.5.4.	"		"	
"	9/R.F.	"	Dugouts in B.25.b.&d.	"		"	
"	10/R.D.F.	"	H.1.c.	"		"	
30/4/17	Bde.H.Q.	ST.CATHERINE	MAROEUIL	ST.CATHERINE.	10.0 am	ANZIN ST AUBIN	
"	190th.T.M.B.	"	"	Bde.H.Q.	10.5 am	"	
30 Apl/1st May	190th.M.G.Coy	Trenches & ST.CATHERINE	ANZIN	ST.CATHERINE		Direct.	

Appendix XIX

SECRET.   Copy No...... 4

190th Infantry Brigade Order No.90.
✱✱✱✱✱✱✱✱✱✱✱✱✱✱✱✱✱✱✱✱✱✱✱✱✱✱

Reference LENS Sheet 1/100,000.   30/4/17.
"   " 51B. N.W. 1/20,000

1. The 1/H.A.C., 7/R.F., 10/R.D.F. and 4/Beds.Regt. will move back in accordance with attached march table.

2. A distance of 300 yards will be maintained by units on the march.

3. Transport of units will join their respective units at their destinations.

4. Billetting parties will be sent on as early as possible to arrange accommodation.

5. Completion of move will be reported to Brigade Headquarters as early as possible.

6. Please acknowledge.

Time issued to Signals... 9 am   2/Lieut.
                                                         for Brigade Major.

1. G.O.C.
2. B.M.
3. S.C.
4-5 63rd Div. G.
6. 63rd Div. Q.
7,8,9, War Diary.
10. 188th Bde.
11. 189th Bde.
12. 99th Bde.
13. 1/H.A.C.
14. 7/R.F.
15. 4/Beds.
16. 10/R.D.F.
17. 190th M.G.Coy.
18. 190th T.M.B.
19. Bde. Transport Off.
20. Bde. Signals Sect.
21. No. 4 Coy. Div. Train.
22. Supply Officer.
23. A.P.M.

MARCH TABLE.

Date.	Unit.	From.	To.	Starting Point.	Time.	Route	Remarks
"	7th Royal Fus	B.25.b.& D.	A.29.b.5.6.	B.25.d.	3.30.pm.	Via ROCLINCOURT.	
"	10/R.Dublin Fus.	H.1.c.	A.22.c.8.0.	H.1.c.	3.15.pm.	Direct.	
"	4/Beds.Regt.	G.6.(Black Line)	G.5.b.	Black Line.	3.pm.	Direct.	

On His Majesty's Service.

Confidential

www.ingramcontent.com/pod-product-compliance
Lightning Source LLC
Chambersburg PA
CBHW081425300426
44108CB00016BA/2301